THE THIRD REICH
A CHRONICLE

12 12

DEUTSCHES REICH

AUSCHWITZ (OBERSCH...
25.2.43. -10

Emilie

dorf Hindenburg 81.

THE THIRD REICH

A CHRONICLE

RICHARD OVERY

First published in Great Britain in 2010 by
Quercus
21 Bloomsbury Square
London
WC1A 2NS

A CIP catalogue record for this book is available
from the British Library

ISBN 978 1 84916 235 7

Designed by Ashley Western

Printed and bound in Portugal

ADOLF HITLER

No period of recent history has been so thoroughly explored as the Third Reich. Although the dictatorship lasted only a dozen years out of the past century of German history, the cataclysmic war that Hitler unleashed, and the genocide of Europe's Jews, had repercussions far beyond Germany's borders and still reverberates in the history of today.

So intense and dramatic were those twelve years of German history that they have forced anyone who looks at them to ask some big questions. First, how did a nation with a reputation for civilized behaviour and a long and glittering cultural heritage come to spawn a violent dictatorship capable of committing remarkable barbarities? This is a question which seems all the more puzzling with the passage of time, since post-war Germany has seen no real residue from the militarism and racism that characterized the Third Reich. In the sixty-five years since its collapse Germans have been Europe's virtuous citizens. Second, why was Hitler allowed to come to power when his party had only just over one-third of the electorate behind it? Of course, there have been plenty of minority parties running the government in the last century. But given the menace that Hitler represented it is necessary to explain why the two-thirds of Germans who did not vote for Hitler could not find a way of blocking his rise to power. Moreover, having failed, millions of them then threw in their lot with a regime that showed from the start its willingness to behave in utterly lawless ways.

Finally there is the complex question of why Adolf Hitler, an apparent nonentity to many of those who met him in private (away from the rostrum and the baying crowds), was able to exert such an extraordinary grip on the German people, a grip that brought them to the edge of complete destruction without ever eroding entirely the bond that bound leader and led together. The fascination that he exerted exists still today in the endless quest to understand the real Hitler. The truth lies not entirely with Hitler, whose personality was bizarre and whose ambitions grew the more he believed that he was chosen by destiny, but with the people he led, many of whom wanted to believe and who accepted the cult of personality as an act of faith rather than a realistic assessment of the kind of man who led them. In this sense Hitler was, as he always claimed, the supreme representative of his people, not someone imposed on Germany as an alien presence. The 'leader cult' has operated in other dictatorships too, in Mao's China and Stalin's Russia, with fatal consequences for those who refused to believe. But in the German case leader and led both colluded in the fiction of Hitler as the German Messiah; many people refused to confront the sheer irrationalism of this belief and as a result found themselves committing awful atrocities in the name of the *Führer*.

In trying to come to terms with these large questions it is important to bear in mind that a significant fraction of Germans were affected by the idealism of the National Socialist revolution and genuinely believed they were building a better world, a new utopia in which there would be no racial enemies, no social tensions, no alien cultural influences but instead a cosy social vision of happy families, healthy blond children and a pure race. The idea that Germany's national revival under Hitler was destined to make Germany the centre of a revived European civilization now seems entirely wrong-headed, but there were idealistic Germans who hoped that for all the rough edges of the national revolution, a better world would result, not just for Germany but for the rest of Europe too. The image that recurs often in the propaganda of the Third Reich is the triumph of order over chaos, of decency and honesty over the malign values of other world views.

This vision of a new promised land is very hard to reconcile with the violence, discrimination and injustice widely exercised by the regime. 'You can't make an omelette without breaking eggs,' Hermann Göring once remarked, but this was a slender excuse for the way the regime behaved to its alleged enemies and rivals, both inside Germany and in the wider world. The truth is that the regime and its supporters thrived not on a virtuous, if misplaced, idealism but on the worst aspects of human nature – resentment, against other powers and more prosperous peoples; envy, of those states who possessed rich empires or adequate resources; fear, of imagined enemies of the German ideal; hatred, of those who refused to follow the faith and betrayed or challenged the utopian vision; and above all unbridled aggression, manifested in the beatings and tortures inflicted on political enemies in 1933 through to the savage murder of defeatists and deserters in 1945. It is small wonder that the history of the Third Reich focuses on war and genocide because that was its central legacy. The German virtues that Hitler lauded were realized as vices.

The chronicle of these bleak years is full of paradox. The Third Reich so wanted to restore order, to create a natural ascendancy for a people that did regard itself as cultured and racially superior (even if not everyone believed in the propaganda of the 'master race'), but it ended up creating chaos of an unimaginable kind and blighting German history with recollections of some of the most barbarous behaviour in the modern age. The result was to bring the German people and those they victimized untold suffering in the name of an unrealized and unrealizable ambition. The generation of Germans that grew up in the 1950s and 1960s put all this aside and focused on developing modern political institutions and a thriving economy, but the long shadow of those twelve years has lengthened with each passing decade. 'How was it possible?' is still a question to which many people, inside and outside Germany, have not yet found a satisfactory answer. What follows may not answer that question completely but it is designed to show what it is that is now known about the Third Reich and how we might use that knowledge in framing our answers.

RICHARD OVERY

University of Exeter

April 2010

A bombed house among the ruins of a German city in 1945. The slogan reads 'For this, Hitler needed 12 years'.

CHAPTER 1

RISE TO POWER

1923–1933

Adolf Hitler was a little-known politician in 1923, leader of a small radical nationalist party in Bavaria with a reputation for street-fighting, anti-Semitism and socialist rhetoric. Within a decade Hitler and his party, the National Socialist German Workers' Party (NSDAP), had become the dominant force in German politics, poised to take power. The ten years after the end of the First World War was a historical roller-coaster for the German people. Following defeat they were forced to accept a humiliating peace treaty that blamed Germany for starting the war. For the next three years the country experienced a high level of political violence between the extreme right and extreme left, against a background of massive inflation and economic hardship. The story of Hitler's rise to power can be explained by a mixture of luck, opportunity and ambition. Many German voters remained loyal to the existing parliamentary parties, and even at the peak before 1933, Hitler's party did not succeed in winning more than 37 per cent of the popular vote. Hitler and his party were marginal to the political system only a few years before, when the 1928 elections gave them only twelve seats in parliament. The economic slump paved the way for Hitler because it created a mixture of despair, anger at the outside world, and fear of communism, which persuaded many German voters that the future of Germany was at stake. Hitler posed as the ultimate saviour of Germany. For many people a Hitler vote was a risk, but it was one that millions took because it seemed the only hope. Without crisis a Hitler dictatorship was unthinkable. German National Socialism was an emergency choice, owing its success to the failure of the other parties and the parliamentary order as much as to its own strengths. Even then, Hitler achieved the chancellorship of Germany only through a backstairs political intrigue by a small band of conservative politicians who thought they could control a movement, and a leader whose political potential they constantly underrated.

1923–1924 The Failed Putsch

On 9 November 1923 a procession of around 2,000 German nationalists led by the hero of the First World War, General Erich Ludendorff, and the young Austrian agitator Adolf Hitler, marched through the centre of the Bavarian capital, Munich, down Residenzstrasse towards the Feldherrnhalle, a monument to past Bavarian generals. They were trying to stage a coup (*Putsch* in German) to overthrow the Bavarian regional government and, if they succeeded, the national government in Berlin as well. The long procession of men, some in the scruffy uniform of the paramilitary groups that supported the uprising, carried flags and banners. Some were armed, including Hitler himself, who carried a revolver, though he had given orders for the weapons not to be loaded. The marchers saw themselves at a turning point in German history, the vanguard of a German national revolution to avenge the defeat of 1918.

To understand what Hitler, the self-appointed leader of the *Putsch*, was doing in Munich on that grey and snowy day in 1923 it is necessary to turn the clock back to the last days of the First World War. Adolf Hitler, a young corporal in a Bavarian army regiment, was lying in hospital recovering from a gas attack. When he heard the news that the German leaders' request for an armistice had been granted, to come into effect at 11.00 on 11 November 1918, he was overcome with inexpressible grief and anger. Like millions of other German soldiers, he had believed in the rightness of the German cause. The European war that broke out in early August 1914 was a war, so it was believed, engineered by the entente of Russia, France and Great Britain to emasculate German power and to impose the crude materialism of the Allies on a cultured and civilized people. Defeat when it came was a profound shock to millions of Germans who had not been told the full truth about the state of the German war machine, or of the difficulties in getting the home front to sustain any longer a draining and expensive war. For nationalists like Hitler, who had abandoned his native Austria to live in Germany in 1913, and willingly served in a German rather than an Austrian unit for four years from 1914, the armistice was treason to the fatherland. Like thousands of others, Hitler blamed defeat on socialist workers and Jewish agitators, who, it was always alleged afterwards, had 'stabbed Germany in the back'. Defeat turned Hitler into an angry, disillusioned veteran, determined if he could to help Germany revive its natural place in the world and to take violent revenge on the Marxists and Jews who were accused of causing defeat in the first place.

Germany faced serious political crisis as a result of the bitter divisions between left and right over how to react to the fact of defeat. The German social-democrats and liberals wanted an end of the monarchy and the establishment of a parliamentary republic; a new constitution was drawn up founding what became known as the Weimar Republic, after the city where it

Pages 10–11: A group of storm troopers (SA) in 1926 with a homemade swastika flag and uniforms they have bought themselves. The SA embodied the comradeship, but also the violence, of the Hitler movement.

was formally adopted. German Communists, on the other hand, wanted a revolution like the one in Russia in 1917, which would create a workers' state. The revolutionary wave could only be held back, paradoxically, by an alliance between the social-democrats, the army and right-wing nationalists. Communist leaders were murdered and vigilante groups, the *Freikorps*, composed of veterans who had kept their uniforms and weapons, were set up to destroy working-class resistance and intimidate any other alleged threats to Germany's future.

On 28 June 1919, the new German government was compelled to sign the Versailles Treaty drawn up by the Allied side without negotiation. The Treaty disarmed Germany, took away valuable territories in Alsace Lorraine and Silesia, abolished Germany's colonial empire and imposed in Article 231 of the Treaty the notorious 'War Guilt' clause, in which Germany was compelled to admit responsibility, together with its allies, for causing all the damage endured by the Allied powers. Germany was then required to pay extensive reparation for the damage caused. Despite widespread hostility to the Treaty across the political spectrum in Germany, it had to be signed or risk an Allied invasion. One of the chief architects of acceptance, Matthias Erzberger, was murdered by *Freikorps* members on 27 August 1921; another politician closely associated with the new system, the Foreign Minister Walter Rathenau, was assassinated by the same group on 24 June the following year.

REPARATIONS

Under the terms of the Versailles Treaty signed on 28 June 1919 Germany and her allies (Austria, Hungary, Bulgaria) were obliged to pay reparations for the damage caused by the war in Western Europe. The sum finally fixed in May 1921 for Germany to pay was 132 billion gold marks, of which 50 billion marks had to be paid off first at the rate of 2 billion marks a year with an additional levy equal to 26 per cent of the value of German exports. When the German currency collapsed in 1923, a new schedule known as the Dawes Plan was drawn up in April 1924 which allowed Germany to pay very small amounts for the first years of recovery, reaching 2 billion marks again by 1927. Growing economic difficulties, combined with the reluctance of the German government to honour reparation obligations, led to a renegotiated schedule in 1929. The so-called Young Plan reduced total obligations to 112 billion marks, to be paid off at the rate of two billion a year until 1988. The Young Plan involved a generous loan to Germany to help cope with reparation payments but over the years of the slump Germany succeeded in paying very little. The obligation to pay reparations was regarded by most Germans as a profound injustice because it reflected the Allied view that Germany alone was 'guilty' for starting the First World War. It is estimated that Germany paid around 20 billion between 1921 and 1931, when reparation payments were suspended for a year. At the Lausanne Conference in June 1932 reparations were finally abandoned by the Allies.

When Hitler emerged from hospital he returned to Munich where, in contrast to the account he later gave in the autobiographical volume *Mein Kampf*, he found himself siding with the radical revolutionary movement there as the spokesman for his regiment's 'soldiers' council'. Briefly arrested when the regular German army overthrew the Bavarian revolution and restored order, he was released in order to become an army agitator among returning German prisoners-of-war, whose political outlook was regarded as unreliable. Hitler immediately found his calling; he gave impromptu speeches on political subjects which proved to be an instant success.

On 12 September 1919, he was ordered to attend a meeting of a fringe radical right-wing group, the German Labour Party (DAP). A month later, on 19 October, he joined the party as member number 555 (membership began from 501); by the middle of November he was invited to become one of the party's leading figures, responsible for propaganda. He soon earned a reputation as a popular local agitator, capable of bringing in crowds to hear him denounce Versailles, condemn the 'November criminals' and call for the expulsion of Jews

Above left: The German diplomat Kurt Freiherr von Lersner, chief of the German delegation in Paris, signs additional protocols to the Versailles Treaty in a hall in the French Foreign Ministry in Paris in July 1919.

Above right: A group of marchers on their way to the Feldherrnhalle in Munich on 9 November 1923, intending to take over the government of Bavaria as a prelude for a 'March on Berlin' and the seizure of power.

HITLER ON THE JEWS, 1920

The Jew brings Democracy and with it stifles Reason
Democracy = majority decision = Public opinion = Press = Capital = Jew
German democracy – means persuading the majority with reason
Jewish democracy – means killing the majority with reason
Democracy means breaking the nation's resistance
To that end – abolition of the death sentence
But final aim subjugation of all nations
Hence
Democracy Dictatorship of the Proletariat
Final resistance Class struggle
National intelligence
Must be destroyed
The Jew as leech
Bolshevism
The bloody Jew....
And present-day Germany? Fight between dictatorship and democracy
No Between
Jew and German
Who has grasped this?
The parties on the Left?
The parties on the Right?
Election slogan Middle class against proletariat
Class against Class instead of Germans against Jews

Source: Werner Maser (ed) *Hitler's Letters and Notes* (Bantam, New York, 1976), pp. 224–7, Hitler's notes
for a speech, 1920

Opposite above: A *Freikorps* group in Germany in the early 1920s. These militia were
made up of veterans from the war and young nationalists who wanted to fight against
left-wing revolutionaries. The figure in the centre wears a swastika armband. The corps
were finally disbanded on government orders in 1922.

Opposite below: A picture of Hitler as a young politician c. 1923, during a propaganda
tour by motorcar. Hitler placed great emphasis on making himself visible to the wider
public in staged appearances and theatrical speeches.

from Europe. The key elements of his political creed – a revival of Germany, war against Marxists and other enemies of the German ideal, and the eradication of Europe's Jewish population – were in place within weeks of his decision to pursue a political career.

The DAP was founded and led by Anton Drexler, a railway mechanic with a mixture of extreme nationalist and anti-capitalist views. Hitler worked with him closely in the first year and a half of his membership. On 20 February 1920 the party changed its name to the National Socialist German Workers' Party (NSDAP) to make clear that its aim was to recruit workers, seduced by Marxism, back to the national cause. Four days later at the new Party's first public meeting, in front of 2,000 people, Hitler read out the 25-point Party Programme, prepared by himself and Drexler. The programme came to constitute the unalterable aims of the movement when, a year later, on 29 July 1921, Hitler staged a coup in the Party against Drexler, whose tactics he regarded as too moderate. He succeeded in getting himself voted as the Party's sole leader and secured unconditional approval of the programme. By that stage Hitler already overshadowed the rest of the Party leadership; the ever-larger crowds who came to National Socialist rallies, came to listen to him. At the same meeting that approved his takeover of the Party, Hitler was described for the first time as *Führer*, the title he later took in 1934 when he became Germany's supreme authority. The term was chosen deliberately: both leader but also, in German, a guide. Hitler had begun political life hoping that he might be a drummer for the national movement, egging it along; by 1921 he saw himself as destined for larger things as Germany's saviour.

After Hitler assumed leadership of the Party it began to take on its future shape. On 3 August 1921 a paramilitary unit was set up, the SA (*Sturmabteilung*), whose job was to protect party meetings and disrupt those of left-wing parties. In the spring of 1922 leadership of the SA was given to a young ex-pilot, Hermann Göring, who volunteered to work for the Party after hearing Hitler speak at a meeting. On 29–30 January 1922 the Party held its first rally, with around 1,000 delegates; the first national party congress was held a year later in Munich, on 27–29 January 1923. The Party rapidly developed a national reputation as a rowdy, violent, radical movement, hostile to parliamentary rule, strongly anti-Semitic and in favour of some kind of national revolution. Hitler himself was arrested twice in 1922, serving a brief period in prison in between 24 June and 27 July. The Party was banned throughout most of Germany with the exception of Bavaria, its heartland. After the Italian Fascist Party leader, Benito Mussolini, staged a 'March on Rome' on 28 October 1922 which brought him the offer of the premiership, National Socialists began to think more seriously about launching a similar 'March on Berlin'. On 3 November Hitler addressed a Party rally on the success of Mussolini and Italian 'patriotism': 'In our country,' he announced, 'we will have to do the same …'

During 1923 the political and economic situation reached crisis point in Germany, making Hitler's idea of a national revolution less fantastic. On 11 January 1923 French and Belgian troops occupied the Ruhr industrial region in north-west Germany, ostensibly to enforce German compliance with the payment of reparations. The German government reacted with a campaign of passive resistance, while the numerous nationalist parties and leagues (including the National Socialists) campaigned noisily against the whole Versailles

The 'Fundamental Programme' of the National Socialist German Workers' Party produced in 1920. The document was drawn up by Hitler and Anton Drexler, but not all of its provisions were implemented when Hitler later came to power.

THE NATIONAL SOCIALIST PARTY PROGRAMME, 1920

The programme of the German Workers' Party is addressed to its era. After the goals of the programme have been achieved, the leaders refuse to set new ones for the purpose of artificially increasing the discontent of the masses, merely in order to make possible the continuance of the party.

1 We demand the union of all Germans – on the basis of the right of self-determination of peoples – in a Greater Germany.

2 We demand equality of the German people with all other nations, the abrogation of the peace treaties of Versailles and Saint-Germain [applied to Austria].

3 We demand land and soil (colonies) for the nourishment of our people and for the settlement of our excess population.

4 Only he who is a racial member can be a citizen. Only he who is of German blood, regardless of his church, can be a racial member. No Jew, therefore, can be a member of the race.

5 He who is not a citizen shall live in Germany only as a guest and must be governed by the law for aliens.

6 The right to make decisions about leadership and law belongs only to citizens. We therefore demand that every public office, no matter what kind, whether national, provincial or local, be staffed only by citizens.

7 We demand that the state pledge itself to assure the productivity and livelihood of citizens above all others. If it is not possible to support the entire population, members of foreign nations (non-citizens) are to be expelled.

8 Any further immigration of non-Germans is to be prevented. We demand that all non-Germans who have entered Germany since August 2, 1914, be forced to leave the Reich immediately.

9 All citizens must possess equal rights and duties.

10 It must be the primary duty of every citizen to work mentally or physically. The activities of the individual may not conflict with the interests of the general public but must be carried on within the framework of the whole and for the good of all.

WE THEREFORE DEMAND

11 Abolition of income unearned by labour or effort;

BREAKING THE BONDAGE
OF INTEREST

12 Considering the enormous sacrifices of property and blood which every war demands from a people, personal enrichment because of war has to be seen as a crime against the people. We therefore demand complete confiscation of war profits.

13 We demand nationalization of all (previously) incorporated companies (trusts).

14 We demand profit-sharing in big businesses.

15 We demand a generous extension of old-age insurance.

16 We demand the creation and maintenance of a sound middle class, immediate communalization of the great department stores and their leasing to small businessmen at low rents; most favourable consideration to small businessmen in all government purchasing and contracting, whether national, provincial or local.

17 We demand land reform suited to our national needs, creation of a law providing for expropriation without compensation of land

for common purposes, abolition of taxes on land and prevention of all speculation.

18 We demand a relentless fight against those whose activities harm the common good. Traitors, usurers, profiteers, and so forth, are to be punished by death, regardless of creed and race.

19 We demand the substitution of a German Common Law for Roman law. Roman law serves a materialistic world order.

20 In order to make it possible for every able and industrious German to obtain a higher education, and thereby to achieve a leading position, the state must take charge of a thorough extension of our entire national educational system. The curricula of all schools must be adapted to the demands of practical life. The school must impress an understanding of the state very early, at the very beginning of rational thought in the child. We demand the education of gifted children of poor parents at the cost of the state, regardless of the parents' status or profession.

21 The state must improve public health through protection of mother and child, prevention of child labour; by imposing a physical fitness programme by means of establishing legal obligations in gymnastics and sports, and by supporting all organizations concerned with the physical training of youth.

22 We demand the abolition of mercenary troops and the creation of a popular army.

23 We demand legal measures against the conscious political lie and its propagation through the press. In order to make possible the creation of a German press, we demand that:
a. all editors and contributors of German-language newspapers be racial comrades;

b. non-German newspapers must have the express permission of the state to appear. They may not be printed in the German language.
c. every non-German investment in or influence on German newspapers to be legally forbidden and be punished by the closing of the publishing house and the immediate expulsion of the non-Germans involved.

Newspapers which conflict with the common good are to be forbidden. We demand legal measures against any tendency in art and literature which has a subversive influence on the life of our people, and the closing down of any meetings or organizations which do not conform to these demands.

24 We demand freedom for all religious denominations within the state as long as they do not endanger the state or violate the ethical and moral feelings of the Germanic race.

The party as such subscribes to a positive Christianity without binding itself to a specific denomination. It opposes the Jewish materialist spirit within and around us and is convinced that a lasting recovery of our people can only come about by an effort from within based on the principle:

THE COMMON GOOD BEFORE THE INDIVIDUAL GOOD

25 In order to carry out these policies we demand: creation of a strong central authority in the Reich. The central parliament must have unlimited authority over the entire Reich and all its organizations.

The formation of chambers according to occupation and profession, to carry out in the individual provinces the basic law enacted by the Reich.

The leaders of the party pledge that they will relentlessly seek the implementation of these points, if necessary at the cost of their lives.

Source: adapted from Barbara Lane, Leila Rupp (eds) *Nazi Ideology before 1933: A Documentation* (Manchester University Press, 1978), pp. 41–43. This version is based on a document taken by the Munich police dated 24 February 1920.

During the hyperinflation of 1923 paper money in Germany became completely worthless. Here small children make a pyramid out of bundles of banknotes. Many people survived by developing a system of barter to replace cash payments.

GERMAN INFLATION, NOVEMBER 1923

November 15, 1923 – Berlin

Unfortunate Germany! In constant turmoil, in constant unrest. A series of attempted Putsches has once more thrown the country into a state of excitement. In Munich the National Socialists, with Adolf Hitler and General Ludendorff, tried a *coup d'état*. On November 9 there were sudden revolts staged by Leftist elements in Saxony, Hamburg and Thuringia.

The value of the mark continues to drop to unbelievable figures, astronomical figures. When you go shopping you have to carry your banknotes in suitcases. Savings accounts have been absolutely wiped out. In order to mail a letter inside Germany I had to pay several million marks for a stamp. Germany's money is worth less than a scrap of paper. Foreigners can buy anything in Germany for a microscopic sum of their gold-backed currency.

Before I left Kitzingen I called on one of Mother's old friends, an old woman who had been one of the wealthiest women in that part of the country. I found the huge house stone-cold. All the rooms were practically empty. I found the old lady, shivering in blankets, by the fireplace in the only heated room in the house.

'For heaven's sake, Aunt Paula!' I exclaimed. 'Where are your rugs, your pictures, your furniture?'

'All gone, child,' she said, 'All gone to the antique shop in Munich, piece by piece. I used to have an income. That is no longer worth anything, and my furniture and pictures have gone for bread, week by week. When the last of it goes…' she shrugged her shoulders hopelessly.

Source: Bella Fromm *Blood and Banquets: A Berlin Social Diary* (Geoffrey Bles, London, 1943), p. 20.

system and the 'November criminals' who had made it possible. The Ruhr occupation accelerated the sudden collapse of the German currency, which had been the subject of a steady inflation since the end of the war in 1919, thanks largely to a vast government debt left over from the war of more than 150 billion marks. By the summer of 1923 the inflation had changed into hyperinflation, with the mark almost worthless by the end of the year. Millions of Germans dependent on pensions, or fixed incomes from investments or mortgages, were ruined; unemployment rose and there was widespread hunger in the cities. The conditions made for political extremism.

Under this charged atmosphere, the small nationalist parties began to collaborate with the idea of creating a political revolution. On 2 September 1923, following a fiery Hitler speech in front of 25,000 people, and in the presence of General Erich Ludendorff (who had been the

HITLER'S POLITICAL ADOLESCENCE

I have met him [Hitler] a few times – not at any of his meetings, of course. The first time was in 1920, at the home of my friend Clemens von Franckenstein, which was then the Lenbach villa. According to the butler, one of those present was forcing his way in everywhere, had already been there a full hour. It was Hitler. He had managed an invitation to Clé's house under the guise of being interested in operatic scenic design. Hitler very likely had the idea that theatrical design was connected with interior decorating and wallpaper-hanging, his former profession.

He had come to a house, where he had never been before, wearing gaiters, a floppy, wide-brimmed hat, and carrying a riding whip. There was a collie, too. The effect, among the Gobelin tapestries and cool marble walls, was something akin to a cowboy's sitting down on the steps of a baroque altar in leather breeches, spurs and with a Colt at his side. But Hitler sat there, the stereotype of a head waiter – at that time he was thinner, and looked somewhat starved – both impressed and restricted by the presence of a real live Herr Baron…Eventually, he managed to launch into a speech. He talked on and on, endlessly. He preached. He went on at us like a division chaplain in the Army. We did not in the least contradict him, or venture to differ in any way, but he began to bellow at us. The servants thought we were being attacked, and rushed in to defend us.

When he had gone, we sat silently confused and not at all amused. There was a feeling of dismay, as when on a train you suddenly find you are sharing a compartment with a psychotic. We sat for a long time and no one spoke.

Source: Friedrich Reck-Malleczewen *Diary of a Man in Despair* (Audiogrove, London, 1995), pp. 23–4

most important senior German commander in the last years of the war), a Fighting Association (*Kampfbund*) was set up including the SA and other paramilitary groups with the purpose of overthrowing the Berlin government. Hitler tempted Ludendorff with the prospect of becoming commander-in-chief of a new national army. During September and October, despite efforts by the government in Berlin to force the Bavarian regional government to disband the *Kampfbund*, ban the National Socialist Party and close down its newspaper (the *Völkischer Beobachter*), the Munich regime allowed Hitler to survive, anxious in case the crisis provoked a renewed threat from German communism.

In the chaotic atmosphere of the last months of 1923, Hitler and his Party leaders prepared to launch the national revolution and the March on Berlin from their Munich base. On 6 November the Bavarian government, under the temporary emergency authority of Gustav von Kahr, warned

that any attempted *Putsch* by Hitler's organization would be suppressed by force. Hitler set the date for his coup as 11 November, but when he learned that von Kahr was to address patriotic associations on the evening of 8 November in the *Bürgerbräukeller*, he decided to change the date for his coup to the earlier one. That evening 600 SA men, armed with rifles and machine-guns, surrounded the beer cellar. Hitler arrived in a red Mercedes car, dressed in his trademark trench raincoat. Inside von Kahr was talking to a bored audience about the perils of Marxism, when Göring and a group of SA men burst in and set up a heavy machine gun. Hitler then strode through the hall, jumped on a chair, fired a round from his revolver into the ceiling and announced the start of the national revolution. Kahr and two other government leaders were browbeaten into endorsing the *Putsch*, and Hitler's ally and former commanding officer, Captain Ernst Röhm, took a detachment of paramilitaries to occupy the Munich military headquarters.

The attempt to seize other military and police installations was a failure, and by the morning of 9 November it was clear that the coup was not even close to success. Kahr and his

Hitler and the local party leader, Julius Streicher (to Hitler's left), review SA men in Nuremberg on 'Germany Day' in 1923. Many SA men wore ordinary clothes and a cap because they could not afford to buy the full uniform.

THE RACIAL STATE

We National Socialists as champions of a new philosophy of life must never base ourselves on so-called 'accepted facts' – and false ones at that. If we did, we would not be the champions of a new great idea, but the coolies of the present-day lie. We must distinguish in the sharpest way between the state as a vessel and the race as its content. This vessel has meaning only if it can preserve and protect the content; otherwise it is useless.

Thus the highest purpose of a racial state is concern for the preservation of those original racial elements which bestow culture and create the beauty and dignity of a higher mankind. We, as Aryans, can conceive of the state only as the living organism of this nationality which not only assures the preservation of this nationality, but by the development of its spiritual and ideal abilities leads it to the highest freedom. …. We National Socialists know that with this conception we stand as revolutionaries in the world of today and are also branded as such.

Source: Adolf Hitler *Mein Kampf* (ed. D.C.Watt, Hutchinson, London, 1969), p. 358

Proklamation
an das deutsche Volk!
Die Regierung der November-verbrecher in Berlin ist heute für abgesetzt erklärt worden.
Eine
provisorische deutsche Nationalregierung
ist gebildet worden, diese besteht aus
Gen. Ludendorff
Ad. Hifler, Gen. v. Lossow
Obsf. v. Seisser

colleagues had escaped and were rallying forces against the coup. Ludendorff suggested a march on the town centre and Hitler, after some hesitation, agreed. It was this march, by a tired and uncertain column of Party members and supporters, that arrived in front of the Feldherrnhalle at a little after midday. They were met by a large detachment of police with heavy machine guns and an armoured car. Someone in the procession fired at the police cordon and the machine guns opened up. Göring, in the front row, was hit in the groin and collapsed; Hitler threw himself to the ground, dislocating his shoulder, and was saved from death by his bodyguard, Ulrich Graf, whose own body was riddled with bullets as he shielded his leader. In all, thirteen of the procession were killed plus two more when Röhm's brief occupation of military headquarters was overcome. Four policemen were killed. Hitler limped away in the confusion and was taken to a friend's house outside Munich, where he was arrested on 11 November, threatening suicide. There were violent pro-Hitler demonstrations in Munich for the next two days, but with his arrest on charges of high treason the *Putsch* finally petered out.

Above: The courtroom in Munich, in a converted barracks, where Hitler and his fellow conspirators were tried from 26 February to 1 April, when judgement was passed. Hitler used the trial as an opportunity to make nationalist propaganda. The trial judge, Georg Neidhardt, was openly sympathetic to Hitler's cause and was later rewarded with a good job in the Third Reich.

Opposite: A proclamation published by the organisers of the Munich *Putsch* on 8/9 November 1923. It reads: 'Proclamation to the German people! The government of November criminals in Berlin is today declared to be set aside. A provisional national government has been established, which consists of General Ludendorff, Adolf Hitler, General von Lossow and Colonel von Seisser'.

Above: A photographic portrait of Gustav Stresemann, taken in 1923.

The failed coup might have cost Hitler his life, and ought to have ended his political career. Hitler, Ludendorff and a number of other conspirators were put on trial in Munich on 26 February 1924. Hitler was given extensive opportunity to declare that he had only been acting as a patriot, and the trial attracted nationalist attention from all over Germany. On 1 April the court sentenced him to five years in prison and acquitted Ludendorff. Requests to ensure that Hitler was deported to Austria after serving his sentence (which was legally possible) were overruled, and on 18 October 1924 the Austrian authorities withdrew his citizenship, making him formally 'stateless'. He began his sentence in Landsberg prison, where he dictated the first volume of his autobiography to his secretary and disciple Rudolf Hess, which was later published in 1925 under the title *Mein Kampf*, 'my struggle'. The Party was banned even in Bavaria and those of his supporters who remained loyal to the cause joined a new patriotic association, the National Socialist Freedom Movement, which on 7 April 1924 won 17 per cent of the vote in regional elections in Bavaria, and 50 per cent in Munich. In Hitler's absence, however, the momentum of the movement slowed, while Party leaders in other parts of Germany, particularly in Berlin, began to prepare for a new era without Hitler's leadership. His opportunity came as a result of the leniency of the Bavarian authorities. In recognition of his exemplary behaviour as a prisoner, he was freed on 19 December 1924 and could once again take up the reins of leadership after serving just nine months of his five-year sentence.

1925–1928 Refounding the Party

The Germany that Hitler returned to in 1925 had survived the crisis of 1923 and begun to establish a greater degree of political and economic stability. The inflation ended in 1923 and a new stable currency, masterminded by the banker Hjalmar Schacht, was introduced. The Allies agreed to reschedule the financial reparations demanded from Germany in the Dawes Plan of April 1924. The inflation left millions of Germans much poorer than they had been before it, but the stabilization allowed normal economic activity to be resumed and the German economy entered its first period of stable expansion since the outbreak of war in 1914. The 1924 parliamentary elections produced a centre–right coalition government whose dominant figure was the German People's Party leader, Gustav Stresemann. He was able to persuade much of the right wing that it was more sensible to work with the former Allied powers rather than against them, and in 1925 negotiated a treaty at Locarno with Britain, France, Italy and Belgium which confirmed the frontiers of Western Europe agreed in 1919, giving Germany some guarantee against further French encroachments. The Locarno Treaty of 1 December 1925 was the first agreement since the war in which Germany had negotiated as an equal partner. On 19 September 1926 Germany was admitted to the post-war League of Nations as a reward for her international good behaviour.

The post-war crisis in Germany also encouraged a mood of indulgent, even decadent social and artistic life. Berlin became famous as a centre for cabaret and the new music craze, American jazz. Many Germans reacted to inflation and impoverishment by trying to forget about the future and live for the present. The despair and nihilism was turned into a vibrant

Above: Guests in a Berlin striptease club in 1920 wear masks to try to conceal their identity. Postwar Berlin developed a reputation for clubs, music and cabaret that challenged conventional morality and encouraged sexual licence.

Opposite: A satirical painting by the German expressionist artist Otto Dix of *The Seven Deadly Sins*. The small central figure in front of the figure of death is clearly Adolf Hitler. Dix was one of the leaders of the revolution in modern art in Germany in the 1920s but the work was treated as degenerate in the future Third Reich.

31

modern art and literature. The German expressionist painters – Otto Dix, Max Beckmann, Max Ernst and a host of others – produced works that were savage indictments of the age, or lurid flights of the imagination. The playwright Bertolt Brecht and the artist Käthe Kollwitz used their communism to write plays and verse, or to paint images that invoked the failures of the bourgeois German world that had spawned crisis in the first place. The satirical artist Georg Grosz lampooned traditional German society in his cartoons and sketches, and in 1923 was put on trial and fined for work that his judge regarded as pornographic. Many Germans, among them Hitler, rejected modernism and deplored both its challenge to existing values and its nihilism, but it turned Germany briefly into the European centre of a richly experimental and creative culture.

For Hitler and his supporters, the stable years of the Weimar Republic worked against the prospect of his national revolution, which flourished on crisis. Hitler's first task was to refound the Party and establish his authority over it. During his imprisonment the northern wing of his supporters in Prussia, the largest German province, had rallied behind one of Hitler's close

GUSTAV STRESEMANN

The son of a Berlin beer trader, Gustav Stresemann became a business lobbyist for the German chocolate industry in 1901 before embarking on a political career with the German National Liberal Party. He became the youngest member of parliament in 1907. His politics was a mixture of aggressive nationalism and concern for the social question. During the First World War he supported the idea of annexing conquered territories and expanding Germany's colonial empire. In 1919 he became president of a new political party, the right-wing German People's Party (DVP). He represented the strand of German nationalism that recognized the importance of not confronting the victorious Allies but working carefully to undermine the settlement imposed on Germany in 1919. In 1923 he was briefly German chancellor, and from November 1923 until his death in October 1929, he was German foreign minister. He was successful in reintegrating Germany in the European states' system. In 1925 he negotiated the Locarno Pact with France, Britain, Belgium and Italy which guaranteed the territorial settlement on Germany's western frontier. In 1926 Germany was admitted to the League of Nations. That year he won the Nobel Prize for Peace. He favoured greater collaboration between European states and wanted greater disarmament if other states would honour their pledge to disarm. In Germany many nationalists regarded him as someone who had betrayed the national ideal, but to many other Germans his politics came to represent a sensible compromise with the prevailing order and the best way to secure German interests. There was general agreement that with his premature death, Germany had lost a major statesman.

collaborators, Gregor Strasser, who became a parliamentary deputy in December 1924 as part of a radical nationalist bloc. Ernst Röhm, briefly imprisoned in 1924 for his part in the Beerhall *Putsch*, had become the leader of around 30,000 paramilitary supporters and did not want to take orders from Hitler. General Ludendorff resigned from the National Socialist Freedom Movement in February 1925 and increasingly distanced himself from Hitler. It took Hitler more than a year to overturn the many threats to his continued role as *Führer*. On 16 February 1925 he benefited from the decision of the Bavarian regional government to lift the emergency ban on the National Socialist Party imposed in 1923. On 26 February the first new issue of the Party paper appeared with Hitler's directives for reconstructing the Party, and on 27 February Hitler delivered his first speech after leaving prison in the same beerhall where the failed *Putsch* had been launched. Thousands of supporters gathered outside, unable to get seats. The speech was one of the most important of his career. Many of those in the hall welcomed his return and endorsed his demand to be considered the sole source of authority for the Party, but others kept their distance. Strasser agreed to collaborate as an equal rather than a subordinate, and

THE STRASSER BROTHERS

Among the cohort of Party leaders who worked with Hitler in the 1920s the most important was the Gauleiter of Lower Bavaria, Gregor Strasser (1892–1934). The son of a Bavarian official, Gregor trained as a pharmacist before joining the Bavarian army in 1914. He rose to the rank of first lieutenant and was decorated with the Iron Cross first and second class. In 1919 he and his younger brother, Otto Strasser (1897–1974), joined the Freikorps and helped to put down the Bavarian communist revolution. He joined the Hitler movement in 1921 and took part in the Putsch in 1923, for which he was imprisoned. On his early release he entered the Bavarian regional parliament as part of a nationalist bloc, and in December 1924 became a Reichstag deputy as a member of the National Socialist Freedom Movement, a cover name for the banned National Socialist Party. In 1925 Strasser joined again with Hitler, though he insisted on being treated as a 'colleague' and not a 'follower'. In 1928 he became the Organization Leader of the Party and set about reorganizing its structure. Strasser was on the left of the Party, attracted to socialism as well as nationalism. In 1932 he began secret negotiations with the Trade Unions and with other political parties to try to find a way of creating a coalition which would allow National Socialism a share of power, possibly under his leadership. In December 1932 Hitler ordered him to stop the discussions and to remain loyal to him. Strasser promptly resigned and gave up political life until his murder eighteen months later. His brother Otto left the Party in July 1930 because he wanted it to be more socialist. He fled from Germany in early 1933 after Hitler came to power, eventually emigrating to Canada.

assumed leadership of the north German wing of the Party, supported by Joseph Goebbels, a virulent anti-Semite and anti-Marxist from the Ruhr, who wanted National Socialism to adopt a more revolutionary profile and who initially saw Hitler as a reactionary figure.

The Party that Hitler tried to rebuild was part of a broader nationalist movement which was fragmented into many small groups and associations, with a limited membership. Hitler wanted to separate his Party from the rest of the nationalist front and give it a clear identity. The opportunity to display the new party came with the death of the first president of the Weimar Republic, the moderate social-democrat Friedrich Ebert, on 28 February 1925. Hitler's Party decided to put up General Ludendorff as their candidate against the socialist, Wilhelm Marx and Ludendorff's former commander-in-chief Field Marshal Paul von Hindenburg. The result showed how far Hitler still had to go. Ludendorff won only 285,000

Hitler greets members of the SA as they arrive at Nuremberg railway station for the 1927 annual Party Congress. Hitler liked to mix with ordinary Party comrades, but the SA was a constant source of unrest and rebellion against the Party leadership.

votes out of the 27 million cast and was eliminated from the second run-off election, in which Hindenburg won by a narrow majority, the beneficiary of votes switched from Ludendorff. The election of Hindenburg gave the nationalist centre and right in Germany a figure to rally round, making the prospects for Hitler's national revolution even dimmer. His own situation was made worse by the decision taken in Bavaria on 9 March 1925 to ban him from speaking; the ban was imposed in most other German provinces and lasted for two years. He was forced to give speeches to private gatherings and lost the opportunity to do what he had done so effectively before 1923, in rallying support through carefully staged and theatrical public appearances.

By the end of 1925 the Party was only half the size it had been in 1923, with 27,000 members organized in 600 small local branches. It was a marginal movement with little prospect of power. Disillusionment in the north German wing of the Party led Gregor Strasser to draft a new party programme in February 1926, with a more aggressively socialist and anti-capitalist message. On 14 February Hitler called together a meeting of delegates from all over Germany at the Bavarian city of Bamberg, to both assert his undivided authority over the movement and quash any idea of Party democracy or a more socialist political agenda. He spoke for a remarkable five hours, an achievement that perhaps stunned his audience into acquiescence. The speech defined the future of the movement. Hitler rejected any alteration in the Party programme of 1920 – it was, he said, 'the foundation of our religion, of our ideology' – and also rejected the idea of popular nationalist revolution in favour of the legal path to power, using democratic institutions to destroy democracy. He insisted that his own person as Leader was an indispensable factor in the Party's future success, and succeeded in extracting oaths of loyalty from all those present, including the more sceptical Strasser. The meeting restored Hitler to his position as *Führer*. On 22 May, a meeting in Munich confirmed that Hitler's party programme was unalterable and established a small National Socialist leadership corps with Hitler as chairman, subject to no constitutional constraints. On 3–4 July 1926 the second national Party Congress was held at Weimar, where Hitler was formally accorded the title of 'Leader'. Reviewing a parade of SA on 4 July, Hitler for the first time stretched out his arm in greeting in what afterwards became, during the period of the dictatorship, the mandatory Hitler salute.

In the second half of 1926 some of the key organizations of the Party were established on a firm foundation. In July the Hitler Youth was instigated, based on a youth branch of the Party first set up in 1922. On 1 November 1926 Hitler refounded the SA without Ernst Röhm who, disillusioned with politics, had left for Latin America. The SA was now led by Franz

---

Overleaf: Hitler, standing in a car, reviews the SA as they march past in the spring of 1926. Hitler had by now succeeded in re-establishing himself as the Party's leader after his period in prison. The banner reads 'Death to Marxism'. The struggle against German communism was seen by many Germans as much more important than the Party's anti-Semitism.

THE MUNICH BROWN HOUSE

The 'Brown House' (*Braunes Haus*) was the name given to the National Socialist headquarters in Munich. The large, solid building was bought by the Party on 26 May 1930 after their previous headquarters at 50, Schelling Street had become too small. The building, in the style of a small palace, belonged to a British industrialist. His widow sold it to the Party for 805,000 marks, a sum that was made available by the German industrialist Fritz Thyssen. The building was remodelled so that it could act as the national headquarters and was finally opened in 1931. It was the site of the Party chancellery and the Party's Reich leadership. A large card-index was built up profiling every member of the Party, which had grown from 129,000 in 1930 to 849,000 three years later. By 1945 there were approximately 8 million members. The Brown House briefly achieved international recognition as the site of the notorious Munich conference on 29–30 September 1938, when it was agreed to cede the German-speaking areas of Czechoslovakia to Germany. In 1945 it was destroyed by Allied bombing and in 1947 the remains were pulled down. The site remained unbuilt until 2005, when it was decided to construct a document centre there on the theme of National Socialism.

Pfeffer von Salomon, who accepted Hitler's demand that the paramilitary organization become subordinate to the Party, even though many of its predominantly working-class recruits were not actually Party members. The SA remained an unruly element, and in May 1927 the SA leader in Munich, the released murderer Edmund Heines, was expelled for his refusal to toe the Party line. In order to provide himself with a loyal security guard Hitler, in November 1925, had set up the *Schutzstaffel* (SS), a small unit drawn from the SA, whose job was to protect above all the person of the Leader. To satisfy the ambitions of the north German wing of the Party, Gregor Strasser was made Chief of Propaganda on 16 September and on 1 November Goebbels was rewarded with the task of organizing the Party in the capital as regional leader (*Gauleiter*) of Berlin. Over the following year the Party made slow progress, building up a national network of supporters and office-holders. In 1928 a national system of regional leaders was confirmed, each *Gauleiter* personally appointed by Hitler and bound to him by an oath of loyalty. The central apparatus of the Party was dominated by Hitler from the Munich headquarters which was rehoused in 1931 in a large villa in the city centre, called the Brown House, after the yellow-brown shade adopted by the Party as the colour of its uniform.

During 1927 the Party focused its efforts on trying to win the German working class away from Marxism. Many Party members came from a working-class background, though the leadership was predominantly middle-class, a cross-section of civil servants, small businessmen, craftsmen, teachers, ex-soldiers or political drifters (like Hitler himself). By 1928 the Party membership had increased to around 95,000 but the conditions necessary to turn that support into effective political success were still absent. In May 1928 there were fresh parliamentary elections and the Party embarked on a national propaganda campaign in the cities. The result was a disaster for Hitler's strategy of the legal path to power. The Party polled only 809,000 votes (100,000 fewer than the nationalist alliance in 1924) and won only 12 Reichstag seats. Hitler was technically stateless and could not be a parliamentary deputy, but Gregor Strasser and Hermann Göring became his principal representatives in the Reichstag. The largest gains were made by the German Social Democratic Party with 153 seats, and in June 1928 a broad coalition government was formed with a socialist chancellor, Hermann Müller, and Stresemann as foreign minister.

The National Socialists began a lengthy post-mortem about what had gone wrong with their campaign. The highest successes had come in the countryside and small towns. It became clear that there was a much broader potential support for the movement here than in the cities, where the German socialist and communist parties were difficult to dislodge. On 31 August 1928 Hitler convened, instead of the annual party rally, a gathering of all Party leaders in the Munich beerhall to discuss Party organization. A former regional leader, Artur Dinter, raised a proposal that Hitler should be advised by a Party 'senate' on questions of political strategy. In the subsequent vote, Dinter's was the only one in favour. In October he was expelled from the Party and Hitler sent a circular letter to all Party leaders asking them to indicate their agreement that his authority in the Party should be unlimited. They all returned their approval. On 16 November Hitler gave his first speech in the German capital, at the Berlin Sports Palace, in front of 10,000 supporters. The decision to focus on Berlin marked an important change for Hitler, whose movement was widely regarded as southern German, with its centre in Bavaria. Over the following year Hitler began to move from the local to the national stage, paving the way for the startling expansion of the movement when Germany was plunged once again into political and economic crisis.

1929–1932 The Search for the German Messiah

Hitler and his Party would never have come to power without the severe economic and political crisis that engulfed Germany from 1929 onwards. The chief problem was the fragile nature of economic revival in Germany after the inflation; economic fears paved the way for political radicalism, both left and right. The economic problems of the republic began before the Wall Street Crash of October 1929, when the American stock market started its precipitous collapse. German recovery had been very dependent on foreign loans, many of them short-term, and on the revival of international trade. During 1929 the supply of loans began to dry up as investors became cautious about sustained German economic growth. German agriculture, and many of the traditional German craft trades, were declining sectors, hit by price falls and the rise of new, cheaper mass-produced consumer goods. Unemployment was high throughout the good years of the 1920s, but by the spring of 1929 it reached 3 million. Relations between business leaders and trade unions were poor throughout the 1920s thanks to the introduction shortly after the war of new legislation on wage bargaining, and in 1928 there were large-scale strikes and lockouts in the Ruhr-Rhineland industrial heartland. The antagonism benefited chiefly the German Communist Party because many workers thought the social-democrats too cautious. In 1928 the communists won four times more votes than Hitler, with 54 seats in parliament.

The first signs of economic downturn in 1929 created growing alarm among a German population that did not want to return to the instability and hardships of the early 1920s. Fear of a communist revival was a powerful one among all political and social groups, particularly the moderate socialists, who needed to keep working-class support to remain in power. Anti-communism remained one of the principal factors pushing voters towards support for Hitler's party, because National Socialism (and especially its violent paramilitary wing, the SA) was identified as the only force in Germany in the late 1920s willing to take the battle directly into communist strongholds. During the spring and summer of 1929 the Party began to make modest electoral gains. In the local elections in Saxony in May they won 5 per cent of the vote, double the national average achieved the year before. On 23 June the Party won control of the town council in the city of Coburg, and a National Socialist became mayor. Following this success Hitler found himself propelled into national politics by a decision to join with other nationalist groups in a campaign against the Young Plan, negotiated by the American financier Owen Young and signed on 7 June 1929, which gave Germany some relief from immediate reparation demands, but committed Germany to paying reparations until 1988. A National Committee was formed, made up of the huge veterans' organization the Steel Helmet (*Stahlhelm*), led by Franz Seldte, the German National People's Party (DNVP), led by the newspaper owner Alfred Hugenberg, and the National Socialists. Hitler was the junior partner in the national coalition, but he was the one to profit most from it.

In September Hugenberg and Hitler launched the campaign for a national plebiscite against 'the Enslavement of the German People'. The aim was to secure signatures against the Young Plan from at least 10 per cent of the electorate (the constitutional requirement) so as to compel parliament to institute a national referendum on the issue. Hitler made the most of the campaign: he appeared on platforms side-by-side with the country's nationalist elite, while Party propaganda took the opportunity to attack the whole Versailles system, the vindictiveness of the Allies and the supine behaviour of the Weimar governments. By 31 October 1929 over 4 million signatures had been secured and the referendum was scheduled to take place in December. The campaign that followed was a failure, for only 5.8 million people voted against the Young Plan, while Hugenberg alienated his more moderate nationalist allies and the conservative president, von Hindenburg, by his strident language. On 10 March 1930 the German parliament voted to accept the terms of the Young Plan.

The radical Party leader of Berlin, Joseph Goebbels. He was highly critical of Hitler's 'reactionary' tactics but eventually came to regard Hitler as the true German messiah. He was rewarded with the job of organizing Party propaganda and became Minister of Propaganda and Popular Enlightenment in 1933.

Hitler, on the other hand, enjoyed unrestricted publicity in the Hugenberg press for four months and had no allies to alienate in his savage attacks on the existing order. By the end of the year Hitler was at last a genuine national figure, and one identified in the eyes of many Germans as someone committed to changing the existing system and the unfair balance of international power, which still made Germany's fate an object of the interests of other states.

The Wall Street Crash of October 1929 coincided with the death of Gustav Stresemann, who was the architect of most of the international agreements secured with the West. His death, coming at the same time as a growing economic panic, undermined what efforts were being made to sustain a moderate centre politics in Germany. In early 1930 a bitter argument over cuts in welfare between the social-democrats and their coalition partners ended with the resignation of the chancellor on 27 March, and the decision of the social democrats to abandon participation in government (which they did not exercise again until the 1960s). The Catholic Centre Party leader, Heinrich Brüning, was invited to form a new government but it was a weak coalition of right and centre parties. The need to push through tough measures to keep down government spending in a time of rapidly rising unemployment and shrinking tax revenues forced Brüning to rely more and more on rule by presidential decree, under Article 48 of the constitution. The practice accelerated the decline of public trust in the parliamentary system, while the strictly deflationary policies made the economic crisis worse. In June 1930 unemployment was double the rate of a year before. Reichstag elections were called for September in an atmosphere of growing crisis.

The electoral tactics adopted by the National Socialists in 1930 differed markedly from 1928. The Party organized associations of National Socialist teachers, students, doctors and lawyers who could be counted on to spread the word among colleagues and peers. Greater emphasis was placed on recruiting the conservative sections of the community and playing down the socialism of the movement. This provoked crisis in May 1930 when Gregor Strasser's brother, Otto, confronted Hitler with accusations of betrayal to the middle classes. He and a number of other radical members left the Party in protest. In late August the SA leader, von Salomon, argued with Hitler over the role of the SA, which he saw as a rival to the established national army, and he resigned when Hitler refused to listen to his views. In Berlin radical SA units under Walter Stennes went on strike in protest but Hitler intervened

---

Opposite above: A shop in 1930 during the long economic recession announces 'Total Bankruptcy Clearance Sale'. High unemployment and short-time working hit many small retailers because regular customers could no longer afford to buy anything but essentials.

Opposite below: A column of women marching through the Brandenburg Gate and down Unter den Linden, in central Berlin in 1931, 'to protest against unemployment. 'Only a strong Germany,' reads the banner, 'can give German men work'. By 1933 around 8 million fewer people were in work than in 1929.

HEINRICH BRÜNING (1885–1970)

Chancellor of Germany from 1930 to 1932, Heinrich Brüning tried to steer his country through the worst economic crisis in its history. The son of a wine merchant, he embarked on an academic career before the First World War then volunteered for the German infantry in 1915. He became a successful and highly decorated soldier, and emerged from the war determined on a political rather than an academic career. In 1924 he entered parliament as a member of the Catholic Centre Party, and became a prominent spokesman on economic affairs. In 1929 he became the Centre Party leader in parliament. When the Grand Coalition of socialists, Catholics and moderate nationalists collapsed in March 1930, Brüning was asked on 29 March to form a new government. He struggled to cope with Germany's deteriorating economic situation and was committed to maintaining financial security rather than using state loans to help achieve economic revival. The economic policies of his government contributed to a rising tide of unemployment and popular political protest. By 1932 the Chancellor faced growing hostility from von Hindenburg, whose support was needed to pass emergency legislation through parliament. When he tried to introduce a scheme to settle unemployed workers on the landed estates of the Prussian aristocracy, Hindenburg forced his resignation on 30 May 1932. He was opposed to the rise of Hitler's movement, and in 1934 he emigrated to the United States to avoid the threat of imprisonment, where he established an academic career at Harvard. He returned to Germany briefly in 1954, but went back to America, where he died in 1970.

personally to keep the radical element in the SA under control, taking over temporary command of the SA himself. The new direction of electoral policy was made clear with the appointment, on 1 June 1930, of Walther Darré as head of the Party's agrarian sector. He set about revolutionizing the Party's activities in the countryside with the establishment of Party cells in every rural district and a Party trustee, usually a local and well-respected farmer, in every village and hamlet. Germany's peasantry were hit particularly harshly by the slump, and the fall in farm prices, together with the National Socialist promise to cut interest rates and protect German producers, turned millions of farm votes towards Hitler. In the rural districts of northern, Protestant, Germany the Party polled an average of 43 per cent of the votes in the 1930 election.

Hitler imposed upon himself a gruelling schedule of high-profile election speeches across the whole of Germany during August and September. The results, when they were declared on 14 September, showed an astonishing increase in the National Socialist vote. From just 12 seats in 1928, the Party now had 107 and a popular vote of 6.4 million; from a small splinter party it had become the second-largest party in parliament, behind the 143 social-democrat seats and well ahead of the increased representation for the German communists, who

DESCENT INTO CIVIL WAR, OCTOBER 1930

Monday, 13 October 1930   *Berlin*

Reichstag opening. The whole afternoon and evening mass demonstrations by the Nazis. During the afternoon they smashed the windows of Wertheim, Grünfeld, and other department stores in the Leipzigerstrasse. In the evening they assembled in the Potsdamer Platz, shouting 'Germany awake!' 'Death to Judah', 'Heil Hitler.' Their ranks were continually dispersed by the police, in lorries and on horseback. At half past eleven I went down Leipzigerstrasse to Friedrichstrasse and stood outside the Fürstenhof for three quarters of an hour. In the main the Nazis consisted of adolescent riff-raff which made off yelling as soon as the police began to use rubber truncheons. I have never witnessed so much rabble in these parts.

In front of the Fürstenhof I watched some of these youngsters, unemployed getting an extra dole, perform regular patrol duty. From time to time a pack of adolescents, pursued by the police, would rush by in wild disorder. Poor devils who had received two or three marks from the Thyssen money-box for proving their 'patriotic' frame of mind. These disorders remind me of the days just before the revolution [of 1918/19], with the same mass meetings and the same Catilian figures lounging about and demonstrating.

If the Government does not take matters firmly in hand, we shall slide into civil war. In any case today's rioting will, I estimate, cost us between five hundred million and a billion marks in stock exchange losses and the withdrawal of foreign assets. The destruction in Leipzigerstrasse as well as the patrols between Prinz-Albrecht-Strasse and Potsdamer Platz confirm that the mischief was organised. Only businesses with Jewish names suffered....Nazis invaded the Palast-Hotel and in the hall roared 'Germany awake!' and 'Death to Judah.' The gorge rises at so much pig-headed stupidity and spite.

Source: C. Kessler (ed) *The Diaries of a Cosmopolitan 1918–1937: Count Harry Kessler* (Phoenix Press, London, 2000), pp. 400–1

increased their deputies from 54 to 77. The result for Brüning was disastrous because the extremes had been strengthened at the expense of the moderate centre parties on which he had hoped to rely for a parliamentary majority. The three largest parties – social-democrats, communists and National Socialists – refused to serve under him, and his government survived only by using rule by presidential decree and relying on occasional support from the German Social-Democrat Party, which did not want to see either National Socialists or communists benefiting from the political crisis. The Hitler movement recorded even higher gains in many of the regional elections held during 1930. The capacity of the movement to mobilize the growing protest votes against parliamentary weakness and mounting poverty surprised even Hitler and the Party leadership, showing the extent to which success relied on the deepening of the crisis rather than on the Party's electoral tactics. Hitler found himself in the strange position of seeking a strong Germany yet profiting from its weaknesses at one and the same time.

Over the following two years Hitler and his movement sought a way to achieve power through a combination of the ballot box and noisy, sometimes violent, street protest. Over the same period the major political parties of the left and centre tried to find a way of preventing him from achieving power. Hitler was clear in his mind that he had to avoid the risk of any hasty and illegal action on the part of the Party and the paramilitary SA, many of whom were not satisfied with electoral politics and wanted some strategy for seizing power. On 30 November 1930 he addressed a congress of the SA where he announced his decision to appoint Ernst Röhm, the former SA leader, as the new SA chief-of-staff. In January 1931 the SA was reorganized to cope with its rapidly growing numbers. Over the following two years the organization grew from 100,000 men to half-a-million, many of them recruited from the army of unemployed, which grew from almost 5 million in January 1931 to reach a peak of over 6 million a year later. SA men could be sure of regular meals and welfare while the comradeship and street fighting against communists gave them a strong shared sense of identity as soldiers of the national revolution. On 5 January 1931 Röhm was formally appointed chief-of-staff, while Hitler retained the supreme command.

Almost immediately Hitler was faced with a crisis in the restless ranks of the SA. On 20 February he issued a directive that the SA was to cease street-fighting for the moment in order to enhance the Party's image of legality. However the directive was challenged by the SA in Berlin and Eastern Germany under the command of Walter Stennes, who had already clashed with Hitler in August 1930 when his SA men had occupied the offices of the Berlin *Gauleiter*, Joseph Goebbels, in protest at the failure to include SA men as candidates in the election.

Three girls watch a formation of SA men march past Hitler in Nuremberg, the home of the annual Party Congress. Many women found Hitler fascinating; some even wrote to ask him to father their children.

Goebbels was himself on the radical wing of the party, in favour of involving workers more fully in the movement. On 15 January 1931 the Party had set up a National Socialist Factory Cell Organization based in Berlin to recruit working-class members; like the SA, the organization was keen to engage in more extra-parliamentary activity. The crisis point was reached when the chancellor, Heinrich Brüning, published an emergency decree on 28 March outlawing the wearing of political uniforms, banning street demonstrations and requiring all parties to obtain police permission before holding political rallies. On 30 March Hitler announced that all Party members should obey the new legislation. Two days later, Stennes led his SA in a revolt in Berlin against the Party leadership. Hitler travelled to the capital and made an emotional appeal for loyalty which succeeded in stifling the rebellion. Stennes was expelled from the SA and the Party, and all SA men in the area that Stennes had commanded were compelled to swear an oath of loyalty to Hitler or face expulsion. The following day Goebbels was ordered to carry out a purge of the SA and the local Party organization. Stennes was replaced by Edmund Heines, who had previously been expelled from the Party for homosexuality and insubordination.

The conflict with Stennes highlighted the tensions in the Party created by the decision to pursue the legal path to power at a time when the economic crisis was creating what many regarded as the ripe conditions for a revolution. Despite the ban on uniforms and demonstrations, the streets of Germany's major cities descended into something approaching a state of civil war between communists and nationalists. Both sides resorted to political murder and the police found it difficult to control the breakdown of law and order. During 1931 46 Party members were killed and 4,800 wounded in the violence. In local elections the National Socialists began to win very large shares of the vote. In Oldenburg on 17 May 1931 they won over 37 per cent; in Hamburg (one of the centres of communist activity) the Party won 25 per cent of the vote in September. The Party now took large numbers of seats in municipal and provincial assemblies as popular confidence in the parliamentary system and the economic future of Germany began to evaporate almost entirely. Party leaders pressed Hitler to engage in more radical tactics, but he remained adamant that only the legal path to power would work in Germany. During the summer months he began to establish contacts with other leading political figures in order to find allies for the eventual moment when the President would be compelled to invite him to form a government. In mid-July 1931 he agreed to form a national front with the veterans' league, the Steel Helmet (*Stahlhelm*), and the German Nationalist Party, former allies from the campaign against the Young Plan. He was invited to meet Brüning in July, and again in October, to see whether his movement could be incorporated as part of a coalition, but Hitler refused to co-operate. On 11 October the alliance with the Steel Helmet and the nationalists was cemented formally in a meeting at Bad Harzburg, where the nationalist 'Harzburg Front' was formed. Hitler ensured that there remained some distance between his party and the conservative nationalists under Hugenberg, but the alliance brought together all those forces in Germany hostile to the failing Weimar constitution, the Versailles settlement and the threat of communist revolution created through economic collapse.

While Hitler was learning to play the role of a national politician he was struck by a personal crisis that might have ended his career if he had not, in the end, restrained his reaction. On the evening of 18 September 1931 Hitler's twenty-three-year-old niece, Geli Raubal, killed herself with Hitler's pistol in his apartment in Munich following an argument with her uncle. The body was only discovered the following morning when Hitler was in Nuremberg. Urgent telephone calls to Hitler's hotel discovered that his cavalcade had just left. A hotel porter was sent in pursuit by taxi and finally delivered the news. Hitler raced back to Munich in turmoil. His relationship with Geli has been open to much speculation, but there is no doubt that she was an important part of his private world, and her loss hit him severely. He withdrew to a villa on Tegernsee for a few days to try to master what one witness called his 'hysterical despair'. There were fears that he might follow her example and kill himself, and for that reason the funeral was arranged in Vienna on 23 September

A painting of a Hitler election meeting, 'Hitler as a speaker at a mass rally', which was later displayed in German schools as a form of propaganda. In the foreground can be seen a heckler being dealt with by three SA men. The main banner reads 'Adolf Hitler shows you the Way', the smaller one 'Adolf Hitler gives you work and bread'.

without Hitler's presence. The following day he arrived in Hamburg to give an election address, but on 25 September he drove to Vienna and the next day went with his family to Geli's new grave to pay his last respects. The full truth of the relationship between uncle and niece has never been discovered.

During the last few months of 1931 the economic crisis continued to worsen as credit dried up, bankruptcies increased and industrial production fell back to the levels of the 1890s. As investors panicked, over 6 billion marks of funds were withdrawn from Germany and only an international agreement signed on 20 June 1931 to suspend the repayment of loans and reparations for a year, usually known as the Hoover Moratorium, prevented the German

A dispirited Hitler and Göring in conversation with the SA chief-of-staff Ernst Röhm in 1932, during the ban on wearing uniforms. The electoral campaigns failed to gain Hitler the job he wanted as German chancellor while the SA remained an unruly element in the movement, capable of alienating the electorate rather than winning it over.

government from facing bankruptcy. The number of registered unemployed, which peaked in the winter of 1931–2, did not include all of those not liable for union registration, nor the millions of German workers forced to work short hours. The scale of the economic devastation and the length of the recession, which shattered the rising expectations prompted by the brief period of economic recuperation in the 1920s, played a primary role in pushing many German voters to the political extremes, both right and left, and undermining still further the prospect of building a moderate centre in parliament. The rise in extremism prompted Brüning to pass a further decree law on 8 December banning all political badges and uniforms, and limiting the freedom of the press and the right of assembly. The move was directed principally at the National Socialists, partly prompted by the discovery of compromising documents in the possession of a Party delegate in the local Hesse parliament, Werner Best, outlining how the movement should act in the event of an attempted communist coup. The publicity generated by the so-called 'Boxheimer documents' did not affect the Party's continued expansion. By the end of 1931 there were 806,300 members.

During 1932 it was evident that the domestic economic and political crisis would have to be resolved in one way or another, but it was not yet evident that the solution was a Hitler chancellorship. The year was dominated by three elections: the first was a presidential election with the end of Hindenburg's term of office; the second two were parliamentary elections, one in July and the second in November.

The presidential election was widely regarded as a test of the current political crisis. In early January Hitler was invited by Brüning to support a second term for President von Hindenburg as a symbol of national unity. Hitler offered to support Hindenburg if new parliamentary elections were called at the same time, but the president rejected the proposal. By early February Hitler had decided to stand for the presidency himself but was prohibited from doing so as he was technically stateless, enjoying neither German nor Austrian citizenship. The National Socialist minister of the interior in the provincial government of Brunswick agreed to appoint Hitler as a special professor at the local Technical University, a post that carried with it automatic German citizenship, and on 26 February Hitler formally assumed his new status at a ceremony in Berlin. A few days before, on 22 February, Goebbels had announced, to an enthusiastic crowd in the Berlin Sports Palace , Hitler's decision to stand.

The election was held on 13 March and showed a remarkable growth in support for the Hitler movement since the last elections in 1930. Hindenburg won 18.6 million votes against Hitler's 11.3 million; Hindenburg's share of the vote was 49.6 per cent, a few thousand short of the majority required for victory. Two other candidates, including the communist leader Ernst Thälmann (who won 13 per cent of the vote), were excluded from the second ballot. Hitler set off on a gruelling electioneering campaign, for the first time using an aeroplane to carry him from city to city in the full glare of publicity. The run-off was held on 10 April with Hindenburg winning 19.3 million votes and Hitler 13.4 million, including an estimated 1 million transferred from the communists. The bulk of the nationalist vote went to Hitler, undermining the conventional appeal of von Hindenburg to right-wing voters. Hindenburg's success rested on the votes of social-democrats, Catholics and liberals, all of them groups

ALBERT SPEER JOINS THE PARTY, 1931

The following day I applied for membership in the National Socialist Party and in January 1931 became member Number 474,481.

It was an utterly undramatic decision. Then and ever afterward I scarcely felt myself to be a member of a political party. I was not choosing the NSDAP, but becoming a follower of Hitler, whose magnetic force had reached out to me the first time I saw him and had not, thereafter, released me. His persuasiveness, the peculiar magic of his by no means pleasant voice, the oddity of his rather banal manner, the seductive simplicity with which he attacked the complexity of our problems – all that bewildered and fascinated me. I knew virtually nothing about his programme. He had taken hold of me before I had grasped what was happening.....

It must have been during these months that my mother saw an SA parade in the streets of Heidelberg. The sight of discipline in a time of chaos, the impression of energy in an atmosphere of universal hopelessness, seems to have won her over also. At any rate, without ever having heard a speech or read a pamphlet, she joined the party. Both of us seem to have felt this decision to be a breach with a liberal family tradition. In any case, we concealed it from one another and from my father. Only years later, long after I had become part of Hitler's inner circle, did my mother and I discover by chance that we shared early membership in the party....

I did see quite a number of rough spots in the party doctrines. But I assumed that they would be polished in time, as has so often happened in the history of other revolutions. The crucial fact appeared to me to be that I personally had to choose between a future Communist Germany or a future National Socialist Germany...

Source: Albert Speer *Inside the Third Reich* (Weidenfeld, London, 1970), pp. 17–19

generally hostile to the Prussian traditions represented by the aged field marshal. The presidential election turned German politics upside-down and made Hitler a difficult figure to ignore in the subsequent efforts to find a workable parliamentary coalition.

The immediate reaction to Hitler's strong showing in the election was to provoke the government, on 13 April, into banning the SA and the SS and prohibiting the wearing of Party paramilitary uniform. The Party reacted with widespread protests while Hitler immediately threw himself into the task of winning the provincial parliamentary elections scheduled for 24 April 1932. The Party won the largest share of the vote in every province except Bavaria. The economic crisis and political instability of the summer of 1932 created a growing political polarization which further undermined the prospect for a political solution. The Party published a poster with the slogan 'Hitler – Our Last Hope' and although millions of German voters were not seduced by the ceaseless propaganda and activism of the movement, the appeal of Hitler as the last resort in a world of chaos, disorder and poverty succeeded in recruiting at

A popular National Socialist poster from the election campaigns of 1932, 'Hitler – Our Last Hope'. For many Germans poverty during the recession drove them to vote for parties they would never have considered in the more prosperous 1920s. A Hitler vote was often regarded as a last resort, a protest against the failure of the other parties.

least one-third of an electorate that a few years before would never have contemplated voting for a former political terrorist, and a party with a reputation for crude anti-Semitism and street rowdyism. Significantly, the Party deliberately played down its racism during the year of elections, attempting to present a more subdued and responsible image.

In the end the crisis devoured the Brüning government as well. On 9 May parliament met in Berlin for the first time since March, amid noisy scenes from the National Socialist fraction protesting against the ban on the SA. The efforts of the Defence Minister, General Wilhelm Groener, to defend the ban were shouted down. Three days later he resigned. During the next two weeks another political general, Kurt von Schleicher, conspired with right-wing politicians to undermine the Brüning government and install a more authoritarian and conservative alternative. Hindenburg needed little persuasion and when his chancellor asked him, on 28 May, to sign a presidential decree to break up the estates of some of the impoverished Prussian aristocracy (so that the land could be distributed to poor farmers) he refused. Two days later Brüning resigned together with his whole cabinet. He was replaced by a conservative aristocrat, Franz von Papen, who immediately set out to undermine the republican system and establish an authoritarian regime based on the interests of the traditional ruling class. Hitler had already been asked if he would support Papen, and had agreed. Papen accepted Hitler's pledge and the conservative elite that now dominated German politics assumed, for the following seven months, that they would be able to control the Hitler movement rather than be swept away by it. As a concession for Hitler's support, the new government lifted the ban on the SA and SS on 18 June 1932 and agreed to call new parliamentary elections (which were set for 31 July).

The Papen government initiated the long slide to dictatorship in the months that followed. Restrictions were relaxed on the National Socialists, but imposed on German communists. Newspapers were censored and the German communists, who continued to increase popular support in the major cities where the economic recession had created exceptional levels of poverty and hardship, were subject to police surveillance and harassment. On 20 July Papen authorized the unconstitutional appointment of a Reich Commissar for Prussia, the largest German province and a bastion of support for the parliamentary republic. The social-democrat government was sacked and threatened with armed force under the terms of a state of siege that Papen had declared in Berlin and the surrounding areas. The army colluded with Papen in destroying the last element of support for the existing system. The Social Democrat Party could find no way to contest the coup; caught between the popular support for the communists (who on Moscow's orders refused to co-operate with the moderate left) and the rising tide of National Socialist violence, the social-democrats adopted a policy of wait-and-see. The establishment of an authoritarian regime in Prussia signalled the final collapse of the Weimar system. The undermining of democracy was not a product of Hitler's appointment in 1933, but had already begun months before he achieved power.

The parliamentary elections confirmed Hitler's party as the largest party in Germany, with 37.3 per cent of the vote and 230 parliamentary deputies. The German communists and social-democrats between them polled 36 per cent, but their refusal to co-operate rendered them powerless as an opposition. Hitler and the Party leadership now hoped that power would at last be handed to them. As by far the largest party in parliament this would not have been a remarkable outcome, but Hindenburg was determined to keep his aristocratic cabinet in being and insisted on Papen remaining chancellor. On 5 August Hitler met Papen and von Schleicher outside Berlin, where he explained that the price of his Party's support in a coalition was his appointment as chancellor, with Party leaders installed as Reich and Prussian ministers of the interior, with control over the police. On 10 August Hindenburg strongly rejected any idea of a Hitler government, suspecting, rightly, that he would use it as an opportunity to impose a single-party state. On 13 August Hitler was offered the vice-chancellorship by Papen but turned it down with contempt. He was then ushered in to see the President; during a humiliating interview Hitler was told to control the behaviour of the SA, act with greater political decorum and to support the present government. He was then dismissed, boiling with rage. He told the SA leadership, who had been expecting at any moment to celebrate the seizure of power, to send their men on a two-week leave while Hitler himself retired to his retreat in the Bavarian village of Berchtesgaden to reflect on what else needed to be done to achieve supreme power.

The following four months of political intrigue and argument failed to secure what Hitler wanted, while the Party's popularity began slowly to deflate. In the last months of 1932 the economy began to show the first signs of a recovery after three years of continuous contraction. In June 1932, in a meeting at Lausanne in Switzerland, the powers had agreed to suspend reparation payments, marking an important step away from the Versailles system. The Party's success in attracting protest votes from disillusioned Germans was always likely to be short-term; even among Party members and the SA there was a growing disillusionment that two years of political activism had brought the movement no closer to taking over Germany.

Some of the revolutionary SA members defected to the communists, while Party membership (which had grown rapidly for more than a year following the electoral successes) became more volatile as large numbers left or failed to pay their monthly dues. In September 1932 Hitler decided to use the Party's large new numbers in parliament to force a new election in the hope that one more effort at the legal path to power would produce the triumphant majority and secure his role as chancellor. On 30 August, when the new parliament met for the first time, Hermann Göring was selected as President. On 12 September the Communist Party tabled a motion of no-confidence in the Papen government and Hitler instructed the Party to side with the communists and to abandon his support of Papen, agreed three months before. Göring at once called for a vote. Papen, sitting on the government benches, tried to intervene by waving a decree from Hindenburg suspending the parliamentary sitting. His plan was to rule with the support of Hindenburg, but without parliament. Göring deliberately ignored him and the subsequent vote of no-confidence showed only 42 delegates in favour of Papen and 512 against. Parliament was dissolved and new elections scheduled for 6 November.

Hitler embarked on yet another round of major election speeches, crossing and recrossing the country. German voters were asked for the fourth time in less than a year to express their

preferences. This time there was no repeat of previous elections, in which the National Socialist vote had always increased. On 6 November the results showed that the Party had lost 2 million votes compared with July. With only 33.1 per cent of the vote, the Party was overtaken by the left-wing parties, which together polled 37 per cent. The main beneficiaries were the communists, who now had 100 deputies in parliament. It was clear that the Party had peaked electorally and that the tactic of forcing elections in order to demonstrate the mass appeal of the Party had failed. The election changed nothing at government level and Papen continued to rule by presidential decree. On 13 November Papen invited Hitler once again to consider becoming vice-chancellor, and again Hitler refused. Between 19 and 21 November Hindenburg met Hitler and Göring a number of times, and for the first time indicated that he might be willing to accept Hitler as chancellor if he could secure a parliamentary majority. Hitler asked instead for the right to be chancellor ruling by presidential decree, as Brüning and Papen had been, but Hindenburg refused. The persistent signs of incipient civil war,

German men and boys in October 1932 fishing for pieces of coal that have fallen from barges into the river. By 1932 Germany was in the grip of a desperate poverty, with millions no longer even eligible for unemployment relief.

which were kept alive by a renewed wave of violence between communists, social-democrats and National Socialists, alarmed Hindenburg and pushed Papen at last to tender his resignation in the face of widespread unpopularity. His successor was the political general Kurt von Schleicher, appointed on 2 December.

Schleicher, like Papen, saw the need to win some kind of collaboration with Hitler, who still enjoyed support from one-third of the electorate. Hitler, however, refused to negotiate. On 3 December Gregor Strasser, who was strongly critical of Hitler's consistent refusal to moderate his demands for a share in power, was offered the vice-chancellorship by Schleicher in a secret deal. A few days later, in a meeting in the Kaiserhof Hotel in Berlin, Hitler (who knew of the negotiations) confronted Strasser and angrily ordered him to reject Schleicher's offer and remain loyal to the Party's strategy. On 8 December Strasser abruptly resigned all his Party posts and withdrew from politics entirely. The crisis exposed all the difficulties Hitler now faced in holding together a Party whose electoral fortunes were declining, and whose

A dishevelled Hitler raises his arm in the Hitler salute at an election meeting in the tiny state of Lippe in January 1933. The 900,000-strong electorate was chosen by Hitler as a target for renewed electioneering, but the Party vote in January 1933 was less than it had been the previous July.

rank and file had become restless over the failed national reawakening promised to them for years. 'If the Party should break up,' he told Goebbels on the day of Strasser's resignation, 'then I shoot myself at once.'

Hitler becomes Chancellor

At the start of 1933 the Hitler movement was facing the prospect of decline and possible fragmentation. The Party was short of funds while the SA was once again a source of potential revolt. In mid-January a major crisis was provoked in the southern province of Franconia when the local SA leader, Wilhelm Stegmann, led a rebellion against the local Party regional leader. Hitler once again tried to discipline the SA but Stegmann refused to be browbeaten and, on 24 January, told a rally in Nuremberg that Hitler's strategy had failed and the movement's 'historic moment' had been missed. In other parts of Germany, units of the SA left the organization and set up independent militia or joined the communists. While the Stegmann crisis unfolded, Hitler and the whole Party leadership campaigned in the local elections in the tiny state of Lippe to try to reverse the electoral slide of the Party. Hitler had to pay some of the election funds out of his own royalties for *Mein Kampf*. A great deal was made of the results on 15 January, which showed that 39 per cent supported the Party, but this represented fewer votes than the Party had registered in the July 1932 election, while the social-democrats increased their vote significantly. An internal Party post-mortem of the recent elections suggested that the movement had reached its zenith, with no more voters to bring onto the bandwagon. There was an evident mood of despondency and uncertainty about any hope of real political power.

The key to the eventual achievement of power lay not with the ballot box but in backstairs intrigue. On 4 January 1933 Hitler agreed to meet von Papen at the house of a Cologne banker, Kurt von Schröder, one of a number of prominent businessmen and financiers who had given their support to the idea of a Hitler government during the course of 1932. The two men had different objects in mind: Hitler wanted to find a way to get the chancellorship; Papen wanted to get revenge on Schleicher for replacing him in December by getting some kind of pledge of support from Hitler. The two found common ground in the desire to overturn the Schleicher government, but the meeting also opened the way to Hitler's participation in its replacement. Papen hinted at the possibility of a Hitler chancellorship, while Hitler indicated that he was not pressing for total power but a role in a coalition of nationalist forces. On 9 January Papen reported to Hindenburg that Hitler did not claim total power, and would be willing to serve alongside conservative ministers. Over the course of the following ten days Papen tried to see if there was the possibility of a new 'national' government in which a combination of right-wing parties could exert decisive influence in parliament. On 17 January Hitler met the leader of the German nationalists, Alfred Hugenberg, to patch up an alliance. Hugenberg had never liked having to co-operate with Hitler, whose movement he regarded as dangerously radical and violent, and the meeting ended with Hugenberg's assurance that Hitler would never become chancellor. On 18 January Hitler met Papen again at the house of a young Party supporter, Joachim von Ribbentrop, an

MEIN KAMPF

The book 'My Struggle' was produced in two volumes in Munich on 19 July 1925 and 11 December1926. It was largely written – or rather dictated to two faithful followers, Rudolf Hess and Emil Maurice - by Hitler while he was in Landsberg jail following the abortive *Putsch* of 1923. A mixture of autobiography and reflections on issues of political theory, race and foreign policy, the book became the 'Bible' of the movement, compulsory reading for all Party members. The title was suggested by the Party's publisher, Max Amann, to replace the more clumsy title chosen by Hitler, 'A Four and a Half Years' Struggle against Lies, Stupidity and Cowardice'. The volumes sold modestly in the 1920s, 23,000 copies of volume 1 by 1929, 13,000 copies of volume 2. A popular edition of two volumes in one was issued in 1930 and by 1933 around 1.5 million had been sold. During the dictatorship the book was used as a prize or a presentation gift in schools and public institutions. In 1936 registrars were encouraged to present a copy to every newly-married couple. By 1945 an estimated 8 million copies had been sold. The book was translated into 15 languages. Its sale or publication was banned in West Germany after the war. A second book, focusing more on issues of foreign policy and war, was dictated by Hitler in 1928, but it was never published in his lifetime. It finally appeared as *Hitler's Second Book* in 1961.

ambitious socialite with links to the conservative circle around Hindenburg. Here he once again stressed that only the chancellorship was acceptable, while Papen insisted that the best he was likely to get was a share of power in a Papen cabinet.

Hitler was in reality less than two weeks away from his goal. The unpromising prospects in mid-January 1933 turned within days into the real possibility of a Hitler government. The last ten days of January represented one of the most critical points in modern German history by opening the door to the establishment of the Third Reich and a Hitler dictatorship. Part of the explanation lies in the antagonism that opened up between Hindenburg and Schleicher during January, over the chancellor's plans to break up some of the old aristocratic estates. This was the same issue that had led to Brüning's downfall in July 1932. Hindenburg was also no longer attracted to the idea of a government based solely on presidential decree and wanted Schleicher to find a parliamentary coalition. Parliament was in recess until 31 January and Schleicher knew that he would have great difficulty finding a majority and avoiding a vote of no-confidence. His tentative feelers to Hugenberg and the German National Party came to nothing; he met Gregor Strasser on several occasions in the hope that he might be able to use him as a threat to Hitler, in order to win Hitler's cooperation. This tactic, too, failed to match reality. On 16 January Hitler publicly repudiated Strasser and the rift became permanent. By late January Schleicher was isolated and the scene was set for his replacement.

On 22 January Papen and Hitler met again at the house of von Ribbentrop. They were joined there by the president's son, Oskar von Hindenburg, and the president's secretary, Otto Meissner, who had both slipped away from an opera performance and discreetly taken a taxi to the rendezvous. Hitler and the younger Hindenburg talked together in a separate room for an hour while the others drank Ribbentrop's champagne. What was said is unrecorded, but Oskar proved a valuable ally in the course of the following week in persuading the stubborn president to accept the possibility of a Hitler government. When Hitler and Oskar Hindenburg reappeared they sat with the others for supper. For the first time Papen agreed that he would support Hitler as chancellor. This was a vital change of heart, for until then Papen had assumed that he would be the one replacing Schleicher. Over the days that followed Papen proved an indispensable ally of Hitler's ambition. On 23 January he met the president and suggested a Hitler government with a majority of the cabinet, including Papen, drawn from conservative circles rather than National Socialists. The hub of Papen's argument was that this would stabilize the political crisis, create the possibility for a parliamentary majority government, and that the Hitler movement would be tamed by office. The conviction that Hitler could be manipulated by more experienced and cynical politicians was,

---

In the evening of 30 January 1933, following Hitler's appointment as German chancellor, hundreds of thousands of supporters marched through the Brandenburg Gate and past the Chancellery building. The march-past finished only in the early hours of the following morning.

as it turned out, a remarkable miscalculation. Papen and other conservatives failed entirely to understand the nature of mass political nationalism, which would not be content with playing a supporting role to the old elite.

Over the next few days Hindenburg's continued resistance to the idea of a Hitler government was slowly eroded. Both his son and Meissner, among his closest advisers, had come over to the view that Hitler had to be appointed. On 28 January Schleicher visited Hindenburg to ask for a presidential dissolution of parliament so that he could rule without it. Hindenburg refused and Schleicher tendered his resignation. Immediately after the interview Papen appeared and Hindenburg finally agreed that negotiations should begin to appoint a new cabinet, with Hitler as chancellor and Papen as vice-chancellor and Prussian commissar. There then followed hours of further discussion: first with Hitler, who accepted only on condition that Göring could be Papen's deputy, in control of Prussia's large police force; then with Hugenberg, who accepted as long as he could be given responsibility for all economic policy. Hitler was still unsure whether Papen was not about to double-cross him and take the chancellorship for himself. There were rumours that General Schleicher might call out the army and declare a military dictatorship. But on the evening of the 28 January Papen returned to Hindenburg with the news that a Hitler coalition was now possible, and

HITLER TAKES POWER, 30 JANUARY 1933

At noon special editions, hastily printed, officially announced Hitler's appointment as Chancellor. The tramp, the pre-1914 failure, the shady character, the 'unknown soldier' of World War I, the semi-ridiculous orator of the postwar Munich beer halls, the member of a party then numbering only seven members, was at the helm, and behind him the movement that he had created now totalled thirteen million Germans.

That evening the National Socialists organized a torchlight parade. In massive columns, flanked by bands that played martial airs to the muffled beat of their big drums, they emerged from the depths of the Tiergarten and passed under the triumphal arch of the Brandenburg Gate. The torches they brandished formed a river of fire, a river with hastening, unquenchable waves, a river in spate sweeping with a sovereign rush over the very heart of the city. From these brown-shirted, booted men, as they marched by in perfect discipline and alignment, their well-pitched voices bawling warlike songs, there arose an enthusiasm and dynamism that was extraordinary. The onlookers, drawn up on either side of the marching columns, burst into a vast clamour. The river of fire flowed past the French Embassy, whence, with heavy heart and filled with foreboding, I watched its luminous wake; it turned down the Wilhelmstrasse and rolled under the window of the Marshal's palace.

The old man [von Hindenburg] stood there leaning upon his cane, struck by the power of the phenomenon which he had himself let loose. At the next window stood Hitler, the object of a very tempest of cheers, as wave upon wave kept surging up from the alleys of the Tiergarten. The parade, which lasted until midnight, was conducted amid perfect order. But there had been so little time to organize it that no one had thought of summoning photographers. On the morrow, therefore, the ceremony was repeated with unabated fervour in order that the memory of this historic night might be perpetuated pictorially.

Source: André François-Poncet *The Fateful Years: Memoirs of a French Ambassador in Berlin* (Victor Gollancz, London, 1949), pp. 47–8.

that Hitler had agreed to represent a broad national bloc, not merely his own party. On the morning of 29 January Papen discussed the final arrangements with Hitler and Göring. He accepted Hitler's insistence on new elections so that he could win a majority and pass an enabling law allowing his cabinet to introduce legislation without reference to parliament or the need for presidential decrees. Papen accepted this, perhaps unaware of just what its consequences would be. In the afternoon Papen succeeded in winning the German nationalists and the Steel Helmet leaders to the idea of a national government in which they would have key ministerial posts. On the evening of the 29 January Papen returned again to see Hindenburg with a list of ministers for the new cabinet. The list contained only three National Socialists and a majority of conservatives; he assured Hindenburg that his choice of defence minister and foreign minister would be respected. It was agreed to convene the new cabinet in the presidential suite the following morning, 30 January 1933.

The group that gathered in the ante-room of Hindenburg's apartment in the middle of the morning of 30 January were an ill-assorted alliance. The Steel Helmet leaders were still unhappy about throwing in their lot with Hitler, and had to be mollified by Hitler's assurance that all the hostile propaganda directed at them by his Party had been none of his doing. Hugenberg's arrival immediately began an argument about Hitler's demand for new elections, which Hugenberg thought would both undermine his party and boost Hitler's. The two men were arguing the case when Otto Meissner arrived to say that unless they stopped squabbling and came to see the President, already fifteen minutes later than the appointed time, the whole ceremony would be cancelled. Hugenberg reluctantly agreed in haste to new elections and the group of prospective ministers trooped into Hindenburg's office. There at 11.30 he administered the oath to Adolf Hitler, who swore to defend and uphold the constitution. The rest of the ministers were then sworn in and Hitler became, at last, the head of the German government.

The announcement of Hitler's appointment provoked neither widespread protests nor much sense of alarm. Popular interest in the endless cabinet reshuffles and intrigues had declined; there was scepticism about just how long Hitler might remain in power. Conservative opinion was mollified by the fact that this was a government of 'National Concentration' which represented a broad spectrum of national opinion and might, as von Papen assured a fellow conservative, box Hitler in rather than unleash him. The first sign that Hitler's appointment might produce a different and more dangerous outcome came in the evening of 30 January, as the Party and SA celebrated what they had been anticipating for years. Hitler stood at the window of his new office while row upon row, thousands strong, the SA and Party marched in procession down the Wilhelmstrasse, flags waving, bands playing and voices blaring out the songs and slogans of the movement. A few yards away President Hindenburg watched from a window the spontaneous display of nationalist fervour which his vexed decision had now made possible. Hitler's legal path to power, ten years after his failed *Putsch*, had finally and unexpectedly triumphed, not from a rising of the national masses but through the intrigues of a handful of ambitious and short-sighted politicians.

CHAPTER 2

BUILDING THE THIRD REICH

1933–1934

The decision to appoint Hitler chancellor in January 1933 did not lead immediately to the establishment of dictatorship, but it transformed German politics entirely. For the first few months Germany retained a multi-party system, and Hitler was leader of a national coalition, with only three National Socialists in the cabinet. But during the months between January and March (when the next parliamentary elections were held) Hitler's party and the paramilitary SA began a ruthless process of cleansing their political enemies by holding them in makeshift concentration camps and prisons, or through political murder. The burning of the Reichstag, the German parliament building, on the night of 27/28 February speeded up the process by allowing Hitler to pass an Emergency Powers bill which effectively suspended civil rights for those deemed to be an enemy of the national revolution. The March 1933 election created the conditions for a more widespread process of cleansing and 'coordination' by creating the possibility of a right-wing nationalist majority. An Enabling Bill, pushed through parliament, gave Hitler's government authority to make laws. By the autumn the other parties in the system were wound up and the independence of the provinces, which had their own governments, was overturned. Yet only in August 1934, when President von Hindenburg died, was Hitler able to declare an open dictatorship and install himself as 'Leader'. The early years of power were tense and uncertain. Unemployment remained high and social unrest was never far below the surface. It took time to complete the destruction of the large working-class parties. Most of all Hitler had to confront a restless movement for more rapid social revolution among the SA and party activists. In June 1934, with army backing, Hitler destroyed the SA leadership. By the end of the year the dictatorship was finally secured, almost two years after Hitler's appointment as chancellor.

1933 The 'National Uprising'

Hitler's appointment as chancellor opened the way to what was called the 'national uprising'. Overnight the long years of pent-up frustration felt by the Party and SA were released in a wave of lawless violence and political vendetta which the police were largely powerless to control, or in many cases actively abetted. The left-wing parties knew they were likely to be the victims of this wave of political terror. On 31 January the Social-Democrat Party called for a united front against any attempt to undermine the constitution, but they hesitated to recommend fighting the new regime outside the law. The communists called for working-class unity and a general strike, but nothing materialized. On 2 February the right of communists to demonstrate publicly was removed by law. On 4 February a new decree law 'for the protection of the Reich' placed severe limits on the communist press and the right of assembly. Tension between the two left-wing parties, from years of sharp political competition, made it difficult for them to bridge those differences sufficiently to obstruct the new government. Many leaders on the left assumed there would be a short period of crisis and repression before the Hitler government in its turn fell from power and more conventional politics could be restored. By the time they realized their mistake, many were in prison or the improvised concentration camps set up in the first weeks of the Hitler government.

Once he had his hands on the chancellorship Hitler had no intention of being displaced, even though there were only three Party leaders in the cabinet - Hitler himself, Göring as Minister without Portfolio and the lawyer Wilhelm Frick as Minister of the Interior. Hitler's first priority was to secure new elections in which it was hoped a majority could be won with all the powers of the state at the Party's disposal. After the failure of deliberately half-hearted negotiations with the Catholic Centre Party, whose support would have given Hitler an absolute majority in parliament, Hitler was able to ask Hindenburg on 31 January for the power to dissolve parliament so that he could secure the necessary majority. Hindenburg complied and on 1 February new elections were set for 5 March. The intervening month gave the regime the opportunity to both tighten its grip on German society and terrify its principal opponents. The SA indulged in an orgy of violence and, to prevent the police from penalizing them, Göring issued a decree in Prussia permitting the security forces to shoot 'enemies of the Reich' without fear of punishment. On 11 February SA were sworn in as police in the Ruhr-Rhineland area to be able to carry on legally their campaign against the Marxist industrial districts. On 22 February 50,000 more SA and Steel Helmet members were drafted as auxiliary police throughout Prussia to complete the work of intimidation and repression with the backing of the state. The SA seized the opportunity to storm working-class districts in the

Pages 64–65: On the morning of 28 February onlookers watch the last stages of the fire that destroyed the Reichstag, the German parliament building.

'ARE YOU ARYAN?'

…the intruders had arrived at the [law court] library. The door was thrust open and a flood of brown uniforms surged in. In a booming voice, one of them, clearly the leader, shouted, 'Non-Aryans must leave the premises immediately.' It struck me that he used the careful expression 'non-Aryans', but also a rather colloquial expression for 'premises'. Someone answered, 'They've already left.' Our ushers stood there as though they were about to salute. My heart beat heavily. What should I do, how keep my poise? Just ignore them, do not let them disturb me. I put my head down over my work. I read a few sentences mechanically: 'The defendant's claim that….is untrue, but irrelevant…' Just take no notice!

Meanwhile a brown shirt approached me and took up position in front of my work table. 'Are you Aryan?' Before I had a chance to think, I had said, 'Yes'. He took a close look at my nose – and retired. The blood shot to my face. A moment too late I felt the shame, the defeat. I had said, 'Yes!' Well, in God's name, I was indeed an 'Aryan'. I had not lied, I had allowed something worse to happen. What a humiliation, to have answered the unjustified question as to whether I was 'Aryan' so easily, even if the fact was of no importance to me! What a disgrace to buy, with a reply, the right to stay with my documents in peace! I had been caught unawares, even now. I had failed my very first test.

Source: Sebastian Haffner (Raimund Pretzel) *Defying Hitler: a memoir* (Weidenfeld, London, 2002), pp. 122–3 (first written by Haffner in 1939)

hunt for opponents who were gunned down or beaten and tortured. The first weeks of Hitler's government made it clear that this was no ordinary transfer of power, but a revolution in the name of a new Germany.

While the waves of violence washed over the population, Hitler took the opportunity to sketch out his initial programme. His public priority, announced on the radio on 31 January, was to overcome the economic crisis, end unemployment and invigorate Germany's depressed agriculture. In private he told German army leaders on 3 February that his aim was first to secure domestic peace and then to create 'living space' (*Lebensraum*) in the East, guaranteeing the future of the German people. On 8 February he told one of his first cabinet meetings that the rearmament of Germany was a priority for the initial four or five years of the regime. Hitler had none of the uncertainty for the future that many Germans felt. He believed that destiny had at last chosen him for a historic role to rescue Germany from disaster. Over the coming five years the economy did achieve a remarkable recovery and Germany was rearmed,

but both ambitions seemed unlikely in the political turmoil and continued economic crisis of early 1933. The Party was short of money to contest yet another election, as were most of the other parties. On 20 February Hitler and Göring met with German bankers and industrialists to outline economic policy (which was at best a hazy mix of plans for public work schemes and agrarian subsidies) and at the same time to collect donations for the Party's election fund. It was difficult for those present to refuse. For the moment, and despite the lawlessness on the streets, Hitler was still a parliamentary politician canvassing for money and votes.

At the height of the election campaign the government was handed a golden opportunity to increase the appeal of its anti-Marxist stance and its promise of order. On the night of 27 February smoke and flames could be seen coming from the Reichstag building in the

Above: Unemployed youth do temporary work repairing shoes in a National Socialist 'Winter Help' workshop in December 1932. The positive efforts made by the Party to provide welfare for the poor encouraged many young workers to switch their allegiance to Hitler.

Overleaf: An election poster from March 1933 shows workers pledging their support for Hitler. Around 40 per cent of voters were drawn from the manual working classes, who abandoned the left-wing parties in the hope of a promised national revival.

GÖRING AT THE REICHSTAG TRIAL, 4 NOVEMBER 1933

On the defendants' bench sat Torgler, Van der Lubbe, Popoff, Tanoff, and Dimitroff. Torgler looked ghastly, a greenish-grey prison pallor on his face – one could imagine that his body and clothes gave out a prison odour. He was tense, scared, nerve-racked. The newspapermen insisted that there was very likely a dictaphone under his chair and that he had been subjected to horrible torture. I didn't believe either. The Bulgarians looked wiry, tough, indifferent. Van der Lubbe was one of the most awful sights I have yet seen in human form. Big, bulky, sub-human face and body, he was so repulsive and degenerate that I could scarcely bear to look at him. He sat there, motionless, his head and hands hanging down between his knees, either in a trance or doped. He seemed to be slobbering at the mouth and the only movement he made was when one of the guards would attempt to raise his head and he would let it fall heavily again....

Diels [Rudolf Diels, head of the Gestapo] told me that Goering was going to appear at the trial in a few days and that everything was being prepared, that I shouldn't miss this by any means: it would be the most dramatic event of the whole proceedings. This time I had a ticket for the floor of the courtroom itself, not in the back with the newspapermen and listeners....I walked in, my heart in my throat, as I was seated much too close to the front. Goering and Diels were on the side conferring, only a few yards from me.

I suppose there were a lot of preliminaries, but I was so fascinated watching these two men that I didn't take my eyes off them until Goering got up to offer his testimony. He was faced by Dimitroff, a brilliant, attractive, dark man emanating the most amazing vitality and courage I have yet seen in a person under stress. He was alive, he was burning; fire of conviction, indignation, and hatred flamed in his posture, his magnificent voice and face. Some people's faces never come alive, they always look dead, pallid or passive, or have a cold reserved intellectualism like the face of Torgler. But Dimitroff was not only a shrewd dialectician and logician, he was a man, a superb dynamic personality.

I shall never forget his living stillness as he stood there listening to Goering, his face expressing a fiery contempt. It was a real fight, a real struggle. Goering took the stand, huge, paunchy, his stomach protruding swollenly, his face sagging; pompous and yet a little nervous. His voice was uncontrolled, his gestures melodramatic.

Dimitroff interrupted him several times and he flew into a rage. He continued his testimony and Dimitroff got up to answer. What they said to each other is on record, but how they looked is perhaps not. Dimitroff, in superb and impassioned, but controlled oratory, pointed out the flaws and dangerously absurd contradictions of Goering's speech. He made such a case, with deadly sarcasm was beginning to reveal so much, that Goering shouted for him to stop. He screamed at him, hoarse, frightened, his face turning so deep a purple that it seemed the blood would burst forth in a stream; choking, trying to drown out the accusing, brilliant, convicting voice of the other. He finally shouted, 'You know what will happen to you if you ever get out of this! I will see to it that you get the justice you deserve!' And by saying this Goering freed Dimitroff from the living death of a Nazi concentration camp. Dimitroff let him continue and then made some insulting remark by which Goering had him evicted for contempt of court. It was a narrow escape for the Nazis.

Source: Martha Dodd *My Years in Germany* (Victor Gollancz, London, 1939), pp. 54–6. Martha Dodd was the daughter of William Dodd, US ambassador in Berlin.

government centre. By the time fire-fighters arrived in numbers the building was thoroughly alight and burned until the following day. A young Dutch communist, Marinus van der Lubbe, was arrested at the scene. The regime immediately announced that the fire was the start of a communist uprising and the following morning Göring ordered the arrest of 4,000 communists. Four were eventually accused with van der Lubbe of burning the Reichstag – the communist leader Ernst Torgler and three Bulgarian communists, including Georgi Dimitrov, who was later to run the Moscow-based Communist International. Their trial began later in the year on 21 September, first in Leipzig and then transferred to Berlin. Only van der Lubbe was found guilty and he was executed on 10 January 1934. The others were acquitted on 23 December after Göring, among others, failed to convince the judges that there was any evidence against them.

The truth about who started the fire was unimportant and many people, both inside and outside Germany, assumed that the National Socialists had done it themselves in order to allow them to fight more ruthlessly against communism. On 28 February Hitler presented Hindenburg with an emergency decree to sign 'On the Protection of People and State'. The president complied, since he was already anxious about the apparent threat posed by communism to the existing order. The 'Reichstag Fire Decree' created a state of emergency and suspended most civil rights. The German Communist Party was prevented from campaigning for the forthcoming election and the social-democrat press was also banned for the last week of the campaign. The police won the right to take people into protective custody without a fixed trial, the device used throughout the period of the Third Reich to get rid of political enemies. For anyone who was not part of the national 'uprising' and a supporter of the new regime, the election was conducted in an atmosphere of growing intimidation and fear. Although the March election is often called the last free election in Germany before the onset of dictatorship, it was anything but free. Even under these circumstances, the Party managed to win only 43.9 per cent of the vote while the left-wing parties, subjected to a barrage of hostile propaganda about an alleged communist coup and denied the right to campaign properly, still won over 30 per cent of the electorate brave enough to defy the new regime. Hitler did not yet have a majority, and was far short of the two-thirds he needed in parliament to be able to amend the constitution.

Over the following weeks the Party and the SA set out to change the political balance by defying the constitution and the rule of law. In most provinces outside Prussia, which was now effectively ruled by Göring as Prussian minister of the interior and deputy commissar, the local assemblies were overturned and a Party commissioner appointed in their place. Police

---

Opposite: A poster from the German Communist Party (KPD) aimed at creating a united left-wing front with the Social-Democrat Party (SPD) against the fascist threat.
'Comrade, give us help!', runs the slogan. 'Together we can overcome it!' Ultimately the competition between the two parties proved too great to make a firm alliance possible.

Feierliche Reichstagseröffnung · Garnisonkirche Potsdam 21. III/195

chiefs in most cities and provinces were the victims of what came to be called 'co-ordination' (*Gleichschaltung*). Any who were not sympathetic to the national revolution were removed and replaced by Party members or supporters. The one major stumbling block was in Bavaria, where the movement had started years before, and where Hitler had launched his abortive *Putsch*. The Bavarian state government, led by Heinrich Held, defied the efforts of the Berlin regime to impose a commissar on Bavaria to 'co-ordinate' it with the rest of the country. This time Hitler was in control in Berlin and could impose his coup in Munich by force. On 9 March large numbers of SA and SS men began to assemble in the centre of the city, brought in from other parts of southern Germany. Around midday Ernst Röhm, Heinrich Himmler (the SS leader) and the local Party regional leader, Adolf Wagner, arrived in Held's office, surrounded by uniformed supporters, and told him to appoint a commissar immediately with full powers in the province. Held bravely refused and in the afternoon met his Bavarian ministerial council, who supported his decision to reject the unconstitutional imposition of a National Socialist commissar. At 5 o'clock in the afternoon negotiations ended and Röhm

The formal opening of the new parliament after the 5 March election was held at the Garrison Church in Potsdam, outside Berlin. Here the president, von Hindenburg (right), can be seen greeting war veterans. Hitler can be seen centre left and to the left the Reichstag president, Hermann Göring.

THE ENABLING LAW, MARCH 1933

Law to Remedy the Need of People and Reich (Enabling Law), 24 March 1933

The Reichstag has approved the following law, which with the agreement of the Reichsrat is herewith promulgated, while it is confirmed that the conditions for a law that alters the constitution have been fulfilled:

Article 1 Reich laws can also be enacted by the Reich government outside the due process laid down in the Reich constitution.

Article 2 The Reich laws decided by the Reich government can deviate from the Reich constitution so long as they are not in opposition to the institution of the Reichstag and Reichsrat as such. The powers of the President remain undisturbed.

Article 3 The laws enacted by the Reich government will be worked out by the Reich Chancellor and published in the Reich Gazette. They shall take effect on the day following the announcement, so long as they do not intend something different.....

23 March 1933
Signed: von Hindenburg, Hitler, Frick, von Neurath and von Krosigk

ordered the SA to march. Held tried to get the army to protect him but the local commander refused. In the evening Held was presented with a telegram from Berlin transferring power to Franz von Epp, one of Hitler's leading Bavarian allies. At 11 p.m. Epp made a historic speech at the Feldherrnhalle where ten years before Hitler and his supporters had been fired on by police machine guns. The following day a new National Socialist administration was set up in Munich.

The illegal transfer of power in Bavaria was followed by a wave of arrests and beatings for all those, including Catholic politicians and journalists, who had opposed the Party over the years. Heinrich Himmler was sworn in as Munich Police President on 10 March 1933, beginning his rapid ascent to become the security chief of the Third Reich. At Dachau, a small town outside Munich, a disused barracks was turned into Bavaria's first concentration camp and political opponents were sent there under the protective custody provision of the Reichstag Fire Decree, to be mistreated and in some cases murdered by their SA and SS guards. On 10 March, in reaction to the danger posed by unlimited violence, Hitler issued an order to his paramilitary supporters to end the revolution from below and to work towards the positive construction of a new Germany. He still needed the formal power to be able to do this himself, and so on 23 March an Enabling Bill was introduced into parliament. The new legislation needed a two-thirds majority because it amounted to a major revision of the constitution. Under its terms the cabinet (but not Hitler alone) could introduce and authorize laws without reference to parliament or the president. Together with the other nationalist parties Hitler had a clear 50 per cent majority, but still not what was needed. When the parliament met in the Kroll Opera House (the temporary replacement for the destroyed Reichstag) Göring reduced the quorum needed by discounting the legally elected communist members. The Catholic Centre Party delegates were intimidated by the presence of armed SA and SS men in the chamber and voted in Hitler's favour. Only 94 social-democrats, weakened by the arrest and imprisonment of some of their deputies, had the courage to vote against. The Enabling Act became law and Hitler was now freed from any constitutional constraints.

Rule by Terror

Despite the gloss of legality granted by the Reichstag Fire Decree and the Enabling Law, the establishment of dictatorship in Germany involved a high level of violence and coercion that not only tore up civil rights but defied the established legal system. On 21 March a decree was published outlawing any malicious comment against the present government, and the same day special courts were founded to deal with allegedly 'political' crimes in which the defendant lost most of the conventional rights of defence in a normal court of law. The Interior Ministry formally recognized the concentration camp at Oranienburg, outside Berlin, as a legitimate prison for political prisoners and the following day, 22 March, Dachau was added as a second camp. All over Germany smaller camps or holding centres were set up, run in most cases by the SA and largely unsupervised by any legal authority.

The concentration camp became a characteristic feature of the Third Reich. The Party had warned its political opponents, even before 1933, that if it ever came to power, camps would be set up. The first months of Hitler's government saw hundreds of small prisons mushroom all over Germany. The exact number may never be known but it has been estimated that between 150,000 and 200,000 Germans were held in custody at some stage during 1933, around 100,000 of them under the protective custody legislation. Local judges and lawyers tried in some cases to impose some kind of legal order on the detentions, but they also ran the risk of ending up in prison themselves, and many local policemen and judiciary sympathized with the

---

Opposite above: A social-democrat Reichstag deputy is driven through the streets of Chemnitz in Saxony following his arrest on 9 March 1933, surrounded by smiling SA men. Hundreds of leading politicians were taken into custody under the terms of the emergency decree of 28 February 1933 as an alleged threat to the state.

Opposite below: Rows of prisoners in April 1933 at one of the major new concentration camps, in a disused factory in Oranienburg, just outside Berlin. They are waiting for a distribution of letters. Most prisoners were freed by the end of the year, after pledging that they would no longer undertake political activity.

IN THE HANDS OF THE SA

17th May 1933

Terrible news today. Last night our colleague , Dr. Gerlich, was nearly beaten to death.

Dr. Fritz Gerlich, publisher of the Catholic weekly paper, *Der Gerade Weg* [The Straight Path], which attacked the Nazis so bitterly, has been imprisoned since the 9th of March in a dark cell on the third floor. He endures his prison life with stoical calm and good humour and is therefore very popular with all the warders.

Last night, towards one o'clock, two SA men visited the warder on duty and asked for Dr. Gerlich. He was to be brought up for examination. The warder did not ask for a written order. He handed Dr. Gerlich over to the two SA men. They conducted him along a corridor to the Administration Section. Then they bandaged his eyes. The prisoner, now unable to see, was taken up and down various staircases to prevent his finding out which room he was being conducted to.

Finally the bandage was removed. Dr. Gerlich looked about him. He found himself in a rather large room. His eyes were dazzled by the glare of spotlights. He was facing a number of lamps turned full upon him. There were people sitting behind them whom he could not see. It was like being on stage. The actor was in bright light, the audience in darkness.

A voice shouted at Dr. Gerlich in a bullying tone. It came from the direction of the lamps, where he could discern vague figures moving.

'Where did you get your information about the Brown House?' [The NSDAP headquarters]

Dr. Gerlich answered quietly: 'No one but myself is responsible for any of the articles which have appeared in my paper.'

'So you won't betray your accomplices?' roared the voice.

'No,' returned Dr. Gerlich firmly.

There was a second's pause. It was deathly still in the room. Then Dr. Gerlich was seized and thrown on to a table. Twenty-five blows with a rubber truncheon were rained down on him.

Dr. Gerlich did not make a sound.

He was pitched into a chair.

He was asked questions.

Dr. Gerlich remained silent.

The same sentence was bawled into his ear time after time. 'Did you get your information from Dr. Bell?'

Dr. Gerlich maintained an obstinate silence.

'We'll soon make you talk, you dog!'

Twenty-five more blows rained down on Dr. Gerlich

The unfortunate scholar, beaten almost unconscious, staggered back to his chair in a half-fainting condition.

'Will you confess now?'

Dr. Gerlich sat still, and made no reply.

A revolver crashed on to the table, and a harsh voice ordered: 'There! Shoot yourself, you blackguard, you!'

Dr. Gerlich spoke at last. His voice had a very decided ring: 'I refuse to shoot myself. I am a Catholic.'

He knelt down on the floor, and began to pray. He was preparing to meet his end. He took no more notice of his surroundings. He was alone with his God. Praying he awaited the shot that would put an end to his life.

The man's profound faith touched his tormentors. Something like a miracle took place. The SA men considered the situation. They conferred. They did not venture to shoot down Dr. Gerlich.

The 'examination' came to an end. They had Dr. Gerlich removed.

Source: Stefan Lorant *I Was Hitler's Prisoner* (Penguin Books, 1935), pp. 120-22.

national revolution and felt no qualms about the treatment meted out to people they regarded as untrustworthy or seditious. The arrests were mainly directed at communists and social-democrats, but there were also many Germans in senior positions in the media, schools or universities for whom status was no protection. Leading directors of the German state radio were taken into detention accused of left-wing bias. Members of parliament also enjoyed no immunity. Accounts by many of those who were subjected to the round of beatings and humiliation, or who merely witnessed it, show that guards often singled out members of the more privileged or educated classes for special treatment by thugs whose social background was more plebeian.

During the summer months an effort was made to rein back the wild terror and impose a more regular regime on the political prison population. Small camps and holding centres were closed down following Hitler's appeal on 6 July 1933 to scale down revolutionary violence. By October 1933 an estimated 22,000 were still held in protective custody, either in regular prisons or in camps. Most of those arrested spent from a few days to a few months in incarceration and were then released on the promise of good behaviour, or so traumatized by the experience that they no longer constituted a political threat. Thousands fled from Germany in 1933 and 1934 rather than face any further threat of punishment. One of the key institutions set up to impose some kind of order on political repression was the Secret Police Office (Gestapa) and the Secret Police Force (Gestapo) which were founded under Göring's jurisdiction in Berlin on 26 April 1933. The new police force was suggested by an official of the Prussian interior ministry responsible for combating communism, Rudolf Diels. There had always been political police in Germany, monitoring political activity and identifying dangerous political dissenters. The new Gestapo was housed next to Göring's official residence in Berlin, at 8 Prinz-Albrecht-Strasse, with between 200 and 300 political detectives. Here it began its work of arresting and vigorously interrogating suspected communist revolutionaries. Within five years it had grown into a nationwide organization, employing 20,000 people, with the right to take prisoners into protective custody and hold them without trial.

The terror unleashed in 1933 was directed at all the enemies, real or imagined, of the Party and its national ambitions. But it was directed in particular at Germany's Jewish population. On 1 April 1933 a nationwide boycott was organized, with Hitler's blessing, against all Jewish businesses and professions. The boycott was directed and publicized by Joseph Goebbels who had been appointed on 13 March to a new ministerial position as Minister for Popular Enlightenment and Propaganda. In the weeks before the boycott, Jewish businesses had been singled out for violent treatment by SA and Party supporters, and Jews had been publicly

---

On 1 April 1933 a nationwide boycott of Jewish shops and businesses was organized throughout Germany on the instructions of the Party leadership. Some customers defied the boycott but ran the gauntlet of the SA men who stood guard outside the premises.

THE GERMAN EXILES

One of the important consequences of Hitler's appointment as chancellor and the wave of lawlessness it unleashed was the voluntary exile of a large number of prominent German political, scientific and cultural figures. They left either because they were political opponents of fascism, or because they were Jewish, or because they disapproved of the violence and cultural prejudices of the regime, represented by the burning of books across Germany on 10 May 1933. The scientists included a large number of Nobel prize-winners, most famous among them Albert Einstein, who was abroad in the United States in early 1933 and refused to return. His books were among those burnt. Other scientists helped the British and American nuclear research programmes during the war. A host of distinguished writers, artists and film directors also left Germany; among the most notable were Thomas Mann and Bertolt Brecht (who both ended up living in California), the artist Max Beckmann (who moved to Amsterdam, then New York) and the architect Walter Gropius, who had helped found the *Bauhaus* movement in the 1920s, responsible for pioneering modern architecture and furnishing. Around 300,000 emigrated in total during the 1930s, not all of them distinguished artists or scientists, but a high proportion of them academics and intellectuals. By 1934 2,000 had come to Britain, and in many cases went on to the United States, 21,000 to France and 8,000 to Poland. Among the political exiles, who were chiefly communists and social-democrats, exile organizations were established in Prague and Paris, which published anti-Hitler journals and kept up contact with resistance groups still inside Germany. The political bureau of the German Communist Party was set up in Paris under Wilhelm Pieck; its general secretary was Walter Ulbricht, who later became the leader of the East German state set up in 1949.

molested or imprisoned. The boycott was staged as a response to criticism of the Hitler regime abroad, which was blamed on Jewish agitators. Notices were stuck on Jewish shop windows warning people to stay away from Jews if they wanted to be regarded as good Germans. Not all Germans complied, but entering a Jewish shop became a mark of political resistance and a danger to those who risked it. The boycott lasted only for a day and was lifted on the evening of 1 April, as planned, but the fear instilled in many Germans about patronizing Jewish shops, or doctors, or lawyers remained more permanent. During April the regime introduced other legislation aimed at Jews. On 7 April the Law for the Restoration of the Career Civil Service enabled the government to get rid of Jews in the administration and justice systems, as well as left-wing officials and lawyers. On 25 April a law was passed limiting the number of German Jews in high schools and universities to 1.5 per cent.

The next target for the regime was the trade union organization. The main trade union movement – the Free Trade Unions – was run chiefly by socialist officials. They had already been the target of attacks in the first months of the regime, but they had a large membership and substantial funds. On 1 May Hitler ordered large-scale celebrations of the National Day of Labour in an attempt to hijack the traditional left-wing May Day rallies. His speech that day, to over a million people gathered on the Tempelhof airfield, was designed to show that the new regime also cared for the working class as long as it identified with the new Germany as part of a united nation. The following day, groups of SA, police and the Party factory cell organization occupied the buildings of the trade union movement and arrested prominent union leaders. The Workers' Bank was taken over by the state and its funds sequestrated. The main white-collar associations were also taken over and their funds seized. The plan was to replace the old unions and associations with a single national labour organization run by Party leaders and officials. On 10 May the German Labour Front (DAF) was founded under the leadership of the Party organization leader, the chemist Robert Ley, who was a notorious womanizer and drunk. The DAF eventually embraced 25 million workers, from the shop floor up to senior management. Its purpose was to end class warfare and create a single corporation to organize rates of pay, working conditions and leisure time. On 19 May a new system of Trustees of Labour was established whose role was to oversee wage fixing, but with no rights for workers to participate. In the factories, local committees elected by the workforce could discuss issues with management and the DAF representatives, but the committee members were mainly drawn from the Party's factory cell organization. The Labour Front effectively stifled all possibility of labour opposition and helped to create a reluctant consensus among groups that had been strong opponents of the Hitler movement before 1933.

There was also coercion directed at German intellectual life, much of which had been hostile to the rise of National Socialism. Hundreds of prominent scientists, writers and artists fled from Germany in 1933 in the belief that the new system was likely to survive for some time. In schools and universities professors and teachers were subjected to strong pressure to resign if they failed to accept the national uprising; in many cases they could be sacked as employees of the local state administration. The Party had already founded, in May 1928, a 'Combat League for German Culture' under the Party ideologist, Alfred Rosenberg, whose task was to define 'pure' German culture and to attack anything deemed to be modernist or degenerate. In 1933 the League increased its membership from 6,000 in January to 38,000 by the end of the year; it began to sponsor small displays of what it regarded as un-German and depraved modern art. In March 1933 Goebbels instructed a librarian, Wolfgang Herrmann, to draw up a list of all books he considered to be typically Jewish, Marxist or un-German and to send the list to all schools and universities. From 12 April to 10 May the student organizations declared a month of cultural cleansing, culminating on 10 May with a national book burning in Berlin, Munich, Frankfurt, Dresden and Breslau. Watched by enthusiastic crowds, large bonfires were lit and queues of students and SA men took it in turns to throw piles of blacklisted books into the flames. Among the first books burned were those of Marx and Freud, a German and an Austrian Jew. Later in September Goebbels moved to control all cultural production in Germany by setting up a Reich Chamber of Culture with departments for press, cinema, literature, visual arts, music and radio. On 13 November 1933 the

organization was formally established and all artists, musicians and journalists had to register with the chamber or risk being denied the right to paint, play or write. Strict censorship was introduced for everything that was produced during the Third Reich, but most artists or writers hostile to the Third Reich imposed self-censorship on themselves rather than risk flouting the narrow guidelines of what now constituted 'German' culture.

Creating the One-Party State

While the national revolution was consolidated in the first half of 1933, Germany was still formally a multi-party political system. Even after Hitler had secured his Enabling Act, the cabinet he chaired was made up of a majority of conservative politicians and experts who might have acted to restrain Hitler's dictatorial ambitions. In the summer of 1933 Hitler moved to eliminate rival parties and find a way to dominate the structure of the state more thoroughly. By the autumn there was only one political movement left and every organization or institution had to fall into line with what National Socialism expected.

The problem of banning the communist and social-democratic parties was made easier by the pretence that they posed a revolutionary Marxist threat. The German Communist Party was outlawed on 28 March and its assets seized, though the legal appropriation of communist property was only ratified on 29 May with the Law for the Confiscation of Communist Property. The leading communists who were not in prison established an exile organization in Paris. The Social-Democrat Party recognized that its prospects for survival were poor but a party conference in April approved the decision to maintain the principle of operating within the law rather than engaging in more direct political resistance. The party's days were numbered. On 10 May its assets were seized by the state, a few days after the party leadership decided to transfer its operations abroad. In late May an exile organization was established in the Saarland, still under international control under the terms of the Versailles Settlement, and later in Prague. On 22 June the government banned the SPD as a political party.

The situation with the other parties was more complicated, as some of them had supported the government of National Concentration and had willingly voted for the Enabling Law. They were persuaded to accept their termination in return for integration into the great national movement represented by National Socialism. The nationalist party voluntarily wound itself up on 27 June and its leader Alfred Hugenberg resigned from the cabinet; other smaller parties followed, the German Democrats on 28 June, the German People's Party on 4 July. Hitler's other erstwhile nationalist ally, the Steel Helmet, was also forced on 27 June to merge with the SA, a process completed a few days later on 2 July. On 4

On 10 May 1933 books were collected from libraries in schools and universities of all those authors regarded as decadent, left-wing or anti-German. In the evening they were thrown onto large bonfires as a symbolic rejection of un-German culture. The book burnings were regarded abroad as a sign of German barbarism.

July the separatist Bavarian People's Party (BVP) was also abolished. Although its members sympathised with much of what Hitler stood for, its Catholicism distanced it from the more secular and violent National Socialists. In May BVP meetings were banned and in late June there began a wave of arrests of BVP leaders and churchmen. The situation with the Catholic Church was nevertheless a delicate one and there was still the third largest party before 1933, the Catholic Centre Party, to consider. Negotiations between the Hitler regime and the Papacy were undertaken to try to assure the Vatican that Catholic interests would be respected, even if political Catholicism was outlawed. On 5 July the Centre Party ended its political existence, but three days later a Concordat was announced between Germany and the Vatican which was formally ratified on 20 July. The agreement guaranteed the right to Catholic worship, education and charity and in return the Papacy undertook not to interfere in domestic German affairs.

On 14 July a crop of laws were promulgated to give legal sanction to the creation of the one-party state. These included the Law against the Formation of New Parties and a law to retroactively sanction the seizure of assets from organizations and individuals deemed to be hostile to the new Germany. For those who had fled abroad to oppose Hitler from greater safety there was a law withdrawing their citizenship, which by the end of the regime in 1945 saw 39,000 rendered stateless. Throughout the rest of German public life the Party replaced officials who were thought to be politically unreliable, in every sphere from local government down to local sports clubs. The emphasis was on 'co-ordination'. Germany before 1933 was a federal state in which all the separate provinces (*Länder*) had their own provincial assemblies and could pass their own local laws. The provinces were represented at national level in a second chamber, the Reich Council. On 7 April a new law was introduced to allow the government to appoint local representatives (*Reichsstatthalter*) who enjoyed special powers to overrule the local assemblies and oversee the introduction of national legislation. In the summer each province was made to introduce a 'Provincial Enabling Law' to extend the same rights Hitler had at national level to the provinces. After extensive negotiations and planning, the powers of the provincial parliaments were eventually overturned by a law of 30 January 1934 on the 'Reconstruction of the Reich' which completed the task of centralizing the whole state apparatus and abolished the Reich Council. In a speech on 7 July 1933 Hitler felt confident enough about the success of co-ordination to declare that 'the Party has now become the State'.

Building the 'People's Community'

The political revolution ushered in in 1933 did not take place in a vacuum. The movement had its own ideas about what the new political system and new society should look like. The concept used to describe this vision of a new age was the 'People's Community' (*Volksgemeinschaft*) and the members of this new society were to be called 'People's Comrades' (*Volksgenossen*). The ideal of Party ideology was to create a strong, united and biologically pure nation based upon the activities of the movement, and to set aside old notions of class difference in the face of a shared racial identity. 'Our socialism,' said Hitler, 'is the socialism of the race'.

FRITZ TODT (1891–1942)

Todt was one of the Third Reich's leading technocrats, entrusted by Hitler with the task of building the new German motorways but also with running most of the country's major state building projects. He was born into a prosperous family in south-west Germany and studied at the Munich technical college before 1914. He served in the German air force during the war, when he was wounded, and after the war went on to qualify as an engineer. He joined the Party in 1922, and became an SS officer in 1931. Hitler appointed him Inspector-General of German Roads in 1933 and then put him in charge of all construction at the head of what became known as the Organisation Todt. In this capacity he was responsible for overseeing the rapid construction of the German Westwall fortifications in 1938–39. The workers of his organization were drawn from the large pool of unemployed. They were subject to strict discipline and moved from site to site, living in rough barracks, often paid very little. From 1939 onwards his organization also began to employ foreign workers, principally Italians. During the war the Organisation Todt built the submarine pens and fortifications along the French coast. Todt was the first person to receive the German Order, a new award created by Hitler to mark particular service to the German people. In 1940 he was appointed Minister of Munitions and it was after a conference on armaments with Hitler on 8 February 1942 that the plane taking him back to Germany crashed. He was a committed National Socialist but not an active Party politician. His appeal to Hitler rested on his skill as an engineer and an organizer; Hitler was fascinated by technical achievements and saw Todt as the embodiment of German technical pre-eminence.

A start was made even before 1933 in trying to decide what constituted a pure race. On 31 December 1931 Walter Darré, the Party's agrarian expert, whose 'blood and soil' ideology saw a direct connection between a healthy population and peasant stock, was appointed head of the Party's Race and Resettlement Office. On 22 March 1933 the Interior Ministry set up a department to deal with issues of 'racial hygiene'. The prevailing scientific view in Germany was that populations that could not control the gene pool effectively, by removing those with hereditary diseases or some level of disability or mental disorder, would fail to compete in the struggle for racial existence. Hitler had read a good deal of eugenic theory in the 1920s and favoured positive policies to protect racial 'purity'. On 14 July 1933 a law was passed to prevent 'Offspring with Hereditary Defects' by allowing compulsory sterilization. Anyone who was classified as a genetic danger could be brought before a Hereditary Court, which would have at least one doctor on its panel of judges, and ordered to be sterilized. Over the course of the Third Reich over 350,000 were subject to compulsory sterilization orders including those with conditions such as epilepsy or congenital blindness. Many more women than men were sterilized, but male paedophiles (regarded as a racial blight) were also subjected to compulsory castration.

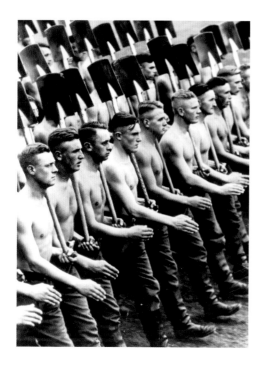

One of the keys to creating a healthy and united people was the immediate need to achieve an economic revival and restore the 6 million unemployed to work. The economy remained in severe difficulties throughout 1933. In August there were still over 4.1 million unemployed and many more still on short time. German finances had been saved only by refusing to pay back debts to other states, and through strenuous efforts to balance exports and imports to avoid a serious balance-of-payments problem. The key figure behind the effort to make sure the recession got no worse was the banker Hjalmar Schacht, who had helped to solve the crisis of inflation in 1923 and who in 1932 had been one of the leading capitalists in Germany in favour of risking a Hitler government. He was rewarded, on 17 March 1933, with the post of president of the Reichsbank, the German central bank. Other appointments of Party sympathizers to key positions were made

---

Above left: In 1933 a volunteer Labour Service was organized, followed in 1935 by compulsory service. Young Germans were sent to work on agricultural and construction projects and were taught discipline on military lines. At Party Congresses, like this one in 1933, they marched with spades displayed as if they were rifles.

Above right: On 23 September 1933 near Frankfurt-am-Main, Hitler dug the first spadeful of earth in a carefully staged inauguration of the new German motorway system, the *Reichsautobahnen*. Fourth from right is Fritz Todt, the man charged with building the network.

THE HITLER YOUTH

The National Socialist party placed much emphasis on the importance of recruiting and training youth in the ideals of the new national revolution. The Hitler Youth was founded in 1926, growing out of the 'Youth League of the NSDAP' set up in March 1922. It was the only Party organization to bear Hitler's name, and was directly subordinate to him. The leader of the Party youth movement from 1931 was Baldur von Schirach, but he was replaced by Artur Axmann in 1940, when Schirach joined the army. The youth movement was also extended to include girls in 1930. The aim was to incorporate almost all young Germans in one or other branch of the organization. For younger boys (10–14 years) there was the German Young People's organization (DJ); for boys of 14–18, the Hitler Youth (HJ); for young girls of 10–14, the Young Girls' League (JM) and for girls of 14–21 the League of German Girls (BDM). Boys of 18 would then do Labour Service, followed by military conscription. The youth movement ran educational courses, organized craft activities and sports, and summer camps. There was also a regular diet of political education to get young people to identify with the values of the movement and to display fanatical loyalty to Hitler. By 1932 there were over 100,000 recruits, but by 1939 there were 7.3 million out of a population of 8.9 million young Germans. The organization played an important part in creating a strong sense of identity with the regime and instilling a belief in the virtue of helping the collective racial ambitions of German society. By the end of the war many young boys and girls from the HJ and the BDM took part in anti-aircraft defence, or, in the case of boys, fought in the front line at the age of 14 or 15 against the approaching Allied armies.

in April 1933 – Fritz Reinhardt as state secretary in the Finance Ministry and Konstantin Hierl as state secretary for the Labour Service. Hierl introduced extensive opportunities for voluntary community service for young Germans and by the end of the year 419,000 youth unemployed had volunteered. In 1935 Labour Service was made compulsory for all eighteen-year-olds. Reinhardt worked on plans for work-creation on public works programmes and on 1 June 1933 the Law for Reducing Unemployment was passed incorporating what came to be known as the 'Reinhardt-Programme'. State funds were supplied for construction projects, land reclamation, road repair and so on, but the achievements were modest in 1933, and even by the spring of 1934 only 630,000 new jobs had been created, few of them more than temporary and with little more than pocket-money as wages. In September 1933 work began on a system of high-speed multi-lane motorways to link all Germany's major cities, under the supervision of the engineer Fritz Todt, but progress was slow. By the end of the year living standards remained low and unemployment still high.

The continued level of crisis in Germany was masked by a ceaseless propaganda in favour of the national revolution. The term 'Third Reich', first coined by the nationalist writer Moeller van den Bruck in 1923, was adopted by the new regime (though van den Bruck shot himself in a mental hospital in 1925 and some of his books were burned on the bonfires in May 1933). The choice was symbolic, with historic links back to the First Reich of the mediaeval German emperors and the Second Reich founded by Otto von Bismarck in 1871, when Germany was unified as a nation state. It was supposed to symbolize the final and highest stage of German evolution. In the new Germany the swastika flag was declared to be the national flag on 12 March 1933. It had been designed by Hitler in 1920, using a black swastika on a white circle surrounded by bright red. The swastika was a mystical symbol from south Asia, thought to bring good luck, and it had been appropriated in the late nineteenth century by elements of the German national movement who wanted to identify with alleged 'Aryan' roots stretching back millennia into a dim Asian past. Hitler took over the swastika and turned its arms from left to right, in the process transforming it (according to Hindu legend) into a symbol of misfortune.

The same year that the flag was adopted, the regime introduced a second national anthem to be sung on all public occasions alongside the well known 'Deutschland, Deutschland über alles'. The choice rested on the song 'Raise the Banner', written by a young Berlin National Socialist, Horst Wessel, who was murdered by communists in 1930. Only one verse of the old anthem was permitted, followed by two verses of the 'Horst Wessel Song'. The panoply of Party symbols was presented as something that symbolized the whole nation and not just National Socialism. At the first Party Congress in Nuremberg from 30 August to 3 September 1933 – the 'Congress of Victory' – these symbols were visible everywhere and the vast crowds of 400,000 of the movement's delegates roared out the new anthem. To show that the Party and nation were now one, Hitler asked Hindenburg to dissolve parliament on 14 October and to hold elections on 12 November. Voters were asked to vote yes or no for Hitler's list (which consisted only of members of the National Socialist Party) and 92.2 per cent of those who voted said yes. On 1 December the government published a new law 'For Securing the Unity of Party and State' in which Hitler's party was declared to be the sole bearer of the German nation and a public corporation rather than a private political association.

Opposite top left: An election poster pairs the field marshal von Hindenburg with the corporal Hitler in October 1933. The slogan reads 'Fight with us for peace and parity'. In late 1933 Hitler made a number of major speeches indicating that he was a man of peace only interested in getting fair treatment for Germany.

Opposite top right: A poster celebrating the national revolution shows a German soldier and an SA stormtrooper standing beneath the old national flag and the new swastika flag, adopted in 1933 as a national symbol. The poster aims to show the unity of the old and new Germany but, in reality, relations between army and SA remained poor.

Opposite below: The first head of the secret police, Rudolf Diels, addresses a crowd of concentration camp prisoners at Christmas 1933 who have been amnestied following the successful elections and plebiscite in October. The camp pictured here was at Esterwegen in Elmsland.

1934 Secret Rearmament

One of the main pledges Hitler had made early in 1933 was to start a programme of German rearmament in defiance of the terms laid down in the Versailles Treaty of 1919. These terms had limited Germany to a 100,000-man army for internal policing duties, a small quantity of weapons defined as defensive, and no tanks, submarines, military aircraft or major warships. During the 1920s and early 1930s the Defence Ministry had kept abreast of technical developments and under the terms of two treaties signed with the Soviet Union – at the Italian city of Rapallo in 1922, and in Berlin in 1926 – German forces were able to develop and try out modern aircraft and tanks away from the prying eyes of Western observers. But in 1933 Germany still remained militarily powerless. Army planners reckoned that Germany could not even defend itself against Poland or Czechoslovakia.

It was nevertheless difficult to redeem Hitler's pledge quickly, and military spending was little larger in 1933 than it had been in 1932. The long period of co-ordination and consolidation in 1933 postponed serious thinking about expanding the military while the economic crisis made large-scale state spending risky. For much of the period the German government argued that the other powers should agree at the Disarmament Conference in Geneva, which first convened on 2 February 1932, to reduce their armaments right down to German levels. This was an unlikely expectation and on 19 October 1933 the German delegation left the conference, refusing to return. The same day Germany announced that it was leaving the League of Nations organization as well. On 18 December Hitler produced a memorandum calling for an end to international competition in armaments, but at the same time authorizing the creation of a 300,000-man army to be fully established by 1938. In March 1934 preliminary programmes were authorized for the air force and the navy as well. During 1933 early work began on developing a military aircraft industry and converting a number of passenger aircraft to military use, a total of 294 aircraft. The March 1934 programme, drawn up in Göring's new ministry of aviation, which had been founded on 5 May 1933, planned for 17,000 aircraft in five years, the majority of which were to be trainer aircraft for the new generation of young German pilots. The naval commander-in-chief, Admiral Erich Raeder, had difficulty persuading Hitler that a navy was of much importance, but in March 1934 a Replacement Shipbuilding Programme was drawn up designed eventually to enlarge the navy beyond what was permitted under Versailles. The major difficulty lay in finding the money to pay for rearmament, and concealing the amounts. A solution was found by Hjalmar Schacht, who proposed issuing short-term bonds to be redeemed against future tax earnings when the

---

Political prisoners building their own prison at Dachau, near Munich, as part of their 're-education' into being useful German citizens. Dachau became the model concentration camp and its commandant, Theodor Eicke, became the first Inspector of Concentration Camps in 1934.

ERNST RÖHM (1887–1934)

Among the cohort of leading Party members, Röhm was one of the few who saw himself as a potential rival to Hitler and a possible leader of the national revolution. The son of a Bavarian civil servant, he served in the war and was wounded three times, rising to the rank of Captain. After the war he became part of the violent veterans' movement associated with the Freikorps and embarked on a long career of political terrorism. He met Hitler in 1919 and became a key Party organizer and a close companion of the future Führer, working with him during the failed *Putsch* in Munich in 1923. He left for Bolivia after the failure of the coup, where he acted as a military instructor. He returned to Germany in 1930 at Hitler's request and became the chief-of-staff of the SA. He more than doubled membership in a year, to 170,000, and turned the organization into a model for political violence and intimidation. Röhm himself encouraged the lawlessness and brutality which he saw as a necessary ingredient in the national struggle to transform Germany. He was always on the revolutionary wing of the Party and paid for his radical and violent political views with his life on 1 July 1934.

economy had recovered. The bonds were issued by a fictitious company, the Metal Research Company, and were known as 'Mefo-bills'. In 1934 Mefo-financing exceeded the regular defence budget, 2.1 billion marks against 1.9 billion. Rearmament became a mortgage against future prosperity.

Rearmament also raised another awkward question in early 1934. For some time the SA and its chief-of-staff, Ernst Röhm, had harboured ideas of turning the SA into an armed militia or 'people's army' working with the regular army, or even absorbing the traditional army into the new Party organization. Röhm now controlled an organization of around half-a-million men, many of them keen to play a more active role in the national revolution. He acted with increasing independence from Hitler, hosting dinners in Berlin attended by ambassadors and senior politicians and holding talks with foreign dignitaries. The army became concerned about SA ambitions and tension between soldiers and stormtroopers sharpened over the winter of 1933–4. On 18 January the Defence Minister, General Werner von Blomberg, who had been appointed by Hindenburg a few hours before Hitler became chancellor, wrote to Röhm asking for the relation between army and SA to be sorted out. On 1 February a new army commander-in-chief was appointed, Werner von Fritsch, who was much more hostile to the SA. The same day Röhm sent a memorandum to von Blomberg spelling out his views on the SA as a popular army to be mobilized and used in wartime, which the army rejected. Blomberg would only accept the SA as a preliminary training ground for future military conscripts. On 28 February 1934 Hitler called together the heads of the army, the SA and the SS for a meeting in the defence ministry. In the course of the discussion Hitler made it clear that he did not want the SA to form a military militia but instead to confine itself to political activity; he wanted a large conscript army to be developed under military control, capable of defending Germany in five years and of waging wars for 'living space' in eight. On 6 June 1934 Hitler finally confirmed the creation of a 21-division army, three times the size of the existing armed forces.

Enemies of the People

While tensions with the SA developed during 1934 the sister organization, the SS, began to develop growing influence within the security apparatus of the new Reich. The SS was led by Heinrich Himmler, who had been appointed on 7 January 1929 as *Reichsführer SS*. In 1929 the special protection squad numbered only a few hundred and was nominally subordinate to the SA chief-of-staff; by 1933 Himmler had turned it into an elite of 52,000 black-uniformed security men, whose symbol was a silver death's head. The SS operated a Security Service (SD) to monitor internal Party security and in July 1932 this was placed under Himmler's deputy, the former naval officer Reinhard Heydrich. Himmler was an ambitious racist and anti-Semite with visions of a pure Nordic German people, and a mystical attachment to the traditions of the Norse gods. He was also a very effective security manager and was rewarded in March 1933 with responsibility for the Bavarian political police, and then in September with control of all the political police forces outside Prussia. His next target was to control Göring's Gestapo in Prussia, responsible for policing almost two-thirds of the German population.

THE SS

The SS, short for *Schutzstaffel* (Protection Squad) became one of the dominant organizations of the Third Reich, wielding by the end of the war wide influence in policing, the armed forces and the economy. It grew out of a special unit set up in May 1923 to act as Hitler's bodyguard, the 'Stosstrupp Hitler'. On 9 November 1925 it was converted into the SS, a special element in the SA responsible for protecting the Party leaders and Party rallies. On 6 January 1929 the young Bavarian Heinrich Himmler was appointed the commander of the SS, a post he held down to the end of the war. When he took it over there were 250 members; by the mid-1930s there were around 200,000. With their distinctive black uniforms and death's head badge, the SS came to see themselves as the 'aristocracy' of the movement. Himmler insisted on strict entry qualifications, and a special race card was designed for all applicants which had to be filled out with details of their physical appearance. Although Himmler wore glasses, these were forbidden for other SS members as a sign of genetic weakness. Himmler ran the SS like an old-fashioned mediaeval order, with special ceremonies, including an SS marriage, and a number of prominent SS castles (*Ordensburgen*) where the SS leadership met to engage in a theatrical evocation of a past age. In 1935 Himmler founded the *Ahnenerbe*, a heritage organization committed to trying to find the true origins of the 'Aryan' people through archaeological research abroad. The SS Race and Resettlement Office was set up in 1933 to attract doctors and academic experts interested in racial hygiene and the ethnic remodelling of central and eastern Europe and they played an important part in formulating the race policies of the regime. The SS also ran the concentration camps and later a whole network of forced labour camps during the war, while senior SS leaders were recruited to lead the *Einsatzgruppen* in the Soviet Union and to run the security apparatus in the East, where they were responsible for the deaths of millions of people. Although many policemen became SS members and officers, the SS never had formal police powers. Camp guards were permitted to bear arms, but only in 1939 did Himmler succeed in persuading Hitler that SS troops should be formed, fighting alongside the regular army. The Armed-SS (*Waffen-SS*) grew to 800,000 servicemen by 1944 and SS units had access to supplies and equipment that regular divisions lacked. The SS divisions won a reputation for brutal and uncompromising combat and were responsible for regular atrocities and war crimes.

The takeover of the Gestapo by the SS was a significant turning point in the establishment of the regime of terror in the Third Reich. During late 1933 Göring was under strong pressure from the Interior Ministry to relinquish his police powers to the central Reich authority. In January 1934 his control of the Prussian police passed to the Interior Ministry, which also absorbed the separate Prussian Interior Ministry, which Göring had headed. On 14 March he declared that the Gestapo was an autonomous organization under his jurisdiction, and to avoid losing control over it he agreed to appoint Himmler as inspector, and deputy chief, of the Prussian political police on 20 April. Two days later Heydrich was confirmed as head of the Secret Police Office. Himmler immediately set out to create a national organization and the Gestapo absorbed the regional political police forces. Himmler and Heydrich paid little attention to jurisdictional niceties and ran the Gestapo as if it was theirs to control. By November 1934 Göring had abandoned any claim to authority over it, and eighteen months later Frick was forced by Hitler to do the same.

The secret police had much to do in 1934, for there were still areas of political opposition and resistance. These included socialist and communist groups which worked underground to

The Air Minister and President of the Reichstag, Hermann Göring, sits in hunting costume for a sculptor. Göring was one of Hitler's closest allies and one of the few genuinely popular leaders of the movement. A prisoner at Nuremberg in 1945, he hoped that one day there would be statues of him all over Germany.

THE CAMPS: WHAT PEOPLE KNEW

'Mother was among those the Americans forced to tour nearby Dachau and I had to go along. I'll never forget those heaps of emaciated corpses….Mother suffered a nervous breakdown. It took a long time for her to recover.'

'And then?' asked Kulle. 'Did she still continue to believe in the Führer or was she cured? She must have known that the camps existed and that horrible crimes were committed there in the name of her Führer?'

Grete shook her head. 'No, nothing could shake her faith in Hitler. "I'm sure the Führer wouldn't have wanted *that*," she said later. Another of her articles of faith was: "True National Socialism was pure and decent!" She clung to that till she died, only three years ago [c.1980].'

'And how did she reconcile the concentration camps with that belief?' Kulle wanted to know.

'She accepted the explanation they gave at the Party meetings,' Grete replied. 'It went something like this: The riff-raff have to be cleared off the streets! Repeat offenders, sex criminals, and the parasites on the Volk, like usurers or profiteers, will be re-educated in the camps to do honest work. They will be taught discipline and cleanliness – and, of course, not a hair on anyone's head will be harmed.'

'That's what I heard at home, too, when I was ten or twelve,' Kulle's wife remarked. 'My parents spoke of the camps as having an important educational function. Of course, in my house there was more talk of "dangerous enemies of the state", and I also heard that they were dealt with severely.'

'But you must admit,' Kulle said, 'that no one could really claim afterward that he or she had not even known that such camps existed.'…

'But were the papers allowed to report that so-and-so had been sent to a concentration camp?' his wife asked. 'I thought such things were shrouded in secrecy.'

'No,' I said, 'from the beginning of the "Third Reich" you could find something in the paper every day: "Enemy of the Volk Goes to Concentration Camp", or "Concentration Camp Inmates Treated Well". There were also photos showing prisoners who had been selected specially for their repellent appearance.'

Source: Bernd Engelmann *In Hitler's Germany: Everyday Life in the Third Reich* (Methuen, London, 1988), pp. 34–5 (Engelmann grew up in the Third Reich. This extract is from a conversation with friends years later)

disseminate literature, host discussions and keep a residual organization in being. Communist union members set up the Revolutionary Union Opposition in Berlin and Hamburg, but it was penetrated and broken up by the Gestapo with 800 arrests. A second communist network in the Ruhr-Rhineland industrial region which published regular newspapers, one called *Freedom* and another *Revolutionary*, was also penetrated and eliminated in 1934. In March the Trotskyist 'Funke' organization was broken up and its members arrested. Later in the year a further wave of arrests broke up what was left of the skeleton communist movement. Out of 422 German Communist Party leaders, 219 were arrested and imprisoned, 125 emigrated, 24 were murdered and 42 abandoned the party. Although much of the workforce was not reconciled to the reality of low wages and the end of wage-bargaining, it proved difficult to rouse active opposition in a situation where employment opportunities were rising and the threat of punishment severe. On 8 January 1934 the exiled social-democrat leadership in Prague called on supporters in Germany to overthrow Hitler with a popular revolution, but they were quite out of touch with the reality of life under the dictatorship and nothing resulted from the appeal.

The SA chief-of-staff, Ernst Röhm (third from right) greets an SA comrade in a meeting at Dortmund. The SA were ambitious for a more thorough-going revolution and distrustful of the reactionary forces that Hitler needed for support. In 1934 Röhm was purged by SS men led by Heinrich Himmler (far left).

The regime also faced opposition from a more unlikely quarter. The Protestant churches in Germany, representing approximately two-thirds of the population, were in general favourable to the national revolution. In April 1933 the pro-Hitler 'German Christians' called on the regime to amalgamate all the Protestant churches into a single Reich church. Hitler, who was sceptical of all religious belief, was happy to oblige and on 14 July 1933 a constitution was published for a new Reich Evangelical Church to be led by a pro-Hitler cleric, Ludwig Müller. He was installed as Reich Bishop at a ceremony in Wittenberg on 27 September 1933. Sections of the Protestant churches objected to the new organization and, under the leadership of Pastor Martin Niemöller, a Pastors' Emergency League was set up which by early 1934 had recruited 7,000 clergy, around 40 per cent of all evangelical churchmen. The League rejected a united church and the authority of the Reich Bishop and on 30 May 1934, in a meeting at Barmen in Westpahlia, created a breakaway 'Confessing Church' (*Bekennende Kirche*) and published a Theological Declaration rejecting the idea that religion should be subordinate to the dictates of a political system. The schism in the Protestant churches was completed by the demand of some extreme anti-Semitic clergy to reject the Bible as a piece of Jewish superstition. The Reich Bishop under these circumstances could not be confirmed and Hitler, who had little interest in the theological arguments, abandoned the attempt to create a unitary church. This did not stop the Gestapo from treating churchmen as a potential political threat. Niemöller was arrested in January 1934, but soon freed after widespread protest. More church arrests followed, culminating in 1934 with the arrest of the outspoken and popular Catholic priest from Cologne, Josef Spieker, who on 28 October 1934 gave a powerful sermon in favour of the view that the only true German 'Leader' was Jesus Christ. He was arrested by the Gestapo on 19 November and put on trial. Although his case resulted in acquittal, he was re-arrested and sent to a concentration camp largely peopled by arrested communists. He was re-tried in January 1936, imprisoned and finally released in February 1937. Anxious about his safety he fled across the border and ended up in South America. Despite the Concordat signed in 1933, the Gestapo continued to monitor Catholic opinion and to harass or arrest prominent Catholic critics.

The 'Night of the Long Knives'

The main crisis in 1934 came not from communist or religious resistance but from within the National Socialist movement itself. Following the decision by Hitler that the SA should not become a popular militia (or be allowed to bear arms) there was a good deal of uncertainty about what role the SA could now play. Among the rank and file there was continued impatience, as there had been before 1933, with what was viewed as the failure to pursue a more revolutionary course or to reward the SA for all the sacrifices the movement had made during the so-called 'Years of Struggle' in the 1920s. There is little hard evidence that Röhm himself contemplated a coup against Hitler, but he did see himself as a special category of Party leader, representative of a broad popular movement whose capacities were politically underutilized.

There is no doubt that Röhm was the victim of a coup against his leadership, but the circumstances and explanation for what happened in June and early July 1934 remain obscure.

VON PAPEN SURVIVES THE PURGE

Goering was in his study with Himmler. He told me that Hitler had had to fly to Munich to put down a revolt headed by Roehm, and that he himself had been given powers to deal with the insurgents in the capital. I protested immediately at this, and pointed out that as I was the Chancellor's deputy, in his absence such powers could only be granted to me. Goering would not hear of this, and declined flatly to delegate his authority. With the police and air force troops under his command, he was certainly in the stronger position. I then said that it was essential to tell the President what was happening, declare a state of emergency, and bring in the Reichswehr [the Army] to restore law and order. Again Goering refused. There was no need to disturb Hindenburg, he said, since, with the help of the SS, he was in complete control of the situation.

Tschirschky, who was outside in the waiting room, told me afterwards that while I was with Goering, Himmler had gone to the telephone and had spoken to someone very quietly. Tschirschky could only distinguish the words, 'You can go ahead now.' This was apparently the signal for a raid on the Vice-Chancellery...

In the Vice-Chancellery – and all this had to be pieced together later – Bose [von Papen's aide] had been shot out of hand for 'offering resistance'. My secretary, Baroness Stotzingen, and Savigny and Hummelsheim had been arrested and carried off to gaol or concentration camps....The offices were searched for secret documents and then sealed. A row of safes in the basement – the building had been a bank – were blown open and found to be empty....

My home was surrounded by an SS detachment armed to the teeth. The telephone was cut off, and in my reception room I found a police captain, who had orders that I was to have no contact with the outside world and that no one was allowed to see me.....I spent the next three days completely alone. I had no idea what was going on in Berlin, or in the country as a whole, and expected to be arrested and probably shot at any moment. I had no doubt that Goebbels, Himmler and Heydrich had made up their minds that it was time for the Marburg reactionary to be liquidated. As I learnt later, the only man who stood between me and this fate was Goering. He probably felt that my liquidation would only complicate matters more...When the telephone was reconnected, I received a call from Goering. He had the effrontery to ask why I had failed to appear at that day's meeting of the Cabinet. For once I replied in highly undiplomatic terms.

Source: Franz von Papen *Memoirs* (André Deutsch, London, 1952), pp. 315–7.

After the arguments over the role of the SA, relations between the regular army and paramilitary forces remained strained. The army leadership was anxious that nothing should block the plans to expand the regular army, and was suspicious of a force that was five times the size of the army and some of whom were armed. On 29 May Hitler ordered all SA military exercises to cease and the SA were told to take an extended period of leave in July. On 4 June Hitler and Röhm had a long discussion in which Hitler later claimed that he warned his SA chief-of-staff to tone down the behaviour of the SA. Röhm reacted by going on leave to a spa town at Bad Wiessee to overcome a number of chronic health problems, but not before he told his troops that on his return the SA would be stronger than ever. He went for his cure and rested and bathed for three weeks, but he told friends that he feared some kind of conspiracy was being hatched against him.

The exact nature of the conspiracy is unclear, nor is it known how far Hitler was involved. But senior Party figures, Göring among them, were clearly implicated. Himmler's appointment as deputy for the Gestapo allowed the SS to act with increasing independence from the SA, which Himmler needed if his organization was to become his political power base. He drew up lists of SA leaders who might be purged in a crisis. The army was fed on a diet of rumour and embellished reports on the attitude and behaviour of the SA in order to drive a further wedge between the two organizations. By June the army leadership seems genuinely to have believed in the possibility of an SA rebellion and wanted Hitler to act before it was too late. The sense of crisis was in large measure artificial, but on 18 June it was made more volatile by the decision of the vice-chancellor, von Papen, to make a defiant speech at Marburg University (written by Edgar Jung, one of his officials) critical of the arbitrary and authoritarian nature of the Hitler regime. The publication of the speech was immediately banned but a version appeared before the ban could be enforced. Nothing connected Papen and Röhm, but when Hitler went to see Hindenburg at his East Prussian estate at Neudeck to explain why Papen had been silenced, he was subject to more pressure from the army leadership to do something about the SA.

On 23 June the army was put on high alert and three days later army leaders were shown documents purporting to prove that Röhm had been illegally arming SA units. No doubt Hitler too was fed incriminating evidence by Göring and Himmler, who had their own reasons for getting rid of the SA leadership as a potential political rival. On 28 June Hitler and Göring travelled to Essen for the wedding of the local *Gauleiter*. Army units were issued with emergency supplies of munitions and SS men were given army weapons. Hitler telephoned Röhm from Essen, asking him to convene a meeting of SA leaders at Bad Wiessee for 30 June. During the next twenty-four hours more spurious reports were fed through to Hitler to create a plausible belief that the SA was secretly planning some revolutionary act. Early on the morning of 30 June Hitler and Goebbels, who had been let into the secrets of the crisis only the night before, flew to Munich while Göring returned to Berlin. At around 6.30am Hitler arrived in a fleet of cars full of armed SS men outside the hotel where Röhm and other SA officers were staying. Hitler and two other men then entered the hotel and ordered the headwaiter to knock on Röhm's door on the first floor. When a sleepy Röhm opened the door, Hitler burst in waving a pistol: 'You are under arrest, you pig!' He was given a few minutes to dress himself and was then brought down to the hotel lobby. The rest of the SA guests were taken by detectives and SS men onto a coach and driven to Stadelheim prison in Munich, where Hitler had spent some time a dozen years before. Röhm was driven in Hitler's motorcade to the same prison and placed in a heavily guarded cell. Hitler stayed in Munich before flying back to Berlin in the evening. During the day he appointed the loyal SA commander Viktor Lutze as Röhm's successor.

When Hitler arrived in the capital he was met by Himmler and Göring who reported on what had happened in northern Germany. During the day SS hit squads had murdered key figures who were claimed to be part of some plot, including von Papen's two assistants, Herbert von Bose and Edgar Jung (who had drafted Papen's critical speech), Erich Klausener, a prominent Catholic activist, General von Schleicher and his wife, General von Bredow, and Hitler's former rival in the Party, Gregor Strasser. In Munich a group of SS killers arrived at Stadelheim prison on the evening of 30 June, took the arrested SA men out one by one, then shot them in the prison courtyard. Further shootings continued in Berlin and Breslau (one of the alleged centres of the SA coup) until on 2 July Hitler ordered an end. He found it difficult to order the execution of Röhm, who had shared with him the early struggles of the Party in Munich. But Himmler and Göring persuaded him that it was necessary and Hitler ordered a loaded gun to be left in Röhm's cell so that he could kill himself rather than be shot. The gun was delivered in the early evening of 1 July by the SS commandant of Dachau, Theodor Eicke, and two other SS men. The victim was given ten minutes in which to shoot himself. Röhm refused the offer, bared his chest and waited for his murderers. After ten minutes Eicke and another SS man opened the door, aimed their pistols at Röhm's heart and fired. He had to be given a final shot before his body was removed and quickly buried in a nearby cemetery. For its role in the murders the SS was rewarded, on 20 July, with separation from the SA. It was made an independent organization and Himmler became subordinate only to Hitler.

The total death toll on what came to be called the 'Night of the Long Knives' has been estimated at around 85 victims, though the figure is almost certainly higher, as the SS took the opportunity to settle old scores against its parent organization. The murder of the politicians Schleicher and Strasser was later justified by the argument that they had been plotting with a foreign power to overthrow Hitler, but their deaths were precautionary, to get rid of two men who had tried to obstruct Hitler's path to power in December 1932. The strangest aspect of the two days of murders was Hitler's direct involvement. His behaviour was not that of a German chancellor but once again the actions of a political gangster, as he had been a decade before. Nevertheless the public reaction to what had happened, based on fabricated reports of a dangerous political conspiracy, was largely positive. Many Germans, both inside and outside the Party, found the SA an organization difficult to trust or discipline. On 1 July the defence minister, von Blomberg, announced to the army that Hitler had saved the country 'with soldierly decisiveness'. On 3 July Hitler introduced into the cabinet a retrospective Law for Measures for the Defence of the State which legalized the wave of assassinations. On 13 July, in a meeting of the German parliament in the Kroll Opera House, Hitler announced that

By the summer of 1934 the propaganda machine had turned Hitler into a political superstar and the symbols of the movement – brown uniforms, swastika flags – could be seen in every city and village of Germany. All public buildings and offices had to display a portrait of Hitler or risk an inquiry.

anyone who threatened the Third Reich would face 'a certain death'. For the period of crisis, Hitler continued, he himself had become 'the supreme judge of the German people'. The legalization of the murders placed Hitler firmly above the law and marked a major step towards the establishment of his personal dictatorship.

The Cult of the Führer

During the month following the murders the opportunity arose to make Hitler the Third Reich's supreme authority. Until then President Hindenburg was the chief representative of the state and capable, if he so chose, of replacing his chancellor. He was also formally the supreme commander of the armed forces. By July 1934 it was clear that Hindenburg was near to death. Hitler travelled out to his estate at Neudeck on 3 July to receive the aged soldier's blessing for crushing the threat from the SA and toning down the revolutionary nature of the regime. Like so many of the old elite, he failed to understand that Hitler and his allies posed just as radical a political threat in the long run as the more vociferous SA. With Hindenburg certain to die in the near future, Hitler had to decide how to respond to the constitutional challenge this might represent.

The solution Hitler arrived at was to get the cabinet to approve a law which would make him both chancellor and president in the single office of *Führer*, fusing together the powers of the presidency with those he already enjoyed. He visited Hindenburg one last time on 31 July but the president was now so close to death that he called Hitler 'my majesty' in the mistaken belief that it was the Kaiser who had come to see him. The following day Hitler returned to Berlin and pushed the new law 'On the Leadership of the German Reich' through cabinet. In the morning of 2 August Hindenburg died and the law came into force, making Hitler the sole supreme authority in Germany. This act also made Hitler formally the supreme commander of the armed forces. On 3 August the three commanders-in-chief of the army, air force and navy swore a personal oath of allegiance to Hitler and not to the German nation, as had been the custom. On 19 August the whole of the armed forces took the oath of direct loyalty to the new *Führer*, followed on 27 August by all German state officials. The rule was extended to all ministers as well, and on 16 October 1934 the process of swearing in was completed when members of the government gave their individual allegiance to Hitler. The creation of the new office made Hitler an absolute dictator, able both to make the law and to enforce it, and he increasingly disregarded the cabinet, which was supposed to introduce legislation collectively according to the terms of the Enabling Act. In 1933 there had been 72 cabinet meetings, in 1934 only 19 and in 1935 a mere twelve. Reich laws came to be replaced increasingly by the decrees of the *Führer*.

A group of boys stare at the country residence of President Hindenburg at Neudeck where the flag has been lowered to half-mast following his death on 2 August 1934. Some of the boys are without shoes, evidence that poverty was still a serious problem in Hitler's Germany.

FIELD MARSHAL PAUL VON HINDENBURG (1847–1934)

The name of Paul von Hindenburg is bound up with the decision to appoint Hitler chancellor in 1933, but this decision came right at the end of a long and full career, and only a year before his death at the age of 87. Hindenburg was born in Prussia into the military aristocracy. He served in the wars of German unification against Austria in 1866 and France in 1870–1. He became a General Staff officer but never rose far through the military system and retired in 1911 as commander of the German Fourth Army. He was recalled in 1914 when war broke out in August to command German forces in East Prussia against the Russian attack. His victories at Tannenberg and the Masurian Lakes made him into a national hero, and in 1916 he was appointed army commander-in-chief. In this role he became a virtual dictator in Germany, working together with his Quartermaster General, Erich Ludendorff. It was Hindenburg who persuaded the German Emperor, William II, to accept the need to abdicate in late 1918. Hindenburg then retired again but on the death of the socialist President Ebert in 1925, he was persuaded to stand as a candidate. He won an overwhelming endorsement from the nationalist right because of his reputation as a national hero and was president from 1925 until his death in 1934. He favoured conservative policies on secret rearmament and challenging Versailles, but he interfered little in politics until in 1932, at the height of the economic slump, his small circle of advisers convinced him to make an active stand against the threat from the left. After putting von Papen into power in May 1932, Hindenburg played the key role in January 1933 in appointing Hitler, even though he retained misgivings about the popular street politics practised by the National Socialists. Over the last year of his life he spent much of his time at his Prussian estate at Neudeck, where he died in August 1934, widely mourned by the German people.

The weeks after the SA purge saw the cult of personality reach new heights. Hindenburg's stage-managed funeral at the Tannenberg Memorial, on the site of his famous battle in August 1914 that stopped the Russians reaching Berlin, was designed to give the impression that Hindenburg was passing on his legacy to Hitler – from political father to political son. Hindenburg had written a political testament, whose validity still remains uncertain, and this, too, was used to show that Hitler was the natural successor. Hindenburg talked of 'my chancellor' and welcomed Hitler's national revolution as the opportunity to accomplish 'the mission of our people'. On 15 August the testament was published in the press. Four days later a national plebiscite was organized to win popular endorsement for the new office of 'Leader'. The result was as expected: 89.9 per cent voted yes and 10.1 per cent voted no. This was the largest 'no' vote of the various plebiscites organized during the Third Reich and the last time that a significant fraction of the population, 7.2 million, expressed their disapproval of Hitler. From 5 to 9 September the Party Congress 'Unity and Strength' was held in Nuremberg. Despite the recent crisis, the Congress was the most lavish ever staged, with hundreds of thousands of the Party faithful taking part each day in carefully rehearsed, and theatrical, processions and parades. The event was to be filmed as a record of Hitler's new Germany and the popular German film producer Leni Riefenstahl was chosen by Hitler to make it. The attempt to film the 1933 congress had been a cinematic disaster and Hitler rejected the subsequent film, so at first Riefenstahl refused, anxious about the technical difficulties and risk of failure. Hitler insisted and she went to work installing elaborate equipment to allow cameramen to film from unusual angles or to run the cameras along tracks.

The result was one of the finest propaganda films of the 1930s, *Triumph of the Will*. The film showed the long period of enthusiastic preparation, ardent young Germans waiting for a chance to shine in front of Hitler, then column after column of the main Party organizations converging on Nuremberg and taking their place in the vast Congress stadium – Hitler Youth, the League of German Girls, the women's section, the Labour Service, the SA and SS, the Party welfare organization, the car corps, the motorcycle corps: and so on. By 1934 the Party numbered around 2.4 million members, but millions more were to be found in the auxiliary branches and associations. Every area of German life was now permeated by National Socialism and the cult of Hitler. The climax of the film was the climax of the Congress when on the final day, 10 September, Hitler himself addressed the massed ranks on the parade ground and the packed benches in the stadium. In a flood of light, on a small stage set above the crowd, Hitler gave a typical performance. He used the Congress as the opportunity to finally lay aside the crisis of the summer: 'in the next thousand years, there will be no more revolutions in Germany'.

A panoramic view of the Party Congress held at Nuremberg in early September 1934. This is a still from the propaganda film *Triumph of the Will* made by Leni Riefenstahl at Hitler's request. The shot conveys the sheer scale and discipline of the Congress, which was given the title 'Unity and Strength' following the recent purge of the SA.

"Triumph des Willens"   Foto: Reichsparteitagfilm

AT THE COURT OF ADOLF HITLER

Hitler was as unpunctual and unpredictable as ever. There were no set hours. Sometimes he would appear at breakfast. If he didn't, he would come down for a few minutes, having filled himself up in his suite with hot milk and gruel and digestive powders, and if I had something on my mind this was often a good time to catch him…The high point of the day was lunch and here the main sufferer was a little fat fellow named Kannenberg, the chef. He had run quite a decent restaurant in Berlin in the old days and then become a cook at the Brown House. He never knew what time lunch was to be served. It would be ordered for one and Hitler would sometimes not turn up until three. I have known him to cook lunch three times and throw away two of them but he was still expected to keep proper accounts. It was a completely movable feast with a shifting population. Sometimes Goering would be there, sometimes the Goebbels', less often Hess, and Roehm as good as never. (Roehm had his own private court round in the Standartenstrasse with his boy friends…). The regulars would hang around and get hungrier and hungrier. Otto Dietrich [Hitler's press secretary], who usually joined us, was the wisest. His stomach could not stand the strain, so he always went over to the Kaiserhof at a quarter to one and had a snack, turning up at half past one for all emergencies.

Even during the coalition period none of the conservative ministers ever appeared. The migrant guests were usually types like the regular staff, old party hacks, an occasional Gauleiter from the provinces, which of course suited Hitler excellently. There was hardly anyone to challenge what he said….The environment of power had its contributory effect on Hitler's character. He sat in the inner circle of authority, surrounded by three rings of guards. The adulation involved in the Führer principle would have turned steadier heads than his. His information was filtered and he was exposed the whole time to the influence of Goebbels and the congenital radicals. He lost whatever contact with ordinary people he had ever had. His public speeches became fewer and farther apart and where he once synthesized the feelings of his audience he now preached to the converted. He did not really know what was going on in the world and used to call for all the German newspapers, overlooking the fact that they came out of the one sausage factory, and read them through, looking for the one thing he could not find, which was reality.

Source: Ernst Hanfstaengl *Unheard Witness* (J. B. Lippincott, Philadelphia, 1957), pp. 228–31. Hanfstaengl was part of Hitler's circle and a noted art critic. He fled from Germany in 1937 after falling out with the Party.

The final weeks of 1934 saw a calmer atmosphere after the dilemmas and uncertainties of the first half of the year. The focus swung back towards the need to secure economic stability as a precondition for political stabilization. On 2 August Schacht was provisionally appointed Economics Minister to bring greater co-ordination in economic policy, and on 24 September 1934 Schacht published the 'New Plan', which was a comprehensive programme to control German exports and imports as well as the movement of currency and capital in and out of Germany. Although the economy remained largely based on private enterprise, the regime introduced a widespread system of compulsory groups and corporations to increase the centralization of production. On 27 November a Reich Economic Chamber was established to oversee the activity of six major economic groups. Other laws made it clear that the free market no longer existed. On 10 August a new law on the movement of labour restricted the

---

The minister of economics, Hjalmar Horace Greeley Schacht (front row, second from left), on a visit to the Reich Artisan Festival in Brunswick on 28 October 1934. His old-fashioned appearance among the uniformed Party leaders was deliberate. Schacht tried to keep a distance between himself and the movement, and in 1937 he was finally forced to resign for failing to support Hitler's armaments plans.

free choice of workers to change jobs if they were deemed to be essential in their existing occupation. On 24 October membership of the German Labour Front (set up in 1933) became compulsory for every worker and weekly dues were deducted from their wage packets. A law on 5 November 1934 established a Price Commissioner to oversee the setting of prices for products and services, and price control remained a feature of economic life down to 1945. By the end of 1934 there were no major areas of economic life not controlled in some form or other by state regulations or state-sponsored institutions. Economists in Germany named the system 'the managed economy'.

The economic controls were necessary partly to ensure that rearmament could be carried out even in a weak economic environment. On 2 November Hitler authorized the construction of six submarines, the start of a programme that would make it possible, if ever necessary, to wage war against the major naval powers of Britain and France. The same month Joachim von Ribbentrop was sent to London to see if informal negotiations might indicate the possibility of an Anglo-German agreement on naval shipbuilding. Up until the end of 1934 Germany's early rearmament was secret because it violated the terms of the Treaty of Versailles. If the former Allied powers had chosen to do so they could have compelled Germany to abandon these new military programmes. Hitler might have become the supreme authority in Germany but there remained clear limits to what could yet be achieved in the international arena. On Christmas Eve Hitler lunched with old friends from the Party in Munich after a year in which he had succeeded in creating a firm dictatorship, ending the threat of revolutionary agitation from the radical elements in the SA and securing the sworn support of the key institutions of German public life – the armed forces, the civil service and the ministries. This was a fragile consensus which rested entirely on the willingness of millions of Germans, both prominent and more ordinary, to regard Hitler now as Germany's saviour.

A poster for the new German motorways aimed at the British tourist market in the mid-1930s. German propaganda to the outside world tried to present an image of modernity and peace, masking the reality of discrimination and repression.

SPEED ALONG GERMAN REICHSAUTOBÄHNEN

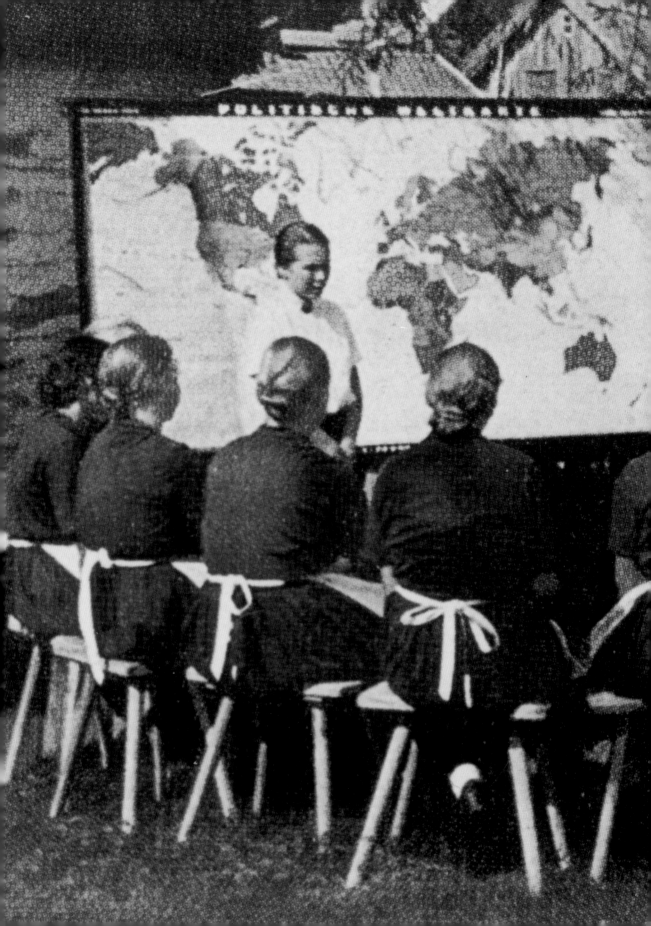

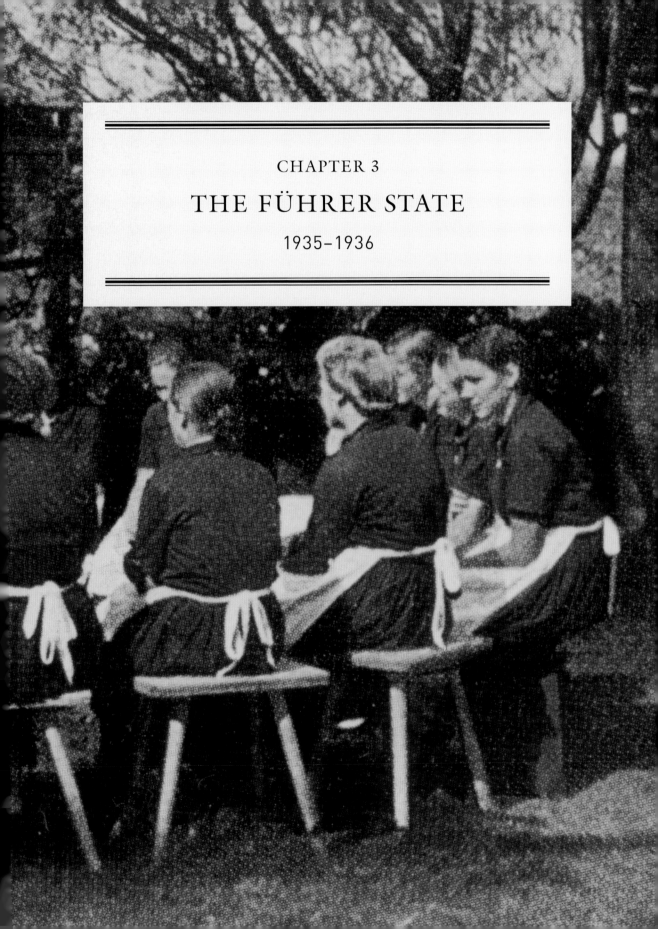

CHAPTER 3

THE FÜHRER STATE

1935–1936

From 1935 onwards Hitler began to exercise a much more personal dictatorship. The propaganda apparatus built up a cult of personality, but the growing popularity of the new leader did not have to be entirely manufactured. Many ordinary Germans came to accept that Hitler might really be able to deliver a richer and more powerful German state and enthusiasm for the successes of the regime meant that many of those who formerly voted for other parties, even on the left, now supported Hitler. With the economy reviving, the main priorities of the regime shifted to areas of rearmament and foreign policy. Hitler as yet had no definite foreign policy programme but he did want to overturn the hated Treaty of Versailles and the powerless state that Germany had faced throughout the years since 1919. This meant accelerating rearmament and remilitarizing the frontier zones of Germany, demilitarized as a result of the Treaty. The other priority for the regime was to ensure that when war eventually came the home front would not undermine the German military effort. In 1935 the first steps were taken to strip German Jews of citizenship and civil rights. Jews were regarded as a potential threat, for Hitler and other radical nationalists assumed that the Jews, among others, had been responsible for the German collapse in 1918. The regime hoped that Jews would emigrate and did everything to force them out of the country. In 1936 the concentration camp system was regularized and placed under Heinrich Himmler, leader of the SS, who also took on supreme police powers throughout Germany. The camps filled up not with Jews, but with political opponents and so-called 'asocials' – habitual criminals, prostitutes, vagrants, alcoholics. These, too, were deemed to be a threat to a people destined to be a master race. Biological health and rearmament were seen in the Third Reich as important contributions to the waging of a future total war.

1935 Destroying Versailles

On 1 January Hitler made a speech insisting that Germany was willing to pursue the course of peace. He had made similar pronouncements in the first years of his regime and many foreign observers hoped that he was sincere in his protestations. In reality the year 1935 was to see the first major steps taken to overturn the conditions imposed on Germany under the terms of the Treaty of Versailles. Uncertainty in the minds of the outside world about German intentions was finally removed and German military and territorial ambitions became a growing source of international anxiety.

The first test of the Versailles order came in January 1935 when a plebiscite was organized by the League of Nations in the former German territory of the Saarland. The plebiscite had been specified in the post-war settlement, in order to give the population the right to decide if they wanted to return to German rule after 15 years of League administration. Hitler placed great emphasis in his speech on 1 January on the importance to be attached to the result, but heavy and continuous German propaganda made a yes vote almost inevitable and on 13 January over 90 per cent voted in favour of reunion. The results were announced on 15 January. Hitler heard the outcome at his Berchtesgaden retreat and immediately gave an emotional radio speech over the telephone from the local post office. Many socialist and communist opponents of National Socialism had taken refuge in the Saar region and had to escape again from the new German authorities, or risk capture and imprisonment in a camp. By the time the area was formally reunited with the Reich on 1 March 1935, around 5,000 opponents had emigrated. A Party commissar was appointed for the region and laws passed in Berlin since January 1933 were now applied to the Saar province. The first step had been taken in reintegrating the territories lost in 1919 back into the Reich.

The most dramatic challenge to the Versailles settlement came a few weeks later when Hitler publicly announced the reintroduction of conscription and the rearming of Germany. Much had already been done since 1933 to prepare the way for this declaration but the decision to make German military revival public was a direct challenge to the existing international order and to one of the central planks of the post-war treaty. At a cabinet meeting on 26 February Hitler announced that the new armed forces would also include a separate air arm, the *Luftwaffe*, whose commander-in-chief was to be the Air Minister and Hitler's close political ally, Hermann Göring. On 9 March 1935 the existence of the *Luftwaffe* was announced and on 16 March a new law was promulgated, 'The Law for the Construction of the Armed Forces'. The new law affirmed that the existing army and navy services were to be overhauled and expanded and, together with the new air force, were to be known as the *Wehrmacht*

Pages 112–113: A group of German girls in the Labour Service sit and listen to an open air lesson in geopolitics, c.1935

ANTI-SEMITISM ON THE MARCH, 1935

The relationship between the Heilbronn Jews and the rest of the population used to be good and actually as far as neighbours are concerned it has not changed much. No one, however, dares to contradict the anti-Semitic propaganda, nor even to discuss it. The Nazis and the SA started systematically to go in parties to an island on the Neckar, and from there we could hear, across the water, mass choir singing and shouting of anti-Semitic songs and slogans. This continued for ten successive nights.

Then one day here in Heilbronn, squads of Nazi troops, each about a hundred strong, marched through the town. In the main streets they shouted their slogans: 'Perish Judah,' 'Out with the Jews,' etc. Jewish shop windows were smashed and then they went to the Jewish houses. Stones were thrown into the rooms, and I myself have seen how a man, who was accused by the Nazis of being friendly with the daughter of a civil servant, was dragged out of a house and beaten until he lay prostrate on the ground. Some of the houses had scrawled over them: 'If you venture out on to the street we'll beat the life out of you.' How many have actually been maltreated I don't know. Almost a week has passed since that Sunday, but even now no Jew dares to go out on the street after dark. Many of them haven't left their houses during the whole of this time. Others do so only when it is absolutely unavoidable.

Source: *The Yellow Spot: A collection of facts and documents relating to three years' persecution of German Jews* (Victor Gollancz, London, 1936), p. 70 (eyewitness account from September 1935)

THE SAAR PLEBISCITE

Between 13 and 15 January 1935 voting took place in the Saarland in the south-west corner of Germany in a plebiscite organized to allow the population of the province to decide if they wanted to be reunited with Germany. In 1919 in the Treaty of Paris (Versailles) the rich industrial area of the Saar was separated from Germany as a potential source of reparation supplies for France. The area was one of the main coal-producing regions and the coalmines were ceded to France. In 1920 a League of Nations mandate was created giving control of the area to Britain and France. They were represented by a League Commission of five members and in 1935, when the League mandate had run its course, the chair of the commission was Sir Geoffrey Knox. The intention was to allow the largely German population of the area to determine its own future in a popular vote. The area housed many refugees from Hitler's Germany, but German propaganda had turned most of the population into enthusiasts for the new German order. When the results of the plebiscite were announced they showed overwhelming victory for reunion with Germany, 90.73% in favour and only 0.41% in favour of union with France. The large turnout of 98% of the voters showed that this was a genuinely popular decision. A Reich commissar, Joseph Bürckel, was appointed and on 1 March 1935 the Saarland was formally reintegrated into Germany. In 1941 the Moselle region was added and the area became known as Westmark. After the Second World War the Saar again returned briefly under French control and was reintegrated with the German Federal Republic in 1955.

(Armed Forces). The law also specified the reintroduction of conscription, abolished in the Versailles Treaty. The plan was announced for a new 36-division army of 580,000 men to be completed by 1939. This was to expand the 300,000-man army secretly planned for in 1934. At the same time the new armed forces would be able to develop and use modern weapons denied them under the disarmament clauses of Versailles. At his aircraft factory in Bavaria Willy Messerschmitt was in the process of designing the Me 109 fighter, the mainstay of the German fighter arm in the later Battle of Britain.

After issuing the law, Hitler reviewed a military march-past on Unter den Linden in the centre of Berlin before returning to Munich. The declaration of rearmament was a difficult moment which carried with it real risk of international retaliation. Between 18 and 21 March

Anti-Semitism was promoted at every opportunity after 1933. Here an illustration from a children's book of 1935 shows the caricature of a rich Jew enticing a pure blond German girl with the promise of a string of pearls.

Above: A group of miners from the Saarland in January 1935 demonstrate their
enthusiasm for Hitler's Reich in the run-up to the referendum in the region about
reuniting with Germany. The sign reads 'We vote on 13 January for Germany'. In the end
over 90 per cent of Saarlanders voted for union.

Opposite: Adolf Hitler in conversation with senior commanders at the army manoeuvres
on the Lüneburg Heath in northern Germany, 6 September 1935. To the left is General
von Blomberg, to Hitler's right is General von Fritsch. Both were later to fall victim to
Party intrigue.

formal protests were lodged by Britain, France and Italy against the reintroduction of conscription. Relations with Britain had been temporarily strained by the publication in early March of a British parliamentary White Paper on German secret rearmament, and on 5 March Hitler had rescinded the invitation to the British Foreign Secretary, Sir John Simon, who with Anthony Eden was coming to Berlin to discuss a possible naval treaty. The decision was eventually relaxed, and Simon and Eden arrived in the German capital on 25 March for a two-day visit in which the British raised questions about German rearmament. Hitler still maintained that his chief objective was peace, but insisted that peace could only be achieved if Germany had parity of status on armaments with the other major powers.

The difficulties could not be overcome so simply. Between 11 and 14 April representatives of Britain, France and Italy met at the Italian lakeside town of Stresa to discuss the consequences of Germany's unilateral action. They condemned the reintroduction of conscription and agreed to co-operate to limit Germany's possibility of further action without the agreement of the Treaty powers. The so-called 'Stresa Front' eventually came to nothing since the British government was already engaged in negotiations with Germany over the prospect of an agreement on naval armament. France placed more reliance on reaching an agreement with the Soviet Union, the sworn enemy of Hitler's Reich, and on 2 May the Franco-Soviet Mutual Assistance Treaty was signed. Although the new pact had the potential to become a military agreement for limiting German attempts to revise Versailles, staff talks never materialized between the two sides and when later, in 1939, France hoped to cement a real military alliance with the Soviet Union, the 1935 pact was shown to have been politically worthless.

The introduction of conscription also raised issues in domestic politics. On 1 April 1935 the Jehovah's Witness organization was banned, partly because its members were committed to refusing military service. Some prominent Witnesses were sent to camps where they were designated with a special coloured triangle, like other categories of political prisoners. The Jehovah's Witnesses wore a lavender triangle and were continually victimized not just for their pacifism but because of their staunch refusal to abandon their faith. On 21 May a new Defence Law came into force which excluded German Jews from serving in the armed forces (but did not exclude the children of mixed German-Jewish parentage, some of whom ended up fighting in the German army in the Second World War). A further decree on 25 July laid down precise conditions for who could serve in the armed forces; full and three-quarter Jewish Germans were specifically excluded. The same law of 21 May also announced that Hitler was now to be the Supreme Commander of the Armed Forces. This raised important constitutional questions since the overall military commander and War Minister, General Werner von Blomberg, expected to exercise that command himself. Not until 1938, and von Blomberg's resignation, was Hitler able to exercise direct control over the armed forces without having to go through his War Minister. Yet the Defence Law of 1935 paved the way for Hitler's role as supreme warlord between 1939 and 1945.

During the period of diplomatic wrangling over German rearmament, German society was briefly enthralled by the society wedding of the year. Herman Göring, recently appointed commander-in-chief of the *Luftwaffe*, was married to the actress Emmy Sonnemann in Berlin

CHURCHILL ON HITLER, 1935

It is not possible to form a just judgment of a public figure whose life has attained the enormous dimensions of Adolf Hitler until his life work as a whole is before us. Although no subsequent political action can condone wrong deeds, history is replete with examples of men who have risen to power by employing stern, grim, and even frightful methods, but who, nevertheless, when their life is revealed as a whole, have been regarded as great figures whose lives have enriched the story of mankind. So may it be with Hitler.

Such a final view is not vouchsafed to us today [1935]. We cannot tell whether Hitler will be the man who will once again let loose upon the world another war in which civilization will irretrievably succumb, or whether he will go down in history as the man who restored honour and peace of mind to the great Germanic nation and brought it back serene, helpful and strong, to the forefront of the European family circle. It is on this mystery of the future that history will pronounce. It is easy enough to say that both possibilities are open at the present moment. If, because the story is unfinished, because, indeed, its most fateful chapters have yet to be written, we are forced to dwell upon the darker side of his work and creed, we must not forget nor cease to hope for the bright alternative.

Source: Winston S. Churchill *Great Contemporaries* (Butterworth, London, 1937), p. 261

on 10 April 1935. Göring had been married once before, to the Swedish aristocrat Carin Beamish-Fock, but she had died prematurely in 1931, leaving him distraught. His vast country manor house, built in the early years of the new Reich, was called Carinhall in her memory. Carin's remains were interred there with great pomp in June 1934. His second wedding was a grand affair, nicknamed 'the Crown-Prince wedding' by the German public. Hitler was the best man, and no expense was spared on the lavish preparations and the celebrations that followed. Emmy was to bear Göring a daughter in 1938, though cruel rumours circulated that she was the fruit of a secret liaison with Mussolini or even the consequence of artificial insemination.

The most important consequence of the declaration of German rearmament was the decision taken in London to try to reach a firm agreement with Germany over limitation of naval armaments. This was in direct violation of the Versailles settlement but it was pursued because the Royal Navy feared that, unless some agreement could be secured, there would be no way of limiting German naval expansion or of knowing exactly what Germany was developing. Any agreement would nevertheless give official international sanction to Germany's right to rearm and might alienate Britain's other League partners. The German Navy for its part was very far from constituting any real threat and was happy to have

The National Socialist foreign affairs expert and special envoy to London, Joachim von Ribbentrop, on his way to the British Foreign Office on 4 June 1935. His success in negotiating the Anglo-German Naval Agreement persuaded Hitler to make him ambassador in London in 1936.

ANGLO-GERMAN NAVAL AGREEMENT, 1935

The Anglo-German Naval Agreement, signed on 18 June 1935, was the first time any of the western states formally acknowledged the German right to rearm in violation of the Versailles settlement. The agreement allowed Germany to build up to 35% of the tonnage of the Royal Navy, but no more. It was negotiated in London by Hitler's personal emissary, Joachim von Ribbentrop, the Party's foreign affairs spokesman and later the German Foreign Secretary from 1938 to 1945. The British motive in agreeing to the treaty was to find some way of ensuring that German naval rearmament might be controlled in some way. It was also hoped that agreement might form a foundation for a more positive effort to get Germany back into the international order and reduce the risk from Germany's sense of grievance against the Treaty. But for Hitler, for whom legal niceties were less important, the agreement seemed to indicate that Britain was drifting towards some more general settlement with Germany at the expense of France or the United States. At this stage Hitler still hoped to be able to reach an agreement with Britain which would allow him a freer hand in Europe. The Treaty of Paris (Versailles) of 1919 had restricted Germany to just 6 heavy cruisers of no more than 10,000 tons and 6 light cruisers of no more than 6,000 tons. Germany was denied submarines, naval aircraft, battleships or aircraft carriers. Under the terms of the Anglo-German Naval Agreement, Germany could now begin to build other kinds of vessels. Construction of the first German submarine had already begun in April 1935. In reality, the effort to build a navy of the size allowed was still too great for the weakened German economy and by 1939 the German Navy was still in the early stages of developing a large ocean-going fleet once again.

agreement that would allow the early expansion to take place without a naval race with Britain, the leading naval power. Hitler took an unusual step in preparing for the discussions that led to the signing of the agreement. On 1 June 1935 he named the Party's foreign affairs spokesman, Joachim von Ribbentrop, as Extraordinary Plenipotentiary Ambassador to London to negotiate a naval treaty. Ribbentrop was in charge of the Party's foreign affairs department and on 1 June it was given formal status as the 'Ribbentrop Office' (*Dienststelle Ribbentrop*). He was a former wine merchant with knowledge of foreign languages and an inflated ego. His diplomatic skills were negligible but Hitler preferred to rely on a Party appointment rather than the officials of the conservative German Foreign Office, whom he distrusted. Ribbentrop's behaviour during the negotiations was arrogant and patronizing, but the British side were keen to reach agreement and overlooked his many gaffes. On 18 June 1935 the Anglo-German Naval Agreement was signed and Hitler had achieved international recognition for the new German armed forces.

The Nuremberg Laws

The second important development during 1935 was the construction of a legal framework for excluding German Jews from citizenship or the right of intermarriage with ethnic Germans. The legal instruments were established at the annual NSDAP rally at Nuremberg in September 1935, but the process of discrimination and exclusion continued throughout the year.

German anti-Semitism was not only expressed in legal documents. From the spring of 1935 onwards a fresh wave of violence was unleashed against both individual German Jews and Jewish businesses by SA-men and Party activists. Acts of violent intimidation included beatings, parades through the streets, the smashing of windows and the daubing of anti-Semitic graffiti. The object was to encourage Jewish emigration, and between June 1933 and September 1939 around 287,000 Jews did leave Germany for safer destinations. But in 1935 some German Jews had returned after fleeing from Germany in 1933 and they now found themselves subjected to a second wave of persecution. This wave included further acts of deliberate discrimination. Jews were denied membership of German student fraternities by a regulation of 8 July 1935. On 25 July the Propaganda Ministry set up an office to supervise all 'non-Aryan' cultural and intellectual activity, although many Jewish intellectuals, artists and writers had already chosen emigration.

The high point of anti-Semitic policy was reached in mid-September when the Party faithful arrived at Nuremberg for the annual Party rally. The rally was named the 'Congress of Peace', perhaps to echo Hitler's regular assertions during the year that peace was the principal aim of his foreign and military policy. Exceptionally on this occasion, the German Parliament was summoned south from Berlin (although most of its members were delegates to the Congress anyway) to ratify three new laws. The Congress opened on 10 September amid the usual clamour of marches, flags and torchlight parades. On 15 September the new laws were presented to the German Parliament as it met in extraordinary session. The first law confirmed that the national flag of Germany would now be the swastika banner of the Party. This formally replaced the black, red and gold flag of the Weimar Republic, which symbolized for many Germans the flawed republican regime. The old imperial flag was considered to be too reminiscent of the failed monarchical system. The Party's red flag with a white circle and swastika in the middle, originally designed by Hitler himself, was used to symbolize the marriage between the Hitler movement and the German nation. Goebbels issued guidelines on the use that could be made of the swastika, banning any commercial exploitation of the Party symbol.

The second two laws were designed specifically to limit the civil rights of Germany's Jewish citizens. The first was the Reich citizenship law which limited those who could become citizens, enjoying full civil rights, to those of German blood. The second law 'for the Protection of German Blood and German Honour' outlawed marriage or sexual relations outside marriage between Jews and Germans. This legislation permitted popular anti-Semitism to be directed at new targets, and German Jews accused by the local population of having sex with ethnic Germans were forced to wear placards and paraded through the street to the jeers of their neighbours. In addition, the victims were subject to the direct punishment of the state. What became known as 'race shaming' (*Rassenschande*) could eventually lead to

THE NUREMBERG LAWS

Law for the Protection of German Blood and German Honour, 15 September 1935

Imbued with the realization that the purity of German blood is a prerequisite for the continued existence of the German people, and inspired by the inflexible will to protect the German nation for all times to come, the Reichstag has unanimously passed the following law which is herewith promulgated:

1

(1) Marriages between Jews and subjects of German or related blood are forbidden. Marriages concluded in spite of it are null and void, even if concluded abroad to circumvent this law.

(2) Only the state attorney may initiate an annulment claim.

2

Extramarital sexual intercourse between Jews and subjects of German or related blood is forbidden.

3

Jews may not employ in their households female subjects of German or related blood under 45 years of age.

4

(1) Jews are forbidden to fly the national flag of the Reich or display the national colours.

(2) They may, however, show the Jewish colours. The right to do so is protected by the state.

5

(1) Anybody violating the injunction listed in 1 will be punished by detention in a penitentiary.

(2) Any male violating the injunction listed in 2 will be punished by either a prison term or a penitentiary term.....

Source: Reinhard Rürup (ed) *Topography of Terror: Gestapo, SS and Reichssicherheitshauptamt on the 'Prinz-Albrecht-Terrain': A Documentation* (Verlag Willmuth Arenhövel, Berlin, 1989), pp. 114–16

incarceration in a concentration camp or, later in the war, public execution. The first of the 'Nuremberg Laws' applied not only to Jews but also to other aliens living in Germany. It could also be used to strip German opponents of the regime of their citizenship if they were not 'willing or suitable' to assist the national revolution. The second law was aimed more particularly at Germany's Jewish population. The position of the few blacks living in Germany in the 1930s was never clearly defined. Some of them enjoyed citizenship status as inhabitants of the former German colonies, but the Party was hostile to any idea that blacks and Germans could intermarry or have sexual intercourse. The community of 600 so-called 'Rhineland bastards', the result of liaisons between German women and black French soldiers during the occupation of the Ruhr in 1923, was subject to compulsory sterilization in 1937 to avoid further 'race contamination', but there existed no legal ground for doing so.

The decision to push through the Nuremberg Laws was not Hitler's, but driven by anti-Semitic officials in the Interior Ministry who wanted a clearer definition of German citizenship. The issue of definition was a difficult one. Hitler struck out the last sentence of the draft law he was shown at Nuremberg which said 'This law is for full Jews only', but this left open the difficulty of deciding whether 'half-Jews' or 'quarter-Jews' were citizens or not. A supplement to the law was issued on 14 November 1935, making it clear that any German who had two Jewish grandparents, who was also an orthodox Jew, or married to someone Jewish, or was the offspring of a marriage with a Jew, was defined as Jewish. All other half- or quarter-Jews could still be citizens and would be obliged to serve in the armed forces.

The Pace Quickens

By the autumn of 1935 the international situation began to become more sharply defined. In October 1935, thinking that he had neutralized the risk of opposition from Britain and France, Mussolini launched an invasion of the African state of Abyssinia (now Ethiopia). The League of Nations moved to introduce a variety of economic sanctions against Italy, which was still a member, and relations between Italy and the Western states quickly deteriorated, though sanctions in reality proved difficult to enforce. Germany supplied raw materials, particularly coal, to Italy but Hitler was wary of becoming too involved in the League dispute. He nevertheless gave Mussolini more support than the other states in Europe and the close alignment of the two 'fascist' states the following year had its roots in the willingness of both countries to recognize the interest of the other.

This was particularly important for Hitler because he hoped to take advantage of the crisis over Ethiopia and the failure of Britain and France to act decisively to reverse Italian

Enthusiastic crowds with arms raised in the Hitler salute welcome German soldiers as they cross the bridge over the Rhine at Mainz during the remilitarization of the Rhineland on 7 March 1936. Though remilitarization violated the Versailles Treaty, the other powers did nothing to prevent it happening.

REMILITARIZATION OF THE RHINELAND

The Western governments had, as [Hitler] commented at the time, proved themselves weak and indecisive. He found this view confirmed when the German troops marched into the demilitarized Rhineland on March 7, 1936. This was an open breach of the Treaty of Locarno and might have provoked military counter-measures on the part of the Allies. The special train in which we rode to Munich on the evening of that day was charged, compartment after compartment, with the tense atmosphere that emanated from the Fuehrer's section. At one station a message was handed into the car. Hitler sighed with relief: 'At last! The King of England will not intervene. He is keeping his promise. That means it can all go well.' He seemed not to be aware of the meagre influence the British Crown has upon Parliament and the government. Nevertheless, military intervention would have probably required the King's approval, and perhaps this is what Hitler meant to imply. In any case, he was intensely anxious, and even later, when he was waging war against almost the entire world, he always termed the remilitarization of the Rhineland the most daring of all his undertakings.

Source: Albert Speer *Inside the Third Reich* (Weidenfeld, London, 1970), p. 72

aggression by challenging the Versailles settlement once again. His aim this time was to remilitarize those areas of the Rhine frontier with France which Germany had been forced to demilitarize under the terms of the Treaty. The action is often presented as the 'reoccupation' of the Rhineland, but the area had remained an integral part of the German state since 1919. What the western powers, and France in particular, would not allow was the stationing of German forces and the construction of fortifications. Consistent with the declaration of German rearmament in March 1935, Hitler wanted to be able to station his forces anywhere in Germany. On 19 February 1936 the German ambassador to Rome was summoned back to Berlin, where he was told that he should discover Mussolini's possible reaction to a German military move into the Rhineland. The ambassador, Ulrich von Hassell, returned to Rome and three days later Mussolini confirmed that he would take a passive approach to any remilitarization even though it violated the Locarno Treaty of 1925, to which he was a signatory, and the ill-fated Stresa Front. For Mussolini, German action would involve France and Britain in a crisis in Europe while his forces completed the ruthless conquest of Abyssinia.

On 2 March 1936 Hitler summoned his military commanders-in-chief to a conference to determine the course to be adopted for remilitarization. The War Minister, von Blomberg, issued orders for what was codenamed *Winterübung* (Winter Exercise). In the evening of 6 March Hitler ordered the remilitarization to take place the following day. Three battalions of soldiers and two squadrons of aircraft were to make the symbolic gesture of crossing the Rhine to the far western bank. They were under orders to retreat if faced with serious intervention by the French army. The formal German justification was the conclusion of the Franco-Soviet Pact in 1935, which the German government claimed violated Locarno as well. When Hitler spoke to the German parliament at noon on 7 March, he promised the other major powers that Germany would be willing to sign a 25-year bilateral non-aggression pact with all or any of the neighbouring states and to rejoin the League of Nations. Britain was non-committal; unsure of British support, France backed away from direct confrontation over the remilitarization and what might have been a serious international crisis became a *fait accompli*, accepted by the other major states. On 14 March, in a speech in Munich buoyed up by his recent success, Hitler told his audience: 'I go with the certainty of a sleepwalker along the path laid out for me by Providence.' He added that his principal aim was peace, but a peace based on equality, a refrain that he continued to repeat regularly over the following years while creating the conditions that made war ever more likely.

To secure popular endorsement for his coup in the Rhineland, Hitler insisted on a new round of one-party parliamentary elections and a plebiscite. The rules were changed to avoid much evidence of negative voting. Any blank ballots were deemed to be 'yes' votes and only those which stated no, or were disfigured in any way, counted as votes against. Out of the almost 44.5 million votes cast, 98.8 per cent were in favour. Some districts recorded a 100 per cent vote, although local officials almost certainly disregarded the voting slips that said anything but yes. Hitler took the vote as a positive reflection of a wide approval of the regime. On 1 April he presented the British government with a 'peace plan', but the offer was not taken

THE CONDOR LEGION

When the Spanish civil war began in July 1936, one of the nationalist rebel leaders, Francisco Franco, asked Hitler to supply help to the rebels. Since Hitler was keen to safeguard Spanish trade and hoped that war there would result in victory for a regime sympathetic to Germany and Fascist Italy, Hitler agreed. Codenamed Operation *Feuerzauber*, some 19,000 German volunteers from among the German armed forces eventually saw action in Spain. In November 1936 the German contingents were organized under the title Condor Legion. Much of the aid came in the form of air forces, including a bomber group, a fighter group, reconnaissance and seaplane squadrons. Around 100 aircraft and 5,100 airmen under the command of General Hugo Sperrle played an important part in helping Franco to push into northern Spain during 1937. In the course of this campaign, German units commanded by Wolfram von Richthofen, cousin of the more famous 'Red Baron' air ace Manfred von Richthofen, attacked the Basque city of Guernica, destroying much of the town and killing an estimated 250 people. Over the course of German intervention some 232 aircraft were lost (but only 72 in combat), and 298 Germans killed. The Condor Legion became a useful training ground for German personnel and also allowed the German air force to test its modern generation of aircraft in battle conditions, including the Messerschmitt Me109, the Junkers Ju87 dive-bomber and the Heinkel He111 medium bomber. The new 88 mm anti-aircraft artillery was also tested against ground targets and was to prove a formidable anti-tank weapon later in the Second World War. Most forces were withdrawn by late 1938. A memorial to the fallen of the Condor Legion can still be seen in Madrid.

seriously. Although the remilitarization restored a measure of German national dignity, Germany was not yet accepted on equal terms with the victor states. This failure of what the Germans called *Gleichberechtigung* (equality of status) remained a constant irritant throughout the 1930s and, in the German view, evidence of the cynical self-interest of the West.

This sense of grievance perhaps helps explain the decision taken a few months later to help the Nationalist rebels when a civil war broke out in Spain. On 17 and 18 July elements of the Spanish armed forces attempted a coup against the Popular Front republican government. Led among others by General Francisco Franco, the rebels found themselves facing not only resistance from servicemen and policemen with sympathies for the legal government, but with the armed resistance of workers and peasants who feared a right-wing dictatorship. Franco was not in strict terms a fascist, as he is often painted, and he distrusted the small native fascist movement, the Falange. His wishes, and those of many of his allies, were to restore a conservative Spain with respect for property, Church and nation. Nevertheless both Mussolini and Hitler decided that they would offer support for Franco's rebellion in preference to a Spain that they regarded as increasingly communistic.

When news arrived on 25 July from two Moroccan businessmen, sent to Germany by Franco, that the rebels needed German military assistance, the German foreign ministry was reluctant. The foreign minister, Constantin von Neurath, feared that German assistance would unnecessarily antagonize Britain. One of the businessmen managed to alert Hitler's deputy, Rudolf Hess, and the two were invited to meet Hitler at the Bavarian city of Bayreuth, where he had gone on 19 July for the annual festival of Wagner's music. Hitler was watching a performance of *Siegfried* and not until late at night was it possible for the emissaries to hand over a letter from Franco. In the early hours of the morning Hitler argued the case with von Blomberg and Göring, who was also unenthusiastic about intervention. Hitler convinced himself that a communist Spain had to be avoided at all costs, and persuaded his colleagues as much. Orders were sent out to transfer 20 Junkers Ju52 transport aircraft, 6 Heinkel He51 fighter-bombers and anti-aircraft guns to Franco's troops. Göring overcame his uncertainty and suggested the codename *Feuerzauber* (Magic Fire) for the operation. Over the following weeks the German leadership came to appreciate the advantages of helping Franco. It was possible to test out new weapons and tactics without a major commitment of forces, as well as to safeguard exports of vital minerals (particularly the valuable Spanish iron ores) necessary for German rearmament. A special company was established to handle trade between nationalist areas of Spain and Germany, known by the acronym ROWAK, and the flow of trade was maintained throughout the subsequent three years of the civil war. Though German help in 1936-7 allowed the rebels to establish a firm foothold in Spain, Franco's eventual victory in the spring of 1939 did not owe a great deal to German military assistance.

The Apparatus of Terror

While Hitler increasingly turned his attention to issues of foreign policy, the Party tightened its grip on the home population. The process of placing responsibility for police and security matters in the hands of Party leaders was finally completed on 17 June 1936 when Heinrich Himmler, head of the SS, was appointed Chief of the German Police and Reich Leader of the SS. Although nominally subordinate to the Interior Minister, Wilhelm Frick, the appointment in reality gave Himmler unlimited powers over the whole police apparatus. On 26 June the Gestapo and the criminal police were merged together in the new organization under the title of 'security police' and put under the direction of Himmler's ambitious young deputy, Reinhard Heydrich; the 'ordinary police' were led by a senior SS officer and police official, Kurt Daluege. Himmler had at last achieved his goal of uniting all the police and security forces fighting against the 'enemies' of the national revolution.

Even before Himmler's appointment the process of expanding and institutionalizing the terror had continued. On 10 February 1936 a new law freed the Gestapo from judicial review and allowed the secret police to decide what constituted a political crime, who the political criminals were and whether they should be taken into protective custody. At the same time the remaining concentration camps were given a firmer legal and institutional basis. An office for the camps was set up in December 1934 under the control of Theodor Eicke, the commandant of Dachau. In June 1935 Hitler approved Reich funding for the camp system and in November insisted against the efforts of the Interior Ministry that the camps were independent of the normal legal system. In the spring of 1936 Hitler confirmed that the camps were the sole responsibility of the SS and on 29 March the SS camp guards were officially renamed the SS Death's Head Units (*SS-Totenkopf-Verbände*). In June, when Himmler took over supreme control of the police forces, the concentration camps also became his direct responsibility. Many of the old camps were closed down, except for Dachau, which was reconstructed using camp labour. Instead Himmler envisaged the construction of a series of new camps to hold an estimated 50,000 prisoners. Himmler thought that if war came again it would be necessary to arrest thousands of potential troublemakers and saboteurs. The camps were also to become places where all those Germans could be put whose behaviour was believed to weaken the biological strength of the nation, from prostitutes and abortionists to the workshy and

Opposite left: Hitler and a group of Party leaders, including Goebbels and his wife, at a performance of Wagner's *Rienzi* in the National Theatre in Munich on 5 May 1936. Hitler's love of opera forced him to dress in formal evening wear rather than the Party uniform he usually wore for public events.

Opposite right: A dog wanders the burning streets of the Basque city of Guernica, destroyed by German bombers of the Condor Legion helping Spanish Nationalist forces during the Spanish Civil War on 26 April 1937. Current estimates suggest that around 250 people were killed in the attack, which shocked world opinion.

alcoholics. In July 1936 work began on the construction of the Sachsenhausen camp, soon to be supplemented by Buchenwald and a women's camp at Ravensbrück.

The terror apparatus began to spread its net more widely as Himmler's power grew. The efforts of the Gestapo uncovered a number of surviving socialist and communist cells. In the autumn of 1935 the communist 'New Beginning' network in Berlin was broken up and over the following months its members arrested and sent to camps. A year later the 'Red Fighters' organization was broken up. Himmler was particularly interested in the opposition of Christians and had a department in the Gestapo organisation responsible for 'Churches'. Most German Christians supported the regime, but the newly founded Protestant organization (the Confessing Church, founded in May 1934 in protest at the regime's efforts to control church policy) sustained a campaign emphasizing Christian doctrine. Over the following two years the

Above left: Theodor Eicke, the first commandant of Dachau concentration camp and the first Inspector of Concentration Camps, appointed in April 1934. Eicke was an embittered veteran of the war years and a brutal overseer of the early camps. He drew up regulations for prisoner behaviour which involved harsh tortures for those who failed to obey.

Above right: A group of concentration camp prisoners at Dachau in Bavaria look at a notice explaining the 'path to liberty'. The path was made up, according to the instructions, by 'obedience, diligence, honourableness, order, cleanliness, sobriety, truthfulness, willingness to sacrifice and love of the Fatherland!'

DECREE ON APPOINTMENT OF CHIEF OF POLICE

I

In order to have the police functions in the Reich placed on a unified and centralized basis, a Chief of German Police is being appointed within the Reich Ministry of the Interior who will simultaneously be entrusted with the direction and handling of all police functions within the jurisdiction of the Ministry of the Interior of the Reich and Prussia.

II

(1) The Deputy Head of the Prussian Secret State Police, *Reichsführer-SS* Heinrich Himmler, is herewith appointed Chief of the German Police within the Reich Ministry of the Interior.

(2) He is directly and personally responsible to the Ministry of the Interior of the Reich and Prussia.

(3) He will deputize within his range of duties for the Minister of the Interior of the Reich and Prussia in the absence of the latter.

(4) His official title will be: *Reichsführer-SS* and Chief of German Police within the Reich Ministry of the Interior.

III

The Chief of German Police in the Reich Ministry of the Interior will participate in all meetings of the Reich Cabinet whenever his sphere of responsibility is affected.

IV

I commission the Minister of the Interior of the Reich and Prussia with the execution of this decree.

Berlin June 17 1936
Führer and Reich Chancellor, Adolf Hitler

Source: *Topography of Terror: Gestapo, SS and Reichssicherheitshauptamt : A Documentation* (Willmuth Arenhoevel, Berlin, 2003), p. 61, Decree of June 17 1936 concerning appointment of Chief of German Police.

HEINRICH HIMMLER (1901–1945)

One of the most notorious of all Hitler's henchmen, Heinrich Himmler became leader of the SS and the mastermind of the whole terror apparatus in the Third Reich. He was responsible for implementing the Final Solution which led to the death of an estimated 5.7 million Jews. He was the son of a Bavarian schoolmaster from a devout Catholic family. He trained for service at the end of the First World War but the armistice came before he could fight. He always profoundly regretted this and made great efforts to demonstrate his masculinity and soldierly temperament in his later career. He gained an agricultural diploma from college, briefly worked as a poultry farmer, but on joining the National Socialist party in 1925 he became devoted to the national cause. Himmler read widely on issues of race and history and developed a deep personal loathing for the Jews. He was also attracted to the idea of breeding a pure, physically perfect race, an idea that he tried to put into practice later in his career. He maintained a lifelong interest in Germany's mysterious pagan past. In 1929 he was appointed head of the black-uniformed SS (Schutzstaffel) which was tasked with looking after Hitler's personal security. When Hitler became chancellor, Himmler took on a police role with the Munich force, where he founded the concentration camp at Dachau. In 1936 he became supreme head of all the police forces in Germany, including the Gestapo, the secret police, which had been established by Hermann Göring in 1933. The SS organization soon became the elite of the Third Reich, able to run the police and security apparatus on the basis of a cruel political oppression and policies for so-called 'race hygiene' – cleansing German society of those deemed to be a threat to the race, particularly Jews. In October 1939 Hitler appointed him Reich Commissar for the Protection of Germandom and he began a programme to resettle all Germans in Europe back in the Reich and to expel unwanted racial groups from the conquered areas. From summer 1941 his SS killing squads in Russia began the process that led to the Final Solution. In 1943 he was also made Minister of the Interior and in July 1944 head of the Replacement Army (or home army) inside Germany. By the end of the war he was the most powerful man in Germany after Hitler. He began scheming to negotiate a separate peace with one or other of the Allies, and when Hitler found out he was stripped of all his offices. At the end of the war he went into hiding but was caught by British soldiers. He killed himself by biting a cyanide capsule before he could be questioned.

The leader of the SS and Germany's police chief, Heinrich Himmler, in conversation with the Reich sports leader Hans von Tschammer und Osten during the Party's winter games at Rottach-Egern, February 1937. Himmler was obsessed with keeping fit and hoped that the next German Olympic team would be made up only of men from the SS.

Above: A cell in the Gestapo headquarters at 8 Prinz-Albrecht-Strasse in central Berlin. The building became the hub of the empire of terror constructed by Heinrich Himmler. The cells were built in the basement in 1933 to hold prisoners taken in under 'protective custody' laws. The routine torture of prisoners known euphemistically as 'intensified interrogation' was carried on in the offices above.

Opposite: A traditional village ceremony in Leissling known as 'begging for eggs' has been transformed under National Socialism into a charade on 'expulsion of the Jews'. The regime encouraged popular anti-Semitism wherever it found an enthusiastic audience.

new church opposed the attempt to create a single German Protestant Church, led by a Reich Bishop appointed by Hitler. The attempt failed and a new Church Minister, Hans Kerrl, appointed in December 1934, set up local committees to check on what the different Protestant denominations were doing. The Confessing Church resisted even this. On 5 March 1936, two days before the Rhineland remilitarization, the Confessing clergy read out from their pulpits a rejection of National Socialist claims to be the ultimate authority in all things. The Gestapo had warned the churchmen not to publish the document and 700 were arrested for defying the ban. A second statement condemning the racial policies of the regime was sent to Hitler on 28 May and further arrests followed. Most clergy were released but over 400 clerics from a number of denominations were held in Dachau concentration camp. In August and September 1936 they were joined by numerous Jehovah's Witnesses, who were now rounded up in large numbers and sent to camps for their persistent defiance of the regime.

The authorities also extended the race laws, first promulgated at Nuremberg in September 1935. The racial priorities took many forms. On 12 October 1935 the Reich radio controller issued a decree banning the playing of so-called 'Nigger-Jazz' on German radio. Germans who chose to listen to jazz in defiance of the regime's cultural ban were not usually persecuted, but it was taken by the authorities as a sign of decadence and associated in the minds of the Gestapo agents with homosexuality, which was hunted down with increased vigour during 1936. Further legislation extended the ban on 'corrupting German blood' imposed first on German Jews. On 18 October 1935 a law was passed prohibiting those with a serious mental or physical disability, or with medical conditions thought to be hereditary, from marrying and having children. They were to be compulsorily sterilized to ensure that they no longer contaminated the German gene pool. On 1 January 1936 the Interior Ministry published a further decree banning Gypsies (Sinti and Roma) and 'coloureds' from intermarriage or sexual relations with Germans. Increasingly the police force found itself monitoring the biological health of the nation rather than the political resistance.

Olympic Interlude

In 1936 Hitler's Germany hosted both the winter and summer Olympic Games. This was an unusual coincidence. The decision to award the summer games to Berlin had been made as long ago as 1931, but there were strong feelings at the time that Germany was too poor, after years of economic crisis, to host both events. A decision was finally taken by the Olympic Committee in June 1933, after Hitler had come to power, and was widely regarded as an early endorsement of the new regime. The site chosen was Garmisch-Partenkirchen in Bavaria. The Winter Olympics opened there on 6 February 1936 in the presence of Hitler himself.

The decision to grant both games to Germany opened up a number of political issues. There was concern about the possibility of a boycott and the American team only participated after a close vote at the American Athletic Union meeting in December 1935 against further investigation of German political conditions. Individual athletes did protest by not attending, but in the end the major boycott was by Swiss and Austrian skiers who objected to the new Olympic ruling that anyone who taught skiing professionally could not be considered an amateur for the purposes of the Games. Nevertheless the German authorities were anxious that there should be no political friction to spoil the international good will they might win as Olympic hosts. In Garmisch-Partenkirchen all anti-Semitic signs were removed just before the games began and the local SA thugs were told to be on their best behaviour. Later, for the summer games in Berlin, the same procedure was adopted and the capital became briefly a site of racial tolerance again. The political pressure on the German population nevertheless continued. Anyone found openly criticizing the regime in conversation with foreign journalists or athletes was liable to arrest. One German journalist foolish enough to complain about reporting restrictions was sentenced to life imprisonment just as the summer games began.

The Winter Games almost failed because of a lack of snow, but a heavy blizzard two days before ensured that the Games would go ahead. Hitler hesitated about going and after a Jewish student assassinated a leading National Socialist, Wilhelm Gustloff, in Switzerland on 5 February, security for Hitler's journey and stay at Garmisch-Partenkirchen was particularly tight. In the absence of Austrian and Swiss stars, the medals table was dominated by Norway

A poster advertising the 1936 Olympic Games held in Berlin. The Games were seen by Hitler as an opportunity to display the new 'Aryan' man and Germany won more golds than any other country. The 1940 Olympics were scheduled for Tokyo, capital of Germany's Axis partner Japan, but the war intervened and they never took place.

BERLIN·1936
1·16 AUG.

OLYMPISCHE SPIELE

AUSKÜNFTE UND WERBESCHRIFTEN DURCH ALLE REISE- UND VERKEHRSBÜROS

GOEBBELS AT THE OLYMPIC GAMES

2 August 1936

March of the Hitler Youth in the Lustgarten. Imposing theatre…Then comes the flame from Olympia. A moving moment. It rains lightly. Nevertheless Berlin in a party fever. Worked briefly at the Ministry. Then reception and food with the Fuehrer. Very impressive. I chat with the actresses. Annoyed at the table plan arranged by Meissner. Journey to the stadium. Through hundreds of thousands. First rain, then it clears. The stadium offers a wonderful vista. Crown Prince from Italy; made a good impression on me. Prince Paul from Greece: almost a German prince. Everyone exhilarated by the impression. The flags. The festival begins. Particularly demonstrative was the greeting for the French and Italians. Cool reception for the English. Rather painful. Screams as the flame arrives. Thousands of carrier pigeons fly high above. An Olympic hymn by Strauss….Hallelujah by Handel. Great, rousing celebration. Triumphal return…Often on the balcony. The crowd raves. It is deeply moving. Girls were fetched up and cried in front of the Fuehrer. A beautiful and great day. A victory for the German cause.

Source: Elke Fröhlich (ed). *Die Tagebücher von Joseph Goebbels* (K. G. Saur, Munich, 1987), vol 2, pp. 652–3.

(which came first) and by Germany, which came second with three gold medals to Norway's seven. While the Games continued, Hitler took the opportunity to discuss for the first time his thoughts about the remilitarization of the Rhineland with the military leaders who were present for the occasion. They were there to watch the military patrol skiing competition which, although not an official Olympic event, was staged as a display for the crowds. The Norwegian government refused to send a team on the grounds that it confused militarism with the peaceful character of the Olympiad, the only political boycott of the entire Winter Games. In the absence of the Norwegians, the German military skiers were hopeful of winning, but the event was won in the end by the Italians.

The summer Olympics represented an event of much greater scale and significance. Plans for a giant stadium and sports field began in 1933 and because Hitler took a particular interest in architecture he played a central part in determining the design. He wanted a complex that could hold half a million people, but in the end the design could accommodate 250,000. The first architect drew up plans for a modern stadium reflecting the latest architectural fashions, but in October 1934 Hitler rejected the idea as too modernist and brought in a young architect, Albert Speer, who had already worked successfully for Party ministers and was to design the new Reich Chancellery in Berlin. Speer remodelled the stadium plans to make it look more evidently neo-classical. The construction fell behind schedule and emergency priority of labour and materials was given to the project. It was completed on time at a cost of 27 million marks. The total cost of hosting the Olympics has been estimated at 100 million marks, making it at the time the most expensive Olympiad ever.

The summer Games began on 1 August with an extravagant pageantry in the presence of Hitler. On the following day the events started; the first gold medal was won by a German in the women's javelin, and a second gold medal by a German shot-putter. Hitler congratulated the medal winners personally. But in the evening he left the stadium before the award of medals to two black American athletes who came first and second in the high-jump. This was regarded as a deliberate act to prevent the Führer from having to congratulate black competitors, and the Olympic Committee protested to Hitler the following day. Hitler then announced that in future he would not congratulate any of the medal winners, to avoid more difficulty. When the black athlete Jesse Owens won medals in the 100 and 200 metres, and the long-jump, the failure of Hitler to congratulate him was not a snub directed at Owens himself, but a result of Hitler's earlier decision not to take any formal part in the ceremonies. German competitors nevertheless did well and Germany topped the medal table with 33 golds against the United States' 24. In total Germany won 89 medals, America only 56. The final day of the Games, on 16 August, ended with further pageantry. Hitler was present and did not speak but when the final flags were lowered and the stadium lights were extinguished, the crowd began to shout out 'Heil Hitler'. The audience then rose to its feet with arms outstretched in the Hitler salute and sang unscripted first the German national anthem and then the Party hymn, the Horst Wessel Lied. As soon as the Games finished, the paraphernalia of anti-Semitism was re-established. The half-Jewish German representative on the International Olympic Committee, Theodor Lewald, was withdrawn to be replaced by the German soldier General Walther von Reichenau. The link in the minds of the regime between sport and militarism was thus made explicit.

Preparing for War

When the Games were over Hitler went south to his Bavarian retreat at Berchtesgaden. Here a new complex had been completed, known as the Berghof, built on the site of Hitler's mountainside chalet to Hitler's own design. The new design was an imposing country residence boasting a terrace with remarkable views across the Alps. Hitler used it more and more over the coming years as a place to discuss policy and plans, or to entertain foreign visitors. It was here on 24 August, only a week after the end of the Olympics, that he authorized military service to be increased from one year to two. If the Winter Olympics had turned Hitler's mind to the Rhineland, the Berlin Games inspired the first overt preparations for a future war.

At some time at the end of August – the exact date is not known – Hitler wrote one of the few documents he composed himself throughout the whole period of his dictatorship. The memorandum has been known ever since as the Four-Year-Plan Memorandum, because it contained a call to prepare Germany militarily and economically for war in four years. Hitler simply styled it 'a strategical memorandum'. It represented his current thoughts about the international situation and the threats Germany faced, but most of the document concerned

Hitler's own ideas about how to ensure that when Germany became involved once again in major war, she would be better prepared to meet the challenge than had been the case in 1914. The main target of Hitler's strategic overview was the Soviet Union, whose rapid economic and military development under Stalin's Five-Year Plans had very quickly altered the strategic balance in Europe. Hitler argued that Germany was at the forefront of the defence of European civilization against 'the attacks of Bolshevism'. A grand war between Germany and the Soviet Union was, he thought, unavoidable in the long run. As a result, he concluded, 'the extent of the military development of our resources cannot be too large, nor its pace too swift'. For Hitler all other economic and social considerations, including the prospect of making the German people more prosperous, would have to take second place to preparation for war.

The memorandum clearly derived from the regime's growing public hostility to the Soviet Union and the threat it posed. Hitler later used this argument as the centrepiece of the speeches he prepared for the Party rally at Nuremberg, which began on 8 September under the title 'Congress of Honour' and ended with a savage attack on the Soviet system in his final Congress address on 14 September. Hitler's hostility to the Soviet Union was to be echoed after the war in Western fears of communism and the institution of the Cold War. Nevertheless Hitler had to decide what to do with the memorandum once it had been drafted. Late in August he summoned Hermann Göring to Obersalzberg to discuss the memorandum. He had been in regular contact with Göring during the summer over issues to do with the economy and rearmament, because on 4 April he had already appointed him Commissioner for Raw Materials and Foreign Exchange to supervise the flow of goods and currency necessary for rearmament. He was chosen because he had good business contacts and was, above all, an ambitious and ruthless politician, utterly loyal to Hitler. Over the summer months Germany's economic situation worsened as growing demand for consumer goods from a population with money to spend once again competed with the labour and materials needed to build up Germany's armed forces rapidly. The desire to avoid any social or political crisis over Germany's still fragile economic situation prompted Hitler to extend Göring's power over the economy so that the four-year programme of war preparation could be completed on schedule.

Hitler told Göring during a walk on the hillside at Obersalzberg that he wanted to vest him with special powers over the economy and rearmament. On 4 September Göring announced to the cabinet that he had been granted supreme authority on Hitler's orders to carry out what was to be called the second Four-Year-Plan (the First Plan had been a plan for employment, launched in 1933, but it had had no overall director). On 9 September the plan was announced to assembled delegates at the Party Congress with a fanfare of publicity. On 18 October Göring was formally invested with the title Plenipotentiary for the Four-Year-Plan and ten days later, in the Berlin Palace of Sport, he announced to the world the terms of his new commission. The armed forces reacted to the new programme with little enthusiasm, since they regarded war preparation as something only they should be responsible for. Blomberg forwarded a memorandum to Hitler drafted in December 1936 asking for control over rearmament to be vested only in the War Ministry, and for economic preparations to be left in the hands of the Economics Minister, Hjalmar Schacht. Hitler ignored the intervention while Göring embarked

HERMANN WILHELM GÖRING (1893–1946)

For much of the period of the Third Reich Hermann Göring was regarded as second only to Hitler. He played an important part in the seizure of power and was rewarded with a number of high offices. In 1939 Hitler named him as his successor. Göring was born in 1893, the son of a German diplomat who became governor of German South-West Africa. He joined the army in 1912 and entered the war in 1914 as a junior officer. In October 1914 he began flying training and by the end of the war was a captain and commander of the famous Richthofen Squadron, following the death of the 'Red Baron', Manfred von Richthofen. At the end of the war he tried his hand at display flying and worked for a while as a commercial traveller. In 1922 he met Hitler for the first time and was captivated by his radical nationalist rhetoric. As a distinguished First World War flying ace, Göring was attractive to the Party and soon after joining he was made commander of the small SA, the Party's paramilitary units. He was wounded in the thigh in the Beer Hall Putsch and had to flee from Germany. He returned in 1927 and took up his role in the Party again. He was one of the 12 deputies elected in 1928, but in 1932, with the National Socialists the largest party in the German parliament, he became Reichstag President. In this capacity he helped in the intrigue to get Hitler appointed as chancellor. In Hitler's cabinet he was Minister without Portfolio but he was also Prussian Minister of the Interior, which gave him extensive police powers to repress the opposition. Later in the year he was made Reich Air Minister and in spring 1935 he was appointed Commander-in-Chief of the new German Air Force. He then headed the Four-Year-Plan set up in October 1936, making him one of the most powerful politicians in Germany. He was a ruthless, showy and ambitious personality. Unlike the ascetic Hitler, Göring acted like royalty, with a rich lifestyle and a liking for gaudy clothes, fine artwork and hunting. He played a full part in running the air force during the war, but his increasingly flamboyant and luxurious lifestyle eroded his former energy and ambition while the failures of the Battle of Britain and the air relief of Stalingrad sapped Hitler's support. Though he was never sacked by Hitler, his political authority was bypassed. At the end of the war he tried to take over power from Hitler, who was trapped in his Berlin bunker. When Hitler learned of his intention he ordered Göring's arrest. The end of the war brought him into American captivity and he was tried at Nuremberg. On 15 October, the night before his execution for war crimes, he committed suicide by taking cyanide. How he obtained the poison has never been properly established.

THE FOUR-YEAR-PLAN, AUGUST 1936

I hold it necessary that 100% self-sufficiency be introduced with iron decisiveness in all the areas where this is possible, and through this not only to make the national supply of these most important materials independent of abroad, but that through this can be saved that foreign exchange which we need in peacetime for importing foodstuffs. I would like to emphasise that I see in this task pure economic mobilization, with no cutting back in armaments firms in peacetime for saving or stockpiling raw materials for war....Almost four valuable years have gone by. There is no doubt that we could be independent from abroad already today in the area of fuel, rubber and partly, too, in iron ore supply. Just as we produce at the moment 7 or 800,000 tons of oil, so we can produce 3 million tons. Just as we manufacture today a few thousand tons of rubber, we could produce 70 or 80,000 tons annually. In the same way we have increased from 2 million tons of iron ore output to 7 million, we could process 20 or 25 million tons of German iron ore, and if necessary 30. There has been enough time to ascertain what we cannot do. It is now necessary to work out what we can do.

I therefore lay down the following task:

I The German army must be ready for combat in four years.

II The German economy must be capable of war in four years.

Source: W. Treue 'Denkschrift Hitlers über die Aufgaben eines Vierjahresplans' *Vierteljahreshefte für Zeitgeschichte*, 1 (1955), pp. 209–10

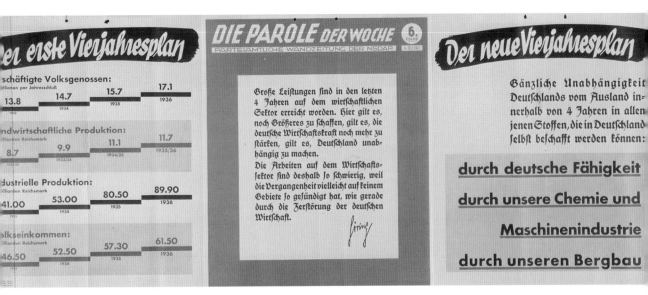

Der erste Vierjahresplan

schäftigte Volksgenossen:
illionen per Jahresschluß

13.8 14.7 15.7 17.1
      1934 1935 1936

ndwirtschaftliche Produktion:
illiarden Reichsmark

8.7 9.9 11.1 11.7
     1933/34 1934/35 1935/36

dustrielle Produktion:
illiarden Reichsmark

41.00 53.00 80.50 89.90
       1934 1935 1936

olkseinkommen:
illiarden Reichsmark

46.50 52.50 57.30 61.50
       1934 1935 1936

DIE PAROLE DER WOCHE
PARTEIAMTLICHE WANDZEITUNG DER NSDAP

Große Leistungen sind in den letzten 4 Jahren auf dem wirtschaftlichen Sektor erreicht worden. Hier gilt es, noch Größeres zu schaffen, gilt es, die deutsche Wirtschaftskraft noch mehr zu stärken, gilt es, Deutschland unabhängig zu machen.

Die Arbeiten auf dem Wirtschaftssektor sind deshalb so schwierig, weil die Vergangenheit vielleicht auf keinem Gebiete so gesündigt hat, wie gerade durch die Zerstörung der deutschen Wirtschaft.

Göring

Der neue Vierjahresplan

Gänzliche Unabhängigkeit Deutschlands vom Ausland innerhalb von 4 Jahren in allen jenen Stoffen, die in Deutschland selbst beschafft werden können:

durch deutsche Fähigkeit

durch unsere Chemie und

Maschinenindustrie

durch unseren Bergbau

on a prolonged political struggle with his critics, which was eventually resolved by the forced resignation of both Schacht and von Blomberg a little more than a year later.

At the core of the Four-Year-Plan was a policy of what was known as 'autarky'. In the 1930s this was a term used to describe an economic policy of self-sufficiency in which states that had restricted access to world markets, or lacked important strategic materials, would try to produce more from the home market or find substitute raw materials. Hitler's purpose in setting up the plan was to try to derive more of Germany's resources essential for war from the domestic economy, above all the increased production of iron ore, more coal for the production of synthetic oil and rubber and increased agricultural produce so that the population could withstand a wartime blockade. Göring set up a formal administrative apparatus under the control of his Prussian state secretary, Paul Körner, and appointed key men from industry, the armed forces and the bureaucracy to run the major departments from the Prussian State Ministry building in Berlin. In order to be able to carry out the large-scale

Above: A weekly wall paper produced by the National Socialist Party announces in February 1937 the tasks of the Second Four-Year Plan established in October 1936. The first plan was to tackle the problem of unemployment, the second was to build up German food and raw material output to achieve a high level of self-sufficiency or 'autarky'.

Opposite: A panorama of the I. G. Farben works at Bitterfeld showing factory chimneys and cooling towers. The chemical giant became a central component in the plans for building up German industry to make Germany independent of foreign sources of supply, particularly the production of synthetic rubber and oil.

diversion of resources to armaments and war materials he also issued decrees to extend his direct control over exports, foreign currency, prices and wages. The first wage stop was published on 29 October and the same day a new Price Commissioner was appointed, the Gauleiter of Silesia, Josef Wagner, whose office continued to monitor and control prices right down to the end of the war. On 1 December 1936 a decree was published on 'Economic Sabotage' which targeted those who hoarded gold and foreign currency, or hid their wealth abroad. The heaviest penalty for anyone found guilty was execution.

The Four-Year Plan was one of the most important documents of the dictatorship, for it set Germany on a path to war and signalled to the German people that economic revival would have to be postponed until Germany had solved the problem of 'living-space'. It was the point at which Hitler took his ambitions to a new stage. On December 17 he spoke to an assembly of economic leaders about the new plans for economic mobilization. 'The word impossible does not exist here!' he told them. This was the onset of Hitler's fantasies of turning Germany into a world power. The changed policy at home was also matched by a changing international constellation, accelerated by the Spanish Civil War and Hitler's strong anti-Soviet stance. On October 24 the Italian foreign minister, Count Galeazzo Ciano, visited Hitler at Berchtesgaden with a view to drawing the two regimes more closely together on a common front against communism. Hitler charmed him and the following day a treaty was signed between Germany and Italy, committing them to consult and cooperate over their work in Spain. To emphasize the importance of the link Ciano handed Hitler a cache of 32 British documents taken by the Italian secret service to show how hostile Britain was to German intentions. Hitler in return hinted that Germany would recognize the Italian conquest of Abyssinia and would also recognize the Franco regime in Spain. Recognition followed on 18 November. Mussolini hoped to get more from cooperating with Hitler than from the Western states and after the treaty was signed began to speak for the first time of the 'Rome–Berlin Axis'.

The chorus of anti-communist propaganda in Germany culminated with an international anti-communist conference in Munich and the opening of an anti-Bolshevik exhibition on 9 November in Hitler's presence. A few weeks before, on 23 October, the Japanese ambassador and the German Foreign Ministry provisionally agreed a pact between their two countries directed against the Moscow-based Communist International (Comintern). The closer links between Japan and Germany were not welcomed by the German Foreign Office because it challenged Germany's traditionally close relations with China, but in late 1936 Hitler wanted to make a more definite gesture against the Soviet Union and its recent alliance with France. On 25 November the Anti-Comintern Pact was formally signed. Although it was aimed to contest the propaganda efforts of the Comintern – which had endorsed in 1935 the strategy of collaboration with socialist and liberal parties in Europe under a Popular Front – there was a secret protocol which committed both countries to maintain a friendly neutrality in the event that the other became involved in a war with the Soviet Union.

The Anti-Comintern pact was a gesture to underline Hitler's current hostility to the Soviet Union, but it also symbolized a closer relationship with the other states engaged in undermining the existing international order. In the autumn of 1936 treaties with Italy and Japan began to give shape to what was to become the Axis alliance of World War II. Hitler's path to war had already begun.

Hitler at the 1935 annual Party congress in Nuremberg talking with members of the Party factory representatives. Behind him is Dr Robert Ley, head of the German Labour Front, whose organization represented all those who worked, from the shop-floor to the directors' office.

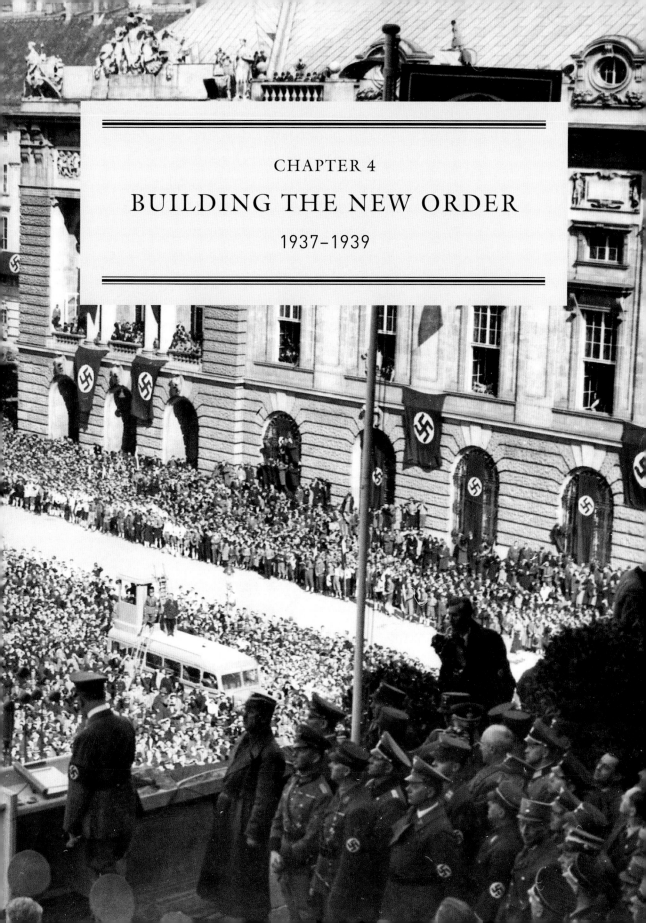

CHAPTER 4

BUILDING THE NEW ORDER

1937–1939

During the course of 1937 and 1938 Hitler began a programme to establish German domination in central and eastern Europe, and to extend the territory of the new Reich. This shift from internal to external policy was made possible by the rapid rearmament of the German armed forces and was made necessary by the need for more resources, raw materials and labour directly under German control in order to make further rearmament viable. Hitler probably had no particular vision of empire at this stage, but saw German expansion in opportunistic terms. The unwillingness of the other major powers to intervene with force had already been shown in the Italian invasion of Ethiopia in 1935–6 and the reaction to the remilitarization of the Rhineland. The Soviet Union had descended into the years of the so-called Great Terror, which made it much less of a threat. In November 1937 he announced to the military his hope that Austria and Czechoslovakia would come under German domination in the near future. In March 1938 German forces occupied Austria and annexed it to the German Reich, with the widespread approval of much of the population. In September a much riskier confrontation took place with Czechoslovakia which ended with an international agreement at Munich to cede to Germany the German-speaking areas of the Czech state. The following March, stung by the Polish refusal to become a satellite of Germany, Hitler began planning a war to crush Poland and extend German rule even further. Despite clear evidence that Britain and France were prepared to fight rather than allow him to expand further, he invaded Poland on 1 September 1939. The decision was a rash one yet it opened the way for German domination of Europe, an achievement Hitler could not have imagined two years before.

1937 Economic Rearmament

The year 1937 marked a break with the earlier years of consolidation. Until then the regime had relied on collaboration with other powerful interest groups, including the army, heavy industry and the traditional conservative elite. During the course of 1937 the balance of power inside the Third Reich swung towards the Party and its leaders, many of whom were anxious to complete the national revolution and impatient of the early years of caution. By early 1938 the key areas of the economy, military leadership, and diplomacy were dominated by ambitious Party men and Hitler had created the political conditions he needed to speed up the transformation of German life and to allow him to embark on the programme of turning Germany into a dominant European power.

The testing ground for the new direction was the issue of rearmament and economic restructuring which had been signalled by the establishment of the Four-Year Plan in 1936. The creation of the necessary industrial and resource capacity to support a major war effort was the precondition in Hitler's view for any more active foreign policy. This restructuring was largely Göring's responsibility. In January 1937, in the first edition of a new journal called *The Four-Year Plan*, he announced his intention to exercise 'the unitary leadership and organization of the entire economy'. This was a grandiose claim which neither the army nor the conservative business elite (who supported the Economics Minister, Hjalmar Schacht) were happy with. For much of 1937 Göring manoeuvred to reduce their influence and secure higher levels of economic rearmament. To do so meant diverting the investment activity of the country away from largely civilian goals and finding ways of limiting the import of inessential goods by encouraging 'autarky'. Both strategies made it difficult to satisfy the interests of ordinary German consumers. Although workers were satisfied at the recovery of regular paid work, living standards were pegged to ensure that the fragile economic revival could be exploited for defence purposes and not merely to indulge popular consumer appetites.

The armed forces had, up until then, dominated the evolution of German rearmament. On 22 February 1937 the War Minister, von Blomberg, sent Hitler a second memorandum insisting once again that only the armed forces had responsibility for war preparations and that Göring's role should be confined to expanding the output of coal and iron ore under the supervision of the War Ministry. Hitler ignored the memorandum, but for Göring it marked von Blomberg as a potential political rival who might have to be eliminated. A second political threat came from the Economics Minister, Hjalmar Schacht, who had been appointed Plenipotentiary for War Economy on von Blomberg's recommendation in 1935. Schacht was also unhappy with the claims now being made by the Four-Year Plan, as well as the large

---

Pages 148–9: Hitler addresses a vast crowd in the Heldenplatz in central Vienna on 15 March 1938 following the occupation of Austria by German troops three days before.

Above: By 1937 the cult of personality in Germany had reached new heights. Here Hitler, surrounded by baying supporters, salutes an audience of the Party faithful. His extraordinary celebrity status encouraged women to write to Hitler asking him to father their child. Hitler preferred to present himself as a single man married to the cause of Germany.

Left: German women queuing in line in January 1938 with bowls and spoons for a helping of soup during a Winter Help campaign under the slogan 'Today Berlin Eats Soup!' The Winter Help organization was set up by the Party before 1933 and became a major source of charitable assistance for needy 'racial comrades'.

additional public loans necessary to fund it. Schacht had close links with the leaders of German heavy industry and they also feared that the new Plan might mean the introduction of higher levels of state interference in the economy. The battleground chosen by Göring was over the question of 'autarky'. Hitler, in his memorandum on the Plan, had called for greater exploitation of domestic sources of iron ore, the key raw material for the iron and steel needed in the event of war. Heavy industry, which owned most of the ore fields, was unenthusiastic, since the additional ore was poor in iron content and expensive to process. In a speech to leading industrialists on 17 December 1936, Göring warned that if they refused to co-operate they might be made to do so. On 17 March 1937 he made his threat more explicit when he met the heads of the iron and steel industry: 'the state must take over when private industry has proved itself no longer able to carry on'.

On 30 April Hitler, in a speech to the Reich Chamber of Labour, used the opportunity to announce publicly that the private economy would remain free only if it co-operated in solving the problems of the nation; if it refused, Hitler continued, 'it will cease to be free'. German business at last began to take notice. Some major German firms, including the armaments producer Gustav Krupp and the chemical giant I. G. Farben, already had generous contracts for producing material needed for war preparations. Many of the rest preferred to rely on an expanding consumer market and exports, resisting the regime's growing emphasis on creating an economy geared to a major war. On 23 July 1937 Göring called the leaders of heavy industry together in Berlin and announced that he was establishing a large state-run enterprise to exploit all Germany's remaining iron ore deposits. It was to be called the Reich Works (*Reichswerke*) 'Hermann Göring' and would be partly funded by a levy on private industry. Over the course of the following two years, the Reich Works became one of the largest industrial combines in Europe, absorbing the iron, steel, coal and machinery industry of the areas taken over by Germany. German industrialists were generally hostile to the new state-run cuckoo in the capitalist nest, and on 24 August 1937 they met together to draft a memorandum rejecting the plan. All but two of those who attended were sent telegrams by Göring that morning, pointing out that opposition constituted economic sabotage (a crime that carried, since the law of 1 December 1936, a maximum of capital punishment). Göring had been using secret tape recordings and telephone tapping to follow the resistance of the industrialists, and his first instinct was to order their arrest. He was dissuaded from such a dramatic course, but the telegrams did their work. The memorandum was not supported and when the two principal opponents arrived in Göring's office a few days later, he triumphantly played back to them taped versions of their secret meetings.

The shifting balance in favour of the Party and its supporters reflected the tightening grip of the movement on many areas of German life. During the early months of 1937 the contest between the churches and the new regime sharpened. On 15 February Hitler ordered the Minister for Church Affairs, Hans Kerrl, to prepare elections for a General Synod of the German Evangelical Church in the hope that a more pliant and less critical assembly might be produced. On 21 March Pope Pius XI published the encyclical 'With Burning Anxiety' (*mit brennender Sorge*), which finally challenged the collaboration agreed in 1933 by criticizing the anti-Christian

'ASOCIALS'

Throughout the years of the Third Reich an effort was made to identify and penalize elements of the population defined by the term 'asocials' (*Asozialen*). These were the workshy, alcoholics, vagrants, prostitutes, habitual offenders. They were regarded as a menace to the construction of a pure racial state and a threat to public safety. A great many were in fact physically or mentally disabled in one form or another and unable to play a full part in conventional society. This concern about the 'asocial' element was not confined to Germany. In Britain the government identified the 'social problem group' as a segment of the population which should be discouraged from reproducing and subject to forms of welfare penalty. Middle-class anxiety about the poorest and least advantaged sectors of society produced suggestions for radical and coercive action all over Europe. The difference in Germany lay in the racial priorities of the regime. 'Asocials' were among those targeted for compulsory sterilization (and sex offenders were also compulsorily castrated). In 1937 some 7,000 'asocials' were rounded up by the police and sent to concentration camps. By 1939 they made up the largest section of the camp population. The hope was that many of them would die in the camps of overwork or illness, and thousands did. 'Asocials' whose disability was profound were also to be found among the victims of 'euthanasia killing' from 1939 onwards. Those who were not sent to camps or prisons were subjected to harsh welfare regimes and stigmatized and victimized by the authorities. Exact figures on the number who died during the twelve years of the Reich are not available. The figure runs into the tens of thousands.

attitude of the regime, and called on all Catholics in Germany to reassert a sense of truth and justice. The encyclical was read out in churches across Germany and there followed a wave of arrests of Catholic clergymen, some of whom also ended up in Dachau concentration camp. Over the summer months of 1937 around 800 clergy from the breakaway Confessing Church were arrested by the security police. When Martin Niemöller, the Church's leader, preached an outspoken sermon in Berlin on 27 June 1937, he was arrested four days later and sentenced to eight months in prison. Hitler intervened to ensure that after he had served his time he would be sent to a concentration camp, from which he only emerged (fortunate to be alive) in 1945.

To underline the incompatibility of religion and National Socialism, on 18 June 1937 the regime issued a ban on any member of the Hitler Youth simultaneously belonging to a religious youth movement. Since by 1937 membership of the Hitler Youth and League of German Girls was over 6 million, the ruling left the churches with only a fraction of young Germans to organize. Education was also a contested ground with the churches, particularly the Catholic Church. In 1937 further steps were taken to create an elite education based entirely on the movement. On 15 January 1937 Hitler approved the establishment of a network of 'Adolf Hitler Schools' where the leaders of the future would be trained. The first one was

opened on 19 April. The schools were intended to inculcate in their pupils an understanding of the values of the movement and of dedication to the race; they encouraged military virtues and a tough physical regime. On 3 May the leader of the Hitler Youth, Baldur von Schirach, laid the foundation stone for the first of a planned 543 Hitler Youth Homes, where the same values would be implanted. All religious education was banned in the Hitler Youth and by 1939 teaching by clergymen had been removed from almost all German state schools. Despite continued protests by prominent churchmen, the popular reaction in 1937 was more muted than it been a few years before in the face of a Party committed to contesting the claims of Christianity and willing to use extreme coercion in doing so.

Art for the 1000-Year Reich

On 30 January 1937 Hitler appointed Albert Speer, the young architect who later designed the new Reich Chancellery, to the prestigious post of Inspector-General of Construction for the Renovation of the Capital. At the party rally in September 1936 he had promised that Berlin would be remodelled to make it a fit capital for the new Germany. For Hitler, architecture had a special symbolic value. He wanted to construct grandiose buildings and boulevards that would endure like the ruins of ancient Greece and Rome. Hitler, the failed architect in pre-1914 Vienna, was determined that he would play a leading part in designing the new capital and it was his vision of colossal neo-classical architecture that Speer was compelled to work with. The architectural legacy of the Third Reich, some of which can still be seen in Germany today, was for Hitler the most important contribution he could make to building the 1000-year Reich.

The law for the reconstruction of Berlin was finally promulgated on 4 October 1937 as part of a comprehensive law for the 'reconstruction of German cities'. Berlin took priority, but Hitler decreed that a further seventeen sites would be model cities of the future. The principal centres, designated as 'Führer cities', were Munich, Hamburg, Nuremberg and (following the incorporation of Austria in 1938) Hitler's home town of Linz. Twelve capitals of major Party regions were also added, which would have additional funding to create an architecture appropriate to their status: Augsburg, Bayreuth, Breslau, Dresden, Düsseldorf, Cologne, Münster, Stettin, Weimar and Würzburg. The plans for Berlin, which Hitler once described as

---

Opposite above: Girls practising javelin throwing at a school for sports run by the German Food Estate in 1937. Although the Party campaigned for women to play a subordinate role to men, they were supposed to become fit and healthy as young girls in order to become future mothers, bearing sons for the Fatherland.

Opposite below: A Party rally for the Hitler Youth agricultural service attended by Rudolf Hess (centre), Himmler (left) and Hitler Youth leader Baldur von Schirach (right). Hitler Youth were involved each year in helping to gather the harvest and do other labouring jobs in the countryside.

the future 'capital of the world', were grandiose. Through the centre of the city it was planned to build a huge axial road, 120 metres wide, at the end of which was a vast People's Hall, based on a sketch Hitler had made in the 1920s. The hall was to house 200,000 people, with a dome 250 metres wide and 74 metres high, seven times the size of the dome of St. Peter's in Rome. Berlin and all other Party cities were to have large squares at the centre where rallies and military parades could be held. Berlin's would house 500,000, that in Dresden 300,000; and so on. For this ambitious construction programme, Hitler suspended the private property rights of those unfortunate enough to have a house or a business in the way of the new buildings.

Hitler had applied the same rule to the inhabitants of Berchtesgaden, where he had built his official residence, the Berghof, overlooking the town. The building, to Hitler's own design, was opened in July 1936. Businesses or buildings needed by the Party, or too close to the secure enclosure built around his estate, were bought up and the owners made to move. On 8 March 1937 one of the last, the owner of a guest house, was forced to sell up after a long boycott by Party visitors to the town. A young photographer compelled to abandon his photo business complained personally to Hitler, ending up with two years in Dachau concentration camp. Hitler's second major project was the new Reich Chancellery in Berlin, designed by Speer under Hitler's close supervision. The new Chancellery, which Hitler wanted built on a scale that would impress all visitors with the sheer power of the new Reich, was built on Voss Street in central Berlin. First planning began in 1934; by 1937 half the buildings that occupied the street had been bought up and torn down. On 11 January 1938 Hitler finally appointed Speer as the overseer for this project too and a year later it was completed thanks to the efforts of 4,500 building labourers and craftsmen working round-the-clock to meet the deadline.

The year 1937 also marked the point at which Hitler defined what was (and what was not) acceptable art for the Third Reich. On 18 July 1937 in the newly-built House of German Art in Munich, whose foundation stone Hitler had laid in 1933, an Exhibition of German Art was officially opened. Hitler played a central role in selecting what should be included, and in the process defined the limits of what pictures or sculptures could be produced in the future. German artists were invited to submit pictures to be considered for the exhibition. Out of 15,000 entries the organizers reduced the number to 900 and showed them to Hitler. He rejected some as too modernist, recalled some of those initially rejected by the judges as too sentimental or dull, and finally chose 884 works for the display. They were predominantly landscapes, which were Hitler's favourite, and portraits (though only one picture of the Führer was permitted). Hitler also selected monumental statues of naked males, in the neo-classical style, and naked women posed like the nymphs and goddesses of ancient Greece. On the day of the opening he watched a pageant parade past him representing 2,000 years of German history. The following day, 19 July, a second display opened in Munich close to the House of German Art, under the title 'Exhibition of Degenerate Art'. The purpose was to show that modern art, much of it assumed to be Jewish, was a diseased abuse of culture which had no place in the new Germany. Goebbels confiscated 16,000 works of art by German modernists, chose 650 for the exhibition and either sold off the remainder or ordered them to be burned. The exhibition also contained pictures by psychiatric patients designed to show

An architectural model of the New Reich Chancellery building designed by Albert Speer as Inspector General for the Renovation of the Reich Capital. The model of the bronze horse was to be completed by Hitler's favourite sculptor, Josef Thorak. Hitler wanted a building that would overawe those who visited it with the sheer power of the new Reich.

ALLEMAGNE

The German pavilion at the World's Fair in Paris in 1937. The pavilion, situated directly opposite the Soviet one, was used as an opportunity to display the culture of the new Germany with giant statues of 'Aryan' men, modelled on the art of classical Greece.

Joseph Goebbels and Hermann Göring in conversation before the opening of the 1937
Party Congress on 7 September 1937. The two men were by now among the most
influential in Germany, keen to transfer more responsibility and power to Party leaders
at the expense of the conservative supporters of the regime with whom they had
collaborated since 1933.

that modern art was also the product of deranged minds. Over the following months 600,000 Germans went to see the wholesome art chosen by Hitler, but more than 2 million went to see one of the finest and largest collections of 'degenerate' modern art ever mounted.

Planning War

On 24 June 1937 the War Minister, Werner von Blomberg, sent a directive to the armed forces to prepare for a possible war against the neighbouring state of Czechoslovakia. This was only a contingency plan, aimed at the most radical democratic state in central Europe, which housed a large number of refugees from Hitler's Germany who used the base to smuggle anti-Nazi literature across the border and to maintain contact with socialist and communist resistance cells. Although Blomberg did not expect a real war against the Czechs, this was the first time that the new German armed forces considered projecting their growing military strength against an external enemy. Later that summer, from 20 to 26 September, the armed forces undertook their annual manoeuvres to test out the possible use of tanks and aircraft as a mobile, hard-hitting attack force. Hitler was present on 26 September with Mussolini, who had arrived the day before on his first state visit to Germany.

Mussolini's visit was a further stepping-stone to the creation of the future coalition that fought the Second World War. On 25 September the two leaders met to discuss their spheres of interest. Hitler agreed that Mussolini should have a free hand in the Mediterranean, and Mussolini was prepared to concede German interest in Austria (a concession he had long resisted). Both dictators agreed that efforts should be made to draw closer to Japan. No formal agreement was signed between them, but Mussolini's visit sealed the Rome–Berlin Axis that had been informally established a year before. On 28 September the two men gave speeches at the Tempelhof Airfield in Berlin. Mussolini attempted to give his speech in German, but a heavy downpour of rain smeared his notes and he struggled with the language to announce that one day he and Hitler might have to fight side-by-side. He left the following day but later, on 6 November, he notified Hitler that Italy would now join the Anti-Comintern Pact which Germany and Japan had signed in 1936, aligning both states against the Soviet Union in addition to their growing enmity towards Britain and France.

On 5 November Hitler called together an evening meeting of his military commanders-in-chief at the Reich Chancellery. Together with Göring, von Blomberg and the naval commander-in-chief Erich Raeder were the army commander, General Werner von Fritsch, the Foreign Minister, Count Constantin von Neurath, and Hitler's army adjutant, Colonel Friedrich Hossbach, who took detailed notes of the meeting. The discussion was called to resolve arguments over resources for rearmament, but Hitler used it as the opportunity to lay out his vision of where Germany's foreign and military policy was leading. For the first time he outlined clear intentions to embark on initiatives in central Europe, by force if necessary, to bring Austria and Czechoslovakia into the German sphere. These territories, he argued, could supply Germany with living space and resources. He set no firm date, but told his commanders that something had to be settled by at least 1943–5. He explained that if opportunities arose that reduced the risk of taking over Austria or Czechoslovakia, then

FIELD MARSHAL WERNER VON BLOMBERG (1878–1946)

Blomberg was the first and only War Minister in the Third Reich, from 1935 to 1938. A Prussian officer from a military family, he joined the army as a young man and graduated to a General Staff position by 1908. He served with distinction on the Western Front during the First World War before joining the post-war 100,000 man army. He became chief of training in 1925 and then headed the troop office in the Defence Ministry from 1927 to 1929, playing an important part in secret military collaboration with the Soviet Union. He was posted to East Prussia in 1929 after falling out with General Kurt von Schleicher. He met Hitler in 1931 and was enthusiastic about the national revolution he symbolized. In January 1933 he was made Minister of Defence and promoted to General of Infantry. Blomberg played an important part in overseeing the early years of illegal German rearmament after 1933 and was a firm supporter of the new Hitler regime. It was his idea that the army should swear an oath of allegiance to Hitler in August 1934 after the death of von Hindenburg, and he supported Hitler during the crisis with the SA on the Night of the Long Knives. He was keen that responsibility for military affairs should be kept firmly in military hands and resented the independence enjoyed by the Luftwaffe and the later encroachment on rearmament policy by Göring's Four-Year-Plan organization. He was appointed commander-in-chief of the armed forces in May 1935 when rearmament was formally announced and in 1936 became the first Field Marshal of the Third Reich. He fell from office in 1938 following a scandal and travelled widely outside Germany. He was arrested in 1945 and died in American detention in March 1946.

Germany could act sooner rather than later. In the brief discussion that followed, those present were divided in their response. Göring enthusiastically endorsed Hitler's arguments; Blomberg and Fritsch were critical, emphasizing the risks of provoking the large French army; Neurath thought Hitler exaggerated the opportunities likely to occur in the international arena. The meeting showed Hitler (as he had perhaps intended) just how cautious his conservative allies would be in reasserting German power in Europe.

The first indication that Hitler had definite aggressive plans was not widely welcomed among the conservative elite that had hitherto supported him. The Army chief-of-staff, Ludwig Beck, voiced his opposition to Hitler's plan in a memorandum circulated on 12 November, just a week after the meeting in the Chancellery. Schacht was also dissatisfied not only with trying to control the cost of German rearmament, but with the open encroachment by Göring on his ministerial responsibilities in the name of the Four-Year-Plan and accelerated economic preparation for a future war. Schacht had tried to sabotage the autarky projects by refusing to release funds for them. He would not accept that he could be subordinate to a man he regarded as a sheer amateur in economic affairs. In July he deliberately suspended his

163

THE HOSSBACH MEMORANDUM, NOVEMBER 1937

The Führer began by stating that the subject of the present conference was of such importance that its discussion would, in other countries, certainly be a matter for a full Cabinet meeting, but he – the Führer – had rejected the idea of making it a subject for discussion before the wider circle of the Reich Cabinet just because of the importance of the matter. His exposition to follow was the fruit of his four and a half years in power. He wished to explain to the gentlemen present his basic idea concerning the opportunities for the development of our position in the field of foreign affairs and its requirements, and he asked, in the interests of a long-term German policy, that his exposition be regarded, in the event of his death, as his last will and testament.

The Führer then continued:

The aim of German policy was to make secure and to prepare the racial community and to enlarge it. It was therefore a question of space.

The German racial community comprised over 85 million people and, because of their number and the narrow limits of habitable space in Europe, constituted a tightly packed racial core such as was not to be met in any other country and such as implied the right to a greater living space than in the case of other peoples. If, territorially speaking, there existed no political result corresponding to this racial core, that was a consequence of centuries of historical development, and in the continuance of these political conditions lay the greatest danger to the preservation of the German race at its present peak....Germany's future was therefore wholly conditional upon the solving of the need for space, and such a solution could be sought, of course, only for a foreseeable period of about one to three generations...

Germany's problem could only be solved by means of force and this was never without an attendant risk. The campaigns of Frederick the Great for Silesia and Bismarck's wars against Austria and France had involved unheard-of risk....If one accepts as the basis of the following exposition the resort to force with its attendant risks, then there remain still to be answered the questions 'when' and 'how'....

Case I: Period 1943–45
After this date only a change for the worse, from our point of view, could be expected.

The equipment of the army, navy and air force, as well as the formation of the officer corps, would be nearly completed. Equipment and armament were modern; in further delay there lay the danger of their obsolescence. In particular, the secrecy of 'special weapons' could not be preserved forever. The recruiting of reserves was limited to current age groups; further drafts from older untrained age groups no longer available....

Nobody knows today what the situation would be in the years 1943-45. One thing only was certain, that we could not wait longer.

On the one hand there were the great Armed Forces, and the necessity of maintaining them at their present level, the ageing of the movement and of its leaders; and on the other, the prospect of a lowering of the standard of living and of a limitation of the birth rate, which left no choice but to act. If the Führer was still living, it was his unalterable resolve to solve Germany's problem of space at the latest by 1943-45.

Source: *Documents on German Foreign Policy*, Ser. D, vol I, pp. 29-39. Notes of a meeting on 5 November 1937 in the Reich Chancellery taken by Col. Friedrich Hossbach.

activities as Plenipotentiary for War Economy, and when that had no effect he tried to suspend his work as Economics Minister to put pressure on Hitler to support him. On 26 November 1937 he resigned after weeks of argument and uncertainty. Göring took over his ministry as a temporary measure; when he arrived in the ministerial office he telephoned Schacht to announce triumphantly 'I am now sitting in your chair'.

The political consequences of Schacht's resignation were important because the economy was one of the few remaining areas of state that had not been subject to the increasing involvement and direction of Party leaders and officials. Schacht remained President of the German Central Bank, but in this post he had far fewer opportunities to challenge the drift towards a war economy, and he was sacked from this position on 20 January 1939 after publicly criticizing the scale of German rearmament. There were now few limits that could be placed on military spending; in 1937 it was held at just over 10 billion marks, in 1938 it reached 17.25 billion and in 1939 38 billion. Germany was being transformed, in a short period of time, into a military superpower. On 21 December 1937, in response to the ambitions Hitler had articulated at the meeting in November, the War Ministry drew up 'Case Green', a detailed plan for possible war against Czechoslovakia.

1938 The Blomberg–Fritsch Crisis

The lack of enthusiasm for Hitler's plans of expansion shown by the army leadership was overcome in an unexpected way in the early weeks of 1938 when both Blomberg and von Fritsch were the victims of clumsy intrigues by two Party leaders, Göring and Himmler. After eliminating Schacht, Göring was also ambitious to get rid of Blomberg and take over the War Ministry himself, and was able to use Himmler's security service to assist him. The opportunity presented itself in late 1937 when Blomberg made the fatal decision to marry his young secretary, Erna Gruhn.

At some point in the previous December, von Blomberg had been incautious enough to confide in Göring that he wanted to marry a 'lady with a past' who was already several months pregnant. He wanted Göring to arrange for one of the woman's other suitors to be removed from the scene and he was transferred against his will to a job in Argentina. Blomberg prepared for his wedding in January, unaware that the security service (at Göring's instigation) had now prepared a file on Erna Gruhn, who had posed earlier in the 1930s for pornographic calendars and was on police records as a prostitute. On 12 January 1938 the wedding took place with both Hitler and Göring as witnesses. On 26 January Göring confronted Hitler with the evidence that his War Minister had married dishonourably. Hitler was horrified: 'If a German field marshal can marry a whore,' he is reported as saying, 'then anything is possible.' The crisis was made worse by the fact that the same day he had a difficult conversation with the army commander-in-chief, von Fritsch, who was the victim of a second smear campaign orchestrated by the two Party leaders. An old Gestapo file from 1935 contained circumstantial evidence that Fritsch was homosexual. When he went on holiday to Egypt in December 1937, to recover from the strains of a difficult year, he was followed by German security agents. They reported nothing untoward, but in a staged confrontation von Fritsch was brought face-to-face with the man who had implicated him three years before. The witness confirmed that Fritsch was indeed his homosexual contact. When Hitler interviewed Fritsch, the latter refused to defend himself against a charge he regarded as a slur on his good name and he was sent on indefinite leave. The Gestapo file was in reality a crude case of mistaken identity, but Himmler deliberately manipulated it to get rid of a strong opponent of the SS. By the time efforts were made by his colleagues to exonerate Fritsch, it was too late. The General never recovered from the incident and walked deliberately towards Polish guns in the campaign in September 1939, in order to die honourably in battle.

For Hitler the Blomberg affair was more difficult to resolve. Blomberg was pressured by his military colleagues to resign after compromising the reputation of the army. Following his resignation, Hitler sent him and his young bride abroad for a year, uncertain about how to proceed with a fresh appointment to the War Ministry. Blomberg gained his revenge on Göring by suggesting, before he departed, that Hitler himself take over the post. Hitler may already have reached this decision on his own, for in the course of just a week he decided to reorganize entirely the structure of military command. On 4 February 1938 he announced that he would now take on the responsibilities of the War Ministry, which was abolished as an institution. In its place Hitler established a Supreme Command of the Armed Forces (*Oberkommando der Wehrmacht*), with himself as the active supreme commander. The decree setting up the new headquarters contained Hitler's express intention to 'directly exercise command authority over the entire armed forces personally'. On the day of his appointment he sacked 14 generals and demoted 40 others who were of doubtful loyalty. The new headquarters was to be run by General Wilhelm Keitel as Hitler's personal chief-of-staff. The army commander-in-chief to replace Fritsch was a more sympathetic and less forceful character, General Walter von Brauchitsch. Göring was rewarded with the rank of field marshal, making him Germany's most senior military figure following the disgrace of Blomberg, even though he had failed to become War Minister. The Supreme Headquarters took over many of the officials of the former War Ministry, and within months comprised twelve major departments with 1,500 members. Hitler was now in an unrivalled position to push through his military plans for expansion.

The same day that he announced the new military organization, Hitler made another important change. The Foreign Minister, von Neurath, had also shown little enthusiasm for Hitler's plans. On 4 February he was retired from his post and replaced by Joachim von Ribbentrop, head of the Party's foreign affairs bureau and the German ambassador in

Overleaf: A 'home evening' for the Hitler Youth in a town in Hessen-Nassau in August 1937. The boys are to discuss an article from the rabidly anti-Semitic newspaper *Der Stürmer* as part of their programme of political education. The generation that grew up during the Third Reich was heavily indoctrinated with crude racial propaganda.

London. This was a post he had taken up on 2 August 1936 with the assurance that he would be able to secure a close relationship between Germany and Britain. His failure in this enterprise did not deter Hitler from appointing him as Neurath's successor; as a Party leader, Ribbentrop would be more likely to support Hitler's views, while his personality (vain, insecure, easily influenced) would allow Hitler in effect to dictate the course of German foreign policy. With Ribbentrop's appointment, Hitler completed one of the most important political turning points in the twelve-year history of the Third Reich: the control of German military and foreign affairs had passed into the hands of an amateur strategist and an amateur diplomat who, over the following seven years, would steer Germany on a course to disaster.

The Seizure of Austria

The political crisis in January and February 1938 was the backdrop to a sudden deterioration in relations between Germany and Austria, which may explain Hitler's desire to bring control over military and foreign affairs safely under the influence of the Party elite. Relations with Austria had been strained since the assassination by Austrian National Socialists of the chancellor, Engelbert Dollfuss, in 1934. The Austrian National Socialist Party was banned, though it continued to operate clandestinely. The new chancellor, the Christian Social Party leader Kurt von Schuschnigg, was hostile to German attempts to pressure Austria to accept a closer relationship with the new Reich. However on 11 July 1936 he had been forced to reach an agreement in which Austria undertook to maintain a 'friendly' attitude towards Germany, to free National Socialists from Austrian jails and to appoint a number of National Socialist ministers to his coalition government. During 1937 pressure increased to try to turn this agreement into a formal union, and when Mussolini made it clear to Hitler in the autumn that he was no longer concerned with the future of Austria, a major international stumbling bloc was removed.

During February 1938 the relationship with Austria worsened as the internal political conflict intensified between those for or against union with Germany. On 12 February Hitler summoned von Schuschnigg to Berchtesgaden, subjecting him to a long and intemperate diatribe on Austria's betrayal of the German ideal. As an Austrian, Hitler felt keenly the desire to build a Pan-German state by uniting Austria with Germany. He compelled Schuschnigg to accept the appointment of a leading National Socialist sympathizer, Arthur Seyss-Inquart, as Minister of the Interior and the legalizing of the Austrian National Socialist Party. On 16 February the new appointment was made, giving police and security powers throughout Austria to a close ally of the Third Reich. Hitler had not yet made up his mind what to do, since outright invasion carried grave international risks. On 24 February, in discussion with leading Austrian National Socialists, he indicated that he would prefer a peaceful transition for Austria from independence to union with Germany. Ribbentrop had not yet returned from London, so that foreign policy had to be conducted in his absence. The crisis was the first test of Hitler's new position as Germany's supreme warlord.

The initiative was taken from Hitler by Schuschnigg's sudden decision, announced on 9 March 1938, that he would hold a plebiscite on 13 March to get the support of the Austrian

A line of cars passes a column of light tanks near the village of Dichthalling on their way into Austria on 12 March 1938. Hitler was anxious that there should be no violence when German forces entered his native country, and in the event millions of Austrians welcomed the Germans with enthusiasm.

THE SUDETENLAND

The Sudeten German areas of Czechoslovakia were originally part of the Czech Bohemian kingdom, settled by ethnic Germans from the thirteenth century onwards. When Bohemia was absorbed into the Habsburg Empire, the Sudeten Germans became subjects of the emperor in Vienna. During the nineteenth century ethnic tensions emerged between the Sudeten Germans and the Czechs; the Germans increasingly identified with the greater German nationalism expressed in 1848 and the movement for German unification. Before the First World War there already existed dangerous tensions between the two communities. In 1918 these tensions emerged in sharper form when it became clear that the newly formed state of Czechoslovakia wanted to keep the territories occupied by Sudeten Germans, despite the commitment of the peacemakers to self-determination. The ethnic Germans were forced to remain under Czech rule under the terms of the Treaty of Saint-Germain in 1919. The German minority were never reconciled to their new status and formed their own political parties to represent their ethnic interests. By the 1930s the Sudeten German Party (SdP), led by Konrad Henlein, openly agitated for German autonomy. Henlein, a gymnastics instructor, was not initially a National Socialist but the failure to achieve any of the concessions demanded by the Sudeten Germans pushed him into the arms of Hitler. On 24 April 1938 the SdP published the Carlsbad Programme which called for equality of status between Germans and Czechs. The Czech refusal to accept the programme provoked deteriorating relations between the two populations and led directly to the Czech crisis of September 1938 and the division of Czechoslovakia.

people for the continuation of Austrian independence. Hitler reacted angrily to the idea of a plebiscite which might (it was feared) give a majority for Schuschnigg. The same day he discussed the issue with military leaders and on 10 March he ordered Operation 'Otto' to be set in motion. Two army corps in Bavaria were mobilized and prepared to move into Austria at short notice, though Hitler was anxious to avoid bloodshed if possible. Early in the morning of 11 March Hitler decided that the union (*Anschluss*) with Austria would go ahead. The Austrian government was asked to abandon the plebiscite, which it reluctantly agreed to do. Momentarily uncertain about the outcome, Hitler allowed Göring to take the initiative. In imperious telephone calls to Vienna, Göring demanded the resignation of Schuschnigg and the appointment of Seyss-Inquart as chancellor. The Austrian president at first refused, but then realized that the situation was beyond his control. Seyss-Inquart was installed as chancellor. At 8.45 in the evening Hitler ordered the occupation of Austria, but waited until he had heard from Mussolini before giving the marching orders. Late in the evening news arrived that Mussolini would not act if Germany occupied Austria, and although this was already a diplomatic certainty, Hitler was effusively grateful. At 2 o'clock

VOTING FOR THE ANSCHLUSS

Interrogation of Albert Göring, Nuremberg 25 September 1945

Q I just want to identify those 'fake elections' you talked about. When and where were they?

A I am talking about the elections now, after the Anschluss of Austria. That is the elections when the population of Austria agreed to the incorporation of Austria into Germany. Personally, I voted 'No', but it was terribly difficult because even the voting itself was faked, and under the most trying of circumstances. It was fixed so that it was almost impossible to vote 'No'.

Q Well, did you have a choice, a 'Yes' or 'No' choice?

A The whole thing took place in a rather large hall. There was an entrance, and when you came in there was a round table at which sat several officials, and they registered you. They would hand you an envelope which had a sheet of paper in it; and there were two circles in it, a large circle meaning 'Yes', and the smaller circle meaning 'No'. Then at the other end of this hall was a telephone booth, and you were supposed to go in there and make your cross, put the ballot in the envelope, return, and drop it into a box which was provided at the end of the table. It was handled in this manner. However, when somebody came in, the officials would greet him with 'Heil Hitler', and then give him a ballot and they said, 'You are voting "Yes", there is no reason to go to into the booth at the end of the hall'; and everybody would make a cross in the larger circle. Then they would give the ballot to the official, and he would put it in the envelope, and put it in the box. Nobody dared to go to the booth in order to vote secretly. Well, I came into this place, and I was the only one among hundreds of people who dared to go into this booth. The official gave me the paper and said I could fill it out right there, and I told him that law and order must be kept, and I proceeded to the booth, and I made my cross in the 'No', then sealed the envelope and dropped it in the box. This is the way that voting was handled at that time.

Source: Imperial War Museum, FO Box 156, testimony of Albert Göring, 25 September 1945, pp. 23–4.

in the morning of 12 March German troops began to cross the Austrian frontier unopposed. That same day Seyss-Inquart assumed presidential powers as well, arranging for parliament to vote for a bill revoking Austria's sovereignty and declaring the state to be a province of the German Reich.

Hitler flew to Munich and then proceeded, in a long motor cavalcade, to cross the Austrian frontier in triumph. He was hailed on both sides of the border by jubilant crowds. He arrived in Linz, near the place of his birth, and visited his parents' grave. On 13 March, at a hotel in Linz, he signed into law the bill uniting the two states. On 14 March he arrived in Vienna to a hysterical welcome; in front of massed crowds gathered in the Heldenplatz he welcomed Austria back to the German fold. On 16 March he flew back to Berlin, where he was greeted as a national hero. Hitler announced that he had now created 'Greater Germany', the aim of German nationalists in the nineteenth century. The enthusiasm for union

A crowd of German onlookers on their way on 16 March 1938 to greet Hitler's arrival at the Wilhelmsplatz in Berlin following the union with Austria. Some can be seen carrying footstools to help them get a better look at the Führer.

expressed by the public in Austria masked how divided Austrian society was over the *Anschluss*. Many socialists and Catholics opposed the move, and Austria's large Jewish population waited for the new German masters to impose the same regime of discrimination and expropriation already practised in Germany. Almost immediately following the union, German security officers and officials moved in to make a wave of arrests. A new concentration camp was set up at Mauthausen, with a reputation for working its inmates to death. Jews were forced to clean the streets of Vienna by crowds of noisy Austrian anti-Semites. Göring gave a speech in Vienna on 26 March announcing the integration of the Austrian economy with the programmes of the Four-Year Plan, and his officials began a concerted drive to take over most of the important heavy industry and engineering works in Austria from their private owners. Schuschnigg himself was imprisoned briefly by the Gestapo and eventually sent to Dachau concentration camp, but survived the war. Seyss-Inquart was made Reich governor of Austria (now renamed the Ostmark) and was eventually executed at Nuremberg in 1946 for crimes against humanity.

Hitler wanted the union to be publicly endorsed, despite the opposition within Austria. A plebiscite was ordered for 10 April to coincide with the Third Reich's last one-party parliamentary election. The voting was organized in such a way that electors only had a choice of saying 'yes' or 'no' to the *Führer*'s list, rather than voting for named candidates. Those known to be likely to vote no were detained or prevented from voting; inside the polling booths those who voted 'no' could easily be identified. Hitler went through the motions of electioneering, speaking at rallies in fourteen major cities. The result of the plebiscite was overwhelming support, 99.08 per cent in favour of union (and within Austria 99.75 per cent). The figures conformed with what Hitler wanted to hear, but the real results from many areas were suppressed. The lowest 'yes' vote was 68 per cent in one constituency, and others recorded actual votes of 70 or 80 per cent. Even these figures, however, reflected a widespread approval of Hitler's policy and marked the highest point of his popularity in the pre-war years.

The Czech Crisis

The successful seizure of Austria, with no serious protest from the other major European powers, marked the first stage in Hitler's aspiration to turn Germany into a major power again, capable of dominating the necessary 'living space' in central and Eastern Europe. The absence of opposition to his first initiative as Supreme Commander also encouraged him to go further and faster than he might otherwise have done. The incorporation of Austria opened up the issue of Czechoslovakia which Hitler had signalled the previous November. The Czech state was now surrounded on both sides by German territory. Its internal difficulties were, like those of Austria, a source of weakness in confronting its powerful German neighbour. The 3 million German-speaking inhabitants, the 'Sudeten Germans' (former citizens of the Austrian Empire), were anxious for greater autonomy; Slovakia, united with the Czechs under the terms of the Versailles Settlement, also contained nationalist elements keen to win Slovakian independence. Although the Czech state was a parliamentary democracy, unlike the remaining new states set up in 1919, it was a fragile coalition that kept the state together.

Even before the plebiscite over Austria, Hitler had decided that the Czech question would have to be decided 'in the not-too-distant future'. On 28 March he met Konrad Henlein, leader of the Sudeten German Party, in Berlin. Henlein's party represented the great majority of Czechoslovakia's German population, which wanted autonomy within the Czech state or, if autonomy was refused, the possibility of uniting(like the Austrians), with Greater Germany. The Sudeten Germans were told to escalate their demands during 1938 so that the Czech government would be compelled into confrontation. Henlein did so on 24 April, demanding autonomy for the Sudeten regions. Hitler's object, however, was to create conditions in which a war might be possible, though this was not the Sudeten Germans' choice. As Germany's new supreme commander, Hitler wanted to be able to show the more timid soldiers and diplomats that he had the strength of will needed to solve Germany's problems. Hitler also believed that the international situation was favourable to a sudden coup: Italy was now a firm ally, Britain and France were distracted by other issues and had made little protest over the union with Austria. Above all, he wanted Germany's new armed forces to be blooded by action in a small and victorious conflict.

On 21 April OKW ordered the armed forces to prepare a revised plan for 'Case Green' for the destruction of Czech resistance. While the plans were being worked out, Hitler made a much-publicized state visit to Rome from 3 to 9 May. Unlike his visit in 1934, Hitler came this time with solid achievements behind him. On the final day he extracted from Mussolini the promise that he would also remain indifferent to a German solution to the Czech question. On his return to Germany the situation quickly escalated. Over the weekend of 20/21 May the Czech government was alerted to what was thought to be a direct military threat from Germany, and ordered partial mobilization of the armed forces. The threat at that point was imagined, not real, though on the same day(20 May), a new version of Case Green had been presented to Hitler, with the stated intention 'to smash Czechoslovakia by military action in the immediate future'. News of the Czech mobilization infuriated Hitler, and he accelerated his plans for actual war. On 28 May he called together his military commanders, as well as Ribbentrop, and his predecessor, von Neurath, for a conference in which he called for war against the Czechs by 1 October 1938, unless international circumstances made it impossible. Two days later he approved the revised draft of Case Green for the destruction of Czech resistance in four days, with a combination of armoured thrusts and heavy air attacks.

While Hitler prepared for his small war against Czechoslovakia, he also ordered, on 28 May, the start of work on a major line of fortifications on Germany's western frontier, known as the *Westwall*. The project was designed to ensure that France did not take the opportunity to invade Germany during a period of growing international tension. The construction was assigned to the Organisation Todt, which was also building the German motorways. Hitler recommended designs for the emplacements. The whole project at its peak consumed half the output of the German cement industry and employed 500,000 people. Hitler launched a number of other important projects at the same time. On 22 May he opened the new construction site for the Munich underground railway; four days later he laid the foundation stone for a huge factory complex at Wolfsburg in northern Germany,

where the Strength Through Joy movement was to build the People's Car (*Volkswagen*). The car, designed by the racing-car designer Ferdinand Porsche on Hitler's instructions, was to cost no more than could be afforded by a skilled worker and be produced in millions. The factory complex was completed a year later, but the coming of war interrupted mass production, which did not begin until after 1946. On 31 May Hitler approved construction of the world's largest suspension bridge over the River Elbe at Hamburg, and on 14 June laid the foundation stone for the House of German Tourism. In Hitler's mind waging war as Germany's warlord went hand-in-hand with a programme of grandiose architecture, as it had done in Roman times.

The crisis over Czechoslovakia intensified during the summer. On 13 June Hitler discussed the campaign with senior generals and on 28 June attended military manoeuvres near the Czech border. The priority was to avoid Western intervention. On 28 May he had told the generals that neither Britain nor France was in a position to intervene from lack of military preparation or will. But the Weekend Crisis of 20/21 May had alerted both states to the

Hitler with the architect Albert Speer discussing the remodelling of Berlin. Hitler wanted all Germany's major cities to be rebuilt to resemble the cities of ancient Rome, with a forum, a military parade ground and a large congress hall. The model of Berlin was stored in an underground room in the Reich Chancellery during the war to allow Hitler to review it even while the new German Reich crumbled around him.

'DEAD AGAINST WAR': BERLIN, 27 SEPTEMBER 1938

BERLIN, *September 27*

A motorized division rolled through the city's streets just at dusk this evening in the direction of the Czech frontier. I went out to the corner of the Linden where the column was turning down the Wilhelmsstrasse, expecting to see a tremendous demonstration. I pictured the scenes I had read of in 1914 when the cheering throngs on this same street tossed flowers at the marching soldiers, and the girls ran up and kissed them, The hour was undoubtedly chosen to-day to catch the hundreds of thousands of Berliners pouring out of their offices at the end of the day's work. But they ducked into the subways, refused to look on, and the handful that did stood at the curb in utter silence unable to find a word of cheer for the flower of their youth going away to a glorious war. It has been the most striking demonstration against war I've ever seen. Hitler himself reported furious. I had not been standing long at the corner when a policeman came up the Wilhelmsstrasse from the direction of the Chancellery and shouted to the few of us standing at the curb that the Führer was on the balcony reviewing the troops. Few moved. I went down to have a look. Hitler stood there, and there weren't two hundred people in the street or the great square of the Wilhelmplatz. Hitler looked grim, then angry, and soon went inside, leaving his troops to parade by unreviewed. What I've seen tonight almost rekindles a little faith in the German people. They are dead set against war.

Source: William Shirer *Berlin Diary: The Journal of a Foreign Correspondent, 1934–1941*
(Hamish Hamilton, London, 1941), p. 119

possible dangers, and over the summer efforts were made to see if the Czech government could make reasonable concessions to the Sudeten Germans to avoid a more serious crisis. France was allied to Czechoslovakia, as was the Soviet Union (whose intervention was regarded by all sides as unlikely, given the recent purge of the armed forces). As the negotiations stagnated between the Czech regime and the Sudetenlanders, Britain decided to intervene directly to broker a solution. In August, under the auspices of the League of Nations, a commission was sent to Czechoslovakia headed by the British politician Lord Runciman, whose purpose was to work out some way of satisfying Sudeten demands for greater independence and Czech fears for their national sovereignty. Henlein was instructed to reject any compromise solution in order to maintain pressure on the Czechs.

By this stage the moment of opportunity to isolate the Czechs that Hitler detected in the spring had disappeared. At home there was growing unease among the military leadership. On 10 August, and again on 15 August, he discussed the forthcoming campaign with German officers, some of whom remained sceptical that Czech fortifications would crumble very easily, or that the uncompleted *Westwall* would actually hold up the French army if it chose to move. On 18 August the army chief-of-staff, General Ludwig Beck, abruptly resigned in protest at Hitler's risky military planning. His replacement, General Franz Halder, was also privately anxious about the risks involved, and flirted with the idea of a coup to replace Hitler (but he remained loyal to the task he was asked to perform). Military planning continued throughout the early weeks of September, while conditions inside Czechoslovakia threatened to degenerate into civil war. On 12 September, following an inflammatory speech by Hitler on the Czech 'menace' at the annual Party rally, violence broke out in the Sudeten areas. The Czech government reacted by declaring martial law throughout the German-speaking zones. A few days later Henlein and other Sudeten leaders fled to Germany, unwilling to ignite a general civil war.

On 14 September, with Hitler's planned invasion only two weeks away, the British prime minister, Neville Chamberlain, asked if he might fly to Germany to meet Hitler face-to-face to try to find a solution to the issue. This was a dramatic gesture on Chamberlain's part – he had never before flown in an aeroplane – but Hitler agreed, even though British intervention might make it more difficult to launch his war against an isolated Czech state. German crowds turned out to cheer Chamberlain on the route to Berchtesgaden, where Hitler greeted him with great courtesy. The two men agreed that self-determination would be granted the Sudeten Germans and Hitler promised to stop short of an invasion. A week later the two men met again at Bad Godesberg, based in hotels on opposite sides of the River Rhine. This time Hitler was determined to solve the issue quickly and, if necessary, by force. In a tense confrontation he told Chamberlain that he would occupy the Sudetenland by force within eight days if the Czech government did not concede everything he asked for. On 23 September, after further deadlocked arguments, Hitler said he would postpone action until 1 October. Chamberlain promised to pressure the Czechs to accept the loss of the Sudeten areas, but neither the Czech government nor his own cabinet would accept the ultimatum. On 26 September, and again the following morning, Hitler met with Chamberlain's special envoy,

Sir Horace Wilson, who assured Hitler that violent, unilateral action on his part would bring British and French intervention on behalf of the Czechs.

The situation by the afternoon of 27 September was acute all over Europe, where populations expected war at any moment. That afternoon and evening Hitler had to wrestle with the reality that his small war might provoke a general European war. He was brought news in the evening that the Royal Navy had mobilized. The following morning a delegation arrived to see him, headed by Hermann Göring, urging him to reconsider in the light of the risk of general war. Among the population at large there was evident anxiety; after experiencing years of 'bloodless victories' the prospect of a real war did not provoke any enthusiasm. When Mussolini let it be known (at the instigation of the British) that he was willing to broker an international conference to settle the Sudeten issue, Hitler with great reluctance decided to accept. A

Left: An anxious Neville Chamberlain, British prime minister, accompanies Hitler after a midnight meeting in the Hotel Dreesen at Bad Godesberg on 23/24 September 1938. They failed to reach firm agreement on a solution to the Sudeten German question, which Hitler hoped to solve by waging war on Czechoslovakia.

Right: Adolf Hitler, watched by von Ribbentrop, puts his signature to the notorious Munich Agreement which allowed him to occupy the German-speaking parts of Czechoslovakia on 1 October 1938. To his right stands Chamberlain, behind him is Benito Mussolini, the Italian dictator, and to his left Edouard Daladier, prime minister of France.

THE MUNICH CONFERENCE, FROM THE SECRET DOSSIER

Munich's streets gave no inkling that a four-power conference was about to take place. On Hitler's orders all public demonstrations of enthusiasm were banned over the next few days. In this way he wanted to make the foreign statesmen understand that National Socialist Germany was not impressed by international conferences. He had just one word he used for both parliamentary sittings and conferences: 'talking shops'.

Chamberlain landed at Oberwiesenfeld airport near Munich, and was met by Ribbentrop and the Bavarian State Councillor Christian Weber in the uniform of an SS-Brigadeführer. This Munich entrepreneur and fanatical anti-Bolshevik was considered a suitable person to welcome His Britannic Majesty's Prime Minister. The Hotel Regina was reserved for Chamberlain and his staff. Göring met the French premier Edouard Daladier at the airport, and Daladier took up residence at the Hotel Vier Jahreszeiten. The conference was convened on 29 September in the Brown House, the headquarters of the National Socialist Party.

Before the conference began, Hitler fetched Mussolini and drove with him to the Führer Building [part of the Party headquarters], where they waited in Hitler's study for the arrival of Chamberlain and Daladier. At about 1.00 p.m. drum-rolls from the parading SS guard of honour announced the arrival of Chamberlain, accompanied by Ribbentrop. Chamberlain handed over his coat and climbed a flower-bedecked staircase to Hitler's study. Along the corridors stood SS men with expressionless, rigid faces, who had been given orders to create the impression that they were ready to march. Chamberlain responded to their shouts of 'Heil Hitler!' with an amicable nod. Hitler tried to adopt a military bearing like his SS men. Each time he appeared he sought to impress upon Chamberlain that he had been enraged by the Czechs. Seated with Mussolini in the middle of the room, he waited for Chamberlain to approach him without rising from his seat before coldly and impassively offering him his hand in the flashlight of the photographer Hoffmann. Mussolini too showed reserve when greeting Chamberlain. Now the door opened and Daladier stepped in. Hitler received him in the same way as he had greeted Chamberlain.

Without further ado, Hitler asked the heads of government of Britain, France and Italy to take their places around the table near the fireplace. Hitler sat as always with his back to the window, so that his face appeared in shadow. In the armchair to his left was Chamberlain, looking worried and confused. Daladier and Mussolini took their places on the sofa also to the left of Hitler's seat; they both looked dignified and decisive. Thus began the infamous Munich Conference.

Source: Henrik Eberle, Matthias Uhl (eds) *The Hitler Book: The Secret Dossier Prepared for Stalin from the Interrogations of Hitler's closest personal aides* (John Murray, London, 2005), pp. 33–4

conference of Germany, Britain, France and Italy (but not the Czechs) was called for 29 September in Munich. Hitler was observed to be ill-tempered for the rest of the day because he had had to back away from waging his first war, under pressure from his own advisers and the other major powers. His first test as Germany's new warlord ended before it had begun.

The meeting in Munich the following day took discussions back to the Hitler–Chamberlain meeting of 15 September. Sudeten self-determination was agreed, which meant in effect union with Germany, though there remained many arguments about the precise geographical limits of the Sudeten areas. Hitler undertook to occupy the areas without invasion from 1 October onwards. An agreement was formally signed at 1.30 in the early hours of 30 September. A little later Hitler entertained Chamberlin briefly in his personal apartment, where he agreed to sign a piece of paper renouncing war between the two countries and agreeing to consult on all major differences. Neither Hitler nor Chamberlain took the piece of paper very seriously, but it was intended by the British side to make clear any breaches of good faith that Germany might indulge in over the months following the Munich agreement. Hitler's good faith was limited; his appetite was whetted rather than assuaged by Munich. On 2 October he told Goebbels that he would destroy the rest of the Czech state when he could. On 21 October he ordered the armed forces to draw up new contingency plans for occupying the rest of Czechoslovakia and seizing the Memelland area ceded to Lithuania in 1919. Three days later he asked Ribbentrop to open discussions with Poland over the possibility of establishing a motorway and rail route across the Polish Corridor, also ceded in 1919, and returning the port of Danzig to German rule. In the Sudeten areas which Germany occupied in early October, German officials moved swiftly to occupy key economic installations while security men searched out remaining anti-Hitler elements in the German population. The area was integrated with Greater Germany and later, in May 1939, Konrad Henlein was appointed head of the administration of the Sudetenland and the local party *Gauleiter*.

Kristallnacht

Foreign policy absorbed much of the energy of the regime during 1938, but the central ambition to solve the 'Jewish question' remained clearly on the agenda. In November 1937, while Hitler was formulating his plans for Austria and Czechoslovakia, he told Goebbels that

---

Opposite above: German soldiers march past a group of Sudeten Germans on 1 October 1938 at Haidmühle. Following the Munich Agreement, German forces occupied the Sudeten areas prior to their incorporation into the Greater German Reich. After the war the Sudeten Germans were driven from the area and had to settle in Germany.

Opposite below: A caricature of a German Jew above a copy of the anti-Semitic newspaper *Der Stürmer* placed on placards in a refugee camp for Sudeten Germans in September 1938, prior to the annexation of the Sudetenland by Germany. 'Germans!' runs the slogan. 'Your Enemy is the Jew!'

the Jews had to be driven out of not only Germany, but the whole of Europe. When Austria was annexed the regime embarked immediately on a drive to force Austrian Jews to emigrate and to confiscate their businesses. Violence towards Jews in Austria exceeded that in the Reich, but the freedom to engage in unrestricted anti-Semitic violence was soon imported into Germany. During the summer of 1938 it reached levels that finally led Hitler himself, on 22 June 1938, to order a stop because of criticism abroad. After the Munich Conference violence by Party activists against Jewish businesses and synagogues began again, and it was against this background of escalating race hatred that the pogrom of 9–10 November must be understood.

The immediate cause of the most serious anti-Semitic violence of the pre-war period was the assassination of a German diplomat in Paris, Ernst von Rath, by a young Jewish protester. Rath died from his wounds on the evening of 9 November, while Hitler was in Munich for the annual celebration of the *Putsch* of 1923. The news prompted anti-Jewish riots, and Hitler, prompted by Goebbels, decided that in this case the police should stand by. 'For once,' Hitler told Goebbels, 'the Jews shall come to feel the anger of the people.' Goebbels gave an impassioned speech at the end of the evening in Munich, encouraging the Party to express its spontaneous anger towards the Jews. All across Germany that night shops were smashed and looted, synagogues burned down and Jews beaten or murdered. The destruction of shops left glass shattered across the pavements of most major German cities, and gave rise to the term 'the Night of Broken Glass' (*Kristallnacht*) by which the pogrom is better known. By the time the violence petered out the following day at least 90 people had been killed, 300 synagogues burnt down and 7,500 businesses damaged or destroyed. At the same time around 20,000 male Jews were rounded up and sent to concentration camps for short periods of punitive detention.

The pogrom received a mixed reception from the German public, many of whom were shocked, not so much by the anti-Semitism but by the disorder and violence that it unleashed. It aroused strong condemnation abroad. Göring, as head of the Four-Year Plan, was unhappy about the degree of damage to commercial property that the pogrom provoked. But the events of 9 November paved the way for an intensification of anti-Semitic measures in the Reich. On 12 November Hitler entrusted Göring with responsibility to tackle the so-called 'Jewish question'. At a meeting in the Air Ministry, Göring discussed further measures against the Jews with Goebbels, Heydrich, and a number of other ministers. The result of the meeting was an order that Jewish owners had to clean up the streets and repair their properties at their own expense. In addition a levy of one billion marks was imposed on all Jewish wealth as a form of atonement for what had happened. The same day a decree banned Jewish children from German state schools, while Jews were to be excluded from business activity. On 3

A smashed shop window on 10 November 1938 following the 'Night of Broken Glass' pogrom against German Jews and their businesses. Many ordinary Germans disliked the violence and damage to property but there was little or no protest against the attacks on the Jews.

THE NIGHT OF BROKEN GLASS, 11 NOVEMBER 1938

The reports so far available from the State Police Offices have given the following overall picture about 11.11.1938: In numerous cities the plundering of Jewish shops and businesses took place. Drastic action was taken to avoid further plundering. At the same time 174 people were arrested on account of the plundering. The scale of destruction of Jewish businesses and houses cannot yet be expressed in figures. The figures listed in the reports: 815 businesses destroyed, 29 warehouses burnt down or otherwise destroyed, 171 residential houses set on fire or destroyed, indicate, except for cases of fire, only a part of the actual available destruction. Because of the urgent need to report, the reports available up to now have had to limit themselves to general statements such as 'numerous' or 'most businesses destroyed'.

The figures given here might therefore be very greatly exceeded.

191 synagogues were set on fire, a further 76 completely demolished. In addition 11 communal houses, cemetery chapels and similar were set on fire and a further 3 completely destroyed. Around 20,000 Jews were arrested, as well as 7 Aryans and 3 foreigners. The latter were for their own safety taken into custody.

There were 36 deaths reported, also 36 badly injured. The dead and injured are Jews. One Jew is still missing. Among the dead Jews there is one Polish citizen, among the injured two.

Report from Reinhard Heydrich, chief of the Security Police, to Hermann Göring, 11 November 1938, in *Dokumente des Verbrechens:1933–1945, Band II* (Dietz Verlag, Berlin, 1993), pp. 152–3

'ARYANIZATION'

From the very start of the Third Reich pressure was placed on Jewish business owners, shopkeepers and professionals to sell their concerns to ethnic German owners. The process was known as 'Aryanization', the takeover of Jewish activities by 'Aryan' Germans. It also involved the regime and the Party putting pressure on German-owned businesses to get rid of directors or shareholders who were Jewish. The overall object was to cleanse the German economy of any Jewish participation. This was done at first without any legal backing; Jewish commercial houses, shops and factories found themselves starved of official or public orders, or subject to intermittent boycott, or physically menaced. Many Jewish owners sold assets at well below their market value in the first years of the Reich. In April 1938 German Jews were legally obliged to register all their assets and portable wealth and on 3 December 1938 a second decree on 'The Deployment of Jewish Wealth' gave legal foundation to the compulsory 'Aryanization' of Jewish businesses. Over the following year around 100,000 Jewish businesses were closed down or sold. Jewish jewellery, gold and silver was also taken against a small nominal payment and used to buy essential imports for German industry. The procedure was repeated across German-occupied Europe throughout the war, using a wide variety of devices to dispossess Europe's Jewish population. An estimated 7–8 billion marks of assets was taken over from German Jews; the quantity seized in Europe has not been estimated with any accuracy. Jewish wealth and assets played an important part in sustaining Germany's war effort after 1939. Only a fraction was ever restituted after the war.

December this last provision was confirmed with an order for compulsory purchase of Jewish firms and their 'Aryanization'. There were also many petty restrictions on the German Jewish population, which was to be denied the use of dining cars or sleeping compartments on trains, banned from public swimming baths and spas, and segregated as far as possible from 'Aryan' apartment blocks and housing. According to Göring, who announced the new crop of measures to Party leaders on 6 December 1938, Hitler wanted the states that complained about German Jewish policy to open their doors to Jewish emigrants: 'Why are you constantly going on about the Jews? Have them!'

The more sinister side to the radical increase in anti-Semitic measures was the language Hitler now chose to use when he talked about the Jewish question. In January 1939 he discussed the Jewish problem with the Czech foreign minister. 'The Jews will be exterminated here,' he explained, as revenge for stabbing Germany in the back in 1918. On 30 January 1939, during his annual speech marking the day he received the chancellorship, he made his threat public. If Jewish bankers, Hitler told the Reichstag, succeeded in plunging Europe into a second global war, the result would not be 'a victory of Jewry' but the opposite, 'the annihilation of the Jewish race in Europe'.

1939 The Occupation of Prague

For Hitler 1939 was to be a year in which German 'living space' in central Europe was expanded regardless of the attitude of the two Western powers, whose intervention had obstructed the small war he wanted against the Czechs. On 24 November and 17 December 1938 he issued directives and instructions for the military takeover of Czechoslovakia, the Free City of Danzig and the Memelland area. His aim with Czechoslovakia, now without the fortifications which had been built along the Czech–German frontier in the Sudetenland, was to exploit the nationalist ambitions of the Slovaks in order to break up the existing state and extend effective German control over the remaining Czech areas. At the same time he began to explore ways of inducing Poland to concede the areas of former German territory which it had acquired after the Versailles Settlement. The return of the Polish Corridor, Danzig and Upper Silesia to Greater Germany was not expected to result in war. Hitler assumed that the evidence of German military and economic power would be sufficient to force his weaker neighbours to bow to reality.

The Czech case unfolded much along the lines that Hitler expected. On 12 February Vojtěch Tuka, a leader of the Slovak People's Party, and Franz Karmasin, spokesman for the German minority in Slovakia, visited Hitler in Berlin, where he encouraged them to declare independence and break up the Czechoslovak state. The German armed forces prepared the ground for the occupation of the Czech areas while Slovak agitation became violent enough for the regime in Prague to declare martial law on 10 March. Hitler sent two emissaries to the Slovak capital, Bratislava, to press the Slovak nationalists to declare their independence at once, but they continued to hesitate. On 13 March Hitler called Józef Tiso, the leader of the Slovak People's Party, to Berlin and berated him for his timidity. Tiso promised to declare Slovak independence the following day, and was given a document prepared by the German foreign ministry for the purpose. On 14 March the German army was in position on the Czech frontier. Hitler summoned the Czech president, Emil Hácha, to Berlin, together with the Czech foreign minister, František Chvalkovský. At one o'clock in the morning of 15 March, Hitler received them together with Keitel, Ribbentrop and Göring. It was the latter's task to paint a grim picture of the bombing of Prague by German aircraft if the Czechs did not give in and accept Slovak independence, as well as a German protectorate over the Czech provinces of Bohemia and Moravia. Hácha fainted at the thought of the destruction of his capital and had to be revived by Hitler's doctor. The two visitors finally agreed to abandon Czech sovereignty and to hand over Czech military equipment. At 4 o'clock the document was signed and Keitel at once ordered military occupation, which began two hours later.

Hitler almost immediately arranged for his entry into Prague. This was to have none of the glamour of his triumphal entry into Vienna. He arrived in Bohemia in a snowstorm and proceeded by car, almost unnoticed, to the former royal palace, Hradčany Castle. Here, accompanied by Himmler and Heydrich (whose task was to organize the arrest of thousands of Czechs considered dangerous to the new German occupiers), Hitler welcomed leaders of the small German community in the city. On the morning of 16 March he formally proclaimed the Protectorate of Bohemia and Moravia and two days later appointed the

DANZIG

Danzig was an ancient Hanseatic German port on the Baltic coast of East Prussia. It had been part of the German Empire in 1918, when Germany was defeated. The victorious Allies compelled Germany to give up the port and to create a 'Free City' which could be used by the newly-constituted state of Poland as an outlet to the sea for its trade. A small hinterland was added and the Free State was set up in 1920, run by a League of Nations committee of three and a permanent League Commissioner. The population was majority German and in May 1933 the Danzig National Socialist party gained a majority of seats in the Danzig Senate. After that Danzig underwent something of the same transformation that had taken place in Germany, although it was impossible in the Free City to impose the same degree of political terror and one-party rule as existed in the Reich. In 1938, against the wishes of the League commissioner, the Danzig government introduced the notorious Nuremberg Laws into Danzig, forbidding Germans and Jews to marry or to have sexual intercourse. Many of Danzig's Jews fled abroad in the 1930s. Relations between the minority Poles and majority Germans were initially tense, then went through a period of more stable collaboration, but finally after 1933 became more bitter and confrontational. The German population of Danzig campaigned openly to rejoin Hitler's Germany and reunification was the first act declared when the Second World War broke out on 1 September 1939.

former foreign minister, von Neurath, to the post of Reich Protector. On 17 March Hitler travelled to Vienna, where a Treaty of Protection between Germany and the now independent Slovakia was drawn up. He returned to Berlin the following day after four days of hectic activity. Almost immediately he ordered the annexation of Memelland from Lithuania, whose government made no protest, and on 23 March Hitler arrived in the port of Memel to address the local German population. In the course of just a week Germany's strategic situation was transformed; for the first time non-Germans had been forcibly brought under German control and the first steps taken to construct a new European order dominated by Germany.

The plans for Poland proved much more difficult to achieve. On 5 January Hitler invited the Polish foreign minister, Józef Beck, to Berlin to begin serious negotiations for an extra-territorial rail and road link across the Polish Corridor and agreement to terminate the 'free city' status of Danzig and return it to Germany. Up until 1939 relations with Poland had been cordial; in 1934 a Non-Aggression Treaty had been signed and Poland had used the Munich Settlement as an opportunity to share in the spoils by compelling the Prague government to cede the small territory of Teschen, on the Czech–Polish border. The German leaders hoped that Poland would become a tame satellite, conceding the territories that they thought properly belonged to Germany, as well as joining the Anti-Comintern Pact against the Soviet

HITLER AND THE ENGLAND PROBLEM, APRIL 1939

This determined and implacable 'No' which Hitler thought he heard whenever he called up the image of 'Perfidious Albion', filled him with a rage that was 'heroic and sacred'. His manner and countenance were changed, his voice became heavy and threatening, while a strange light shone in his eyes. Rage unleashed his soul, which threw off the constraint of *limits* which it had provisionally imposed upon itself and showed itself for what it really was, violent and ungovernable...

'Oh, well! If England wants war, it will have it. It won't be so easy a war as it thinks, not one on the old pattern. England will no longer have the whole world at its side. At least half the world is with us. And it will be a war of destruction such as nobody can imagine. Besides, how can England think of a modern war when she cannot mount two divisions on any front?

'As for us, our misfortunes have been of use. We shall fight with arms other than those of 1914. We shall fight ruthlessly, to the end, with no consideration. We have never been as strong as we are now. To the invincibility of our armies must be added the skill of our technicians, engineers and chemists. We shall astound the world with our methods and inventions. So on what do they rely to hold us in check? Their Air Force? They may perhaps succeed in bombarding a few towns, but how can they measure up to us? Our Air Force leads the world, and no enemy town will be left standing!'

As though seeking in advance to rid himself of such a responsibility, the 'Führer' added sorrowfully:

'And to think that it is I – I who am accused in Germany of being an impenitent admirer of the British Empire, I who have so often tried to establish a lasting understanding between the Reich and England (an understanding which to-day I still consider necessary to the defence of European civilization) – to think that it is I who must envisage such a conflict! And this entirely on account of the incomprehension and blind obduracy of the leaders of Great Britain!'

Source: Grigore Gafencu *The Last Days of Europe: A Diplomatic Journey in 1939* (Frederick Muller, London, 1947), pp. 65–6

Union, which most Poles regarded as a permanent threat to their security. By the time Beck arrived on 5 January, however, it was clear that the German tactic was to make limited requests which step-by-step turned into larger and more pressing demands. Beck indicated that the questions raised by Germany were not open to negotiation. When Ribbentrop requested that Beck return to Berlin on 20 March to discuss the return of Danzig to the Reich, only a few days after establishing the Czech Protectorate, Beck could see that German intentions were hardening and refused to come. On 26 March the Polish ambassador, Józef Lipski, told Ribbentrop that any unilateral alteration to the status of Danzig as a Free City would be a cause for war. This was the end of negotiation. The Polish ambassador in Berlin did not see either Hitler or Ribbentrop until the eve of the German invasion of his country. On 3 April Hitler issued a directive to the armed forces to prepare for 'Case White', the invasion of Poland, with an anticipated date of 1 September 1939.

The Road to War

Hitler's decision to prepare for a war against Poland was an indication of his strong desire to have some kind of war to justify his credentials as Germany's military commander-in-chief. His frustration at not having had a short war against Czechoslovakia may have played a part in his willingness to think of war with the Poles as soon as it became clear that German demands were not easily to be fulfilled. On a number of occasions during January and February 1939 he addressed military audiences on the value of waging war, not only to achieve German 'living space' but as something necessary for the full reassertion of Germany's historic mission as Europe's greatest power. These fantasies of conquest played an important part in Hitler's determination to have a war with Poland, even when the international repercussions became increasingly dangerous.

The Polish question, like the Czech question the year before, could not be isolated from the wider international context. On 31 March, Neville Chamberlain gave a unilateral guarantee of Polish independence in the House of Commons. Guarantees were extended, together with France, to Romania and Greece on 13 April. The British guarantee so infuriated Hitler that it immediately prompted the directive for 'Case White', which the OKW began work on the day after the guarantee was announced. This time, however, Hitler was determined to isolate Poland from any possible assistance in order to ensure that the war would be a short, localized conflict rather than a general European war. At a meeting with his military commanders on 23 May 1939, called to discuss the Polish war, he announced that isolation was decisive: 'It must not come to a simultaneous confrontation with the West.' At the same time Hitler did little to avoid such a confrontation. On 28 April he made a major speech to the German parliament revoking the German–Polish Non-Aggression Treaty and the Anglo-German Naval Agreement, signed in 1935. At the same time he rejected an appeal that had been sent on 15 April by the American president, Franklin Roosevelt, for Germany and Italy to give a ten-year guarantee not to attack a list of neighbouring European countries. Instead, on 22 May and at Italian instigation, the two states signed an agreement to give each other military assistance in the event that one or the other became involved in a war. The 'Pact of Steel' was not particularly welcomed in Berlin, but it was hoped that the alliance would further inhibit British or French intervention in the affairs of Eastern Europe. Hitler told Mussolini nothing about the projected plans for war with Poland.

Over the summer months the armed forces prepared for the coming conflict. German–Polish relations were deliberately inflamed by the German side which encouraged the German minority in Poland to destabilize the regions where they lived, just as the Sudeten Germans and the Slovaks had been encouraged before. In Danzig the majority German population became increasingly obstructive to the Polish port officials and customs officers who supervised Polish trade through the port. The perpetual diet of anti-Polish propaganda directed by Goebbels in the German press not only succeeded in creating popular indignation against the Poles, but also prepared the ground among the German population for the planned invasion in late August or early September. The growing opposition of Britain and France to any German action directed at Poland was made clear in public statements throughout the summer. British and French contacts with the Soviet Union opened up the possibility that Germany might face an encircling alliance to prevent the conquest of Poland, but Hitler remained confident that this time he had the measure of Britain and France. Their abandonment of the Czechs in 1938, and their failure to act over the occupation of Prague, had become hard evidence for Hitler that the West would noisily protest against German actions but would not turn their words into actions. The evident determination to act against Poland encouraged a number of leading conservatives, who had been unhappy about the risks run over the Czech crisis the year before, to establish contacts abroad to encourage a firm response to Hitler's Polish policy and hint that the Hitler regime might, with encouragement, be overthrown. The leading spokesmen for this view were the former mayor of Leipzig, Carl Goerdeler, the former chief-of-staff of the army, Ludwig Beck, and the German diplomat Adam von Trott zu Solz. The Western states, however, used this evidence not to support the German opposition, but to convince themselves that if they stood firm in support of Poland, Hitler might yield or become the victim of a palace coup.

The one factor that Hitler had to take into account was the possibility that the Soviet Union might decide to reach an agreement with the West and revive the old alliance of the First World War. Although Hitler wanted war in 1939, he did not want a world war, for which the German economy and military were not yet fully enough prepared. The idea that it might be possible to reach some kind of rapprochement with the Soviet Union, after spending years publicly announcing that Jewish-Bolshevism was the greatest threat to European civilization, was already under consideration by German leaders at the beginning of the year. By April however, with a firm decision to prepare for war with Poland, the prospect of gaining Soviet neutrality or even Soviet collaboration became more inviting. That month attacks on the Soviet Union ended in the German press and in Hitler's speeches. In May the German ambassador in Moscow, Count Friedrich von Schulenberg, began to drop hints to the Soviet side. On 30 May he was instructed to try to start definite negotiations. Talks were difficult, partly because British and French missions were trying at the same time to secure an alliance with the Soviet Union directed against Germany, and partly because the Soviet leadership found it difficult to believe the German side

THE GERMAN–SOVIET NON-AGGRESSION PACT, 23 AUGUST 1939

The Government of the German Reich and the Government of the Union of Soviet Socialist Republics, desirous of strengthening the cause of peace between Germany and the USSR, and proceeding from the fundamental provisions of the Neutrality Agreement, concluded in April 1926, between Germany and the USSR, have reached the following agreement:

Article 1
Both High Contracting Parties obligate themselves to desist from any act of violence, any aggressive action, and any attack on each other either individually or jointly with other powers.

Article 2
Should one of the High Contracting Parties become the object of belligerent action by a third Power, the other High Contracting Party shall in no manner lend support to this third Power.

Article 3
The Governments of the two High Contracting Parties shall in the future maintain continual contact with one another for the purpose of consultation in order to exchange information on problems affecting their common interests.

Article 4
Neither of the two High Contracting Parties shall participate in any grouping of Powers whatsoever that is directly or indirectly aimed at the other Party.

Article 5
Should disputes or conflicts arise between the High Contracting Parties over problems of one kind or another, both parties shall settle these disputes or conflicts exclusively through friendly exchange of opinion or, if necessary, through the establishment of arbitration commissions.

Article 6
The present Treaty is concluded for a period of ten years with the proviso that, in so far as one of the High Contracting Parties does not denounce it one year prior to the expiration of this period, the validity of the Treaty shall automatically be extended for another five years.

Article 7

The present Treaty shall be ratified within the shortest possible time. The ratification shall be exchanged in Berlin. The treaty shall enter into force immediately as soon as it is signed.

Moscow 23 August 1939

For the Government of the
German Reich
v. Ribbentrop

With full power of the
Government of the USSR
V. Molotov

Additional Protocol

On the occasion of the signature of the Non-Aggression Pact between the German Reich and the Union of Soviet Socialist Republics, the undersigned plenipotentiaries of each of the two Parties discussed in strictly confidential conversations the question of the boundary of their respective spheres of influence in Eastern Europe. These conversations led to the following conclusions:

1 In the event of territorial and political rearrangement in the areas belonging to the Baltic States (Finland, Estonia, Latvia, Lithuania), the northern boundary of Lithuania shall represent the boundary of the respective spheres of influence of Germany and the USSR. In this connection the interest of Lithuania in the Vilna area is recognized by each party.

2 In the event of a territorial and political rearrangement of the areas belonging to the Polish state, the spheres of influence of Germany and the USSR shall be bounded approximately by the line of the rivers Narev, Vistula and San. The question of whether the interests of both Parties make desirable the maintenance of an independent Polish state and how a state should be bounded can only be definitely determined in the course of further political developments. In any event both Governments will resolve this question by means of a friendly agreement.

3 With regard to South Eastern Europe, attention is called by the Soviet side to its interests in Bessarabia. The German side declares its complete political disinterest in these areas.

4 The Protocol shall be treated by both Parties as strictly secret.

Source: *Nazi–Soviet Relations 1939–1941* (US Dept of State, Washington DC, 1948), pp. 76–7

could be serious. Only in August 1939, when it was clear that war with Poland was imminent and when talks with the British and French had reached stalemate, did Soviet leaders at last realize that the hints about German–Soviet agreement might be real.

On 2 August 1939 Ribbentrop told the Soviet trade official Georgi Astakhov that the interests of the two states could be harmonized from the Baltic to the Black Sea. Three days later a German trade negotiator suggested a secret political protocol to any economic agreement the two sides might reach. It was suggested that a Soviet sphere of interest might be assigned in Romania, the Baltic States and Poland. On 11 August, the day a military mission arrived from Britain and France to discuss possible joint action, the Soviet Foreign Minister, Vyacheslav Molotov, finally made it known that an agreement was a possibility. Over the week that followed, talks with the British and French collapsed. On 17 August Molotov presented Schulenberg with a draft non-aggression treaty with a secret political protocol; two days later a comprehensive trade agreement was signed between the two sides, giving Germany access to Soviet agricultural produce and oil, and the Soviet Union access to modern German military equipment and machinery. Hitler then asked if Ribbentrop could come to Moscow urgently and on 21 August Stalin agreed, at last convinced that the German side was not bluffing. On 22 August Ribbentrop boarded a plane for Moscow to sign what is now regarded as a historic agreement between the two dictatorships.

As Ribbentrop flew to Moscow, Hitler called together his military commanders for a final briefing on the forthcoming war. It was a meeting designed to allay any remaining doubts his generals might have over the wisdom of risking general war. He assured them that Britain and France would not fight for Poland. 'Our enemies are tiny little worms,' Hitler said. 'I saw them at Munich.' He announced that the Soviet agreement would make it impossible for the West to act and ordered 'the destruction of Poland' to begin in the early morning of 26 August. The following day, 23 August, Ribbentrop and Molotov negotiated a final agreement. In the evening Ribbentrop telephoned Hitler to get his approval for placing two further Baltic ports in the projected Soviet sphere of influence. Since Hitler had little intention of honouring the agreement in the long term, the concession mattered little to him. At midnight on 23 August the German–Soviet Pact was signed, including a secret protocol assigning spheres of influence and dividing Poland in two. An hour later, Ribbentrop telephoned the news to Hitler. The following morning Hitler waited to hear that the British and French governments had fallen, but instead Chamberlain reiterated British support for Poland. In the evening Hitler returned to Berlin to prepare for his brief war of conquest against Poland.

The Coming of War

The week of hectic activity that divided the signing of the Pact from the invasion of Poland on 1 September reflected once again Hitler's hesitation faced with uncertainty about the behaviour of the Western powers. His assurance that Britain and France would engage in 'theatre' rather than intervene militarily nevertheless hardened in the final days before the invasion, while those around him became more sceptical about the prospects of keeping the Polish conflict localized.

During the week of negotiations with Moscow the German armed forces had been moving into position. On 19 August the first units began transfer towards the Polish frontier; the second echelon was ordered forward on 24 August. The plan was to begin the invasion in the early hours of 26 August without a formal declaration of war. On 25 August the Chancellery in Berlin was a bustle of activity as Hitler waited for the last arrangements to be in place. During the morning Hitler met the British ambassador and offered to guarantee the British Empire if Britain would allow him to solve the Polish question without intervening. At 3 o'clock in the afternoon he gave the order to start the attack at 4.30 the following morning. But over the next few hours added complications arose. At 5.30 the French ambassador arrived to confirm French commitment to Poland; at 5.45 the Italian ambassador had to tell Hitler that, despite the terms of the Pact of Steel, Mussolini was not prepared to engage in war at present. The Italian leadership had been piqued at not being told about the invasion until

German soldiers dislodge a frontier post on the road between Zoppot and Gdingen on the German–Polish border during the first hours of the German attack on Poland on 1 September 1939. Though many Germans did not relish the prospect of a general war, there was wide enthusiasm for a war against Poland.

POLAND UNDER THE GERMAN YOKE, OCTOBER 1939

October 10

It appears that the Germans will be here for a long time. They are seeking quarters for 150 men. We have a new city commandant. From the first moment they put the Jews to work cleaning the city. Today, for the first time in weeks, we had a normal market as we usually do on Tuesdays. Many villagers came to sell their goods…

October 11

The town is crowded with Germans. They are quartered in all the larger houses. Most of them are from Austria and some from Vienna. In general the Germans are trying to clean up the city. For this work they are using only Jews. Jews must sweep the streets, clean all public latrines, and fill in all the street trenches. Plastered everywhere are German notices giving an idea of what we can expect in the future.

We must return all arms. We must record all contagious diseases. The police curfew is from 10 p.m. to 5:30 a.m. The restrictions applying to Jewish shops change from day to day. Sometimes the Jews are allowed to open their shops, and sometimes they are not. It seems most of the orders are aimed at the Jews….

October 13

The German military commander told the mayor that a concentration camp will probably be established in Szczebrzeszyn. This is very sad news…..
The Germans posted several new regulations. I am noting only a few:

'All men of Jewish religion between the ages of fifteen and sixty must report at 8 a.m. on the morning of October 14, at city hall with brooms, shovels and buckets. They will be cleaning city streets.'

'All people of Jewish religion can move freely on the city streets only between 6 a.m. and 6 p.m. Their houses and apartments shall be open for police inspection at all times.'

'All radio receivers shall be deposited at city hall in two days, with the names of the owners attached. Jews shall add under their names "Jude".'
Jews are staying home, not going out.'

Source: George Klukowski (ed.) *Diary from the Years of Occupation 1939–44: Zygmunt Klukowski* (University of Illinois Press, Chicago, 1993), diary from the town of Zwierzyniec

mid-August, but the Italian armed forces were in no shape yet to take part in a major conflict. Finally, at 6 o'clock, Ribbentrop told Hitler that Britain and Poland had just concluded an Anglo-Polish Treaty to confirm Britain's commitment to war if Germany attacked. Temporarily disconcerted by the cascade of unhelpful news, Hitler decided to cancel the instructions for invasion at 7.30 in the evening. The cancellation reached the military authorities very late in the day (and one unit stationed in Slovakia actually did cross the Polish border on 26 August), but the halt was effective.

Hitler was unhappy about having to stop the invasion but he needed time to assess what the news meant. Over the next few days he redoubled efforts to detach Britain from its commitment, but on the following morning he was again more confident that he could cope without Mussolini's assistance, and that Britain and France were playing a dangerous game of bluff. On 27 August the state of readiness was prepared again. On 28 August Hitler confirmed that the new date for the invasion was the morning of 1 September. In the West there was a growing sense that it was Hitler who was bluffing and when Hitler appeared on the 28 August to accept a British suggestion that talks should begin between Poland and Germany the hopes for peace revived. But on 29 August when Hitler met the British ambassador, Sir Nevile Henderson, he insisted that a Polish plenipotentiary had to arrive within 24 hours, prepared to sign an agreement at once. The Western states and Poland rejected what was in effect an ultimatum for the Poles to do what the Czechs had been made to do earlier in the year. On 30 August the Polish government ordered general mobilization. The following day Hitler confirmed, in War Directive No 1 for the Conduct of the War, the intention to destroy Poland, and at 4 o'clock in the afternoon gave the marching orders for the attack to begin at 4.45 on the morning of 1 September. In the evening Himmler's security forces staged a mock attack on German frontier installations at Gleiwitz with officers dressed in Polish uniforms. A number of camp prisoners, also in Polish uniforms, were murdered and left at the scene to make the skirmish seem real. The bogus raid was used by Hitler as the pretext for the German assault.

The German armed forces attacked from three different directions with 1.5 million men, and more than 1,500 aircraft, against an army that was not much smaller, but supported by only 400 aircraft (many of them obsolescent) and very limited numbers of armoured vehicles against the five Panzer (armoured) divisions available to the German side. The first achievement was the seizure of Danzig, which was declared part of the Reich early in the morning of 1 September. Over the following few days Polish units defended bravely but were no match for German operational skills and the relentless bombing of the German air force. The news of invasion arrived early in the morning in London and Paris, and by the evening formal letters had been delivered in Berlin asking Germany to cease its attack and withdraw its forces. In the absence of an ultimatum or declaration of war, Hitler began to doubt that the West would actually fight, as he had assured his colleagues right up to the final hours before the Polish campaign began. On 2 September there was still no definite news from the Western capitals. Only on the morning of 3 September were two ultimatums delivered, the British one at 9 o'clock in the morning, the French at 12.30. The British ultimatum expired at

11 o'clock without a German response, the French ultimatum at 5 o'clock in the afternoon. Hitler was now faced with a general war he had not wanted. He left for the front in the evening, assuring an anxious Goebbels that the West would just fight a war of blockade, not a proper conflict.

The Destruction of Poland

Polish forces proved no match for the German army, which encircled large numbers of Polish soldiers in set-piece battles. On 17 September, at Ribbentrop's prompting, the Soviet Union finally took advantage of the terms of the German–Soviet Pact and invaded Poland from the east, meeting by this time little serious resistance. By the third week of September Polish forces were pushed back to the central areas around Warsaw and Modlin. On 25 September German bombers and dive-bombers attacked Warsaw, causing widespread destruction. On 27 September Warsaw surrendered, followed a day later by the forces at Modlin. Final resistance petered out by 5 October. Around 70,000 Poles were killed and 694,000 captured; an estimated 90,000 escaped from Poland and in many cases made their way to the West. German dead and missing totalled 13,000; Soviet losses were around 750. On 28 September German and Soviet representatives met in central Poland to finalize the demarcation line. Meanwhile Ribbentrop arrived again in Moscow the same day to sign the German–Soviet Treaty of Borders and Friendship, which sealed the division of Poland and assigned Lithuania to the Soviet sphere.

The war against Poland was not only a military conflict. Some weeks before the invasion Hitler had agreed with Himmler the creation of special action squads (*Einsatzgruppen*) made up of security personnel, which would follow the armed forces and deal with issues of security in the rear areas. The groups were in effect given the power of summary arrest and execution, employed to murder elements of the Polish elite, senior Polish officers and Polish clergy, as well as prominent Polish Jews. The operation was code-named 'Tannenberg' and it marked the start of the vicious race war that the SS was to conduct over the whole course of the ensuing six years of warfare. On 27 September the whole security apparatus was transformed into a security ministry, the Reich Main Security Office (RSHA), under Reinhard Heydrich. On 3 September Heydrich had already issued a secret decree which allowed the Gestapo the power to execute saboteurs and enemies of the people without trial, a new right that was exploited ruthlessly throughout the newly occupied area. On 7 October Himmler was granted additional powers to cope with the racial restructuring of Poland and the other territories under German control. As Reich Commissar for the Protection of Germandom he assumed

---

Opposite: A group of Danzig SS militia shelter behind a tank in an assault on the Post Office building in Danzig, where a group of armed Poles refused to surrender when Danzig was taken over by the German majority on 1 September 1939. The Office was finally overwhelmed later in the day and Polish resistance was confined to the Westerplatte Fortress.

responsibility for deporting racial groups that occupied land destined for new German colonists, who were to be found from among the large German-speaking minorities that inhabited most Eastern European states. Eventually Himmler moved 600,000 ethnic Germans back to the Reich or to former Polish territory.

The success of the racial remodelling of Europe was also bound up with the fate of the almost 3 million Polish Jews who had now come under German control. On 21 September Heydrich ordered all Polish Jews to be settled in designated ghetto areas. Poland itself was to be territorially dismembered: the western areas of Silesia, Posen and Prussia, and the city of Danzig, were all reintegrated into the Reich on 8 October 1939. On 12 October a rump Polish region, designated the 'Generalgouvernement', was established under the control of Hans Frank, with its capital at Cracow. Here it was intended to concentrate most of the Polish

Jewish population, as well as deported Jews from Germany, Austria and the Czech Protectorate. On 1 December all Jews in the Generalgouvernement were ordered to wear the yellow star, and that month some 87,000 Jews were deported there from the areas of Poland reintegrated with the Reich. On 21 December a young SS officer, Adolf Eichmann, was appointed to run department IV D4 in the RSHA, responsible for Emigration and Deportation; the office was later changed to IV B4, responsible for Jewish affairs and deportation, and the heart of the later genocide.

While the savage pacification of Poland was taking place, Hitler was forced to decide how to respond to the British and French declaration of war. Since neither state did anything to assist Poland during September, he returned to his earlier conviction that they were not

Two Polish civilians are marched along by German soldiers in Katowice, Poland, on 4 September 1939. Right from the start of the campaign the German army and security forces arrested those suspected of anti-German activity and members of Poland's governmental and intellectual elite. Thousands were murdered during the next few months.

German anti-Semitic policy focused during the 1930s on getting German Jews to emigrate to Palestine, or to other western destinations. This journal supplement from 1933 issued by the Jewish authorities encourages Jews to consider emigration. By 1939 over half of Germany's Jews had left the Reich.

Chanukah-Tage im jüdischen Dorf

Palästina

**Bild-Beilage
der Jüdischen Rundschau**
Berlin W 15, Meinekestraße 10

Nr. 5/99 vom 12. Dezember 1933

חנכה

THE CENTRAL OFFICE FOR JEWISH EMIGRATION

The efforts to force German and Austrian Jews to emigrate were increased from the autumn of 1938 with the founding of the Central Office for Jewish Emigration run by the SS leader Adolf Eichmann. He was born in Germany but grew up in Austria, where he joined the Austrian National Socialists and SS. He returned to Germany in July 1933 and found a position in the SS security service in Berlin. His responsibility was for the Jewish question and in this capacity he established links with Zionist organizations and even travelled to Palestine to investigate prospects for Jewish emigration. In August 1938 he set up and ran the Centre in Vienna which was responsible for issuing all exit visas for Austrian Jews. They were compelled to pay for the privilege by leaving most of their wealth and possessions behind. If they could not afford the hostage price, they had to find funds from wealthy Jews who could sponsor them. Within a few months around 100,000 Austrian Jews had left. Eichmann opened a second branch of the Jewish Emigration office in Prague in March 1939. The success of the Austrian office led to the establishment on 24 January 1939 of a Reich Central Office for Jewish Emigration in Berlin, under the supervision of Reinhard Heydrich. By 1939 some 286,000 German Jews had emigrated, 60,000 of them to Palestine under the terms of an agreement made between the SS and German Zionist movement. By 1941 there were just 164,000 German Jews left in the Reich out of almost 500,000 in 1933.

serious about waging war. On 5 October he returned from a victory parade in Warsaw and the following day announced a peace offer to the Western powers, aimed principally at reaching a special agreement between Britain and Germany. While not all Western leaders were opposed to the idea of a compromise agreement (since little could be done to save Poland) the governments rejected the peace proposal on the grounds that war had been declared to rid Europe of the menace of Hitlerism, not to endorse Hitler's victories. On 9 October Hitler issued War Directive No 6 for a campaign against France, violating the neutrality of Luxembourg, The Netherlands and Belgium. The new campaign, codenamed Case Yellow, was modified again on 18 October and the date for it to start fixed for 12 November 1939. Almost all Hitler's senior commanders thought the campaign was premature, with tired forces not fully equipped and the prospect of poor autumn fighting weather, but Hitler remained adamant that the enemy was if anything even less prepared for combat. Only on 7 November was Hitler forced by the reality of poor weather conditions to accept a postponement to mid-December. In the end the campaign was postponed at least 29 times and was not finally mounted until 10 May 1940.

Hitler's determination to attack France at all costs in the autumn prompted a number of military commanders to contemplate more serious action against their commander-in-chief. A number of generals submitted memoranda critical of Case Yellow; others were appalled by the behaviour of German security men in Poland towards Jews and the Polish elite. During late October and November the most hostile among the conservative resistance began to contemplate an actual coup against Hitler before he risked everything in an unwinnable war. One elderly soldier, General Kurt von Hammerstein-Equord, recalled to active duty in September 1939, planned to invite Hitler to his headquarters in Cologne and there arrest or murder him. Hitler declined the invitation. The other conspirators met secretly, exchanged views, deplored Hitler's grip on the German people, but could find no way to run the risk of unseating him. On 20 November Ludwig Beck wrote a memorandum predicting Germany's utter defeat in the war that had now started, but he could find no one among the cohort of generals with access to Hitler who was prepared to act.

In the end the initiative was taken by a lone assassin, a disgruntled carpenter named Georg Elser. Working alone, he contrived to set up an explosive device in the casing of a pillar in the famous cellar in Munich where Hitler gathered to address the Party's old fighters every year in commemoration of the failed *Putsch*. On 8 November 1939 Hitler spoke as usual but decided to leave earlier than planned. Thirteen minutes after he left the bomb exploded, killing seven and injuring 63 more. Hitler was alerted on his way back to Berlin and interpreted his decision to leave the beer cellar prematurely as the hand of Providence safeguarding Germany's saviour. Elser was not executed straight away but kept as a prisoner by the Gestapo in the concentration camp at Sachsenhausen as 'Hitler's special prisoner'. He was eventually murdered on Himmler's orders on 9 April 1945, shortly before the end of the world war he had sought to avert.

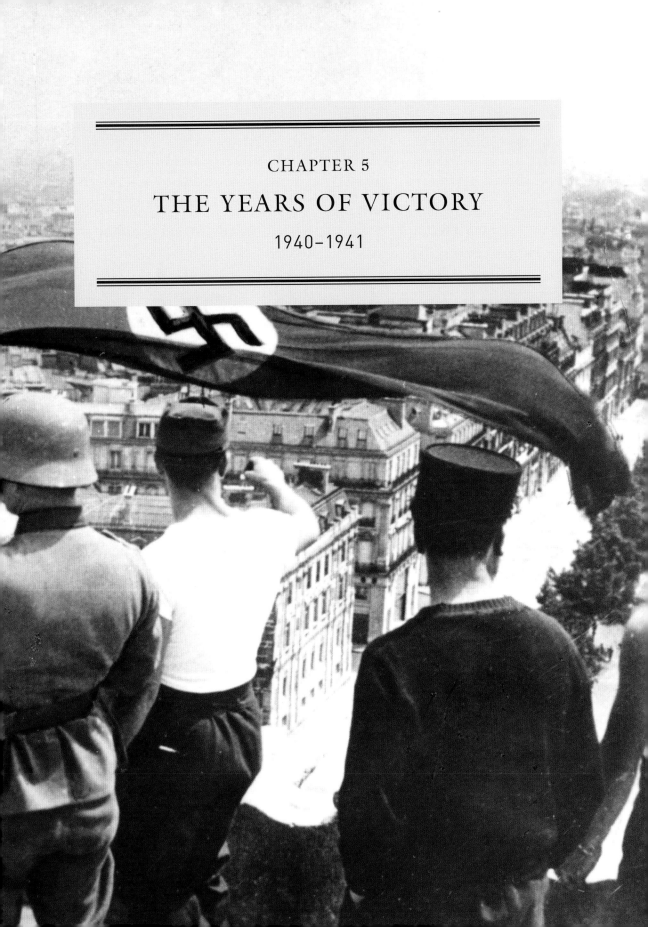

CHAPTER 5

THE YEARS OF VICTORY

1940–1941

War with Poland in September 1939 presented Hitler with the prospect of a World War he had not wanted. In 1940 he gambled on being able to defeat Britain and France in a daring frontal assault against the Anglo-French line. The gamble paid off with French defeat in June 1940 and the expulsion of the British from continental Europe. Victory in the West opened up for Hitler the possibility of constructing what was called the 'New Order' in Europe. German leaders knew, however, that Britain and the Empire were not yet defeated. In the summer of 1940 Hitler tried to offer peace on his terms to Britain, and when it was rejected explored the possibility first of invading in September 1940, then, when invasion was abandoned, of bombing Britain into submission. This failure coincided with growing anxiety about the ambitions of Stalin's Soviet Union in Eastern Europe. In December 1940 Hitler finally authorized an all-out assault on the Soviet Union in early summer 1941 to destroy the Communist threat and to remove the last prospect Britain might have of a European alliance with a great power. Hitler saw himself destined to create a great German empire in the east which would supply the resources needed to secure Germany's role as a world superpower. The German people were happy with the defeat of France because they hoped the war would end. The extension of the conflict in 1941, including the involvement of German forces to help Mussolini defeat Greece and the invasion of Yugoslavia in April 1941 to eliminate the threat from an anti-German coup in Belgrade, presented the German people with the prospect of a longer and more costly conflict. Invasion of the Soviet Union in June 1941 was the largest military operation in history and promised a remarkable victory, but by December, when the army was halted and turned back from Moscow, the years of easy victory came to an end.

1940 The German Home Front

The first winter of the war in Germany saw no serious fighting, but the German population were made to accept from the outset increased mobilization, regulation and limited rations to ensure that the home front was better prepared for large-scale war than had been the case in 1914. Having been forced by poor weather and incomplete preparations to postpone the attack in the West in November 1939, Hitler then hoped to launch the campaign on 17 January. However, the Allied capture of the detailed plans for the operation, following the crash-landing of a German plane in Belgium on 10 January, forced a further postponement until the spring while the planning was overhauled and more military resources allocated. The additional months of preparation saw German society brace itself for a conflict that was widely expected to mimic the stalemate endured on the Western Front between 1914 and 1918.

For Hitler, as for many other German nationalists, the home front was regarded as critical during the war. Veterans of the previous conflict refused to accept that German armies had been defeated in the field and blamed instead the so-called 'stab-in-the-back' by unpatriotic socialist or Jewish elements at home. As a result, great attention was paid from the start of the war to the distribution of foodstuffs to keep the population from protesting, and to the rooting out of elements in the population thought to be either a threat to domestic security or a burden on the national war effort.

Rationing began right from the start of the war and covered a wide range of goods. Food, soap and textiles products were rationed from 28 August 1939, but meat and fats were already rationed. Rationing was extended further and given a firm legal foundation with the publication on 4 September 1939 of the War Economy Decree. The myth still survives that the German population was not subjected to strict rationing, but the reality was entirely different. A complex system of points rationing was introduced to cover purchases of every kind and to ensure that adequate food was made available for different categories of the population. Heavy workers (coalminers, steelworkers etc) got additional rations, children got smaller rations. The families of servicemen got welfare equal to 60 per cent of pre-war income, paid partly by the armed forces, partly by local government. The bulk of the welfare came in the form of coupons for coal, potatoes, milk, bread, rent and school fees. The level of diet for all German consumers was not generous. Average consumers could get 500 grammes of meat a week (though this was almost halved by the end of the war), 125 grammes of butter, 250 grammes of beet sugar and one egg. Potatoes were not rationed, with the result that most Germans not living in the countryside had to make do with a monotonous starch-based diet for much of the war. Consumers were forced to accept standard and adulterated foodstuffs,

Pages 204–5: A group of German soldiers with French gendarmes look out over Paris, following the surrender of the city to the German army on 14 June 1940.

known as *Einheit* products, which included jam, margarine, powdered milk, pudding powder and coffee substitute. Most fresh foods and fish were hard to obtain and the armed forces were given priority for all luxury foods, including chocolate. Cigarettes were rationed to three per day for men, 1.5 per day for women. In restaurants it was necessary to pay for all meals with ration coupons, a separate coupon for each food item on the plate.

All other consumer goods were restricted either through rationing or by limiting their sale. Many inessential goods were displayed in shop windows to give a sense of business as usual, but they could not be purchased during wartime. Passenger car production fell from a peak of 276,000 in 1938 to only 67,000 in 1940, of which the armed forces took 42 per cent. Clothes rationing was introduced on 1 November 1939. Each man and woman had a clothing allowance of 100 points a year which would allow them to buy only two or three items. A man's coat or suit cost 60 points and could only be bought if the old one was given in at the same time. Shoes were strictly rationed, with priority for work boots and shoes, which could not by law be worn outside the office or factory. Many Germans were forced to wear wooden clogs or sandals as their old shoes wore out. The German public was also subjected to a strict regime of waste recycling. All household refuse had to be divided into five categories: paper, rags, bottles, scrap metal and broken furniture. All these restrictions remained in force throughout the war.

The War Economy Decree of September 1939 also laid the foundation for the transfer of economic resources to war production. This meant the reallocation of labour and the switch from civilian production to all forms of military output. On 3 February 1940, Hermann Göring as head of the Four-Year-Plan organization ordered the maximum output of armaments over the coming year. On 20 March a fresh decree ordered the temporary closure of inessential businesses and offices to free labour for the war effort. Göring, in co-operation with the Labour Minister, ordered regular 'combing-out' operations to force firms to shed workers they did not need in wartime. During 1940 the proportion of German workers engaged in either direct or indirect production for the armed forces shot up from 22 per cent in May 1939 to over 50 per cent a year later. The fall in male employment in the large German handicrafts sector was particularly marked. In January 1940 the number had fallen by almost one million since the previous July. Most went into armaments production or into the armed forces. The number of women working in the heavy industrial sectors also rose by over one-

Opposite above: German women queue for rationed bread in a German bakery. Bread was one of many staple foods rationed from the start of the war and formed a major part of the average German diet throughout the war period.

Opposite below: Young German women marching to work on a farm in the late 1930s. A 'duty year' was introduced for all women of 18, who were sent to help in agriculture or welfare services or as domestic workers. All unmarried women were expected to contribute something to the war effort, and rural labour proved the most important.

third between 1939 and the spring of 1941, reflecting a shift in the pattern of female employment that continued throughout the war. In 1940 women were already in evidence driving buses and trams, delivering the mail and directing traffic. On the land large numbers of women worked the farms themselves once male rural workers were conscripted; young girls performing their obligatory 'Year of Duty' were commonly sent in 1940 to work in agriculture. Without the large female workforce on the land, the supply of food to the cities would have been jeopardized during 1940 and 1941.

The shift to an economy based on the war effort suffered from the failure to define very clearly who was responsible for carrying the process out. This had been one of the failures in the First World War, when no central administration was established in 1914 to make sure the home front contributed what was wanted. In the spring of 1940 the army encouraged Hitler to address the problem by appointing an individual responsible for the production of armaments. On 17 March 1940 Hitler appointed Fritz Todt, the man who had built the *Autobahnen* in the 1930s, as Minister of Munitions. The appointment was hedged around with difficulties, since aircraft production remained outside his control and under the influence of Hermann Göring, who was unprepared to relinquish what he saw as an important part of his personal political empire. Nor could Todt control the output of the principal industrial materials – coal, steel, chemicals, machinery – which remained loosely supervised by Göring's Four-Year-Plan organization. None the less Todt did have an immediate effect on German war production. He decided to reorganize production into a series of production rings and committees, each responsible for one important weapon or component, and each run as far as possible by industrialists and engineers who knew what they were doing. The chief problem Todt confronted was the military establishment. The armed forces had their own large and elaborate organization for overseeing weapons production, centred on the work of Colonel-General Georg Thomas at Hitler's Supreme Headquarters. The armed forces were reluctant to sacrifice technical excellence or minor tactical requirements for the sake of increased production and Todt found himself fighting a continual battle to prevent the military from undoing the effects of his own efforts to centralise and streamline German production.

While the population was faced with mounting restrictions and the economy converted to war production, the regime also embarked on a programme to ensure that there should be no

Opposite above: The head of the Reich's construction organization, Fritz Todt, hands out iron crosses to workers for distinguished service maintaining and building the German Westwall defensive line. Todt was a civil engineer and an enthusiastic National Socialist who in 1940 became Minister of Munitions. He died in an air crash in February 1942.

Opposite below: The German Minister of Economics, Walter Funk [right], in a car with the Italian Minister for Trade and Finance, Raffaello Riccardi. Funk recruited other Axis states to his ideas for building a new Axis-dominated economic order.

THE 'NEW ORDER' ECONOMY

The speed with which German forces occupied much of Continental Europe left much German planning in confusion. In a short span of time it was necessary to organize the economies of the occupied regions and to integrate them with the needs of the German war economy. In the summer of 1940 the German Economics Minister Walter Funk announced the creation of an economic 'New Order' in Europe. His object was to make the German mark the chief currency of the continent and eventually for the Berlin finance centre to eclipse the City of London. German corporations began to explore the possibility of setting up continent-wide trading agreements, dominated by German interests. In March 1941 a new Europe-wide insurance company was set up to carry the insurance risks traditionally carried by Lloyd's of London. The same month Hermann Göring authorized the establishment of the Continental Oil Company, which took over and consolidated large parts of the European oil industry into a single umbrella organization. In all the occupied areas special levies were imposed and in Berlin blocked accounts were established to ensure that imports would not have to be paid for in hard currency until after the end of the war. The occupied areas paid out 53 billion marks during the course of the war, most of it from the richer areas in the west – France, Netherlands and Belgium. In every occupied area workers were either taken back to work in Germany, a total of over 5 million by 1944, or worked on producing goods for the Germans in the factories and on the farms of the occupied lands. An estimated 20 million Europeans worked for Germany during the war in addition to the millions who were deported to German factories. To fund what could not be seized or taken on credit, the German authorities hunted for gold which could be used to buy goods on world markets. Much of this was stolen from Jewish owners or taken as gold fillings from the dead in the extermination camps. The gold was melted into ingots and sent mainly to Switzerland, where it could be used to pay for international purchases. The trade in looted gold was only finally exposed in the 1990s when Swiss banks were forced to reveal the history of these transactions.

possibility that the German war effort might be sapped by internal resistance or debility. The population of the German concentration camps trebled during 1940 from 21,000 in August 1939 to around 60,000 a year later. The Gestapo rounded up known communists and social-democrats, many of whom had been released from the camps in the 1930s, and put them back behind barbed wire. In anticipation of the large increase in prisoners, Himmler ordered an expanded programme of camp building. A new concentration camp was built at Stutthof, near Danzig, in September 1939. On 27 April 1940 Heinrich Himmler ordered work to begin on a camp at Auschwitz, in occupied Poland, and on 4 May the SS officer Rudolf Höss was appointed the camp's first commandant. Construction began two weeks later, on 20 May. The camp was initially scheduled to hold Polish prisoners-of-war and political prisoners, but its function expanded continuously during 1940 and 1941 as the camp population grew. Other camps were added over the course of the year to complete the main wartime system .

Among the new wave of prisoners were further 'asocials' whose presence in the German population was regarded as a menace when Germany was at war. Orders were given to begin the expulsion of gypsy populations to the east as they were regarded as intrinsically unreliable. In May over 2,000 were deported to occupied Poland, the first of a wave of compulsory transfers in the first years of the war. The war also provided the opportunity to accelerate the programme of 'euthanasia' authorized by Hitler in October 1939. The deliberate killing of the mentally and physically disabled was designed to release medical and hospital resources for German soldiers, but it also fitted with National Socialist prejudice against the idea that the disabled population should live while healthy 'Aryan' men were sacrificed on the fighting front. In January 1940 the official euthanasia programme, known under the acronym Aktion T4 (T=Tiergarten, the Berlin address where the programme was run), was set in motion with the first killings at Grafeneck in Württemberg. The T4 operation was covered in a veil of secrecy. The Berlin headquarters operated under the cover name of the Charitable Patient Transport Company. The doctors and officials who undertook the programme, whose end result was the death of more than 80,000 disabled in Germany alone, anticipated methods which were later applied to the extermination of the Jews. The patients were sealed in a small airtight room into which carbon monoxide gas was pumped until they were all certified dead by a doctor. Three centres were set up early in 1940, two more added in September. In 1941 the programme was extended to the murder of all mentally ill or criminal prisoners in the camps. In June 1940 all Jewish mental patients, whether disabled or not, were added to the list of victims.

The regime's top priority was the Jewish question. Hitler had long ago blamed the Jews for German defeat in 1918 and German leaders endorsed his view that the greatest care must be taken to ensure that Jews did not do the same again. In the occupied east, German authorities began to create sealed ghettos for the local Jewish population. On 8 February the ghetto was created at Lodz and walled in; on 19 May 1940 orders were given for the erection of the Warsaw ghetto. This ghetto was sealed off by a high wall and large numbers of Jews from the surrounding area forced to move inside, creating conditions which subjected the population to lethal levels of hunger and disease. Hitler also wanted the Jews deported from Germany. In October 1939 he had authorized the Gestapo Jewish Office, headed by Adolf Eichmann, to start deporting Jews from Austria and the Czech lands, but later extended this to all Jews living in Greater Germany. On 17 October the first trainload of 4,700 Austrian and Czech Jews arrived in Lublin in occupied Poland. Hitler then rescinded the order because he realized that he might have a large Jewish population exactly where he wanted to launch a later military assault on the Soviet Union. But the deportations began again in 1940. On 12/13 February 1940 the first Jews were deported from Germany to the area around Lublin, which was designated as a reservation for Jews from outside the region, but the operation then stopped again. The full programme of deportation was only activated two years later under the deadlier terms of the 'Final Solution'.

AN INSPECTION DAY AT RAVENSBRÜCK WOMEN'S CAMP

According to the rank and significance of his visitors, Kögel [the camp commandant] would be dressed in ordinary or gala uniform complete with all his clinking load of medals. Coming smartly to attention, clicking my heels, and keeping my arms at my side, I would report in the appropriate subaltern voice: 'Block Senior Margarete Buber, No. 4,208. Report obediently Block No. 3 occupied by 275 Bible Students and three Politicals, of whom 260 are at work, eight have hut duties and seven permits for inside work.'

Kögel would stare at me with his watery blue eyes, his clean-shaven jowls twitching, and grunt something. Then I would go ahead on the routine inspection, opening one door after the other, and the first three lockers. As we approached the prisoners properly and legitimately present, I would snarl '*Achtung!*' whereupon they would spring up like jacks-in-the box. All the visitors, whether male or female, SA, SS, or what-not, would invariably be impressed by the shining tin and aluminium. Kögel was usually the only one to put questions to the prisoners. If anyone else attempted to do so, he would immediately intervene. Each time he would ask one of the women present, 'Why were you arrested? And invariably the answer would come: 'Because I am a Witness of Jehovah.' That would be all the questioning, for Kögel knew from experience that these incorrigible Bible students never missed an opportunity for a demonstration. 'Carry on,' he would order, and the prisoners would then go on with their knitting or whatever other work had been specially prepaed for such a contingency.

After that the visitors would look into the dormitory, and invariably there would be loud exclamations at the spotless order they found there. At which Kögel would shout:

'Block Senior! How much time have the prisoners between reveille and roll-call?'

'Three-quarters of an hour, Herr Commandant.'

And then Kögel would point to the beds. 'Three-quarters of an hour, ladies and gentlemen,' he would declare with pride. 'And in that time look what my prisoners do: bed-building, dressing, washing, locker-cleaning, coffee-drinking and then roll-call. And look at these exemplary beds. Or perhaps you think there are boards under the blankets?' And then he would go over to one of the beds and turn back the covers and smack the mattress with his whip. 'Look at that straw sack. See how it's packed. That's merely one of the results of the work we do here to educate the prisoners back to a life of order and cleanliness.'

Then he would regularly stride to the window, which was immediately opposite the window of the next hut, whose far window was immediately opposite the window of the one beyond, and so on right down the line, so that visitors could gaze right through all the huts on that side and see never-ending lines of bunks. With a proud movement of his arm, Kögel would embrace the lot, saying in an impressive voice: 'And all those huts are just as clean and orderly as this one; you can take my word for that.'

And his visitors would crowd round the window and look through with admiration at the evidence of the great work being done in concentration camp Ravensbrück to educate the enemies of the State and other inferior elements to be good and useful citizens of the National Socialist People's Community.

After 'A' Wing, exactly the same ritual was performed in 'B' Wing. And once the cigarette-smoking, stamping, clinking mob had trooped off, the prisoners locked in the toilets would tumble out again in great relief, the work would be shoved to one side and the pots with food would reappear on the tables or on the stove. Once again we had survived an inspection.

Source: Margarete Buber-Neumann *Under Two Dictatorships: Prisoner of Stalin and Hitler* Trs. Edward Fitzgerald. (Pimlico, London, 2009), pp. 198–200

War in the West

During the winter months of 1939/40 the German military leadership wrestled with the problem of mounting a campaign against French and British forces with any prospect of success. The striking victory later achieved in June 1940 has obscured the extent to which German military leaders recognized the risky nature of what they were doing against a well-armed enemy. The capture of the German plan in January made the venture potentially more hazardous. Without Hitler's relentless demand for aggression, German generals might well have stayed put in Germany and waited for the French and British to take the initiative.

The solution to the planning problem was finally found after General Erich von Manstein, chief-of-staff of Army Group A, stationed on the western frontier, discussed with Hitler his own idea for a more radical plan of attack. Instead of the plan favoured by the army leadership for a conventional assault through Belgium into the northern French plain, Manstein favoured a concentration of Germany's armoured striking force further south through the Ardennes forest. The woods were generally regarded as impassable for heavy vehicles and the French frontier was only lightly defended at this point and Manstein hoped the Allies would be caught by surprise and their line split in two. Hitler grasped at the idea since, so he claimed, he had been thinking along similar lines. Despite the opposition of senior German generals, Hitler insisted on imposing what was codenamed Operation Sicklecut (*Sickelschnitt*) and on 24 February 1940 this became the German plan of operations. The hope was to launch the attack at some point in April or May.

The schedule was affected once again by other factors. Hitler was distracted by events in Scandinavia which he felt posed a threat to Germany's northern flank. The war between the Soviet Union and Finland, which began on 30 November 1939 with a Red Army invasion of the Finnish southern frontier, threw the whole northern region into sharp relief. Hitler sympathized with the Finns but was also bound by treaty to the Soviet Union. On 27 January he ordered the armed forces to begin preparing contingency plans for the occupation of Norway and Denmark. The German Navy leadership strongly favoured the plan, since it gave them a long coastline from which to mount raids on Allied shipping. Fears that the Allies might themselves pre-empt German plans and occupy the region were fuelled by the informal assistance they gave to the Finns. The Soviet–Finnish war ended on 12 March and on 26 March Hitler finally decided to launch the Scandinavian campaign before the attack in the West. By this stage the British and French had already begun serious planning for an operation of their own. On 2 April Hitler ordered 'Weser Exercise' to begin a week later and on 9 April German forces entered Denmark unopposed and mounted a sea and air assault on Norway. Despite heavy losses of shipping most objectives had been secured by the end of April.

While Norway was secured, the final preparations were made for the campaign in the West. Three army groups were drawn up on the western German frontier. The southern Army Group C was to engage French armies manning the Maginot Line, to keep French forces tied down there while the armour of Army Group A's 44 divisions pierced the Ardennes. Army Group B in the north with 29 divisions was to invade through the Netherlands and Belgium and on to the northern French plain. It was the task of General Gerd von Rundstedt's Army Group A to

THE INVASION OF SCANDINAVIA

On 9 April 1940 German forces occupied Denmark and began the invasion of Norway. The planning for such an eventuality had been called for by Hitler at the end of January following the postponement of the invasion in the West. There was strong intelligence information to suggest that Britain might launch a preemptive invasion of Norway or threaten German supplies of high-quality iron ore from Sweden essential for military production. On 1 March Hitler approved Operation 'Weser Exercise' and by the end of the month, following the end of the Soviet–Finnish 'Winter War' he decided that it should be launched before the planned campaign in the west in order to secure the northern flank. On 2 April Hitler ordered the operation to start in a week's time. At almost exactly the same time Winston Churchill, as First Lord of the Admiralty, had ordered mine-laying operations in Norwegian waters. Denmark was secured by two divisions with almost no active opposition. A large fleet sailed towards Norway while overhead German paratroopers flew to seize Norway's southern airfields. The invasion in the south was successful despite heavy losses of shipping, including the heavy cruiser *Blücher*, which was carrying the Gestapo personnel for the occupation. In the north British and French forces tried to hold on to Narvik and the area around Trondheim but they were finally compelled to withdraw on 8 June under heavy air attack. On 10 June Norway surrendered. Although Hitler had secured his northern flank, he had done so at a heavy cost to the small German Navy, which lost three cruisers, 10 destroyers and had three other major vessels damaged. The Navy was never again able to mount a serious challenge in surface warfare.

break the Allied line and rush for the Channel coast, encircling the British Expeditionary Force and the French First Army Group. The signal for the attack was good weather. Originally scheduled for 5 May, the attack was finally launched five days later when the forecast promised clear skies for the German air force to support the army effectively. The balance of forces on paper favoured the Western states: 144 army divisions (including Dutch and Belgian) against 141; 13,974 artillery pieces against 7,378; 3,384 tanks against 2,445. The chief German advantage was in the air, but only because German forces chose to concentrate almost all their air forces for the attack while French and British aircraft were kept back from the battle line to protect the rest of French and British territory. Germany had 3,254 bombers, dive-bombers and fighters, the Allies 3,562; the German air force committed almost all of them to the campaign, the Allies only 1,800, and that only piecemeal. No other factor played so large a part in explaining victory as the careful use of battlefield aviation by the German side.

On 9 May Hitler told his commanders to expect 'the most famous victory in history.' The following day German forces swept forward at dawn. Dutch resistance was broken almost at once by the innovative use of German parachute troops. When the Dutch port of Rotterdam was heavily bombed on 14 May, following the failure to communicate to the airborne German

aircraft the fact that the city wanted to surrender, the Dutch government abandoned the fight. The Netherlands' forces surrendered on 15 May. In Belgium a daring attack by glider troops on the heavily defended Eben Emael fortress unhinged Belgian defences. The Belgian army fell back to the River Dyle, to be met by the advancing French First Army Group. Both forces found themselves hard pressed by the German army group advancing out of the Netherlands. The Allies assumed this was the principal axis of German advance and failed to watch what was happening further south. Despite the difficulty of the terrain, which led at times to military traffic jams 50 miles long, von Rundstedt succeeded by 12 May in getting seven armoured divisions, the cream of the German army, through the Ardennes and on to the east bank of the River Meuse. At the southern end of the German pincer near Sedan stood General Heinz Guderian's 1st Panzer Division; furthest to the north at Dinant was Brigadier Erwin Rommel's 7th Panzer Division. This powerful armoured fist was still not recognized by the Allies as an immediate threat until the armour began to pour across the Meuse the following day. The assault severed the Allied front line and German armour raced towards the Channel coast, which was reached by 19 May. The French army, much of it tied up in defending the Maginot Line, responded late and limply to the German threat. French air power was all but

A squadron of Junkers Ju-87 dive-bombers in flight in 1940. The dive-bomber proved a very effective battlefield support aircraft. Apart from its bomb, the aircraft also had a siren which emitted a wailing sound as it dived, instilling terror into those on the ground who could hear it. During the Battle of Britain the plane's slow speeds made it vulnerable to fast fighter fire and the Ju-87 was withdrawn.

defeated and its superior armour dispersed too widely. The long exposed flank of the German 'sickle' was never attacked with any vigour, and by the end of May it was clear that France was facing complete defeat on the battlefield.

It was at this point that Hitler, secure in his forward headquarters in the Eifel Mountains, is usually said to have made the decision to halt the German advance, just as it seemed likely that the entire British Expeditionary Force and a large number of French troops would be forced to surrender with their backs to the sea around Dunkirk. In fact two halt decisions, one on 22 May and a second late on 23 May, were made not by Hitler but by the commanders in the field, whose judgement Hitler endorsed. By this stage, after two weeks of gruelling combat, German armoured forces found the going much harder. A strong British counter-attack at Arras on 21 May alarmed the German command and forced the first slow-down while German forces regrouped to eliminate the British threat. Two days later the commander of the German 4th Army, General Günther von Kluge, told the army group commander, von Rundstedt, that his depleted forces were not strong enough yet to risk a strong thrust at the encircled Allied pocket. A second halt was ordered and Hitler ratified it the following morning, 24 May. Hitler was certainly observed to be nervous about the risk of committing German armour prematurely, but the key decisions about whether to stop the advance were taken by the local commanders. On 26 May the halt order was rescinded and large German armoured and infantry formations at last began the final assault on the Allied pocket. By this stage the besieged defenders had been able to construct a defensive perimeter behind which some 338,000 Allied forces, most of them British, were evacuated in eight days of frantic activity, under constant attack from the German air force. The Dunkirk evacuation salvaged something of Allied pride, but it represented none the less a major defeat. When the evacuation ended on 4 June, more than 40,000 British servicemen entered captivity.

With the defeat of the northern armies, German forces turned south to complete the destruction of French resistance. Fierce fighting continued but the capacity of the French command to reorganize a firm front was much reduced in the face of overwhelming German air power, and the need to keep reserves manning the Maginot Line. On 5 and 9 June two powerful armoured thrusts, one led by General Ewald von Kleist and one by Guderian, broke through the extended French line and raced for Paris. German bombers had attacked the city on 3 June, killing 250 inhabitants, and to save the capital from further damage the French government declared Paris an open city. On 14 June the German army entered an almost deserted city in triumph. There was now little to stop German forces, which poured forward across France. They reached the Atlantic coast at Brest on 19 June and Bordeaux six days later. The shock brought the collapse of the French regime. Marshal Philippe Pétain formed a new administration and sought an armistice on 17 June. Hitler insisted that the document of surrender be signed in the same railway carriage in the small French town of Compiègne where the Germans had been forced to sign in 1918. For Hitler, a veteran of that earlier conflict, it was a sweet revenge. On 21 June a French delegation arrived to be told the terms of the German victory and the following day the armistice was signed. At 5 a.m. on 23 June Hitler made a brief visit to Paris in order to look at the architecture, accompanied by his favourite architect, Albert Speer. He stood for a long time at the tomb of Napoleon in the church of the Invalides. On 6 July he returned in triumph to Berlin to be greeted by millions of his fellow countrymen. He arrived in the afternoon and was met by Party and military leaders. With music playing and church bells pealing, his motorcade wound its way through ecstatic crowds to the Reich Chancellery, where he stood at an open window to acknowledge the tens of thousands crowded into the Wilhelmplatz with upheld arms. The popular mood of euphoria evident throughout Germany reflected a widespread belief that the war was now over and life would return to normal.

Hitler also hoped that victory in France would persuade the British to sue for peace. He told his confidants that he had no desire to destroy the British Empire which, in his view, would bring little benefit to Germany. He told the army chief-of-staff, General Franz Halder, that he favoured 'political and diplomatic procedures' to bring about peace rather than an invasion, which he considered 'very hazardous'. On 7 July he nevertheless directed the armed forces to begin exploratory planning for a possible invasion, while at the same time beginning to prepare a 'peace offer' to the British which he intended to announce in front of the German parliament later in the month. German confidence that Britain might negotiate a settlement was fed by regular informal contacts between the two sides, some of which dated from late 1939, and all of which suggested that the British elite might not want to risk the Empire by further warfare. In late May and June 1940 arguments went on in Churchill's government about the possibility of finding some room for manoeuvre in dealing with Germany. One of the difficulties for Hitler was the fact that Germany was no longer fighting Britain on its own. On 10 June the Italian dictator, Benito Mussolini, declared war on France and Britain, hoping to be able to share in the spoils of any subsequent peace settlement. Hitler's relations with Mussolini had been strained earlier in the year when his Axis partner tried to persuade him to abandon the fight in the West. The German leadership had no particular desire to have Italy join the campaign, because it threatened to make more certain continued British belligerency in defence of the Mediterranean and their African empire. 'The greatest service which Italy could have rendered to us', reflected Hitler in 1945, weeks before the end of the war, 'would have been to have remained aloof from this conflict'.

On 19 July 1940 in a crowded German parliament Hitler made his peace offer. Goebbels had ensured that the speech would be broadcast worldwide. German aircraft patrolled overhead in case British bombers attempted a spoiling attack. He used the opportunity to celebrate Germany's six-week victory over France. He blamed the Jews for forcing the West to fight and he offered to respect the British Empire if Britain would agree to end hostilities. He appealed to Britain, he said, 'as a conqueror'. The same day he promoted a dozen generals to the rank of field marshal and awarded Göring the unique rank of *Reichsmarschall*, marshal of the Reich. The peace offer provoked no immediate reaction in Britain, but three days later the British Foreign Secretary, Lord Halifax, broadcast rejection over the radio. The following day, at the daily press conference organized by the Propaganda Ministry, an official announced: 'Gentlemen, there will be war.'

DIRECTIVE NO 16, 'OPERATION SEA LION'

The Führer and Supreme Commander of   Führer HQ, July 16 1940
the Armed Forces

Directive No 16

PREPARATIONS FOR THE INVASION OF ENGLAND

As England, in spite of the hopelessness of her military position, has so far shown herself unwilling to come to any compromise, I have therefore decided to begin to prepare for, and if necessary to carry out, an invasion of England. This operation is dictated by the necessity of eliminating Great Britain as a basis from which the war against Germany can be fought, and if necessary, the island will be occupied.

I therefore issue the following orders:

1   The landing operation must be a surprise crossing on a broad front extending approximately from Ramsgate to a point west of the Isle of Wight. Elements of the air force will do the work of the artillery and elements of the navy the work of engineers. I ask each of the fighting services to consider the advantage from their respective point of view of preliminary operations such as the occupation of the Isle of Wight or the Duchy of Cornwall prior to the full-scale invasion, and to inform me of the results of their deliberations. I shall be responsible for the final decision. The preparation for the large-scale invasion must be concluded by the middle of August.

2   The following preparations must be undertaken to make a landing in England possible:
(a) The British air force must be eliminated to such an extent that it will be incapable of putting up any substantial opposition to the invading troops.
(b) The sea routes must be cleared of mines.
(c) Both flanks of the Straits of Dover and the Western Approaches to the Channel, approximately on a line from Alderney to Portland, must be so heavily mined as to be completely inaccessible.
(d) Heavy coastal guns must dominate and protect the entire coastal front area.
(e) It is desirable that the English fleets both in the North Sea and in the Mediterranean should be pinned down (by the Italians in the latter instance), shortly before the crossing takes place; with this aim in view, the naval forces at present in British harbours and coastal waters, should be attacked from the air and by torpedoes.

3   …The invasion will be referred to by the code name 'Sea Lion'…

Signed: Hitler
Initialled: Keitel and Jodl

Source: *Fuehrer Conferences on Naval Affairs, 1939–1945* (Greenhill Books, London, 1990) , p. 116

Above: At five o'clock in the morning of 23 June 1940 Hitler made his sole visit to Paris. He stayed only a short time but was enthusiastic about the architecture. He can be seen here in front of the Eiffel Tower. To his right is Albert Speer, his favourite architect; to his left the SS commander Karl Wolff.

Opposite: On 6 July Hitler led a triumphant march past in Berlin on his return from the Western front and the defeat of France. He can be seen standing in the leading car, with a film crew moving along in front of him. Huge crowds came out to celebrate a victory which they hoped would bring an end to the war.

Hitler turns to Britain

Even before Hitler made his peace offer he had already decided that if the British remained obstinate, there would have to be an invasion. On 16 July he issued War Directive 16 for Operation 'Sea Lion'(*Seelöwe*). This idea had been first suggested on 21 May by the commander-in-chief of the German Navy, Grand Admiral Erich Raeder, in a conference with Hitler. The navy had been preparing contingency plans for invasion since November 1939, but Hitler was not yet convinced that Britain could not be made to accept peace by a combination of political pressure, air attacks and a naval blockade. On 11 July Raeder again raised the question of invasion but Hitler thought it should be 'a last resort'. Four days later, for reasons that remain obscure, he changed his mind and ordered the navy to be ready to mount an invasion from any time after 15 August. The directive issued the following day called for a seaborne landing in Sussex and Kent, but the precondition for any invasion was the elimination of the Royal Air Force as a threat to the operation. Raeder's initial enthusiasm waned as the naval staff assessed the difficulties of the operation with an inadequate surface fleet and little detailed information about the landing sites and minefields in the Channel. Raeder told Hitler that for any chance of success 'complete air superiority' was essential.

There has been much debate over just how serious Hitler was about Operation Sea Lion. His preference was for Britain to voluntarily abandon the war, and to this end he encouraged the indirect strategy of economic blockade. During the summer of 1940 the German navy and air force kept up a relentless assault on British shipping and ports. German aircraft sank 580,000 tons of British shipping in 1940. German submarines, though few in number, began a three-year war of attrition against Atlantic convoys. When sustained air attack began from July onwards, Britain's southern ports became key targets. Much of the subsequent bombing campaign against Britain over the winter of 1940–1 was directed at major trading ports, warehouses and storage facilities. It was assumed, as it had been in the submarine campaign during the First World War, that if a sufficient proportion of British food and raw material imports could be cut off, the British government would be forced to give up the conflict. The German leadership was also keen to exploit German air power, which was regarded as greatly superior to British. The German air force was directed on 1 August 'to destroy the English air force as soon as possible', and then turn its attention to the destruction of British ports and stocks of food. Hitler reserved for himself the decision about whether to invade, and he was willing to do so only if the prospect of a cheap or quick victory could be created by the success of German air power.

The confused nature of German strategy towards Britain was compounded with the emergence over the summer months of a possible new direction for German military ambitions. On 31 July, at a meeting of German commanders in Berchtesgaden (ostensibly to discuss the war against Britain), Hitler announced that he was thinking of launching an all-out attack on the Soviet Union 'to smash the state heavily in one blow'. The idea of a war in the east for German 'living-space' had not been abandoned by Hitler as a result of the German–Soviet Pact. As early as October 1939 Hitler had told a gathering of Party leaders that he was waiting for the right circumstances before turning again to the East. During June 1940, while German forces were completing the defeat of France, the Soviet Union formally annexed the Baltic States and Bessarabia, part of northern Romania. The German army began its own contingency planning in late June for a limited strike against the Red Army, to try to ward off further Soviet encroachments. Hitler now wanted to go much further than this, partly (so he claimed) to end once and for all the menace of Bolshevism hanging over Europe, but also because defeat of the Soviet Union would end any prospect that Britain might be able to secure Soviet support for a continued war effort. Defeat of the Soviet Union came to be seen as a condition for the eventual defeat of the British Empire. Even while the campaign against Britain was beginning, German army planners led by General Friedrich Paulus, later defeated at Stalingrad, began detailed preparation for a war in the east. To match the new priorities, on 28 July Hitler ordered plans for the creation of a 180-division army, with a much enlarged complement of 37 armoured and motorized divisions, to be ready by the spring of 1941.

The mixture of strategic aims evident in the summer of 1940 may well explain the eventual failure either to defeat the Royal Air Force or to create an effective blockade of the British Isles. Hitler ordered the German air force to begin its assault on British air power from 5 August onwards, the exact start date dependent on the weather. Göring ordered his units to destroy the RAF and its organization in southern England in an intensive four-day campaign, but the onset of the assault, codenamed 'Eagle Day' (*Adlertag*), had to be postponed until 13 August because of cloud. The air force was organized in three air fleets; most of the aircraft were stationed in Air Fleets 2 and 3 in Belgium and northern France, a smaller number were based with Air Fleet 5 in Norway. The attack which was finally launched on 13 August was compromised by poor organization and weather, and not until 18 August did heavy attacks on RAF stations begin in earnest. Over the three weeks of intensive counter-force operations there were 53 main attacks on RAF bases and a small number of attacks against radar stations. The idea of defeating the RAF in four days soon proved a fantasy, but by early September German air intelligence, basing estimates on exaggerated reports from German pilots, claimed that there were now only 100 serviceable fighters left. The confident belief that the RAF had been all but eliminated led Göring to order his forces to move on to the second stage of the campaign, with heavy attacks on British economic and military targets and in particular against London. He gave the order on 2 September and it was endorsed by Hitler three days later. The first heavy bombing of London took place on 7 September, when 348 bombers raided the London dock area. Hitler used the excuse of a handful of small raids on Berlin,

Overleaf: A painting of Reich Marshal Hermann Göring (centre, in white) with officers and air ministry officials in the main hall of the Air Ministry on Leipzigerstrasse, Berlin. To his right is Ernst Udet, the head of air force procurement, whose incapacity for the job played an important part in holding up German aircraft production and technical evolution.

225

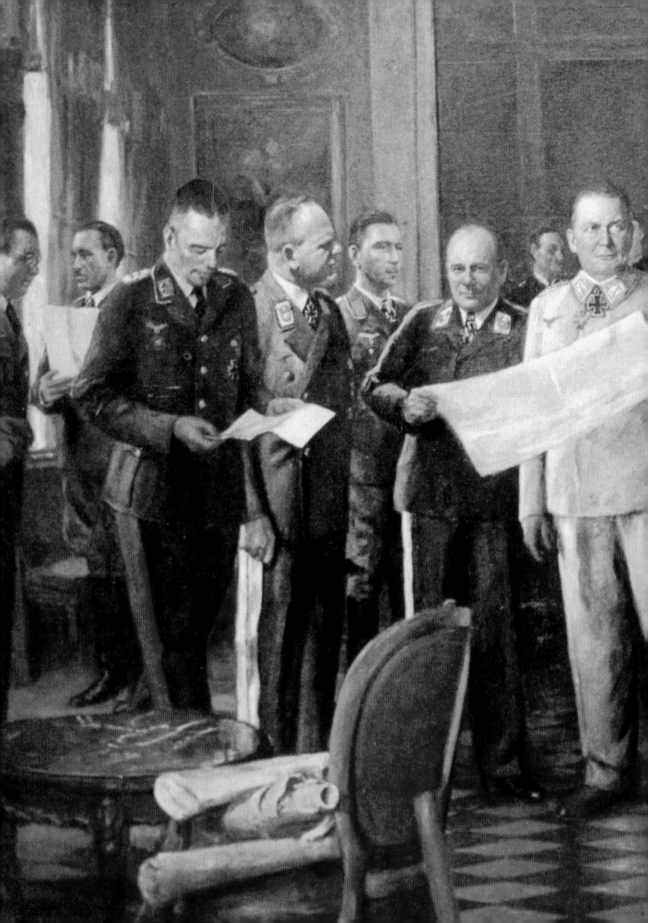

WATCHING THE BATTLE OF BRITAIN

Calais *August 15*

We spend the rest of the afternoon idling on the grass at the edge of the cliff at Cap Gris-Nez. The German bombers and fighters keep thundering over towards Dover. Through field-glasses you can see plainly the Dover cliffs and occasionally even spot an English sausage balloon protecting the harbour. The German bombers, I note, go over in good formation very high, usually about fifteen thousand feet, and return much lower and in bad formation or singly. We keep on the watch for a dogfight, or for a formation of Spitfires to light on the returning German bombers. It's a vain watch. We do not see a British plane all afternoon. Over the Channel to-day the Germans have absolute supremacy. Hugging our side of the coast are German patrol boats, mostly small torpedo craft. They would make easy targets for British planes if any ever ventured over. The sea is calm as glass, and German seaplanes with big red crosses painted on their wings keep alighting and taking off. Their job is to pick up airmen shot down in the Channel. About six p.m. we see sixty bombers – Heinkels and Junker-82's [88's] – protected by a hundred Messerschmitts, winging high overhead towards Dover. In three or four minutes we can hear plainly the British anti-aircraft guns around Dover going into action against them. Judging by the deep roar, the British have a number of heavy *flak* guns. There is another kind of thud, deeper, and one of our officers thinks this comes from bombs falling. In an hour what looks to us like the same bombing squadron returns. We can count only eighteen bombers of the original sixty. Have the British accounted for the rest? It is difficult to tell, because we know the Germans often have orders to return to different fields from those they started from. One reason for doing this apparently is to ensure that the German flyers will not know what their losses are.

Boyer and I keep hoping some Spitfires will show up. But now the sun is turning low. The sea is like glass. The skies quiet. The afternoon on the cliff has seemed more like a bucolic picnic than a day on the front line of the air war. The same unequal struggle that we saw in Belgium and northern France. Not a British plane over, not a bomb dropped.

Source: William Shirer *Berlin Diary: The Journal of a Foreign Correspondent 1934–1941*
(Hamish Hamilton, London, 1941) pp. 372–3

The air force ace Adolf Galland in conversation with other officers. His early successes in combat earned him quick promotion to become General of Fighters in 1942. During the Battle of Britain he raced Helmut Wick and Werner Mölders to become the highest scoring German pilot.

mounted in late August in retaliation for bombing London, to announce in a speech on 4 September that British cities would be obliterated, but this was propaganda. The decision to shift to city-bombing had already been taken in accordance with the schedule for 'Sea Lion', which was now fixed for 15 September.

The new direction in German air strategy, designed to pave the way for invasion two weeks later, was taken in ignorance of the true situation. German pilots were much less inclined to accept the argument that the RAF was close to defeat. Between 8 and 31 August the German air force lost 900 aircraft, including 443 fighters, the heaviest losses yet inflicted. By early September the RAF had more fighter aircraft available than in August, 738 against 672. As a result British air forces were able to impose a heavy toll on German bombers when they shifted to the attack on ports and targets in London. The German air forces lost 298 aircraft in the first week. On 15 September, known later as Battle of Britain Day, a large force of German bombers and fighters attacked London in three waves but lost 25 per cent of the attacking force. The combat that day made it evident not only that the RAF was undefeated, but that the German air force could not sustain losses on that scale. Small daylight attacks continued for some weeks, but the main weight of the bombing campaign shifted to night.

The manifest failure to eliminate British air power finally forced Hitler to postpone 'Sea Lion' until a possible invasion the following year. On 30 August the date was pushed back five days from 15 September; on 6 September Raeder confronted Hitler with the view that invasion should be avoided because air supremacy had not been achieved. On 14 September Hitler assembled the commanders-in-chief to announce that the conditions were not yet ripe for invasion. Three days later he confirmed postponement and on 12 October ordered the armed forces to keep up the appearance of an invasion threat while scaling down all the preparations. He told them that invasion would be reconsidered in the spring if Britain had not been forced to give up by air attack and blockade. Consideration was now given to the idea of destroying Britain's position in the Mediterranean, by gaining Spanish acquiescence in the seizure of Gibraltar, and defeating British Empire forces in North Africa defending the Suez Canal. The German population, which had been buoyed up over the autumn months with news of German victories in the air and the promise of imminent invasion, began to accept the disappointing reality (according to the reports of German home intelligence) that Britain might now survive another winter of the war.

Forging the Axis

While German forces sought a way to subjugate Britain, German leaders were faced with the political challenge of reorganizing the Europe their armies had occupied. In the course of only a few weeks some six states – Denmark, Norway, The Netherlands, Belgium, Luxembourg and France – had been conquered. German leaders had not anticipated this outcome and during the summer and autumn of 1940 began to work out the political shape of what came to be called the 'New Order'. The ambition was not simply to impose a temporary military occupation, but to transform the political geography, economic structure and racial hierarchy of the European continent.

GERMANY'S AXIS ALLIES

Germany did not fight the wars of 1941 entirely alone. Even in 1940 Germany's Italian ally insisted on sending a small contingent of aircraft to fight in the late stages of the Battle of Britain, though it contributed almost nothing. In spring 1941 German armies found themselves fighting alongside Italian in the conquest of Greece, which Italian forces had proved incapable of achieving. For the invasion of the Soviet Union, Hitler ensured that he would have military assistance from some of his new Axis partners. Between November 1940 and March 1941, Hungary, Romania, Slovakia and Bulgaria joined the Tripartite Pact. Bulgaria was the only one not to contribute forces to the invasion of the Soviet Union, though it gave political support. Between them Germany's Axis allies supplied around 690,000 troops, including Finnish forces, which were not linked by treaty with Germany, but served as 'co-belligerents'. Finland wanted to win back the territories lost to the USSR in the 'Winter War' rather than join in the German invasion. The largest components came from Hungary and Romania. Romanian armies served under German Army Group South while Hungarian forces formed part of Army Group Centre. Mussolini also wanted to be included in the campaign despite Hitler's reservations. He sent three divisions of 62,000 men in an Italian expeditionary corps, but in 1942, with greater pressure on the Germans, he increased the contribution to 9 divisions of 230,000 men and reorganised the corps into the Italian 8th Army. The Axis contributions were made partly to increase political influence with Hitler or to gain political advantage, but there was also a fund of powerful anti-communism which drove on the Axis. Later volunteers from Spain as well as other German-occupied countries fought in Russia. But after the defeat in the Stalingrad campaign in late 1942, which hit Romanian, Italian and Hungarian forces hard, the contribution of Germany's Axis partners declined in importance.

In the East the decision had been taken after the defeat of Poland to incorporate Danzig, Polish Silesia and the Warthegau directly into Greater Germany. A rump Polish area, the General Gouvernement, was created out of central Poland, administered by the leader of the National Socialist lawyers' association, Hans Frank, with its capital in Cracow. In the West Luxembourg was absorbed into the Reich as well as Alsace-Lorraine and the small areas of southern Belgium annexed from Germany in 1919. German commissioners were appointed to run Norway and The Netherlands, and German authorities installed in Denmark to oversee the work of a Danish government. Belgium and the northern and western areas of France were declared zones of military occupation, leaving a small independent French state south of the River Loire, with its capital at Vichy. Thousands of German officials and security men were sent out into the occupied areas to organize the exploitation of European resources and to run an apparatus of repression against all forms of resistance.

Hitler and the Spanish dictator Francisco Franco inspect a guard of honour at the frontier town of Hendaye, between France and Spain, on 23 October 1940. Hitler hoped to be able to recruit Franco for the Axis cause in return for the help given by Germany during the Civil War, but Franco refused.

To give international backing to the idea of the German New Order, German diplomats worked during September to create a firm Axis alliance with Italy and Japan. Following extensive negotiations in Tokyo, a Pact was formally signed in Berlin on 27 September 1940. Usually known as the Tri-Partite Pact, the principal terms were a mutual agreement to respect Germany and Italy's right to construct a New Order in Europe and the Japanese right to do the same in Asia. The three states agreed to co-operate in the construction of the New Orders 'with all political, economic and military means', though in reality there was little assistance given in either direction, neither in 1940 nor during the years that followed. Once it was signed, German leaders tried to get other European states to associate themselves as allies of Germany by adhering to the Pact. On 20 November, in a ceremony in Vienna attended by Hitler himself, Hungary signed the treaty, marking a clear commitment to the Axis cause. On 23 November Romania joined and a day later Slovakia. Both these states were closely tied to German interests already through trade agreements and military assistance. On 1 March the following year, Bulgaria also joined the Pact, creating a solid bloc of German-dominated states across Eastern Europe.

Hitler hoped to be able to extend the network of alliances in the west as well. It was important for the Mediterranean strategy outlined in the autumn to win the collaboration of Vichy France and Spain, now ruled by Francisco Franco, victor in the Spanish civil war. On 23 October Hitler met Franco on the Spanish–French border at Hendaye in an attempt to persuade him to allow German troops to cross Spanish territory to capture Gibraltar. After hours of fruitless negotiation, Franco remained adamantly opposed to anything that compromised Spanish neutrality. Hitler later complained that he would prefer to have his teeth extracted than ever to negotiate again with Franco. The following day he met Marshal Pétain and the French prime minister, Pierre Laval, at Montoire but once again left empty-handed after trying to convince the French leaders that they should join a German alliance system directed against the British Empire. A third attempt was made with the Soviet Union to see if Stalin could be tempted to join the Pact and direct Soviet energies to undermining the British Empire in India instead of insisting on further demands in Europe. On 13 October an invitation was sent to the Soviet foreign minister, Vyacheslav Molotov, to come to Berlin and on 12 November he arrived for a state visit. Ribbentrop invited the Soviet side to divert their interests to India and the Persian Gulf, but Molotov made it clear that the Soviet Union was interested in possible military bases in Bulgaria and Turkey, Soviet control of the mouth of the River Danube and of the Dardanelles Strait between the Black Sea and the Mediterranean. He left two days later without agreement. On 25 November Stalin wrote to Hitler spelling out Soviet conditions for joining the Tri-Partite Pact but Hitler refused to reply.

German efforts to construct an alliance system to bring about the isolation and defeat of the British Empire failed to pay off. During November and December Hitler issued directives for detailed operational preparations for the seizure of Gibraltar (Operation Felix), for possible occupation of Vichy France in case France collaborated with Britain (Operation Attila), and for possible assistance to Italian forces in the Balkans and North Africa (Operation Marita). The third of these directives, issued on 13 December, was a consequence of the

WAR DIRECTIVE NO 21 'CASE BARBAROSSA'

Führer Headquarters, 18 12 1940

Directive No. 21 'Case Barbarossa'

The German Armed Forces must be prepared, even before the conclusion of the war against England, *to crush Soviet Russia in a rapid campaign* ('Case Barbarossa').

The *Army* will have to employ all available formations to this end, with the reservation that occupied territories must be insured against surprise attacks.

The *Air Force* will have to make available for this Eastern campaign supporting forces of such strength that the Army will be able to bring land operations to a speedy conclusion and that Eastern Germany will be as little damaged as possible by enemy air attack. The build-up of a focal point in the East will be limited only by the need to protect from air attack the whole combat and arsenal area which we control, and to ensure that attacks on England, and especially upon her imports, are not allowed to lapse.

The main efforts of the *Navy* will continue to be directed against England even during the Eastern campaign.

In certain circumstances I shall issue orders for the *deployment* against Soviet Russia eight weeks before the operation is timed to begin.

Preparations which require more time than this will be put in hand now, in so far as this has not already been done, and will be concluded by 15 May 1941.

It is of decisive importance that our intention to attack should not be known.

Source: H. Trevor-Roper (ed) *Hitler's War Directives 1939–1945* (Sidgwick and Jackson, London, 1964), pp. 93–4

Opposite above: Hitler greeted by the Italian dictator Benito Mussolini at the Brenner Pass on the Austrian-Italian border on 4 October 1940. The two men met to discuss future developments in Axis strategy, including the possibility of getting Vichy France to join the Axis war effort. Hitler told Mussolini nothing about his future plan against the Soviet Union, and Mussolini told Hitler nothing about his planned attack on Greece, scheduled for a few weeks later, on 28 October.

Opposite below: An informal reception in the Hotel Kaiserhof for the Soviet foreign minister, Vyacheslav Molotov, during his state visit to Berlin in November 1940. Molotov (left) is in conversation with Wilhelm Frick, minister of the interior. On the settee are Joachim von Ribbentrop (left) and Heinrich Himmler (right). Despite the many good intentions expressed, Molotov's request to expand the terms of the German–Soviet pact was refused.

decision by Mussolini to invade Greece on 28 October, taken without consulting Hitler. Italian forces immediately found themselves in difficulty and although Hitler was unhappy that he had been left in the dark about Italian intentions, he regarded the subsequent British intervention in Greece as a further threat. He held back from the decision to assist Mussolini in order to see whether Italian forces would succeed in dislodging Britain from Egypt and defeating Greece. But the Greek campaign complicated his calculations and finally exposed the failure of German endeavours to get a combined German–Italian–Spanish initiative to expel Britain from the Mediterranean. On 7 December Franco confirmed that Spain would not join the Axis war effort. At the end of December Hitler put the strategy on hold and turned attention to the plans for the Soviet Union. On 18 December he signed directive no 21, 'Case Barbarossa', named after the mediaeval German emperor, Frederick I. The directive anticipated a single massive blow to annihilate Soviet resistance in a matter of weeks. The object was to occupy the Russian area along the AA-Line, from Archangel in the far north to Astrakhan at the mouth of the Volga in the south. What was left of Russia would be cooped up in Siberia to eke out a primitive existence.

Bombing Britain into Submission

While Hitler sought an alternative route to defeat Britain, the German air force was left to fight the campaign against Britain on its own. On 14 September, with 'Sea Lion' virtually postponed, Hitler gave the air force the opportunity to see whether or not 'ceaseless air attacks' might provoke British capitulation on their own. The air force chief-of-staff, Col. General Hans Jeschonnek, asked for permission to begin attacks with the object of creating mass panic in the British urban population, but Hitler insisted that targets should have some ostensible economic and military sense, reserving for himself the decision of whether or not to launch terror attacks.

To the British the German bombing campaign, which was christened the 'Blitz' (short for *Blitzkrieg*), seemed to be based largely on imposing terror, but there was a pattern to German operations. Greatest emphasis was laid on attacks against ports where stocks of food and materials could be destroyed, along with the shipping designed to transport more. The heaviest bombing was against the ports of London, Plymouth, Southampton, Portsmouth, Hull, Liverpool and Bristol. In addition, attacks were made against major industrial targets, with special emphasis on the aircraft industry. This was the object of one of the best-known raids, against Coventry on the night of 14/15 November, which resulted in the deaths of 554 people. German air force leaders found it difficult to grasp the strategic worth of the campaign, which was fought at night in deteriorating weather conditions. Over 600 aircraft were lost, many

A German artist's impression of the bombing of London during the Blitz of 1940–41. In the background is Tower Bridge while overhead fly Junkers Ju-88 medium bombers. By the end of 1940 the bombing had cost 27,450 dead, principally from attacks on ports and port towns in an attempt to blockade Britain into surrender.

through accidents, while the effect on British production was only very temporary and the effect on morale largely counter-productive, despite the death of 43,000 civilians. Goebbels, together with much of the German public at which he directed his propaganda, remained confident that bombing was a war-winning weapon, 'When will Churchill capitulate?' he wrote in his diary in November. On 11 December he heard Hitler tell a rally of Party leaders that the war was as good as won: 'England is isolated. Will bit by bit be driven to the ground.'

In reality bombing only hardened British resolve, alienated much of American opinion and demoralized the crews assigned to carry it out. When in November 1940 German radio navigation beams were successfully blocked by the work of British scientific intelligence, bombing became less accurate. To maximize the effect achieved by small medium bombers with modest payloads, larger quantities of incendiaries were carried. On 29 December major fires were started in the port and city of London, ending the year with a destructive flourish. For the German population news of the bombing attacks was tempered by the growing evidence of British bombing of Germany. The first British attack was against the city of Mönchengladbach in May 1940, and intermittent attacks continued over the summer and autumn. Although the attacks were generally inaccurate and the attacking force small, the war was brought back to the German people, who remembered Göring's earlier boast that no Allied aircraft would breach German airspace. In 1940 and 1941 the German air force dropped 58,000 tons on British targets, but during the same period RAF Bomber Command dropped 50,000 tons on European targets. The failure to invade Britain, and the growing toll from British air attacks, left the German public at the end of the year with a more ambiguous view of victory in 1940 than had seemed likely in July.

1941 Balkan Interlude

Once Hitler had decided that the campaign against the Soviet Union was the main priority for 1941, he spent much of the following few months secluded at the Berghof in Berchtesgaden. There he received a stream of military visitors reporting on the state of preparations, and of foreign diplomats and politicians keen to secure a position in the new German-dominated Europe. On 13 and 14 January he met Tsar Boris of Bulgaria and the Romanian leader, Marshal Ion Antonescu, both of whom were told about the impending campaign against Russia. Antonescu pledged Romanian support but Boris was reluctant to be drawn, retaining a position of non-belligerence throughout the subsequent campaign. A few days later Mussolini and the Italian foreign minister, Count Galeazzo Ciano, visited Hitler to discuss the Mediterranean strategy. During the visit, on 19/20 January 1941, Hitler confirmed that Germany would come to the aid of Italian forces in Greece and in North Africa, where they faced defeat. At this time he did not tell his Axis partner about the planned Eastern campaign. Yet the promise to Mussolini locked Hitler into a Balkan commitment which threatened to undermine the planned preparation of the great offensive against the Soviet Union, scheduled for May.

Hitler had decided in December 1940 that it might be necessary to stabilize the Mediterranean theatre before moving East. On 11 January he signed directive 22, Operation 'Sunflower' (*Sonnenblume*), to begin a programme of German assistance. A German air unit,

LISTENING TO HITLER:
AN AMERICAN AT THE SPORTPALAST, JANUARY 30 1941

Murmurs ran through the crowd. A military band blared forth. Storm Troopers with shining helmets came through the rear doors, marching to the stage, and took their places beneath the golden eagle. After them came colour-bearers in the tan uniforms of the Nazi Party, some of then carrying stiff standards on long steel poles, others with flying Nazi banners. I was seeing the pageantry of the Nazi Reich.

The crowd rose and cheered as the leaders of the party and the military marched in. There were the bemedalled generals, von Brauchitsch, Keitel, Jodl, and others, moving proudly in the lead. Then big bulky Göring in a resplendent sky-blue uniform, smiling broadly. Little Goebbels hobbled in, paying slight attention to the people around him. Himmler, with his spectacles, small nose and trim moustache, looked more like a bookkeeper than the leader of the dread Gestapo. There, too, were black-browed Hess, Dr. Ley, and finally Hitler himself.

Der Führer walked rigidly, turning slightly to left and right, with one hand stiffly by his side and the other raised diffidently before him in the party salute. He never raised his hand as high as the others. Hitler was far from pretentious. I thought he looked like many a Nazi waiter I had seen. He wore his grey trench coat and peaked cap and was dressed with less show than any of his fellows. I noted that he had a curious little smile. I remarked about it. One of the Nazis near me said it was unusual.

'Der Führer smiles seldom,' he said. 'He must be feeling good to-day.'

The crowd broke into party songs, ending with shouts of 'Heil Hitler!' The place was in pandemonium. Hitler took a seat in the front row on the platform, his arms outstretched on the table before him. Goebbels stood up. In the ringing kind of oratory in which each sentence swells to a climax, he said the German people had decided eight years ago to stand as one man behind the Führer and march with him no matter what came.

At that the crowd was on its feet again, cheering with all its power as Hitler strode to the centre of the platform, stood for a moment before them, and then began to speak. His voice was at first a slow, low rumble. As he went on, he became more emotional. His words suddenly took on vehemence, his arms swept in wide gestures. He clenched his fists and held on to the end of his sentences. With each climax the crowd applauded; some sustained an 'Oooooooh,' which I finally recognized as a kind of 'Bravo!' and some stamped. I looked at the Storm Troopers on the aisles. Many of them were taking no part in the demonstrations. Apparently Hitler was actually moving the crowd to frenzy. I watched closer as he went on, and was finally assured of the hypnotic power the man had in his oratory. At the same time I could not help realizing that Charlie Chaplin had imitated Hitler perfectly in *The Great Dictator*. He had caught the poses just as they were, the long monotonous periods, in the midst of which Hitler would suddenly throw himself into a whirlwind of words and gestures and then as quickly subside again. The picture was perfect.

Source: Harry W. Flannery *Assignment to Berlin* (Michael Joseph, London, 1942), pp. 107-8. Flannery succeeded William Shirer as CBS correspondent in Berlin in October 1940.

Fliegerkorps X, had already been transferred to Sicily to help the campaign against Malta and British shipping. On 12 February he appointed General Rommel, hero of the tank war in France, as overall commander of a German Afrika Korps, stretching German commitments even further. Although nominally under the direction of Italian theatre commanders, German forces acted with increasing independence, until the balance of power between the two sides came to reflect the military reality of German competence and Italian disorganization. Rommel immediately set out to stabilize the North African front. In defiance of orders from Berlin, he launched an attack on 24 March against British Commonwealth forces and drove them back across Libya. Tobruk was placed under siege on 11 April, and despite a visit from General Paulus with orders to instruct Rommel to hold the line, he continued to advance until he reached the Egyptian border by mid-June, threatening the Suez Canal.

This still left the problem of the Greek campaign, where significant British Commonwealth reinforcements continued to arrive. The German plan was to send forces into Bulgaria and invade Greece from the north-east, with German troops beginning to cross the Bulgarian frontier on 2 March. Two days later Hitler met Prince Paul of Yugoslavia, who agreed to join the Tri-Partite Pact on condition that his country would not have to join in the invasion of Greece. On 25 March Yugoslavia's adherence to the pact was marked by a further ceremony in Vienna, in Hitler's presence. But two days later the Yugoslav government was overthrown in a Serb-backed coup and the Pact repudiated. An angry Hitler immediately ordered military preparations for an invasion of Yugoslavia as an extension of Operation Marita against Greece. The operation was improvised in a remarkably short period of time, and on 6 April the campaign opened with a devastating bombing raid on the Yugoslav capital, Belgrade. The same

THE GERMAN CAPTURE OF CRETE, MAY 1941

As German forces moved into place for the expected invasion of the Soviet Union, the conflict in the Mediterranean, triggered by Hitler's insistence on occupying Yugoslavia and helping Mussolini to pacify Greece, continued to absorb German energies. The final operation was among the most difficult of the Mediterranean campaign, a combined arms operation to seize the Greek island of Crete from the British Commonwealth forces that had retreated there at the end of April 1941. The main task was given to General Kurt Student, the pioneer of modern parachute forces, who led his airborne troops to success in Norway and the invasion of Belgium in spring 1940. The island of Crete held around 35,000 Allied forces, including some of the Greek army. They outnumbered the attacking Germans by a wide margin but lacked heavy equipment or sufficient airpower. On 20 May 1941 German paratroopers landed on the island but suffered very heavy casualties. By the following day the airfield at Maleme was in German hands and it proved possible to fly in Ju52 transports with the German 5th Mountain Division. The division's commander, General Julius Ringel, replaced Student, who had disappointed Hitler by losing so many men in the opening assault. Over the following week German numbers rose to 17,500. This proved enough to defeat scattered and increasingly demoralized Allied soldiers and on 31 May the New Zealand commander, Lt General Bernard Freyberg, completed the evacuation of all but 5,000 Allied men. This marked the final domination of Continental Europe by the Axis powers. However, Student's elite force suffered 1,653 dead and total German casualties on Crete exceeded all the casualties from the Balkan campaign. The loss of almost 200 transport aircraft also hampered the early stages of the Russian campaign. Hitler refused to let Student undertake major paratrooper operations again and he ended the war as a ground commander in Eastern Germany.

Opposite left: German heavy artillery wait to cross into Yugoslavia during the lightning campaign 'Operation Marita' on 6 April 1941. The Yugoslav army, though numerically large, was unable to cope with the fast-moving German forces and the heavy air attacks mounted, and surrendered by 18 April.

Opposite right: The commander of Einsatzgruppe D during the invasion of the Soviet Union, SS Brigade Leader Dr Otto Ohlendorf. He was one of many SS leaders with an academic background and qualification, and he later became an official in the Economics Ministry. His group carried out approximately 90,000 executions in the first year of its activity.

THE CRIMINAL ORDERS, MAY 1941

The Führer and Commander in Chief   Headquarters, 13 May 1941

Decree concerning the implementation of Wartime Military Jurisdiction in the area of Operation 'Barbarossa' and specific measures undertaken by the troops.

The jurisdiction of the German Armed Forces serves in the first instance to maintain the *discipline of the men*.

The further extension of the area of operations in the East, the consequent way in which this determines the conduct of the war and the particular characteristics of the enemy, place tasks before the Wehrmacht military courts which during the course of operations and until the pacification of the conquered territories may only be solved with the limited numbers of personnel when military jurisdiction is restricted, for the time being, to its main tasks. This is only possible if *the troops themselves* relentlessly struggle against every threat posed by the enemy civilian population.

Accordingly, the following guidelines are specified for the 'Barbarossa' operational area (combat zone, Army Rear Area and area of civilian government):

I

Treatment of Punishable Acts Against Enemy Civilians.

1 *Punishable acts against civilian persons* are placed outside the jurisdiction of courts martial and field courts martial, until further notice.

2 *Irregulars* are to be mercilessly executed in battle or on the run.

3 All *other attacks by enemy civilian persons against the Wehrmacht*, its members and its attendants are to be silenced on the spot by the most extreme methods, until the attackers have been exterminated.

4 Whosoever fails to implement measures of this kind, or else is unwilling to do so, will be regarded as *suspect and immediately taken before an officer. This officer shall decide whether he is to be executed*. Against *localities* from which the Wehrmacht is attacked in a treacherous or underhand manner, *collective reprisal measures*, authorised by an officer of at least the rank of battalion commander, are immediately to be carried out if the circumstances do not allow the swift seizure of individual culprits.

5   It is *expressly forbidden* to safeguard suspected culprits in order to hand them over to the courts in the event of the reintroduction of jurisdiction covering civilian persons.

6   The Supreme Commander of the Army Group is able, in agreement with the responsible commanders of the air force and the navy, to *reintroduce military jurisdiction regarding civilian persons* where the area is sufficiently pacified.

II

Treatment of Punishable Acts by Members of the Wehrmacht and its attendants against the Civilian Population.

1   There exists *no obligation* to punish offences committed by *members of the Wehrmacht* and its attendants against *hostile civilian persons*, even if the act at the same time is a military crime or offence.

2   In the event of judgements of such acts it is to be borne in mind in any trial that the collapse of 1918, the subsequent period of suffering on the part of the German people and the struggle against National Socialism – with the many blood sacrifices made by the movement – can be traced to Bolshevik influence: and no German should forget this.....

Source: Theo Schulte *The German Army and Nazi Policies in Occupied Russia* (Berg, Oxford, 1989), document c, pp. 321–2

day Field Marshal Wilhelm List's 12th German Army crossed into Greece and southern Yugoslavia, and two days later a full-scale invasion was mounted from the north by German, Italian and Hungarian forces. By 12 April they had reached Belgrade, with Yugoslavia capitulating six days later, its army of more than a million men having inflicted just 151 deaths on the invading Germans. The Axis armies continued on into Greece, which was forced to surrender on 23 April while British Commonwealth troops were evacuated to Crete.

The effect of the Balkan and Mediterranean campaigns was to divert both resources and time away from the planned invasion of the Soviet Union. These preparations dominated Germany's war effort in the first months of the year. It proved impossible to fulfil the requirement for 37 armoured and motorized divisions, but there were many more available than there had been for the Battle of France (30 in total). The assumption among German military commanders was that the Soviet armed forces were unprepared for a major attack and were tactically and technically inferior to their German enemy, though considerably larger. In April 1941 General Günther Blumentritt told the German General Staff that the Red Army would be defeated in two weeks; the Army commander-in-chief, Field Marshal Walter von Brauchitsch, estimated 'up to four weeks'. The enemy was regarded as racially inferior, 'ill-educated, half-Asiatic' as Blumentritt put it. Much emphasis was laid on the element of surprise and as a result the first waves of German army divisions were transferred to the east in stages between February and May, to try to conceal the scale of the movement. The major strike force of armoured divisions, and most of the attack aircraft, arrived only in June 1941, shortly before the launch of the campaign. Until the third week of May German bombers were still attacking targets in Britain nightly.

Once Hitler had made up his mind to destroy the Soviet Union he wanted to fight a war of complete annihilation against an enemy which he regarded as a living manifestation of the Jewish–Marxist threat. In a speech to the generals on 30 March 1941, he explained that the coming conflict was a clash of ideologies so extreme that it had to be fought as a 'war of extermination'. Over the following months there issued from Hitler's Supreme Headquarters a string of directives generally known today by the collective title 'the criminal orders'. Hitler wanted to free the hands of his soldiers and security troops from any moral or legal scruples they might have about exterminating the enemy.

On 13 May he issued a directive on 'Special Measures to be taken by the troops' which freed them from any legal redress if they committed crimes against Soviet soldiers or civilians, encouraging the most extreme acts of retaliation; on 19 May he issued 'Guidelines for the Conduct of Troops in Russia', which gave them the freedom to take ruthless measures against 'Bolshevik agitators, irregulars, saboteurs and Jews'; on 6 June final guidelines were issued to allow soldiers to shoot out-of-hand Soviet political commissars working with the Red Army.

At the same time Heinrich Himmler, as head of Reich security, was granted special powers by Hitler on 13 March to establish the necessary security measures in the conquered areas on his own authority, and on 28 April the army high command was told that Himmler would recruit special security units operating behind the German front line to root out and destroy anti-German elements. These units, known as *Einsatzgruppen*, were recruited from security

SINKING THE *BISMARCK*, MAY 1941

The *Bismarck* was Germany's largest battleship in the Second World War. Named after Germany's famous 'Iron Chancellor', the 41,000-ton ship was launched on 14 February 1939 and commissioned into the German Navy on 24 August 1940. The German Navy commander-in-chief, Grand Admiral Erich Raeder, planned in the late 1930s the construction of a large ocean-going fleet to help restore Germany to world power. In reality the time had passed for the traditional fleet with the advent of the aeroplane. Germany failed to develop aircraft carriers or an effective marine aviation. The *Bismarck*, pride of the German Navy, was destroyed in May 1941 thanks to a single small aircraft. The plan was to use the battleship, together with other major naval units, including the new battle cruisers *Gneisenau* and *Scharnhorst*, as a striking force against Allied shipping in the Atlantic sealanes. These two ships were damaged and the brand-new *Tirpitz* battleship was not yet ready, so *Bismarck* sailed from Norway towards the Atlantic on 18 May 1941 accompanied only by the cruiser *Prinz Eugen*. The senior officer of what was called Operation Rhine-Exercise was Vice-Admiral Günther Lütjens, Fleet Commander of German battle cruisers, noted for his hostility towards National Socialism. He was not confident about the operation and within days his force had been sighted and engaged by British ships. On 24 May, in the Denmark Strait, *Bismarck* succeeded in sinking HMS *Hood* and damaging the new Royal Navy battleship, *Prince of Wales,* but sustained enough damage to slow the speed of the ship. Lütjens set sail for the coast of German-occupied France for essential repairs. The ship managed to avoid detection until 26 May, when following a lengthy radio signal from the German commander a Catalina flying boat spotted it moving towards France and the safety of German air cover. A Swordfish torpedo-bomber from the aircraft carrier HMS *Ark Royal* crippled the battleship's steering equipment and the following morning Royal Navy battleships HMS *Rodney* and *King George V* moved in for the kill. The *Bismarck* sank at 10.39 in the morning, with the loss of all but 115 of her 2,222-man crew. Later research on the wreck suggested that she had been scuttled by the German crew. The loss of the *Bismarck* confirmed that the days of the old-fashioned battle fleet were over. *Bismarck* had been sighted by aircraft and crippled by a small biplane, testament to the changing balance of power between ships and aircraft.

Overleaf: A painting by Claus Bergen of the last moments of the German battleship *Bismarck*, which sank on 27 May 1941 off the French coast.

policemen, SD officers and the Waffen-SS (Armed SS) to act as mobile killing squads. For the coming conflict four groups were created, with a total of 3,000 men. Himmler also had a further task which he and his staff worked on over the months before Barbarossa. Under the title General Plan East (*Generalplan Ost*), Himmler's staff of experts drew up proposals for the racial, economic and geographical remodelling of the whole area planned for German conquest and colonization. The most radical element of the plan was the decision to deport up to 30 million Slavs (including 80 per cent of all Poles) to Siberia in order to free up territory for German colonizers and reduce pressure on food supplies. Here it was hoped many would starve to death. All of these plans and orders were based on the principle of racial superiority. Hitler wanted to carve out a permanent German empire in the east: 'Russia,' he told colleagues, 'will be our India.'

Operation 'Barbarossa'

Hitler had originally hoped to launch the war against the Soviet Union in May 1941, but the Balkan crisis and the slow pace of preparation forced him to postpone the attack beyond the start of good summer weather. On 30 April he finally set the date for the start of the operation as 22 June. Despite numerous intelligence warnings about the impending attack, Stalin feared to provoke the Germans and refused to take any major mobilization measures. A few German soldiers with communist sympathies defected to the Soviet side shortly before the opening of the campaign, but Stalin regarded their statements as so much deliberate misinformation. At 3.00 on the morning of Sunday 22 June German aircraft began a wave of attacks against Soviet airfields, destroying hundreds of planes where they stood, uncamouflaged and in the open. At dawn a vast invasion force of 4 million men, including 650,000 from Germany's allies and co-belligerents, moved forward in three huge army groups, north, centre and south. This was the largest invasion in history.

The initial success of the invasion was almost complete. Some Red Army units defended stubbornly at the frontier but the German operational plan, as in France, was to push forward rapidly with large armoured formations, strongly supported by fighters and dive-bombers, to punch holes in the enemy line and then draw the pincers shut in great encircling movements. Soviet units were quickly overrun and Soviet commanders lost control of the battlefield. Primitive tactics, poor communication and the rapid loss of air superiority allowed Axis forces to advance swiftly in the north and centre, though more slowly in the south where a large Romanian force fought alongside their German allies. By the end of June Army Group North under Field Marshal Wilhelm von Leeb had crossed Lithuania, reaching the Latvian capital of Riga on 1 July. By 19 August the advance armoured divisions had reached the outskirts of Leningrad, which was placed under full siege a few weeks later. To the south, Field Marshal Fedor von Bock's Army Group Centre made even more rapid progress, crossing eastern Poland and encircling the Belorussian capital of Minsk by 28 June. Army Group South, commanded by Field Marshal Gerd von Rundstedt, made slower progress but was approaching the Ukrainian capital of Kiev by mid-July, and by 5 August laid siege to Odessa on the Black Sea.

A GERMAN SOLDIER ON THE EASTERN FRONT, JULY 1941

Vitebsk

Great destruction. Stench of corpses.

In and around Vitebsk around 80 or 100 destroyed Russian tanks.

Tanks lie piled up.

Already many more prisoners. They arrive in crowds.

The mass of loutish civilians also retreat in heaps.

Often those who have been made homeless press on past us.

One sees the strangest combination of things.

The houses are without exception built out of wood.

The people live worse than cattle do with us.

France is gold by comparison.

Russians are great crooks. Everywhere plundering of shops and houses. Our further march leads us on 17.7.41 directly past the burning Dimitrov north of Smolensk...

17.07.1941

Dear Mother!,

I am lying here right in front of the tent I've just made, here you will get a few quick lines from me. If we have had no sleep recently, I have been able to sleep again last night so well. It's really going well for me here. The heat has eased up. The Russians are in retreat.

For today a brief but heartfelt greeting from your Hans-Albert

Source: Konrad Elmshäuser, Jan Lokers (eds) 'Man muss hier nur hart sein...': Kriegsbriefe und Bilder einer Familie (1934–1945) (Edition Temmen, Bremen, 1999), pp. 96–99. Diary entries for Hans-Albert Giese and letter from Giese to his mother, 17 July 1941.

There was a rising sense of euphoria on the German side as the scale of its success gradually emerged. On 23 June Hitler had gone to his new headquarters built in a wood near Rastenburg in East Prussia, codenamed Wolf's Lair (*Wolfsschanze*). Here his staff brought him daily reports of the Axis forces' progress. The army chief-of-staff, Franz Halder, wrote in his war diary in early July that the campaign 'has been won in two weeks' and expected Soviet resistance to gradually evaporate. Within weeks most of the Red Air Force in the West (some 10,000 aircraft) had been destroyed and by the autumn 90 per cent of Soviet tank strength was lost. Over 5 million Soviet soldiers were killed, wounded or taken prisoner. Hitler was confident that the victory he had predicted was about to materialize, announcing on 8 July that he would raze Leningrad and Moscow to the ground to prevent them ever becoming centres of anti-German resistance. So sure was Hitler that the Soviet Union was doomed that on 14 July he set out new production priorities for the German armed forces, giving preference to the air force and the navy for the conflict against the British Empire and an increasingly less neutral United States. To his evening entourage he elaborated his ideas for a post-war German empire in which fast motorways crossed the broad Russian steppe bringing German tourists and holidaymakers to the Crimean coast, while a firm German frontier was set up along the Ural Mountains.

In reality the war was far from over. Despite their losses the Red Army fought with a dogged resistance, imposing 550,000 casualties on Axis forces by the end of September, by far the highest casualties so far sustained in two years of warfare. The long distances and difficult supply lines slowed down the German advance, but did not halt it. On 30 July Hitler decided to stall Army Group Centre and concentrate on clearing the northern and southern flanks. The drive to the south-east into the Ukraine was motivated in large part by the rich industrial and agricultural resources of the region which Hitler wanted to secure before inflicting the final blow against Moscow. Army Group South pushed on into the Ukraine and by 15 September had encircled Kiev and a Soviet force of 650,000 men. Three days later the Ukrainian capital fell and the way was open to occupy the southern industrial belt. On 6 September Hitler ordered Army Group Centre to prepare to move on Moscow later in the month, and on 30 September Guderian's armoured forces began the drive towards the Russian capital and the prospect of final victory. Operation 'Typhoon' (as it was

---

Opposite above: German vehicles, soldiers and supply wagons cross the Soviet border near Urinov-Sokal four days after the start of the invasion, on 26 June 1941. The German army went into the campaign with over 700,000 horses, which were needed to carry supplies, pull artillery pieces and help in extracting heavy vehicles from the Russian mud.

Opposite below: A Russian peasant woman outside her burning farmhouse during the early stages of the German invasion of the Soviet Union. German forces destroyed any villages where they suspected there was partisan or militia activity. The Soviet Union claimed in 1945 that 70,000 villages had been destroyed during the course of the war.

known) was formally launched on 2 October. The following day Hitler travelled by train to Berlin to give his first public speech since the opening of the campaign. In the Berlin Palace of Sport, in front of a rapturous audience, he announced that the Soviet dragon was now slain 'and would never rise again'; the same evening he returned to his headquarters. On 9 October he instructed his press chief, Otto Dietrich, to summon an international press conference in the Propaganda Ministry. 'Hitler', Dietrich later recalled, 'was firmly convinced that the war was as good as over'. The following day in Berlin, in front of a giant map of the Soviet Union displaying the German front line deep in Soviet territory, Dietrich told the assembled journalists that the war was about to end: German forces were drawing tighter the final encirclement around the remnants of the Red Army. German newspapers carried banner headlines the following day: 'Campaign in East Decided! The Great Hour has Struck!'

German troops cross a border river on 22 June 1941 as part of the invasion of the Soviet Union codenamed 'Barbarossa'. They achieved almost total surprise and were able to penetrate rapidly through the incomplete 'Stalin Line' fortifications.

HITLER ON HITLER: TABLE TALK OCTOBER 1941

Night of 13–14 October, 1941

I've acquired the habit of avoiding every kind of vexation, once evening has come – otherwise I wouldn't be able to free myself from it all night…

At present I spend about ten hours a day thinking about military matters. The resulting orders are a matter of half an hour, or three-quarters of an hour. But first of all every operation has to be studied and thought over at length. It sometimes takes up to six months for the thought to be elaborated and made precise. Doubtless the time will come when I shall no longer concern myself with the war on the Eastern front, for it will be only a matter of carrying out what has been already foreseen and ordered. Thus, while these operations are being completed, I shall be able to devote my mind to other problems.

What is fortunate for me is that I know how to relax. Before going to bed I spend some time on architecture, I look at pictures, I take an interest in things entirely different from those that have been occupying my mind throughout the day. Otherwise I wouldn't be able to sleep.

What would happen to me if I didn't have around me men whom I completely trust, to do the work for which I can't find time? Hard men, who act as energetically as I would do myself. For me the best man is the man who removes the most from my shoulders, the man who can take 95 per cent of the decisions in my place. Of course, there are always cases in which I have to take the final decision myself.

I couldn't say whether my feeling that I am indispensable has been strengthened during this war. One thing is certain, that without me the decisions to which we to-day owe our existence would not have been taken.

Source: Hugh Trevor-Roper (ed.) *Hitler's Table Talk 1941–44* (Weidenfeld, London, 1973), pp. 56–8

The Final Solution

The first weeks of the campaign in the Soviet Union coincided with the formal decision to try to find a 'final solution' – *Endlösung* – to the 'Jewish question'. On 31 July a directive was sent to Reinhard Heydrich, head of the Reich Security Main Office and Himmler's deputy, giving him the responsibility for solving once and for all the question of what to do with the Jewish populations of Germany and occupied Europe. Though the document bore Göring's signature, it was drafted in the Gestapo office for Jewish affairs and then given to Göring to sign. The object was to provide a clear administrative chain-of-command for an issue of central importance to the National Socialist leadership.

The document came at the end of a confused period in the regime's treatment of the Jewish populations under German control. In the east Jews were forcibly driven into overcrowded ghettos, their economic resources confiscated or stolen. In November 1940 Hitler approved the idea of deporting Jews from the eastern German and Polish territories to the rump Polish Generalgouvernement. Hans Frank, its German ruler, objected to the idea that his territory should become a Jewish reservation. Arguments continued into the spring and summer of 1941 about what to do with the surplus Jewish population. In the course of the defeat of France yet another possibility had been opened up. Following Himmler's suggestion on 25 May 1940 that Europe's Jews could be deported to an African colony, Hitler became briefly enthusiastic about the idea of sending 4 million European Jews to the French island colony of Madagascar. Here they could be held hostage under German control or decimated by disease and hunger. But the evident difficulty of shipping large numbers of Jews through waters still patrolled by the Royal Navy soon led to the abandonment of the idea. But for the next year the object was still to find some destination for the Jews where they could be deported as a whole, to leave a Europe cleansed of the Jewish menace (*judenrein*). In January 1941 Hitler finally authorized Heydrich and the RSHA as the responsible agency for working out where and how to deport the Jews. The preferred solution was to expel them all after the end of the war to bleak regions in the defeated Soviet Union, where vast numbers would almost certainly perish. Heydrich presented this plan to Göring on 26 March 1941, and after revising the administrative arrangements, it was this document for a 'final solution' that was signed on 31 July. As a result of this new deportation plan the war against the Soviet Union and the war against the Jews became enmeshed together, military success making it possible to complete the racial programme as well.

It was evident that deportation was not to be the only policy. Although there was as yet no specific order from either Hitler or Himmler on the extermination of the Jews, the

---

A German poster from 1942 declares 'Behind the enemy powers – the Jew!' Hitler and others in the Party leadership came to convince themselves that the global spread of war to include the United States was a result of Jewish machinations, a view that played an important part in the decision to launch the camp-based genocide in 1942.

Hinter den Feindmächten: der Jude

REINHARD HEYDRICH (1904–1942)

Heydrich was one of the key members of Himmler's security apparatus until his assassination by Czech partisans in 1942. He was the son of a Dresden music teacher, and was a skilled violinist. Too young to serve in the First World War, he joined the *Freikorps* afterwards and absorbed much of the racism and radical nationalism of the post-war right in Germany. In 1922 he joined the German navy but was forced to resign in 1931 following a scandal in his private life. He joined the National Socialists and the young SS organization and his good looks, ruthless energy and ambition earned him Himmler's approval. In July 1932 he was appointed to head the Party's own internal security service, the *Sicherheitsdienst* (SD), and in 1936, now with the rank of SS Lt General for his services to Hitler during the Night of the Long Knives in 1934, he was made chief of all the security police. In 1939 he became head of the newly formed Reich Main Security Office (RSHA) with responsibility for all security, intelligence and policing activities throughout the Reich. He also played a key part in the plans to eliminate the Jews of Germany and Europe and in July 1941 was given an order from Göring to find a 'final solution' to the Jewish question. He was responsible for summoning the Wannsee Conference in January 1942 where the decisions were taken to move all Jews to the east. Throughout his adult life he was oppressed by the fear that he was part-Jewish and his utterly amoral treatment of the victims of his security apparatus may well have derived in part from his own insecurity about his past. On 23 September he was also appointed Deputy Reich Protector in Bohemia and Moravia, where he undertook a savage pacification of the region. It was while he was in Prague that Czech resistance fighters, armed by the British, shot Heydrich as he drove along on 27 May 1942. He died from his wounds on 4 June and was given a state funeral.

preparations for Barbarossa made it clear that Jews were to be targeted for execution in the areas of German advance. The four SS *Einsatzgruppen* began killing male Jews in large batches from the first days of the campaign, on the assumption (already made clear in the criminal orders) that Jews and Bolsheviks were one and the same. The SS squads also encouraged the local populations in eastern Poland and the Baltic States to undertake their own savage pogroms against the local Jewish population. As the violence spread, SS units began to kill women as well. On 15 August Himmler, on a visit to the Belorussian capital of Minsk, told SS leaders that the killing of women and children was now permissible. By late September 1941 the *Einsatzgruppen*, now joined by other police and SS units under the overall command of SS General Erich von dem Bach-Zalewski, began the systematic extermination of all the Jews they found in the conquered Soviet territory. The most notorious mass murder took place at Babi Yar, outside Kiev, on 29 and 30 September 1941. In alleged retaliation for a terrorist attack, 33,771 Jewish men, women and children were

marched to a long anti-tank trench, forced to undress, their valuables seized, and then made to stand at the pit's edge where they were shot in the back of the head, one layer of dead on top of the last. When the massacre was over, quicklime was spread on the bodies and the pit covered over with earth. By the end of 1941 an estimated 500,000 Soviet Jews had been murdered in cold blood. This programme marked the onset of the genocide of the European Jews.

German soldiers look on while a body is thrown into a common grave somewhere on the Eastern front in the summer of 1941. The German police, security forces and army accepted the harsh conditions of fighting in the Soviet Union, which led to the deaths of millions of Jews, partisans and communists.

THE ARRIVAL OF THE GERMANS:
A JEWISH DIARY, JULY 1941

Preyli shtetl, Latvia

Saturday July 19. An order has been issued that Jews must wear a yellow distinguishing mark. It consists of a five-pointed yellow star, twelve centimetres wide and long. Men are to wear it on their backs, their chests, and their legs, just above the knee. Women will wear them on their chests and on their backs. Many are arrested and put in prison.....

Friday July 25. At five in the morning, we gather on the market square around the fire tower. There is a roll call, then we move off. It is ten kilometres to the peat works. By eight-thirty, they are already dividing us up into work parties. We work in groups of ten: eight girls and two boys. Our job is to turn over the cut turf. It is heavy work. Every minute, a forest ranger comes running up and urges us on. Work stops at 7.00 p.m. A barn has been allotted us as our place to stay for the night. At 2.00 a.m. we are surrounded by a group of strangers, partisans it seems [Latvian militia working for the Germans]. One of them calls for all the Jews to come out, but when none of us answers, they open fire. The scene in the barn was dreadful. Everyone gathered in one corner, and everyone praying to God. Fortunately they were only making fun of us. After the shooting, when no one answered, the men surrounding the barn went away. But we did not sleep the whole night. We went back to work at 5.00 a.m....

Sunday July 27. This is a bloody Sunday for the Latvian Jewish people.
Morning. All the Jews in Dvinskaya Street are ordered to put on their best clothes, take some provisions with them, and go out into the street. Searches of the homes are carried out. At twelve o'clock, all the Jews are herded into the synagogue. One group of young Jews is sent to dig graves behind the cemetery. Then the Jews of two more streets are driven in to the synagogue.

It is 3.30 in the afternoon. All the Jews are chased out beyond the cemetery and shot there. All 250 Jews: men, women and children.

This is terrible. We did not expect things to end this way. The handful of survivors expects death at any moment.

Source: Joshua Rubenstein, Ilya Altman (eds) *The Unknown Black Book: The Holocaust in the German-Occupied Soviet Territories* (Indiana University Press, Bloomington, 2008), pp. 324–5, diary of Sheyna Gram, murdered on 9 August 1941.

Much effort has been devoted to finding a document signed by Hitler which ordered the extermination of the Jews. Almost certainly, no such document existed. The shift from plans for deportation to mass killing was done step-by-step, encouraged by the savage conditions of the war in the East and the willingness of the SS commanders in the field to use the pretence of anti-partisan war to embark on an uncontrolled killing-spree, targeted at Soviet Jews. It was almost certainly done with Hitler's knowledge and approval, but the genocidal character of the war against the Soviet Union, for both Jews and the Slav population, was already implicit in much of the preliminary planning for the campaign. It was also evident from the decisions taken to build special extermination camps in occupied Poland, whose purpose was principally to murder Jews in ways less obtrusive than the open-air mass murders carried out by the *Einsatzgruppen*. The creation of camps and the technology of mass murder coincided with the end, in August 1941, of the T4 Action for murdering the disabled. The termination of the programme, which proved only temporary, came partly in response to growing popular anxiety as news of the murders spread outside the asylums and institutions. The first formal protest had been made on 19 July 1940 by the Evangelical Bishop of Württemberg; on 1 August the German Catholic bishops protested as a whole to Hitler. But it was only following the public protest of the Catholic bishop of Münster, Clemens von Galen, on 3 August 1941, that the programme was officially brought to an end three weeks later. The personnel from T4, with their long experience in gas-chamber killing, were moved to the east to assist in the construction and development of new facilities for mass murder.

The gas technology was applied first to gas vans, mobile trucks that could be adapted to murder their occupants by the simple device of attaching a hose from the exhaust and filling the interior with carbon monoxide fumes. The first experiment took place at Mogilev in September 1941, and by December all four *Einsatzgruppen* were using vans to kill mental patients, prisoners-of-war and Jews. A permanent base was established at Chelmno in eastern Poland where Jews were first killed in gas vans on 8 December 1941. Chelmno then became one of the six main extermination camps. On 13 October Himmler approved a plan to construct a gas-based extermination centre at Belzec, with a number of T4 personnel arriving there in December. The camp at Auschwitz also began to experiment with gas killing in late August or early September 1941. On 3 September some 900 Soviet and Polish prisoners were killed in an airtight cellar into which cyanide granules of the pesticide Zyklon B were thrown. The granules turned to gas at 26 degrees centigrade which was highly toxic even in small doses. Small numbers of Jewish workers were also killed, but Auschwitz was not yet an extermination centre. On 26 September 1941 the order was given to begin construction of a much larger camp next to Auschwitz at Birkenau, and it was this camp that later in 1943 became the principal site of the Jewish genocide.

The Battle for Moscow

The last three months of 1941 represented an important turning point in the German war effort. The confidence shown in October that the Barbarossa campaign was all but won was undermined when the drive for Moscow first slowed down and was then reversed with a Soviet counter-offensive. The launch of Operation Typhoon on 2 October 1941 was intended to complete the destruction of the scattered and demoralized Red Army units defending the path to the Soviet capital. Three armoured groups made up the core of the German attack which quickly destroyed much of the Soviet front. By 17 October large encircling movements at Briansk and Vyazma had netted a further 700,000 prisoners, and it was assumed that the Red Army had little left to fight with. Only 90,000 Soviet troops remained out of the 800,000 who had defended the approaches to Moscow. Then the heavy rains arrived, the period of *rasputitsa*, and the pace slowed. Nevertheless by 18 October Kalinin, to the north of Moscow, was captured along with Kaluga to the south. In late October the frosts came and progress could be made once more. German commanders assumed they would now capture Stalin's capital.

The last push brought German armies almost to the gates of Moscow. By 28 November, Third and Fourth Panzer Armies had reached the Moscow–Volga canal (only 12 miles from the Kremlin) in freezing conditions with deteriorating supply lines. Weakened though the Red Army was, enough reserves could be scraped together to prevent a simple occupation of the city and at Tula, south of Moscow, the Soviet front held firm. Then, undetected by the German side, the Soviet forces (organized by General Georgii Zhukov) launched a sudden counter-offensive on 5 December which drove back German forces by as much as 150 miles, to the line they had held in November. On 8 December Hitler ordered his armies to go over to the defensive along the Eastern Front. When Army Group Centre asked for permission to withdraw further on 18 December, Hitler ordered the troops to stand fast and fight with 'fanatical resistance'. To cope with the sudden crisis Hitler reorganized his high command. Field Marshal von Bock of Army Group Centre was sent on leave and replaced by General von Kluge; Guderian was sacked as commander of the Second Panzer Army. The most important change was Hitler's decision, on 19 December, to replace the army commander-in-chief, von Brauchitsch, and to assume direct command of the whole German army himself, with the aim of making it more National Socialist.

The failure to complete the defeat of the Red Army and seize Moscow has many causes, among which the weather certainly played a part. The German army suffered 133,000 cases of frostbite; it was difficult to maintain vehicles and tanks in sub-zero temperatures, while many German soldiers had inadequate winter clothing. The chief problem was the high level of casualty taken since the onset of the campaign. During the last three months of 1941 German armies had 117,000 casualties (dead, wounded, POW); from June to December 302,000 servicemen had been killed. The wear and tear on aircraft, tanks and vehicles was also high with long supply lines, poor repair facilities and a wide variety of different vehicle type. By October 1941 the German army was very dependent on the more than 700,000 horses brought on the campaign. Many German generals privately blamed Hitler for holding up the advance on Moscow to capture the economic resources of the south. Hitler himself later blamed Mussolini for forcing him to turn to the Mediterranean instead of starting his campaign in the East in the middle of May. This 'catastrophic delay', Hitler claimed, prevented the German army from achieving the victory it deserved.

Even while German forces dug in for the first winter of the Russian war, circumstances in the Far East transformed the war once more. On 7 December 1941 Japanese carrier aircraft attacked

German soldiers attempt to move a motorcycle stuck in the mud of a Soviet road during the Operation 'Typhoon' for the capture of the Soviet capital, Moscow. During the muddy season vehicles were almost impossible to move and the German army came to rely more and more on horses.

the US Pacific Fleet at Pearl Harbor, thereby launching the Pacific War. Four days later, in a speech before the German parliament, Hitler declared war on the United States. Germany was not obliged to do so under the terms of agreements with Japan, and the American President, Franklin Roosevelt, had no intention of involving his country in war in Europe so soon after the shock of the Japanese attack. There were a number of reasons why Hitler made the decision. For some time German leaders had counted the United States among their enemies. American Lend-Lease supplies were helping both Britain and the Soviet Union; American forces were stationed in Iceland and Greenland, and American ships assisted in the Battle of the Atlantic. The declaration of war simplified German policy because it was now possible to fight back without restriction. Hitler's foreign minister, von Ribbentrop, later asserted that great powers did not wait to have war declared upon them, but declared war themselves.

There was also a more sinister aspect to Hitler's decision. On 12 August 1941 Churchill and Roosevelt had signed the Atlantic Charter following a meeting in Newfoundland. The document committed both states to re-establish democracy and human rights in Europe and to destroy 'the Nazi tyranny'. Two days later Hitler was given details of the text and reacted to them with an angry vehemence. He interpreted the Charter as further evidence that an international Jewish conspiracy was at work to create a global war in which Germany would be defeated. On 18 August he discussed the issue with Goebbels and told him that the prophecy he had made on 30 January 1939, that the arrival of a world war would mean the destruction of the Jews, was coming true. He gave Goebbels permission to begin the removal of all Berlin Jews and in mid-September he ordered the deportation of all German Jews to the ghettos and camps in the East. From this point onwards it is possible to detect a radical shift in Hitler's thinking. The course of the war was now bound up with his warped interpretation of the malign role played by the Jews in fomenting and sustaining it. Between 15 and 18 October 1941 the first of the new wave of German Jewish deportation began. Senior officials and politicians began to discuss a new approach to the Jewish question. On 18 November 1941 Alfred Rosenberg, Minister for the Occupied Eastern Territories, noted that 'the biological extermination of the whole of European Jewry' was now to take place in the East. At a meeting with Party regional leaders on 12 December (one day after declaring war on the United States) Hitler announced that the coming of global war against Germany meant that 'the extermination of the Jews must be the necessary consequence'. Exactly when, or in what form, Hitler arrived at the decision to wage an unremitting war of extermination against the defenceless Jewish population of Europe may never be known for certain, but by the end of 1941 the die was cast for a comprehensive programme of genocide.

A German tank, covered with a swastika sign, during the last stages of the German campaign towards Moscow in December 1941. German forces came within a few kilometres of the Kremlin but lacked the resources for one final drive on the capital.

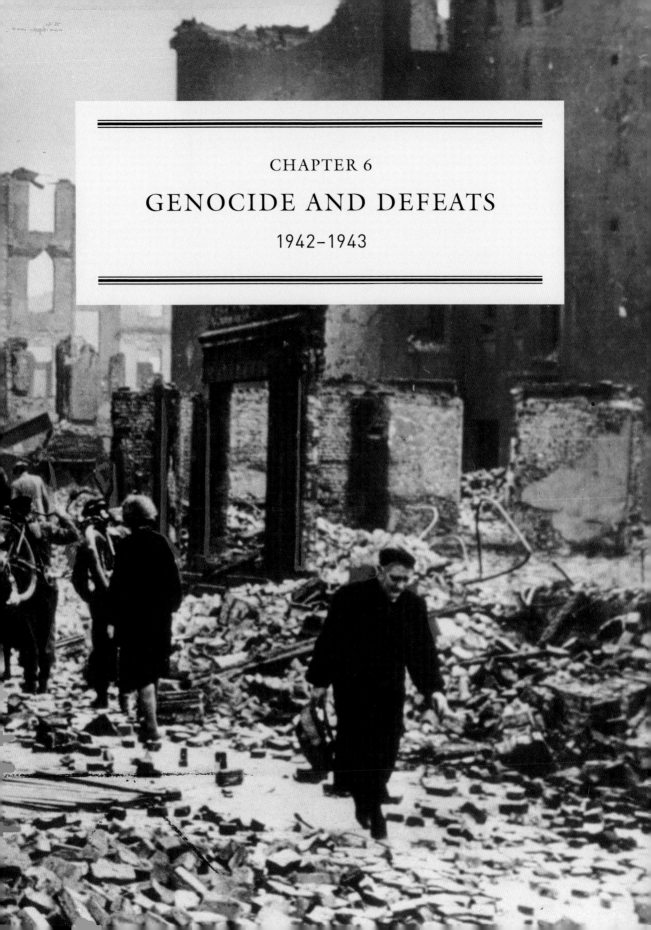

CHAPTER 6

GENOCIDE AND DEFEATS

1942–1943

The ultimate defeat of Germany was not yet evident in 1942. The war economy was geared up to produce more efficiently and in larger quantities; occupied Europe was stripped of anything the Reich needed to sustain its war effort. Mobilization for total war reached even higher levels, while the home population had to accept longer hours, poorer food and the ever-present threat of Allied bombing. This became a serious menace from the spring of 1942 onwards, culminating in the firestorm in Hamburg in July 1943 that killed 45,000 people. To combat resistance in occupied Europe and defeatism at home, the concentration camps began to expand their numbers while millions of forced workers were brought from occupied Europe to work in factories and on farms. In 1942 the forces of Germany and her Allies were still on the offensive, in the Soviet Union, the Pacific and in North Africa. Only by the end of that year was the tide of victory turned. At El Alamein in Egypt Axis forces were routed and forced to retreat back to Tunisia, where they were compelled to surrender in May 1943. The war at sea took a growing toll of German submarines and by May 1943 the Atlantic campaign also had to be abandoned. Deep in the heart of Russia a titanic struggle was fought between German and Soviet forces for the Volga city of Stalingrad. The surrender of German forces there in January 1943 did not make defeat certain, but switched the balance in favour of the Allies. While German forces tried to stabilize the military situation, the first steps were taken to implement the 'final solution' of the so-called Jewish question. Mass shootings in 1941 of Soviet Jews gave way in spring 1942 to the systematic collection and transportation of Jews to purpose-built extermination centres. By the end of 1943 most of the victims of the genocide were already dead. Hitler and the Party leadership saw the war against the Allies as part of the wider war against the Jewish enemy. Although the resources used to murder the Jews could have been used elsewhere, the destruction of the Jews became inseparable from the circumstances of the war.

1942 The Speer Era

The failure to defeat the Soviet Union in 1941 was caused partly by the failure to make the best use of the rich technical and labour resources of Germany and the occupied territories. German war production during 1941 increased more slowly than Hitler had intended, hampered by poor resource allocation and an absence of central organization. After pressing the armed services and industry to make more effective use of the resources they had been given, Hitler finally published a Führer Order on 3 December 1941 for 'Simplification and Increased Efficiency in Armaments Production'. He called for a reduction in the very great number of different types of equipment produced, and improved productivity in German factories. He took a personal interest in trying to get the war economy to respond effectively to the needs of war. In a further order on 21 March 1942 he explained that 'the greatest output is to be achieved with the smallest expenditure of resources.'

Reforming the war economy was a slow and difficult process. On 20 December Fritz Todt, the Munitions Minister, introduced a system of industrial Main Committees, each one responsible for one class of weapon – guns, armoured vehicles, explosives, and so on. The committees were staffed mainly by engineers and industrial managers who understood better than the military the way in which a sophisticated industrial economy worked. In aircraft production Göring's deputy, Field Marshal Erhard Milch, a former director of the Lufthansa airline, set up a comparable centralized system of production rings for aircraft output, each major manufacturer controlling the outer ring of suppliers and contractors. On 6 February 1942 Todt called together the heads of the committees to discuss the establishment of a central organization to control the production and distribution of resources for the war economy. Two days later, flying back to Germany from Hitler's headquarters at Rastenburg, Todt was killed when his aircraft exploded in mid-air. Foul play was suspected but never proved, and Todt received a state funeral in Berlin. That same day Hitler's favourite architect, Albert Speer (who was Todt's deputy for building work), was passing through headquarters. Hitler summoned Speer into his study and appointed him Todt's successor with the new title of Minister for Armaments and Munitions. Despite Speer's protest that he had no experience of military production, Hitler insisted because he wanted an economic overlord whom he could trust. He promised Speer his complete political backing in any future arguments with other Party leaders or the military. Only moments after Speer's appointment, Hermann Göring arrived to demand that he should be Todt's successor; Hitler refused to change his mind.

Speer set about consolidating the work that Todt had been carrying out. On 22 March 1942 he established 'Central Planning', an inner economic cabinet whose task was to

---

Pages 264–5: German survivors make their way through the ruins of Hamburg, destroyed in bomb attacks in late July 1943.

HITLER ON THE GERMAN THOUSAND-YEAR REICH, APRIL 1942

As regards the government of Germany, I've come to the following conclusions:

1 The Reich must be a republic, having as its head an elected chief who shall be endowed with absolute authority.

2 An agency representing the people must, nevertheless, exist by way of a corrective. Its role is to support the Chief of State, but it must be able to intervene in case of need.

3 The task of choosing the Chief shall be entrusted, not to the people's assembly, but to a Senate. It is, however, important that the powers of the Senate shall be limited. Its composition must not be permanent. Moreover, its members shall be appointed with reference to their occupation and not individuals. These Senators must, by their training, be steeped in the idea that power may in no case be delegated to a weakling, and that the elected Fuehrer must always be the best man.

4 The Election of the Chief must not take place in public, but in camera. On the occasion of the election of a pope, the people does not know what is happening behind the scenes. A case is reported in which the cardinals exchanged blows. Since then, the cardinals have been deprived of all contact with the outside world, for the duration of the conclave! This is a principle that is also to be observed in the election of the Fuehrer: all conversation between the electors will be forbidden throughout operations.

5 The Party, Army and the body of officials must take an oath of allegiance to the new Chief within three hours following the election.

6 The most rigorous separation between the legislative and executive organs of the State must be the supreme law for the new Chief. Just as, in the Party, the SA and the SS are merely the sword to which is entrusted the carrying-out of the decisions taken by the competent organs, in the same way the executive agents of the State are not to concern themselves with politics. They must confine themselves exclusively to ensuring the application of laws issued by the legislative power, making appeal to the sword, in case of need. Although a State founded on such principles can lay no claim to eternity, it might last for eight to nine centuries. The thousand-year-old organization of the Church is proof of this – and yet this entire organization is founded on nonsense. What I have said should *a fortiori* be true of an organization founded on reason.

Source: Hugh Trevor-Roper (ed.) *Hitler's Table Talk 1941–44* (Weidenfeld & Nicolson, London, 1973), pp. 388–9, dinner conversation, 31 March 1942

oversee the whole economy, and to decide on priorities for the allocation of scarce resources and materials. In addition to the Main Committees set up in December he added ones for radio, aero-engines, aircraft, shipbuilding and vehicles. Each committee was to be served by a series of Special Committees, each one responsible for just one type of aircraft or tank or vehicle. Speer, who was only 37 when he was appointed, filled the new offices in his organization with other younger men. The slogan for 1942 was 'Rationalization and Concentration' and Speer drove on a relentless programme of centralization and simplification. Output of the Messerschmitt Me109 fighter was increased from 180 per month, built in seven separate factories, to over 1,000 per month in three factories two years later. At the same time improvements in factory layout, the introduction of flow and

Above left: The Minister for Armaments and Munitions, Albert Speer, addresses members of the Todt Organization who are to work on reconstructing the Möhne dam, destroyed by a British bombing raid on the night of 17 May 1943. Speer feared that a systematic campaign against the German water supply would be catastrophic for arms production.

Above right: An SS doctor, Karl Brandt, one of Hitler's own medical team, examines Soviet prisoners-of war in a camp shortly after the onset of the campaign. SS scientists and race experts were interested in classifying all the different racial types in the East in case any could be found suitable for 'Germanization'.

mass production, and savings in the use of raw materials, meant that many more weapons could be produced from the same quantity of resources. Over the next three years armaments production trebled.

The most serious bottleneck facing the German war effort in 1942 was labour. Millions of workers had been drafted into the armed forces (in the end over 17 million Germans were conscripted out of a population of 96 million). Over 14 million German women worked in industry, offices and agriculture, a higher proportion than in either Britain or the United States. The conquest of Europe had brought additional labour under German control, but also absorbed tens of thousands of Germans who were needed to run the occupied regions. The answer was to bring labourers back to Germany to work in German factories and on German farms. On 21 March 1942 the Party leader in Thuringia, Fritz Sauckel, was appointed Plenipotentiary for Labour Allocation. Like Speer, Sauckel was given the full and direct political support of Hitler, without which it was difficult to centralize labour recruitment and distribution. Sauckel's principal task was to find workers outside Germany. Some of them were volunteers, lured by the promise of high pay and regular employment in German factories, but the great majority were sent to Germany against their will, or were recruited from among prisoners-of-war.

Among the first forced workers were those from the conquered areas of the Soviet Union. Hitler had been reluctant in 1941 to allow Soviet POWs or workers to be moved to Germany because he feared they might be a source of sabotage and a racial threat to the German population. But the desperate shortage of labour forced Hitler to change his mind and on 31 October 1941 he had approved in principle the use of Russian labour. It took many weeks to work out the security regulations governing the deportation of workers to Germany and their treatment in German factories, and only on 20 February 1942 were the guidelines finally published. In the interim most of the 3,300,000 Red Army prisoners had died of disease, neglect and deliberate murder in ill-kept, overcrowded camps in the east. The transport of prisoners to Germany began in large numbers only in April 1942, at the same time as the first large transports of Soviet workers who were rounded up and shipped to Germany by force. During 1942 1,480,000 workers and 456,000 prisoners were sent to work in Germany under conditions of close supervision, low pay and the threat of savage

---

Opposite above: A vast ocean of Red Army prisoners-of-war somewhere on the Eastern front. More than 3 million prisoners were taken in the first six months of the campaign but little provision had been made for them and at least two-thirds died of disease, exposure and malnutrition before a decision was taken to move them to the Reich as labour.

Opposite below: Scenes such as this were enacted all over the occupied East. Here Polish hostages are hanged at Zdunska Wola. The German armed forces and security services seized hostages in retaliation for any attack by civilian resisters or partisan fighters. They were permitted to kill 50–100 for every German soldier who died.

punishments. At the same time Sauckel began to recruit workers from Western Europe, a small number as volunteers, the majority recruited by coercion. By the end of 1942 there were 617,000 workers from Belgium, the Netherlands, France and Italy and a further 931,000 French prisoners-of-war, who should have been repatriated under the terms of the Geneva Convention. By the end of the war over 7 million non-German men and women were working in Germany; in Speer's armaments empire the proportion of foreign workers reached approximately one-third.

Operation Reinhard

Hitler's war against the Jews ran parallel with the efforts to boost the war effort on the home front. On 30 January 1942, in a speech at the Berlin Sports Palace to commemorate his coming to power, Hitler publicly declared that the war would now mean 'the destruction of Jewry'. A few days earlier, in a large villa on the shores of Lake Wannsee on the western outskirts of Berlin, Reinhard Heydrich called together a meeting of German ministerial heads to discuss the Jewish question. The meeting had originally been scheduled for 9 December but had to be postponed. Heydrich used it as an opportunity to tell the party and ministerial officials present that Hitler had changed Jewish policy from emigration to one of deportation to the East from all over occupied and Axis Europe. The final solution aimed at ridding Europe of all Jews, including those in Britain and in neutral countries, a total calculated by German officials at 11 million. This outcome depended entirely on securing a comprehensive German victory. On the other hand, the programme of deportation (with the implication of extermination) could be applied to all those Jews unfortunate enough to find themselves directly in the German sphere of influence. How the programme was to be carried out remained unclear, but the decision to inaugurate a programme to remove all Jews to the East opened the way to a second wave of genocidal killings.

The murder of the Jews in the first half of 1942 was made up of a number of different strands that gradually coalesced into a programme of systematic mass murder. In the occupied Soviet Union the extermination of the local Jewish population continued as it had in 1941, with the security police and *Einsatzgruppen* killing Jews wherever they found them by shooting or gassing in vans. In the Polish Generalgouvernement Hans Frank interpreted Hitler's comments in December 1941 as a green light to start clearing his whole fiefdom of the large number of Jews, approximately 2,500,000, who either lived there or had been shipped into the ghettos in the Lublin region from other parts of Eastern Europe. The mass murder of the Jews in Poland was organized under SS commander Odilo Globocnik, a corrupt and fanatical anti-Semite, who was given responsibility by Himmler to run Operation Reinhard (named after Heydrich) at four purpose-built extermination camps – Belzec, Sobibor, Treblinka and Chelmno. The last of these had already begun killing in December; Belzec was ready in March 1942, Sobibor in May and Treblinka in June. These camps were responsible for the rapid mass murder of all the Jews in Poland, except for those deemed capable of being worked to death instead. On 22 July the transfer of Jews from the Warsaw Ghetto also began; by September more than a quarter of a million had been killed. The four Operation Reinhard camps between them accounted for an estimated 1.75 million Jews by the autumn of 1943.

THE SECRET ORDER FOR GENOCIDE

WISLICENY Eichmann then stated that a visit by a Slovak commission in the area of Lublin would be impossible. When I asked him why, he said, after much delay and a great deal of discussion, that there was an order of Himmler according to which all Jews were to be exterminated. When I asked him who was going to assume responsibility for this order, he said he was prepared to show me this order in writing which had been signed by Himmler. I then requested that he show me this order. This order was under the classification of Top Secret. This discussion took place in his study in Berlin. He was sitting at his desk, and I was in the same position, opposite him, as I am now opposite the Colonel [interrogator Lt. Col Smith Brookhart]. He took this order from his safe. It was a thick file. He then searched and took out this order. It was directed to the Chief of the Security Police and the Security Service [Heydrich].

The contents of this order went something like this. I cannot give it precisely since I am under oath, but it is approximately as follows. The Fuehrer has decided that the final disposition of the Jewish question is to start immediately. By the code word 'final disposition' was meant the biological extermination of the Jews. Himmler put the limitation on this order that at the present time able-bodied Jews who could be used for work were to be excluded.

BROOKHART Did Himmler put that order into the Hitler order, or was it included in the text of the order?

WISLICENY 'I designate the Chief of the Security Police and Security Service and the Inspector of Concentration Camps [Richard Glücks] with the execution of this order.' Excepted from this order were those few in concentration camps who were needed within the framework of the labor programme. The particulars of this programme were to be agreed between the Chief of the SD and the Security Police and the Inspector of Concentration Camps. 'I am to be informed currently about the execution of this order.' I saw with my own eyes the signature of Himmler under this order.

BROOKHART What was the date of this order?

WISLICENY I can't say exactly, but it must have been from the end of April or the beginning of May 1942.

Source: Richard Overy *Interrogations: Inside the Minds of the Nazi Elite* (Penguin, London, 2001), pp. 359–60, extract from the interrogation of Dieter Wisliceny taken at Nuremberg, 15 November 1945.

RUDOLF HÖSS RECALLS AUSCHWITZ

I had to appear cold and indifferent to events that must have wrung the heart of anyone possessed of human feelings. I might not even look away when afraid lest my natural emotions got the upper hand. I had to watch coldly, while the mothers with laughing or crying children went into the gas chambers......

I had to see everything. I had to watch hour after hour, by day and by night, the removal and burning of the bodies, the extraction of the teeth, the cutting of the hair, the whole grisly, interminable business. I had to stand for hours on end in the ghastly stench, while the mass graves were being opened and the bodies dragged out and burned.

I had to look through the peep-hole of the gas-chambers and watch the process of death itself, because the doctors wanted me to see it.

I had to do all this because I was the one to whom everyone looked, because I had to show them all that I did not merely issue orders and make the regulations but was prepared myself to be present at whatever task I had assigned to my subordinates.

The Reichsführer SS sent various high-ranking Party leaders and SS officers to Auschwitz so that they might see for themselves the process of extermination of the Jews. They were all deeply impressed by what they saw. Some who had previously spoken most loudly about the necessity for this extermination fell silent once they had actually seen the 'final solution of the Jewish problem'. I was repeatedly asked how I and my men could go on watching these operations, and how we were able to stand it.

My invariable answer was that the iron determination with which we must carry out Hitler's orders could only be obtained by a stifling of all human emotions. Each of these gentlemen declared that he was glad the job had not been given to him.

Source: *Commandant of Auschwitz: The Autobiography of Rudolf Höss* (Phoenix Press, London, 1995), pp. 154–5

The second strand came with the decision to begin the mass transfer of Jews from Greater Germany (including Austria), from former Czechoslovakia and the states of Western Europe. At first some of these new deportees were housed in ghettos already cleared of their Polish Jewish occupants, but gradually the process changed into one of immediate killing, except for a small fraction (usually around 20 per cent) who were set aside for labour in the concentration and labour camps in the East. The first new wave of German Jews began to arrive in March 1942; the first deportation of Slovakian Jewish families began on 11 April; the first 1,000 Jews from France arrived at Auschwitz on 27 March. The mass movement of Jews from Western and Southern Europe did not begin until the summer of 1942. By that time two other extermination centres were ready, at Maidanek and the Birkenau facility at Auschwitz. Birkenau became the most lethal of all the camps, responsible for the death of an estimated 1,100,000 Jewish victims, as well as political prisoners, gypsies and prisoners-of-war. The precise date when gas chamber killing began in Birkenau is not known, but it was in the spring of 1942 when 'bunker 1' and 'bunker 2', two farm buildings on the site, were converted into primitive gas chambers. The two bunkers could accommodate around 2,000 victims at a time; the corpses were then cremated in the main camp or buried in pits. In July 1942 the first new installation, Crematorium II, was ready for operation and further facilities were opened in March, April and June 1943, by which time Birkenau could handle 4,746 bodies a day. The first recorded systematic murder of Jews dates from May, but the first trainload of victims arrived on 25 March, ostensibly to perform forced labour. Over the next four months trains began to arrive with Jews from the West and from Germany. On 17 and 18 July Himmler visited Auschwitz, watched the gassing of a trainload of Dutch Jews, promoted the commandant, Rudolf Höss, and expressed himself pleased with the procedures he had witnessed. From then on most Jews from outside Poland destined for extermination were shipped either to Auschwitz-Birkenau or to the combined labour and extermination facility built at Maidanek, which began operation in August 1942.

The shipping of Jews from outside Eastern Europe involved a complicated programme of registration, collecting and deportation. Much of the programme was orchestrated by Eichmann's office of Jewish Affairs (IV b4), housed in the Gestapo building in Berlin. His deputies were sent out to occupied and allied areas to negotiate with local authorities for the deportation of Jews. Bulgaria was the only one to refuse to release its native Jewish population, but the government in Sofia willingly sent the Jews from Thrace, the territory seized by Bulgaria following Greek defeat in 1941. In all the occupied areas it proved possible to find collaborators, many of them anti-Semitic. The mass transport of Jews from the rest of Europe would not have been possible without the assistance of many non-Germans. In Germany itself the deportation of the Jews from 1942 provoked little resistance; in major cities Jewish property was put on sale in markets and grateful customers bought up furniture and clothing at cheap prices. Other Jewish goods were stored and handed out to Germans who had been bombed out. Although thousands of Jews were concealed from the Gestapo in Germany and elsewhere by neighbours or friends, the penalties for discovery were severe, including the prospect of being shipped east to the camps alongside the Jews they had aided.

The savage nature of German reprisals was made evident when on 27 May Reinhard Heydrich was attacked and wounded by two Czech agents. He died of his injuries on 4 June. In retaliation, the Czech village of Lidice was razed to the ground on 9/10 June and 192 men and 7 women shot. The remaining women were sent to Ravensbrück concentration camp, with the children sent to orphanages. 1,000 Czechs were put on trial and executed while 3,000 Jews were deported from the Theresienstadt camp in Bohemia and exterminated.

Advancing on All Fronts

For much of 1942 German forces were moving forward with the prospect of victory still alive. With Britain undefeated, Germany was forced to fight a number of different wars: a war at sea against British Empire and American shipping; an air war against the limited strategic bombing campaign mounted by the RAF; a land war in North Africa for control of the Suez Canal; and a large-scale combined arms war against the Soviet Union. These many different theatres of war made heavy demands on German resources and manpower, but for the first nine months of the year German forces seemed equal to the many tasks they had to face.

In early 1942 the war in the Atlantic turned in Germany's favour. The German submarine commander-in-chief, Admiral Karl Dönitz, hoped to be able to sink at least 500,000 tons of Allied shipping each month, the level achieved in December 1941. He believed that this level of loss would slow down, or even halt, Anglo-American military operations. The entry of the United States allowed the German submarine packs to move to the United States east coast where inexperienced American captains still sailed singly rather than in convoy, using radios freely to betray their location, and illuminated at night by coastal cities which did not yet operate a blackout. Operation Drumbeat [*Paukenschlag*] netted 1.2 million tons of shipping sunk in the first four months of 1942. The Allies lost 2.6 million tons between January and April, more than during the whole of 1941. German submarine losses were three in January, only two the following month. In 1942 the standard Type VII submarine (with a radius of 8,000 miles and armament of 11 torpedoes) was supplemented by the introduction of the Type IX boat with a radius of 13,450 miles and 22 torpedoes. During the period of greatest success the German navy had the advantage that the B-Dienst intelligence service could read the Royal Navy Cypher No. 2 from September 1941, and at the beginning of 1942 could also read Cypher No. 3. In February the British lost the capacity to read German signals through intercepting encrypted messages from the German Enigma machine when the Navy changed its Triton cipher. This intelligence blackout lasted until the end of the year. Over the course of 1942 submarines sank 7.8 million tons in all waters and British imports fell to one-third of their pre-war level.

Field Marshal Erwin Rommel stands with men of his Afrika Korps in the Libyan desert in 1942. Rommel transformed the campaign in North Africa and came within a few hundred miles of capturing the Suez Canal and gaining access to the British-controlled oil of the Middle East.

Some of these sinkings were recorded in the Mediterranean, where German aircraft and submarines also operated against both Allied shipping and Allied bases, principally the island of Malta. The German Fliegerkorps X, based on Sicily, operated together with Italian bombers to pound much of Malta into rubble. Between 1 January and 24 July 1942 there was only one day on which bombs did not fall on the island. By May 1942 the German air commander in the theatre, Field Marshal Albert Kesselring, declared that Malta was effectively neutralized. The defeat of Allied air and naval power in the Mediterranean was a necessary condition to allow the Axis to continue to supply Italian armies and Rommel's Afrika Korps in Libya. Here the fortunes of Axis forces had continued to fluctuate. Rommel had been driven back across Cyrenaica in late 1941 to the port of El Agheila. On 21 January 1942, reinforced from across the Mediterranean supply route, he launched a powerful counter-offensive which took Axis armies back to Gazala, close to the port of Tobruk. After pausing for further supplies, Rommel launched a second operation on 26 May designed to bring him into Egypt. The remarkable success of the attack opened the way to the Suez Canal. Tobruk was captured on 21 June, and with it 35,000 British Empire prisoners-of-war. German and Italian forces pressed on until they reached the re-formed Allied front at El Alamein and Alam Halfa, deep in Egyptian territory and only 150 miles from Cairo. Rommel was poised by midsummer for the final breakthrough to the Suez Canal and the oil of the Middle East.

The great bulk of German land forces were still concentrated in the Soviet Union, where Hitler hoped to be able to complete the rout of the Red Army he had been denied in 1941. The German front line had stabilized after the initial crisis at Moscow in December, and German forces adapted themselves to the difficulties of fighting in a Russian winter. On 5 April Hitler issued Directive No. 41 for Operation 'Blue'. The principal aim was 'finally to destroy any remaining military power of the Soviets', an ambition that Hitler wanted to achieve by seizing the southern steppe region as well as the oil and resources of the Caucasus region. It would then be possible to cut off all Soviet supplies of oil and starve the Red Army of its most vital resource. There was no mention yet of Stalingrad, but the assumption lying behind the plan to drive south was to follow the defeat of Red Army units by reaching the Volga and swinging north to cut off Soviet forces behind Moscow. German commanders favoured a frontal assault on Moscow to achieve the psychological advantage of capturing the enemy capital, but Hitler was determined to seize the oil and, if possible, to use the southern victory to link up with Rommel's forces driving into the Middle East from Egypt.

Before Operation 'Blue' could be launched there were other battles to be fought. Convinced that German forces were weakened by the winter months, Stalin ordered the Red Army to recapture the city of Kharkov on the southern front. The operation was launched on 12 May but German forces, forewarned by intelligence, prepared a trap for the advancing Soviet armies. After ten days the trap was sprung and the equivalent of three Soviet armies were encircled and captured. Soviet losses at Kharkov were 171,000, matching the scale of losses sustained the previous year. In the Crimea a further Soviet attempt was made to drive back the German army. Three Soviet armies were brought across the ice in early 1942, to the Kerch Peninsula in the east of the Crimea, and on 27 February 1943 they opened up a campaign

HITLER AS GERMAN ARMY COMMANDER, 1942

Though he was now directly responsible for the fortunes or misfortunes of the Army in the East, he seemed to find this compatible with spending weeks and months in the Berghof [Hitler's Bavarian retreat], during which time the Chief of Staff of the Army with the entire OKH [Army High Command] remained behind in East Prussia and was seen by Hitler perhaps once a week. As against this, there were more and more frequent verbal discussions with generals commanding on the Eastern Front, who almost invariably had to come to Supreme Headquarters for the purpose, generally at moments of crisis.

All of this is not to say that Hitler purposely neglected his job of commanding the Army – the time and attention he gave to it are enough to show that. Nevertheless it was only too obvious what a difference there was between him and a *military* commander who throughout his career had prepared himself for this great responsibility and had no other object in life. A man like Hitler could not be expected to grasp the full import of the job which he had taken over; quite apart from the fact that in many respects he was ignorant of the basic principles of the exercise of command, he was overloaded with other responsibilities, and finally it was not his nature. As regards enemy intelligence he only accepted what suited him and often refused even to listen to unpalatable information. As before, time and space were for him only vague ideas which should not be allowed to affect the determination of a man who knew where he was going. As a soldier of the First World War, he felt himself better qualified than any of his advisers to judge the capacity of his troops, and this was the subject of interminable and repetitive dissertations. In the end, however, it was generally pushed into the background and forgotten. He had already shown that strategically he did not understand the principle of concentrating forces at the decisive point; now he proved incapable of applying it tactically, also, so nervous was he of exposing himself to attack anywhere. For years he had kept the whole world on tenterhooks by sudden adventurous decisions but now, when unexpected situations presented themselves, he proved incapable of taking the most urgent decisions in good time. He became less and less prepared to give senior commanders long-term directives and so allow them to act on their own initiative within a broad framework. Even more than within his own headquarters he now showed that he lacked the most important quality of a military leader, knowledge of men and the understanding and *mutual confidence* which spring therefrom.

Source: Walter Warlimont *Inside Hitler's Headquarters 1939–1945* (Weidenfeld & Nicolson, London, 1964), pp. 244–5. Lt. General Warlimont was on Hitler's wartime staff at Supreme Headquarters.

against von Manstein's army group. The results were poor and on 8 May Manstein launched his own counter-attack, Operation 'Bustard Hunt' (*Trappenjagd*), which in two weeks destroyed the Soviet position, netting 170,000 prisoners and driving the remainder back across the Kerch Straits. Manstein then turned to the port of Sebastopol on the Crimean Black Sea coast. Bombarded by the German Eighth Air Corps commanded by Wolfram von Richthofen, and subjected to heavy siege artillery (including the 'Big Dora' gun built by the German firm of Krupp, with an 800 mm barrel and shells weighing seven tons), the city finally succumbed on 4 July. General von Manstein, victor of Sebastopol, was promoted to field marshal.

The evidence from the first weeks of combat in 1942 suggested that Axis armies would have the same easy success they had enjoyed the year before. Optimism grew at Hitler's new forward headquarters at Vinnetsa in the Ukraine. The launch of Operation 'Blue' under the overall command of Field Marshal von Bock, on 28 June 1942, confirmed this judgement. The operation involved a large component of armoured forces, the First and Fourth Panzer armies, with heavy air support. The entire Army Group South was strengthened for the campaign at the expense of Army Group Centre, opposite Moscow, which was forced to dig in for the summer. Within days the Red Army in the south collapsed, already weakened by the disasters at Kharkhov and Kerch; the whole area from Voronezh, north of Kharkov, to Rostov-on-Don, on the southern coast, was captured by 23 July. So confident of victory did Hitler become that at the end of July he divided his forces into two: Army Group A under Field Marshal Wilhelm List was to drive south and capture the Caucasus oil, while Army Group B, commanded at first by von Bock, but then by General Maximilian von Weichs, was to drive east to the city of Stalingrad on the Volga and on to Astrakhan on the Caspian Sea. The whole Caucasus region produced annually more than four times the amount of oil that Germany consumed every year.

Of the two operations, the seizure of Stalingrad seemed the more straightforward. Across the vast Don steppe towards the Volga there were scattered remnants of Red Army units,

---

Opposite top left: A rare colour photograph of three of Hitler's ministers at the forward headquarters in Vinnetsa, Ukraine, in the summer of 1942. To the right is the Air Minister, Hermann Göring, in the centre the Economics Minister, Walter Funk, and at the left the Foreign Minister, Joachim von Ribbentrop. All three played a crucial role in constructing the new political and economic order in Europe.

Opposite top right: A pencil sketch of the German army chief-of-staff, General Franz Halder. He played a key role as chief-of-staff from 1938 until his dismissal in July 1942 after arguing with Hitler over strategy. He was on the fringes of the military opposition and ended the war in Dachau concentration camp.

Opposite below: A poster from January 1943 shows a massive artillery piece used for reducing areas of urban resistance. The image was part of a National Socialist wall newspaper, 'words of the week'. The slogan reads 'The military genius of the Führer, the bravery of our soldiers and the superiority of such weapons decide this war!'

THE SIEGE OF LENINGRAD 1941–1944

Throughout the whole period of victories and defeats in Russia, German forces laid siege to Russia's second city, Leningrad [St Petersburg]. Army Group North arrived at the outskirts of the city by early September 1941. The last rail link was cut on 30 August, the last land link was closed on 8 September. From early September the German army and air force began regular shelling and bombing of the city, which continued right through the period of the siege, 150,000 artillery shells in total. The city held around three-and-a-half million people, who had to produce their own weapons and eat what they could. In November the Red Army succeeded in opening a road across the ice of Lake Ladoga to the east of the city. Supplies across this thin lifeline kept the city going, but the cost was an estimated one million deaths from malnutrition, disease and cold. In 1942 the Red Army made several attempts to dislodge the German encirclement but failed to do so, although they prevented a German plan to storm the city in autumn 1942. Hitler wanted to capture Leningrad in 1942, partly as a political prize but also to allow the German army to link up with the Finns who held the northern part of the line around Leningrad. Operation 'Northern Lights' (Nordlichte) was scheduled for September and was to be led by Field Marshal von Manstein, who had successfully captured Sebastopol earlier in the year. The plan was thwarted by an attempted Soviet breakthrough and Manstein flew south to try to save Stalingrad. At the Red Army's second attempt, on 18 January 1943, a narrow neck of land was freed south of Lake Ladoga and more regular supplies could be brought into the city. Only on 27 January 1944 was the siege finally lifted when a general Soviet offensive drove the German army back from the city perimeter. Hitler's ambition to raze Leningrad to the ground was never realized.

demoralized and disorganized. The German Sixth Army under General Friedrich Paulus forced the pace across the steppe, crossing the River Don on 21 August, and two days later carved out a five-mile salient on the banks of the River Volga north of Stalingrad. Another 370,000 Soviet soldiers were lost in the two months of summer campaigning. Little stood between Paulus and the capture of Stalingrad. In the south the Caucasus campaign, Operation 'Edelweiss', made equally rapid progress at first. In early August First Panzer Army drove towards the oil cities of Maikop and Grozny, and on 9 August Maikop fell to a German attack. Progress then slowed with poor weather and the tough terrain of desert, mountain and rough grassland. The German forces moving south to the Caucasus Mountains reached some of the peaks but could go no further; in the east First Panzer Army tried to reach Grozny and the oil capital of Baku on the Caspian Sea but Soviet resistance stiffened, while long and difficult supply lines inhibited rapid movement. By September both branches of the German attack were held. Those oil wells in German hands had been set alight or blown up by the retreating Russians; the plan to seize Russian oil failed to materialize.

While the regular German army was driving into southern Russia, another war was being waged in the rear of German armies by scattered units of Soviet partisans, concealed in the forests and marshland of the western Soviet Union. This conflict merged with the racial war waged against Soviet Jews and provoked a wave of savage reprisals, orchestrated in many cases by the same security and SS commanders who had led the war against Jews and political enemies in 1941. The framework for the many atrocities committed came with the criminal orders of 1941, supplemented by instructions signed on 16 September 1941 by Field Marshal Wilhelm Keitel (Hitler's headquarters chief-of-staff) that 50–100 'communist' hostages were to be shot for every German death at the hands of civilians or partisans. During 1942 punishments routinely involved burning down whole villages and shooting the male population. In July the whole anti-partisan operation was placed in Himmler's hands. He ordered the term 'partisan' to be dropped and the word 'bandit' to be substituted. On 16 December 1942 he drew up new guidelines for the anti-partisan war which included specific

A German machine-gunner in snow uniform at the top of Mount Elbrus in the Caucasus Mountains in the autumn of 1942. The summit proved to be the limit of German expansion into the region and within weeks the German army was forced to retreat.

permission to kill women and children as well. During the great anti-partisan sweeps in Belorussia and Ukraine in 1942 tens of thousands were murdered, a high proportion of them Jews who were specially targeted as 'bandits'. 'Where the partisan is, there the Jew is too,' claimed SS General Erich von dem Bach-Zalewski, commander of the anti-partisan war behind Army Group Centre in 1942, and from 1943 commander of the entire anti-partisan campaign in Russia. His units ruthlessly exterminated village after village, measuring each victory by the number of victims.

Defeat in the Desert, Defeat in the Air

Within only a matter of weeks of Axis forces reaching their furthest territorial extent, the tide of battle turned against them. The first major defeats were inflicted in two battles fought in the distant Egyptian desert between a mixed Italian–German force and their British Commonwealth enemy. During the late summer, after Rommel's remarkable successes in May and June, both sides paused to reinforce their lines and prepare for the final battle over the Suez Canal. The advantage here lay with the defender, as large numbers of aircraft and tanks, including the American Sherman tank now available for the British, were sent to the Middle East. Rommel's supply lines were constantly harassed by submarines and aircraft as the naval battle in the Mediterranean swung in the Allies' favour. The second change for the enemy side was the decision by Churchill to appoint Lt. General Bernard Montgomery as commander of the British Eighth Army for the contest with Rommel.

The first major battle began on 30 August 1942 when Rommel led his mixed Italian–German force in an attempt to breach the Allied line between El Alamein and the Alam Halfa Ridge. His aim was to encircle the enemy forces by using four armoured divisions (two German, two Italian) to sweep forward through the desert and then turn north towards the coast. Carefully prepared defences trapped the tank force between two major fields of fire and Rommel was forced in early September to retreat with the loss of 450 tanks and vehicles. The stage was now set for an Allied counter-offensive. The balance of forces strongly favoured Montgomery, who commanded 230,000 men and 1,030 tanks against 100,000 German and Italian troops, with 500 tanks (of which 282 were weaker Italian models). The battle began on 23 October when Rommel was temporarily absent on sick leave. He returned two days later to find his forces already heavily pressed back around El Alamein. When, on 2 November, Montgomery released his second planned attack through the weaker Italian front, Rommel realized he faced defeat. Hitler refused to allow him to retreat for a further two days but then accepted reality. Rommel extricated much of his force from the Allied trap and raced westward

---

Opposite: A painting by the German artist W. Krogman of the British bombing raid on Cologne on 30 May 1942. This was the first large-scale raid carried out by RAF Bomber Command and was a shock to the German public. German air force leaders refused at first to believe it had been possible until further heavy raids on Essen and Bremen.

FIELD MARSHAL ERWIN ROMMEL (1891–1944)

Rommel was among the most flamboyant and resourceful of German commanders. He made his reputation as a tank commander but his initial contribution had been in the field of infantry tactics. The son of a teacher, he joined the army in 1910 and served with distinction in the First World War in Romania and Italy. He remained in the post-war army and served as an infantry instructor, writing a manual of infantry tactics. He commanded Hitler's bodyguard battalion during the Polish invasion but was released in 1940 to command the 7th Panzer Division, which he led successfully to the Channel coast. He was promoted to lieutenant general in January 1941 and posted the following month to North Africa as the commander of the Afrika Korps. His remarkable successes in the desert war brought promotion to field marshal on 22 June 1942 following his capture of Tobruk. He led the fighting retreat back to Tunisia and was then evacuated to Italy, where he commanded Army Group B. Hitler liked Rommel and he was popular with both the public and his own troops. He was not an enthusiast for National Socialism but found it impossible not to accept Hitler's leadership. He was chosen to command the defence of northern France in 1944 and tried to organize his forces to repel the Allied landing. He was aware of the July plot and not unsympathetic with the aims. On 17 July he was wounded in an air raid and returned to Germany to recover. When his name was implicated in the plot by one of those captured and tortured he was offered the choice of suicide or trial. He took cyanide on 14 October 1944 and was given a state funeral in Berlin.

across Libya, closely pursued by Montgomery's army and constantly subjected to Allied air attack. Tobruk was retaken on 13 November, and by 23 January the Libyan capital of Tripoli was in Allied hands. At the Second Battle of Alamein, Axis forces lost 400 tanks and 30,000 prisoners fell into Allied hands. This represented the costliest defeat yet experienced by German forces in the Western theatre of operations.

Rommel was forced to retreat all the way back to the French colony of Tunisia, where his forces stopped to dig in behind the Mareth Line, a defensive system built earlier by the French. By the time he arrived, the strategic situation in the Mediterranean had deteriorated yet further. On 8 November a combined Anglo-American seaborne force landed in north-west Africa in the French colonies of Algeria and Morocco. Operation 'Torch' was immediately successful and Rommel faced the prospect of being crushed between an advancing Montgomery and Allied forces approaching from the west. The precarious supply route from Italy across the Mediterranean was subject to ceaseless air and sea attacks. The overwhelming size of the Allies' Mediterranean Air Force ensured that by the end of 1942 air superiority throughout the theatre had passed decisively to the enemy. To counteract any sudden moves by the Allies, Hitler ordered the occupation of Vichy France on 11 November and German forces moved down to the French Mediterranean coastline.

The air threat also emerged over the Reich itself during 1942. The early bombing of German cities in the Ruhr and on the coast achieved very little, but from the spring of 1942 (when Air Marshal Arthur Harris assumed control of Bomber Command) the scale and intensity of bombing attacks escalated. On the night of 30/31 May 1942 Bomber Command sent 1,050 bombers to attack the city of Cologne. Only 868 bombed the city, causing 500 deaths and destroying 12,000 homes and apartments. On 2 June 956 bombers attacked Essen, and on 25 June, 1,006 were sent to destroy the port of Bremen. The amount of damage was limited, but Hitler retaliated by ordering so-called Baedeker raids (after the famous tourist guide) on British cultural centres. Attacks on Bath, Exeter, Canterbury and York did extensive damage but made no difference to British strategy. Over the course of 1942 bombing continued with increasing accuracy, thanks to the 'Gee' navigation aid, plus the addition of new heavy bombers. To hold back the tide of bombing, which had considerable impact on an urban population that had assumed it was virtually immune thanks to extensive anti-aircraft defences and the German fighter force, the German air force was now compelled to do what the RAF had done in 1940. Under the command of General Josef Kammhuber, a line of defences was constructed across northern and western Germany based on daytime and night fighters, and a sophisticated radar screen. At the Peenemünde research station on the Baltic coast work continued on a missile that might help reverse the tide of the air war. On 14 October 1942 the first successful launch of Werner von Braun's A4 rocket was carried out. So impressed was Hitler by the news that he ordered immediate production of 5,000. However, the rocket was still in an immature stage and the need for continued modification and improvement postponed its wartime use for a further two years.

FIELD MARSHAL ERICH VON MANSTEIN (1887–1973)

The son of a Prussian general, von Manstein was born Erich Lewinski. After the death of his parents he was adopted by the von Manstein family, whose surname he adopted as his own. He became a junior army officer in 1906 and fought on the western and eastern fronts in the First World War. He remained in the small post-war army, rising to the rank of colonel by 1933 with a post on the General Staff. By 1938 he was a lieutenant general, and assistant to the army chief-of-staff, General Beck. When Beck was sacked, Manstein was sent off to command a division in eastern Germany. For the Polish campaign he was recalled as von Rundstedt's chief-of-staff, and for the Battle of France he commanded an infantry corps. He was responsible for shaping the German plan of operations against France, with a shrewd understanding of the potential of armoured forces. He led a Panzer corps in the invasion of the Soviet Union, leading his force to the siege of Leningrad. He was then transferred south, where as commander of the German 11th Army he captured the Crimea and the port of Sebastopol. He led Army Group Don in its efforts to rescue Paulus at Stalingrad and recaptured Kharkov in a daring campaign in March 1943. He argued regularly with Hitler, who finally lost patience with him in the retreats of 1944. In March he was sacked as commander of Army Group South and retired for the rest of the war to his estate. He was captured by the British in 1945 and tried for war crimes against civilians. He was sentenced to 18 years' imprisonment in 1949 but on health grounds was freed in 1953. He was regarded by many Western soldiers as the outstanding commander on the German side; he blamed German defeat on Hitler's strategic incompetence.

The Road to the Volga

While Rommel tried to stave off defeat in North Africa, the German campaign in southern Russia, which had begun so auspiciously in July and August, began to face tougher resistance. German armies moved effortlessly at first across the broad plain towards the Volga. The landscape, recalled one veteran later, was a 'barren, naked, lifeless steppe, without a bush, without a tree, for miles without a village'. General Paulus led the German Sixth Army to the perimeter of Stalingrad by 19 August where he prepared to storm the city. To the north the line was breached and the Volga bank secured. On 23 August the German air force launched a 600-bomber raid on the city, killing (according to Soviet calculations) 40,000 people but creating a landscape of rubble which proved ideal for the tactics of urban guerrilla warfare adopted by the Soviet 62nd and 64th armies defending the city. Paulus expected to capture the city in a matter of days; at Hitler's headquarters in the Ukraine (where he waited impatiently, suffering from the heat and the endless insects) an 'exultant mood' was reported. Stalingrad bore Stalin's name and the symbolic significance of seizing Stalin's city played its part not only in Hitler's initial euphoria, but in his subsequent determination to hold it at all costs.

Paulus pushed his force into the city in late August but found that it was not to be easily captured. On 7 September he launched a concerted effort to dislodge the small Soviet force and drive it into the Volga. On 26 September an operation was mounted to seize the north of the city, which succeeded all bar one remaining factory. Fighting had to be carried out block by block, house by house. Though heavily outgunned and outnumbered, Soviet forces learned to exploit the broken urban environment. Hiding by day, they infiltrated German lines by night, recapturing lost buildings and murdering any soldiers they found; snipers were recruited to exact a high toll of any German soldier foolish enough to show himself. Nevertheless, by mid-October the Red Army held on to only a few small bridgeheads, protected by an array of Soviet artillery and rocket fire from the far bank of the river. The balance of air power also began to swing towards the Red air force. By October there were 1,500 Soviet aircraft against the 300 the campaign had started with; German air forces after months of combat faced mounting attrition. Both sides suffered declining numbers and fighting power as they battled in the cold with few reinforcements. On 9 November the Sixth Army finally carved out a large salient in the remaining Soviet frontline, seizing half-a-mile of the Volga bank, but the fighting petered out again three days later as the two exhausted forces battled to a halt.

Unknown to Paulus (and to the entire German army command) the Soviet enemy had devised and prepared a remarkable counter-stroke. Stalin's military deputy, General Zhukov, together with the army staff planned in September to carry out a massive flanking attack against the long and exposed Axis line across the steppe to Stalingrad. The operation was codenamed 'Uranus' and was one of a number of operations with planetary names planned for the autumn, including Operation Mars, a large-scale frontal assault on the weakened German Army Group Centre. During October and November the Red Army successfully concealed the movement of a million soldiers, 14,000 guns, 979 tanks and 1,350 aircraft. The operation was fixed for the northern attack on the flank on 19 November 1942, the south-eastern attack for a day later. The first wave hit the weaker armies of Germany's allies, Romanians and Italians who were holding

---

Opposite above: German soldiers edge forward through the ruins of the city of Stalingrad in October 1942. The destruction of the city created an ideal environment for the hit-and-run guerrilla tactics used by the Red Army. German forces took high casualties from sniper fire and sudden ambushes.

Opposite below left: A German Panzer III tank on the Kalmuck steppe north of Stalingrad in September 1942. German armour could travel swiftly across the open grassland but was slowed to crawling pace in the ruins of Stalingrad itself. The vast distances created exceptional problems of maintenance and supply.

Opposite below right: The commander of the encircled Axis forces at Stalingrad, General Friedrich Paulus, at one of the few airbases that remained operable during the final weeks of the campaign. In Soviet captivity, Paulus came to play a leading role in the Free Germany Committee run by German officers in Soviet hands, and after the war he settled in communist East Germany.

the line approaching Stalingrad. The element of complete surprise coupled with the lack of adequate equipment led to the rapid defeat of Axis forces. By 24 November the two Soviet pincers met on the Don steppe and Paulus, with more than 330,000 men, was encircled in Stalingrad. The German efforts to break the ring failed and Paulus was soon more than 200 miles from friendly forces. His request to Hitler, on 24 November, to break out of Stalingrad was refused; so, too, a second request a month later. He was promised 300 tons of supplies a day to be brought in by German transport aircraft after Göring had assured his leader that this was possible. Hitler ordered von Manstein to organize a Don Army Group to break the Soviet circle and provide a lifeline through to Paulus. In appalling weather conditions, and against determined Soviet resistance, the rescue mission set out on 12 December. By 24 December Manstein was forced to retreat or face a further encirclement. Three days later Hitler was compelled to approve the withdrawal of Army Group A from the Caucasus rather than risk encirclement there as well. The Red Army embarked on Operation 'Little Saturn' to drive Axis forces back over the same steppe they had crossed triumphantly three months before.

Hitler was faced in the last weeks of 1942 with a sudden and dramatic reversal of fortune. On 18 December the Italian foreign minister arrived at Hitler's headquarters in Rastenburg bearing a letter from Mussolini in which he recommended that the Axis seek a separate peace with the Soviet Union and concentrate their efforts on defeating the Western allies. The following day they discussed a possible withdrawal from North Africa. Hitler flatly rejected both proposals. He remained determined to hold out in the East and in particular to hold on to Stalingrad, whose capture had already been prematurely announced on 8 November. The Mediterranean theatre, which he had entered with reluctance in 1941, he now regarded as a vital area to defend. The German empire, which had been on the offensive for much of 1942, was by the end of the year a system under siege.

1943 Stalingrad

The whole of the first month of 1943 was focused on the struggle for Stalingrad and what it represented for the future of the German war effort. The crisis on the Volga obscured the defensive victory further north opposite Moscow, where Operation 'Mars' had cost the Soviet side 70,000 casualties and failed to dislodge the German front. The survival of Paulus's forces in the city depended on being able to keep it supplied with resources by air. Göring promised 300 tons a day, but most days the level was very much lower (averaging only 100 tons), while 488 transport aircraft were lost. By January rations for Axis soldiers in Stalingrad were down to two ounces of bread and one ounce of sugar a day. The troops were ravaged with frostbite and dysentery. Around 30,000 wounded men were flown out but most of those who remained were in little condition to fight by the time the full weight of the Soviet assault on the city, Operation 'Ring', began on 10 January 1943.

German forces were soon cleared from the steppe west of the city and bottled up in the ruins. They fought from desperation and fear, with ever-decreasing resources and will. On 22 January the army chief-of-staff, General Kurt Zeitzler, asked Hitler for permission for Paulus to surrender, but Hitler insisted that the Sixth Army should fight to the last man and last

THE POPULAR MOOD AFTER STALINGRAD

Security Service (SD), Report from the Reich (no. 356), 4 February 1943

I General

The reporting of the *end of the struggle in Stalingrad* has once again had a deep impact on the whole people. The speech of 30 January and the Führer proclamation are pushed into the background because of this event and play in the earnest discussions among the citizens a lesser role than a range of questions which are linked to the happenings in Stalingrad. In the first place the population asks about the *scale of the blood sacrifice*. The estimates range between figures of 60,000 and 300,000 men. As a result, people reckon that the greater part of the fighters in Stalingrad is dead. In relation to the troops fallen into Russian captivity people swing between two perceptions. Some declare that captivity is worse than death because the Bolsheviks will handle inhumanely the soldiers that have fallen into their hands. Others on the other hand insist that it is fortunate not everyone had fallen, so there is still hope that later part of them might return home. The dependants of the fighters in Stalingrad particularly suffer very much from this division of opinion and the consequent uncertainty.

Further in all elements of the population the *unavoidability of the development in Stalingrad and the necessity for the monstrous sacrifice* is discussed. In detail, the citizens are moved to ask if the threat to Stalingrad was itself not properly recognized. The air reconnaissance must have confirmed the approach of Russian armies sent against Stalingrad. The question is also asked, for what reasons the city was not evacuated while there was still time. Above all it is observed that the strength of the enemy must have been underestimated, otherwise the risk would not have been undertaken, of holding Stalingrad even after the encirclement. The population cannot grasp that the abandonment of Stalingrad was not possible and in part do not have a proper understanding of the strategic significance of the struggles, because of a lack of precise orientation about the whole development of the southern sector of the Eastern Front. In part it is doubted that the defenders of Stalingrad in the end tied down strong forces of the enemy.

The third point around which the discussions of the citizens revolve is the *significance of the struggle for Stalingrad in the whole course of the war*. There is a general conviction that *Stalingrad signifies a turning point* in the war. While those of a fighting nature feel Stalingrad as an obligation for the final mobilization of all forces at the front and at home, from which mobilization they hope for victory, the more feeble citizens are inclined in the case of Stalingrad to see the beginning of the end.

Source: Heinz Boberach (ed.) *Meldungen aus dem Reich: Die geheime Lageberichte des Sicherheitsdienstes der SS 1938–1945* (Pawlak Verlag, Herrsching, 1984) vol. 12, pp. 4750–51

JOSEPH GOEBBELS (1897–1945)

Joseph Goebbels was one of the most important political figures in the Third Reich, head of the whole apparatus of propaganda and culture during the entire life of the dictatorship. He was born into a Catholic working-class family in the Rhineland. He was a gifted pupil and went on to study history and literature at Heidelberg University, where he took a doctorate in the 1920s. He suffered polio as a child and had a permanently deformed foot which prevented him from doing military service in the First World War. He was an unstable, radical personality with a deep hostility to the world of bourgeois Germany and a hatred of Marxism, which he associated with the Jews. He joined the National Socialist Party in 1922 and aligned himself on the left wing of the party, strongly anti-capitalist in outlook. His sharp intellect and bitter prejudices soon won him promotion. In 1926 he was appointed regional leader of Berlin-Brandenburg and the following year launched a journal *Der Angriff* (The Attack) which continued to be published after 1933. In 1929 he became Reich Propaganda Leader of the Party, a position he held down to 1945. In 1933 he was made Minister for Propaganda and Public Enlightenment, in which he controlled not only everything that was broadcast or published in the press, but all other forms of cultural production – art, theatre, film and literature. He played an important part in orchestrating the Night of Broken Glass in November 1938 and was an important influence on Hitler's own anti-Semitism. He was a tireless worker who committed himself to selling the myth of Adolf Hitler and to countering all the negative views of the Third Reich generated abroad. He remained dedicated to the most extreme efforts in the war and in summer 1944 was rewarded with the increasingly hollow position of General Plenipotentiary for Total War. He committed suicide with his wife and children in Hitler's bunker on 1 May 1945.

bullet. On 30 January 1943 he promoted Paulus to field marshal, perhaps in the hope that it would give him greater courage to hold out. The following day he surrendered. The Fourth Panzer Army held out for longer, but capitulated on 2 February. The losses at Stalingrad eclipsed anything yet experienced. The German army lost 147,000 dead and a further 91,000 went into captivity, few of whom returned after the war. The scale of the disaster could not be concealed from the German public. After a delay of several days it was announced on the radio on 3 February, alongside excerpts from Wagner's opera *Rienzi*. At his headquarters Hitler could not conceal his rage and disappointment, not least the failure of Paulus to kill himself rather than be caught by the Russians – an early indication of what Hitler himself would do two years later in Berlin.

The sense that the Third Reich had reached a turning point was evident in the efforts to transform Germany into a state utterly dedicated to the struggle for final victory, whatever the sacrifice. The leading spokesman for this view was the Propaganda Minister, Joseph Goebbels.

He tried in late 1942 and early 1943 to persuade other Party leaders that Germany should now be converted into a 'war camp' in which all vestiges of civilian life were stamped out. War would become everyone's defining activity, at home as well as on the fighting front. When he tried to interest Hitler in the proposal in October, and again in December 1942, he found him too preoccupied with the military situation. But in early January, with disaster looming, Hitler agreed to the idea of a decree to encourage the German people to accept the harsh realities of total war. Goebbels involved Hitler's secretary Martin Bormann, the Chancellery secretary Hans Lammers and the Armaments Minister, Albert Speer. On 13 January a decree drafted by the group was signed by Hitler calling on higher than ever levels of compulsory mobilization of men and women on the home front. Five days later, on 18 January, Hitler appointed a three-man committee consisting of Bormann, Lammers and his military headquarters chief, Keitel, to steer through the necessary measures.

The new committee lacked any real power and never functioned as an effective mobilizing agency. Goebbels continued to press for his own involvement in the campaign for total war, and on 18 February he prepared a long speech for a meeting at the Sports Palace where he

At the end of the Stalingrad campaign around 90,000 Axis soldiers entered Soviet captivity. Soviet POW camps were small and soon overcrowded and thousands of German prisoners died of hunger and cold. Only in 1943, as the number of captured Germans increased, were additional purpose-built camps created so that German prisoners could work for the Soviet war effort.

293

THE PEOPLE'S COURT

On 20 August 1942 the National Socialist state secretary in the Ministry of Justice, Roland Freisler, was appointed President of the People's Court [*Volksgerichtshof*]. His predecessor, Otto Thierack, was appointed Minister of Justice. The People's Court, based in Berlin, was founded on 24 April 1934 to try all cases involving high treason or a danger to the state. There were also Special Courts in provincial capitals which had responsibility for trying political offences. During the war the People's Court was also responsible for trying cases of resistance in occupied Europe under the 'Night and Fog' Decree of 7 December 1941, which allowed the German authorities to seize opponents and resistance fighters in northern and western Europe and place them in indefinite detention or subject them to judicial murder. Under Freisler the People's Court began to impose an ever increasing number of death sentences. In 1941 there had been 102; in 1942 there were 2,572, in 1943 3,338 and in 1944 4,379. This last figure included those condemned after the failed July Plot. The People's Court also tried all cases of defeatism – 'undermining national defence' – and the number of these cases increased sharply after the defeat at Stalingrad, 241 cases in 1943 and 893 cases in 1944. One case involved a man who claimed after the bombing of Hamburg that the problem was that German fighters could not fly high enough to engage the enemy. He was condemned to death on 6 September 1943. Freisler himself was killed during the course of an Allied air raid on 3 February 1945 inside the court building while conducting further trials against the conspirators of the July Plot.

planned to launch the current slogan. He drove to the stadium in a new bulletproof Mercedes car, a recent Christmas present from Hitler after Goebbels had survived an assassination attempt the previous December. The hall was filled with the Party faithful and carried a banner hung across the room proclaiming 'Total War – Shortest War'. In an impassioned speech, interrupted by enthusiastic applause, he painted a lurid vision of 'terror, the ghost of famine, and complete European anarchy' if the Soviet Union won. He ended his speech by asking his audience if they wanted total war and was greeted with baying agreement. The audience reaction was noisy and hysterical. German radio stayed on the air so that the German public could hear the mood of frenzied approval. It brought Goebbels no nearer his goal of playing a part in the transformation of Germany's home front. Nor was the message of total war as widely approved as his staged speech had suggested. The secret intelligence reports on German opinion showed growing alarm and uncertainty among the German population after Stalingrad. For most Germans the level of sacrifice and increased efforts of the previous two years already heralded the onset of total war. What Stalingrad did was to make clear for the first time that this was a war that Germany and her allies might not win.

Resistance and Persecution

Stalingrad also had the effect of prompting those few Germans who had contemplated resistance to the regime to act more boldly. Resistance continued throughout the war years, usually in small concealed cells of those hostile to the regime. They were regularly broken up by the Gestapo, and their members executed or sent to camps. Most of the cells were social-democrat or communist in sympathy, but there were groups that were not obviously Marxist. The White Rose circle in Munich was one example. The name was taken from a popular novel of the 1930s and its chief members were two siblings, Hans and Sophie Scholl, children of a mayor who was ousted from his job in 1933. Hans joined the Hitler Youth but later left it to join a small youth protest group, which earned him a spell in prison. He did war service in the Medical Corps but was in Munich in late 1942 where, together with his sister and an academic expert in folk music, Kurt Huber, they drafted flyers protesting against the authoritarian nature of the regime, which they posted on walls around the city. They were caught on 18 February 1943 after they were denounced by a university porter and the Scholls were beheaded four days later. Huber was held for longer but killed in July.

Many protests ended with death or imprisonment, though in some cases the authorities were uncertain how to act. Dissident youth gangs in Leipzig and the industrial area of the north-west (the best known of which styled themselves the Edelweiss Pirates) engaged in acts of

Portraits taken in 1941 of Hans Scholl (1918–1943) and his sister Sophie (1921–1943).

violence against Hitler Youth, scrawled slogans on walls and listened to proscribed jazz. In December 1942 the Gestapo made a sweep of the Ruhr and Rhineland cities, netting 739 boys and girls, many of whom ended up in a youth concentration camp. The most serious form of protest came not from the traditional left or disaffected youth, but from within the heart of the regime itself. The roots of the conservative opposition to Hitler, based in the army, the ministries and judiciary, went back to the failed attempts to overthrow Hitler in 1938 and 1939 before the coming of war. During the period of victory many conservative critics held their fire while they waited to see what would happen, but by 1943 an important group based around the former army chief-of-staff Ludwig Beck and the former mayor of Leipzig, Carl Goerdeler, saw impending military disaster as a sign that they should overthrow Hitler and try to change the direction of German policy, particularly towards the West, where efforts had been made to win Allied support for the resistance.

The circle of those sympathetic to the resisters was much wider than those who participated, but among senior officers there were many who were willing to discuss the possibility of a *coup d'état* and even to act. Some were nationalists, who had initially exhibited sympathy for Hitler's national revolution, but fear that Hitler would destroy Germany overcame their scruples about contemplating the overthrow of their head of state and commander-in-chief. The first attempt to assassinate Hitler came on 13 March 1943, when a basket containing two bottles of Cointreau primed with explosives was smuggled on to Hitler's aircraft when he stopped briefly at the headquarters of Army Group Centre. Two officers, General Henning von Treschkow and Fabian von Schlabrendorff, saw to it that the bottles were properly stowed with their time fuses primed. Hitler flew off to Rastenburg but the device failed to detonate. A few days later, on 21 March, a second assassination attempt was made by Colonel Rudolf von Gersdorff, who turned himself into a suicide bomber for Hitler's annual speech for Heroes' Memorial Day in Berlin. However he failed to get near enough to his victim before Hitler made an early departure. The failures provoked some disillusionment and not until the following year were further serious attempts made to rid Germany of Hitler.

One issue that united the conservative resistance was their revulsion against the murder of the Jews. During the first months of 1943 the system of deportation and extermination spread out over the whole of occupied Europe. The process of rounding up Germany's own remaining Jews was also speeded up. Soon after Goebbels's failed attempt to become the director of the total war effort, he personally organized the final exodus of Berlin Jews to the death camps. As Party regional leader in Berlin he wielded extensive powers. Following Hitler's decision in late January to end the practice of using skilled Jewish labour in German factories, Goebbels ordered the SS on 27 February 1943 to round up all remaining Jews working in Berlin factories and to ship them to the east. By mid-March 36,000 of the 66,000 Jews living in Berlin had been deported eastwards; a further 15,000 elderly Jews were deported to the 'model' camp of Theresienstadt. By 19 May Goebbels declared Berlin to be 'Jew-free'. On 23 May Himmler issued an order to complete the transfer to the east of all German Jews remaining in the rest of the country. Outside Germany the net now extended as far as the Mediterranean. In January plans were set up to deport Greek Jews northwards and

THE WHITE ROSE: THE FINAL LEAFLET, FEBRUARY 1943

Fellow Students!

Our people stands shocked before the downfall of the men at Stalingrad. Three hundred and thirty thousand German men have been led to death and imprisonment senselessly and irresponsibly through the clever strategy of the World War corporal.

Among the German people ferments the question: Do we want to trust again the fate of our armies to a dilettante? Do we want to sacrifice the rest of our German youth to the lowest instincts for power of a party clique? Never again! The day of reckoning has arrived, the reckoning of German youth with the most abhorrent tyranny that our people has ever suffered. In the name of the entire German people we demand back from the state of Adolf Hitler personal freedom, the costliest possession of the Germans, about which we have deceived ourselves in the most wretched way.

We have grown up in a state that ruthlessly stifles every free expression of opinion. HJ, SA and SS have tried in the most fruitful formative years of our lives to make us uniform, to revolutionize us, to drug us. 'Ideological schooling' means the hateful methods of suffocating growing self-awareness and self-worth in a fog of empty phrases. ....

For us there is only one slogan, struggle against the Party! Out of the Party formations in which they want to keep us even more politically silent. Away, out of the lecture rooms of the SS lower leaders and higher leaders and the Party toadies! For us it is about true scholarship and genuine freedom of the spirit! No means of threat can terrify us, not even the closing of our high schools. It signifies the struggle of each one of us for our future – our freedom and honour in a form of the state conscious of its ethical responsibility.....

Fellow students! The German people look to us! They expect from us as in 1813 with the breaking of the Napoleonic tyranny, the breaking of the National Socialist terror with the power of the spirit! .....

Source: Fred Breinersdorfer (ed.) *Sophie Scholl: Die letzten Tage* (Fischer Taschenbuch Verlag, Frankfurt a M, 2005), pp. 29–31

Above: A woman fighter is captured in the Warsaw Ghetto during the uprising that took place in April and May 1943. Those captured were either shot or sent to extermination camps. At least 400 German soldiers and police were killed during the uprising.

Opposite above: A picture of a group of European Jews arrived at the station in the Auschwitz-Birkenau concentration and extermination camp in 1943. The arrivals were made to walk from the platforms to the extermination buildings in Birkenau after those deemed fit for work had been selected by an SS doctor and sent to the Auschwitz labour camp.

Opposite below: A letter from a political prisoner at Auschwitz to his mother in February 1943. The front of the envelope carries a list of rules by the camp commandant governing correspondence for prisoners. Two letters or postcards could be received each month and two sent out. The letters had to be clearly written, no longer than 15 lines and the envelopes left unsealed.

Konzentrationslager Auschwitz

Folgende Anordnungen sind beim Schriftverkehr mit Gefangenen zu beachten:

1.) Jeder Schutzhaftgefangene darf im Monat zwei Briefe oder zwei Karten von seinen Angehörigen empfangen und an sie absenden. Die Briefe an die Gefangenen müssen gut lesbar mit Tinte geschrieben sein und dürfen nur 15 Zeilen auf einer Seite enthalten. Gestattet ist nur ein Briefbogen normaler Größe. Briefumschläge müssen ungefüttert sein. In einem Briefe dürfen nur 5 Briefmarken à 12 Pfg. beigelegt werden. Alles andere ist verboten und unterliegt der Beschlagnahme. Postkarten haben 10 Zeilen. Lichtbilder dürfen als Postkarten nicht verwendet werden.

2.) Geldsendungen sind gestattet.

3.) Es ist darauf zu achten, daß bei Geldoder Postsendungen die genaue Adresse, bestehend aus: Name, Geburtsdatum und Gefangenen-Nummer, auf die Sendungen zu schreiben ist. Ist die Adresse fehlerhaft, geht die Post an den Absender zurück oder wird vernichtet.

4.) Zeitungen sind gestattet, dürfen aber nur durch die Poststelle des K.L. Auschwitz bestellt werden.

5.) Pakete dürfen nicht geschickt werden, da die Gefangenen im Lager alles kaufen können.

6.) Entlassungsgesuche aus der Schutzhaft an die Lagerleitung sind zwecklos.

7.) Sprecherlaubnis und Besuche von Gefangenen im Konzentrationslager sind grundsätzlich nicht gestattet.

Der Lagerkommandant.

Frau

Kubs Emilie

Heinrichsdorf Hindenburg 81.

Mähr. Ostrau

Böhm u. Mähr.

by May around 45,000 Jewish inhabitants from the ancient Jewish quarters of Salonika had been sent to Auschwitz. In late December, after the occupation of Vichy France, Hitler gave Himmler permission to start a systematic deportation of all French Jews. Raids were staged in January and the first trains rolled east in February. The French authorities did not all work willingly to fulfil the German plan, and in May Himmler demanded that all French Jews who had arrived after 1927 should have their citizenship stripped from them and be deported to Germany by July. In May mass transfers of Dutch and Croatian Jews to the east were also under way, and negotiations were begun with the Hungarian government of Admiral Horthy for the liquidation of Hungary's 800,000 Jews.

The situation in occupied Poland also sharpened in early 1943. In January the clearing of 54 remaining Jewish residential districts in the Lublin district of the Generalgouvernement was ordered, and in the same month Himmler approved the liquidation of the Warsaw Ghetto. In March the ghetto in Cracow, capital of the Generalgouvernement, was closed and its population killed. The movement of Jews out of the Warsaw Ghetto, which had begun in 1942, was carried out swiftly and with great brutality. By the end of 1942 300,000 had been sent to Treblinka. Among the 60,000 who remained, a small Jewish Fighting Organization was formed which prepared to resist by force the final destruction of the ghetto. On 19 April, under the command of SS Brigade Leader Jürgen Stroop, around 3,000 SS troops and police moved in to clear the ghetto, to be met by machine-gun fire, Molotov cocktails and grenades (which was all the 1,000 Jewish fighters had). The small armed units, made up of both men and women, fought a bitter war against the SS. The German operation involved moving from house to house in the ghetto, destroying every building where there were signs of resistance and killing all the Jews who resisted. The remaining inhabitants could fight no more by mid-May; they were rounded up and sent to Treblinka and Maidanek for immediate extermination. Around 14,000 died in the fighting, but at the cost of an estimated 1,400 German casualties.

The Jews were not the only victims of the rising tide of brutal racial policy. On 16 December 1942 Himmler ordered the deportation of the Gypsy populations, the Sinti and Roma, to Auschwitz. They were gathered in a special camp at Auschwitz for so-called 'mixed-race' Gypsies, whose behaviour was deemed to be more criminal and anti-social than that of pure-blood Gypsies. Over 13,000 Gypsies were sent to Auschwitz from Germany, 10,000 from other parts of Europe. A large proportion died of typhus contracted in the camp and 5,600 were gassed. In the East, Gypsies were regarded as potential partisans or spies and murdered along with Jews, an estimated 64,700 in total. Thanks to this and similar actions the concentration camp population increased sharply in size during 1943. In August 1942 it had numbered 115,000, by June 1943 199,500. The majority of the new prisoners were non-Germans: Eastern prisoners-of-war sent as a punishment; political opponents from all over occupied Europe; forced foreign labourers whose political outlook or behaviour was regarded as subversive or socially dangerous. The camp inmates had a high mortality rate from disease, malnutrition and the harsh conditions of work. When it was discovered in December 1942 that 70,000 out of the recent camp intake of 136,000 prisoners had died, the SS authorities insisted that a higher survival rate had to be guaranteed so that the prisoners could be used as

THE END OF THE WARSAW GHETTO, APRIL 1943

WARSAW, 19 April 1944: the first anniversary

On Saturday, 17 April, sentries are posted outside the ghetto. Sunday night, units of German police enter the ghetto from Nalewki Street. Meeting with fire, they retreat. On Monday the siege begins. A new ultimatum: unconditional surrender, complete submission to German mercy. The ultimatum is categorically rejected. The Jews are not going to go to the trains. Their answer is *war*. A significant number of shop workers don't see any way out. They have no weapons. Are they to fight with their bare hands? They have no choice; they give in. They go to the Umschlagplatz and on to Trawniki and Poniatów, where they won't last more than six months. The rest decide to fight until the last Jew has the last shell in his pocket.

It will fall to others to describe the battle, to portray the fighters who resisted to their last breath: the children with rifles, the old men and young women with petrol bombs hurling themselves at the tanks, the mothers with their infants rushing into burning buildings to avoid capture. Others will tell about a dozen men charging an entire company, about the night raiders disguised as German soldiers, about the victories and defeats. And finally they will recount how one building after the next was bombed from the air and set alight, one point of resistance after another. They will praise the struggle and those who fought, their deeds and their exceptional heroism....

The fighters have chosen to die, to fall one after the other. That's their decision. But what about the others? Their wives will fight with them, shoulder to shoulder. But what about their mothers and fathers? What of their children? Shall they be left to their fate, which no longer means the gas chambers but being burned alive? Abandon them to the flames? Inconceivable! What then? Kill them ourselves? Hardly – the few bullets left are too valuable, they can't be wasted; each one is marked for a German. What about gas? It's been cut off. There's cyanide – but how to find enough? And when to use it?

So don't be surprised when people compare this to other great historical examples and speak of 'exemplary heroism'. The decisions these people had to make, and the battle they fought, were by no means easy.

Source: Michael Grynberg (ed.) *Words to Outlive Us: Eyewitness Accounts From the Warsaw Ghetto* (Granta, London, 2003), pp. 254–5. Testimony of Jan Mawult written in 1944.

labour for the war effort. Conditions improved marginally in 1943, with monthly mortality rates falling from 10–20 per cent down to 2–3 per cent, but the reality for most prisoners was a wearing regime of physical labour – ten or twelve hours a day on a slender diet with the prospect of vicious punishment or torture for any infringement.

Retreat in the Mediterranean

In the aftermath of defeat at Stalingrad, the possibility of defeat in North Africa loomed larger. The withdrawal of Axis forces to Tunisia in December 1942 made it evident that the theatre could no longer be adequately defended, but the German forces, assisted by the Italian First Army, commanded by Marshal Giovanni Messe, built two strong defensive lines, one in the south, manned by the Afrika Korps, and a second along the western frontier of Tunisia, manned by Col. General Hans-Jürgen von Arnim's Fifth Panzer Army. Axis forces totalled almost 250,000 men, but were short of tanks and heavy equipment and aircraft. Hitler's decision in December 1942 that North Africa would be defended at all costs turned Tunisia into a besieged fortress.

American forces advancing from the West after the Torch landings planned to divide the Axis armies by driving a wedge to the sea through central Tunisia, but instead the inexperienced American commanders found themselves driven back by a sudden offensive launched by the two German Panzer groups. On 20 February, at the Kasserine Pass, Rommel inflicted what was to be the last German victory in Africa. Two days later the German offensive stalled and Rommel moved his forces back to the southern Mareth Line, expecting an attack from Montgomery's Eighth Army. Here, too, Rommel thought attack the better option and on 6 March 1943 drove three armoured divisions against the Allied line. Montgomery had been warned in advance by intercepted Enigma traffic and set a trap. Rommel was forced to retreat back and on 9 March flew to see Hitler to ask for more reinforcements. Hitler refused and sent Rommel on sick leave; his command in Tunisia was taken over by von Arnim. On 20/21 March Montgomery attacked the Mareth Line, outflanking it to the west and forcing a rapid German retreat. By early April, Axis forces were bottled up in the north-west corner of Tunisia around Bizerta and the capital, Tunis. On 8 April Hitler and Mussolini, meeting at Klessheim Castle in Austria, ordered von Arnim and Messe to hold out to the last rather than surrender or retreat. The do-or-die mentality became characteristic of Hitler's approach to the outcome of the war. Two days later at Klessheim he told the Romanian leader that there was no way out save for 'clear victory or absolute annihilation'.

The final battle in Tunisia was almost absurdly one-sided. Axis forces had 150 serviceable tanks against 1,500. Allied air forces were overwhelming, shooting down 432 Axis aircraft for the loss of just 35 of their own. On 6 May 1943 a general offensive was launched from west and south, and the following day both Bizerta and Tunis were in Allied hands. Small pockets of resistance held out for few days but on 13 May 1943 von Arnim surrendered. Some 238,000 German and Italian prisoners were taken, a defeat ranking in scale with the recent disaster in Russia. Only three days later an RAF bombing attack destroyed the Ruhr dams and on 24

May Grand Admiral Dönitz, who had succeeded Raeder as commander-in-chief of the German navy, suspended the submarine war in the Atlantic because of unacceptably high losses of boats and crews. At Berchtesgaden on 31 May Dönitz passed on the news to Hitler. Within the space of a month the German position had been irreversibly undermined and the initiative passed to the Allies. After the disaster in Tunisia, the situation in the Mediterranean theatre continued to deteriorate. German forces were placed in Sicily and mainland Italy to help forestall an Allied landing, and to anticipate any sudden crisis if Mussolini's regime collapsed or faced serious internal unrest. Italian ports and cities were subjected to heavy Allied bombardment as German air strength in the theatre evaporated. On 9/10 July 1943 the

Above: During the last days of the Allied invasion of Sicily most German forces were successfully evacuated to the mainland across the Straits of Messina. Here a ferry has arrived on the Calabrian coast preparing to disembark German soldiers on 16 August 1943.

Overleaf: A long line of German and Italian prisoners-of-war captured during the campaign in Tunisia. The surrender of 238,000 prisoners was the largest single capture of Axis soldiers so far in the war and ended Hitler's hopes of holding the position in the Mediterranean theatre.

Allies mounted a vast seaborne invasion of Sicily under the codename 'Husky'. Thanks to Allied disinformation, Hitler expected some kind of operation in the Balkan area and reinforced the German garrison there. In Sicily around 50,000 German troops and 270,000 Italians faced an invasion force of 180,000 American and British Commonwealth soldiers. The fight for the island was brief, Italian forces having little stomach for the contest. By 22 July Palermo was in Allied hands; by 5 August Catania, on the east coast. German forces fought a skilful rearguard action and by the time Allied forces converged on Messina, opposite the Italian mainland, 100,000 Axis forces had been evacuated, a large part of them German.

During the course of the campaign, six days after the Allied bombing of rail communications in Rome on 19 July, Mussolini was overthrown and put under arrest. The new Italian government of Marshal Pietro Badoglio continued to fight alongside the Germans, but his object was to find some way of extricating Italy from the war. On 3 September 1943 Allied forces crossed into mainland Italy and on 8 September Italy announced an armistice. Immediately German units stationed in Italy disarmed Italian soldiers and treated Italy as yet another occupied state. Some 650,000 Italian soldiers and 100,000 civilians were sent to Germany as forced labour, while Italian workers in northern Italy were compelled to continue producing materials and weapons for the German war effort. On 12 September Mussolini was freed from prison in a daring rescue by SS glider troops led by SS Lt. Colonel Otto Skorzeny, organizer of the special commando groups set up by the RSHA in 1942 known as Friedenthal Hunting Units (*Friedenthaler Jagdverbände*). He was taken from Gran Sasso in the Abruzzi mountains and installed at Salò as head of a fascist Italian Social Republic, entirely subservient to the German occupiers and the German commander-in-chief, Field Marshal Kesselring. In the south of Italy British Commonwealth and American armies pushed slowly northwards, meeting stronger resistance from the Germans. On 1 October Naples fell to the Allies and the German army pulled back to prepared positions on a line north of the port. The stage was set for a gruelling eighteen-month contest up the narrow and mountainous Italian peninsula.

Germany under the Bombs

Throughout the crisis over Stalingrad and the Mediterranean, the RAF and the United States Army Air Forces began more regular and heavier bombing attacks on occupied Europe and the German homeland. The campaign was launched in January 1943 at the inter-Allied Casablanca Conference; the Combined Bomber Offensive was designed to destroy Germany's capacity to make war by attacking her military and heavy industries by day and her major industrial cities, and the morale of the workforce, by night. The offensive was codenamed Operation Pointblank. The first stage in the new campaign was launched by RAF Bomber Command in the spring of 1943, with what was called 'The Battle of the Ruhr'.

The cities of the Ruhr and Rhineland had been hit repeatedly during 1941 and 1942, though the damage had been limited. The 'Battle of the Ruhr' involved much heavier raids with a higher level of death and urban destruction. From January 1943, when American air forces began regular bombing of Germany, urban populations found themselves subjected to

daytime air alarms as well, which interrupted work and left many German workers tired and under stress for long periods of time. From the spring of 1943 the German war effort had to be diverted in ever larger measure to combat the bombing. Some 70 per cent of German fighter strength was concentrated in the West. The need to respond to the bombing produced a flow of technical and tactical innovations. German night-fighters were equipped with radar known as *Lichtenstein*, allowing them to hunt bomber streams in large groups; after the radar was jammed by British scientific intelligence, new equipment, SN2, was introduced with even greater effect. Single-engined fighters were also brought into the battle, flying a tactic known as 'Wild Sow' in which they would attack bombers caught in a cone of searchlights. The result of these innovations was to exact a heavy toll on the attacking bomber force. On the ground,

In response to the Allied bombing of Germany a large official programme of evacuation was organized from the major German cities to safer rural and small-town destinations. There also developed an unofficial exodus of the urban population which by 1945 had created a combined evacuation of almost 9 million Germans from the threatened areas.

AFTER THE FIRESTORM: HAMBURG, AUGUST 1943

I have gone through all these districts, by foot or by car. Only a few main streets were cleared, but mile after mile there was not a single living house. And if you tried to work your way through the ruins on either side, right away you would lose all sense of time and direction. In areas I thought I knew well, I lost my way completely. I searched for a street that I should have been able to find in my sleep. I stood where I thought it must be and didn't know which way to turn. I counted on my fingers the lateral furrows in the rubble, but I could not find the street again. And if after hours of searching you met a person, it would only be someone else wandering in a dream through the eternal wasteland....A week later, these sections of the city were completely closed off. A high wall was built round them; there certainly were enough stones. Armed guards stood at the entrance...One could see convicts in striped suits working in there. They were supposed to recover the dead. People said that the corpses, or whatever one wants to call the remains of dead people, were burned on the spot or destroyed in the cellars with flamethrowers. But actually it was worse. The flies were so thick that the men couldn't get into the cellars, they kept slipping on maggots the size of fingers, and the flames had to clear the way for them to reach those who had perished in flames.

Rats and flies were the lords of the city. Insolent and fat, the rats disported themselves on the streets. But even more nauseating were the flies. They were large and of a shimmering green; no one had ever seen flies like this. They wallowed in swarming clumps on the pavement, sat, copulating, on top of the ruined walls, warmed themselves, bloated and tired, on splinters of window glass. When they could no longer fly, they would crawl after us through the narrowest crevices, soiling everything, and their rustling and buzzing was the first thing one heard in the morning. This didn't stop until October.

Source: Hans Nossack *The End: Hamburg 1943* (University of Chicago Press, Chicago, 2004), pp. 42–4. Translated by Joel Agee, originally written in November 1943.

efforts were made to reduce the level of damage to German society. Mass evacuation was carried out to the safer rural and small-town areas of southern and central Germany. In January 1943 Goebbels was appointed to run an Interministerial Committee for the Relief of Air Raid Damage, and he toured the stricken cities to try to boost morale of the local populations. At the end of the year, on 10 December 1943, Hitler made Goebbels the Director of a centralized 'Inspectorate of Civil Air War Measures'.

During the spring and summer months the bomber offensive increased in intensity. On the night of 17/18 May 1943 a special unit of RAF Lancaster bombers attacked, and breached, the Möhne and Eder dams in the Ruhr valley. The attack resulted in a flooded area fifty miles in length and the estimated death of 1,650 people, including 1,026 POWs and foreign labourers. The damage was quickly repaired and by 27 June the water supply to the region was fully restored. On the night of 24/25 May Dortmund suffered the heaviest raid yet mounted, when 800 mainly four-engined bombers dropped 2,500 tons of bombs in one night. A few days later, on 29/30 May Barmen suffered the first 'firestorm' and 3,500 dead; on 28/29 June Cologne suffered a death toll of 4,370, the highest death rate so far from the bombing attacks. Between March and July there were over 43 main raids. In July the German Labour Front under Robert Ley set up a special 'Ruhr Action Group' to bring assistance to the dispossessed and homeless populations.

The toll exacted in the 'Battle of the Ruhr' paled in comparison with the series of raids on Hamburg between 24 July and 2 August 1943 under the codename Operation 'Gomorrah'. The attacks were co-ordinated by RAF Bomber Command and the US Eighth Air Force so that the city would be hit by night and day. The RAF used a new tactic to defeat German radar, dropping thousands of small strips of aluminized paper ('Window'). The defences were thrown into confusion on the night of the first attack on 24/25 July and never recovered the initiative when attacks were repeated on 27/28 July with heavy loads of incendiaries. The fires could not be quenched and swiftly merged together, creating an intense heat that sucked in the cold air from the surrounding area, generating a fierce hot wind up to 240 m.p.h. that devoured everything in its path. An estimated 45,000 people died in the Hamburg raids and ten square miles of the city were obliterated. Yet within a matter of months production had recovered. By the end of 1943 it was back to 82 per cent of the level before the firestorm.

For the German population the destruction of Hamburg was a profound shock and apocalyptic rumours spread across the country. The refugees from the city described scenes of grotesque horror. Albert Speer confessed in his memoirs that the raid 'put the fear of God in me' and he told Hitler that six more raids like Hamburg would bring armaments production to a halt. The German air force chief-of-staff, General Hans Jeschonnek, was so distressed by the failure of his force to stem this and other attacks that on 19 August 1943 he shot himself. However, the unforeseen effect of the attacks on Hamburg proved to be the exception in 1943. Over the following months the initiative passed again to the German air defence. The 'Battle of Berlin', launched by Bomber Command in November 1943, exacted a heavy toll on the attacking bombers and led to a temporary pause in the British campaign. Greater success was achieved against the US bombers. In two daylight attacks far into Germany against the ball-bearing factories at Schweinfurt, the attacking force suffered heavy casualties: in the attack on 17 August 1943 German fighters and anti-aircraft fire destroyed 19 per cent of the force and damaged around 30 per cent of the rest; on 14 October 1943 a force of 300 American bombers returned to Schweinfurt but suffered a loss of 60 more and damage to 138. Daylight attacks were also temporarily suspended.

From Kursk to Kiev: Disaster in Russia

After the defeat at Stalingrad German forces had been compelled to draw back the front line in the south and regroup for the expected conflicts in the spring and summer. This involved a difficult negotiation between von Manstein, commander of Army Group Don, and Hitler at the headquarters in Rastenburg. In the end Hitler agreed to withdraw from Rostov and to retreat to a defensible line a little farther west. The German forces falling back from the Caucasus were extracted before the Red Army arrived. Further to the north a second major attack in January drove the remains of Army Group B back from Voronezh, where Operation Blue had started the year before, and back almost to the steppe city of Kursk. Then on 2 February the Red Army began a major offensive to take advantage of this breakthrough, pushing through to capture Kursk and Belgorod on 8 February and Kharkov on the 16 February. Soviet commanders grew in confidence as they saw an opportunity to drive the German front right back across the Ukraine. Then on 19 February von Manstein launched a large-scale and unexpected counter-offensive with three Panzer armies and an SS Panzer corps, which recaptured Kharkov (now a city of ruins) on 14 March and pushed all the way back to Belgorod, creating a large Soviet salient in the German line centred on the city of Kursk. It was here that German commanders, with Hitler's approval, decided that the decisive battle of 1943 would be fought.

The plan to pinch off the large Soviet salient and trap a large part of the Red Army was first developed in mid-March 1943, though Hitler was unusually hesitant, unwilling to risk further disasters with the crisis unfolding in the Mediterranean. The object was to concentrate heavy German mobile forces on either side of the neck of the salient and then to pinch it off, trapping the enemy inside and preparing the possibility of further moves towards Moscow. Hitler at first agreed with von Manstein that the new operation, codenamed 'Citadel', should take place in April or May, before the Red Army had had time to dig in, but Hitler wanted to ensure that the operation would be decisive and to prepare for longer. On 15 April he set 3 May as the start date for Citadel, but then postponed it until mid-June. On 21 June he finally set the date for early July. In the meantime German Panzer armies were brought up to strength and numbers of the new heavy tanks, the 'Tiger I' and the 'Panther', plus the self-propelled gun 'Ferdinand', distributed to units. By July there was an enormous concentration of German forces with 900,000 men in 50 divisions, 2,000 aircraft and 2,700 tanks. Soviet commanders had correctly guessed German intentions and for the first time thoroughly prepared a defence in depth around the perimeter of the salient. Into the Kursk area they poured 1.3 million men, 3,440 tanks and self-propelled guns and 2,170 aircraft. Unknown to the German side, the Red Army had also prepared a large reserve force, held back from Kursk, to be deployed once the German attack had been blunted.

GERMAN TANKS

The earliest German tanks produced after 1933 were small, lightly armoured and with limited armament. By the end of the war German armoured forces possessed the largest and most heavily armoured tanks among all the combatant powers. The changeover came during the contest on the Eastern front when it was found that the Soviet T34/76A tank could outgun its German counterpart. Hitler took a personal interest in the development of the new vehicles which now bore the name of beasts of prey. The Tiger I entered service in 1942. It carried an 88mm gun and had 100mm armour, though its great weight made it slow. The Panther D, developed at great speed in late 1942 and early 1943, was introduced in July 1943 at the battle of Kursk. It had a long 75mm barrel and lighter armour than the Tiger. In 1944 the giant Tiger II tank was introduced into combat with 150mm armour (the US Sherman tank had 76 mm) and an 88mm barrel. Under Hitler's pressure to produce ever more colossal vehicles, the 100-ton Maus tank was under development in the last years of the war. The difficulty was to produce enough of the highly sophisticated tanks in an economy strained to the limit by the impact of bombing. In 1942 and 1943 German factories produced 26,500 tanks against 48,500 in the Soviet Union. Too few of the heavy Tiger tanks could be produced for the strategic tasks they faced: 1,350 of the Tiger I and only 485 of the Tiger II. German tanks were also very complex engineering products, difficult to maintain at long distances, and in many cases had to be shipped all the way back to the Reich for repairs. The Tiger II was superseded only at the end of the war by the Soviet JS (Joseph Stalin) II with its 122mm gun and 230mm armour.

For both sides the battle at Kursk was critical. Victory for the German side would come at an important psychological moment with the bombing of the homeland and the threat to Italy, which explains Hitler's uncharacteristic nervousness. On 4 July, the eve of Citadel, his message for the troops told them that Kursk was of 'decisive importance' and must 'bring about a turn in the war'. For the Soviet side defeat at Kursk would have placed in jeopardy 40 per cent of Soviet manpower and 75 per cent of its armour. The risk for the Soviet side was considerable, for the Red Army had failed to hold the Germans in summer campaigning weather in 1941 and 1942. On the night of July 4/5 1943 German forces moved into final positions and prepared to launch the attack at dawn. Warned in advance, the Soviet commander, General Zhukov,

Overleaf: Hitler in discussion with Field Marshal Erich Manstein (on Hitler's right) and army chief-of-staff General Kurt Zeitzler (on Hitler's left) on 19 February 1943 at the height of the Soviet counter-offensive around Kharkov. Manstein was generally regarded as the most gifted of the frontline commanders in Russia but his unwillingness to accept Hitler's ideas without argument led to his dismissal in 1944.

ordered a pre-emptive artillery and air strike. The German side was briefly nonplussed, but the operation began as planned. At 4.30 in the morning of 5 July Field Marshal Walter Model's Ninth Panzer Army drove forward against the northern neck of the salient; instead of the usual Soviet collapse, a titanic firefight developed with the entrenched defenders. Model's army could push forward only a dozen miles and came to a halt on 9 July.

On the southern flank of the salient General Hermann Hoth's Fourth Panzer Army plunged forward against a more weakly held defensive line with nine Panzer divisions, including the three elite SS divisions Leibstandarte Adolf Hitler, Das Reich and Totenkopf. In two days of fierce fighting they drove 20 miles across the neck of the salient, but on 7 July the German columns reached the main defensive line and progress slowed. The Panzer divisions regrouped and punched forward against the small village of Prokhorovka. Here, on 11–12 July, a fierce tank battle took place which exacted a heavy toll from the Soviet defenders but slowed the pace of the German advance. Then on 12 July the SS Panzer corps was pulled back and on

Above: Hitler being introduced to commanders by Field Marshal von Kluge at the headquarters of Army Group Centre at Smolensk in the Soviet Union on 19 March 1943. It was during this visit that two bottles filled with explosive were placed in Hitler's plane but failed to detonate. Von Kluge was implicated in the later July Plot and killed himself.

13 July Hitler cancelled the operation; on 18 July the ground already captured was abandoned. The reasons for Hitler's order have never been entirely clear but the Allied invasion of Sicily, which began on 9 July, played a part. So too did the launch of a massive Soviet counter-offensive at the north of the salient on 12 July, which stunned Model's force and precipitated a rapid collapse. On 5 August the Red Army captured Orel and on 18 August they entered Briansk, pushing German forces back across the Ukraine towards the River Dnepr. In the south the counter-offensive was launched by Zhukov on 3 August and two days later Belgorod was recaptured; on 28 August Kharkov fell to a more carefully planned Soviet advance and remained in Soviet hands. Operation Citadel was a disaster for the German army and the initiative passed decisively to the enemy.

Over the next three months the Red Army pursued the Germans across the Ukraine, reaching the River Dnepr on 22 September. Hitler agreed with von Manstein's request to retreat to a prepared defensive position, the Wotan Line. This was part of a longer 'Eastern

Above: A recruitment poster for the Waffen-SS published in the Netherlands during the war. All over occupied Europe thousands of young volunteers joined the campaign against the Soviet Union, some in the hope of avoiding the worst of the occupation. The poster here shows a portrait of the South African Boer leader, Paul Kruger, who led the Boer resistance to the British in the South African War of 1899–1902.

Wall' (*Ostwall*) which Hitler wanted to establish along the 1,000-mile length of the eastern front, from the Sea of Azov in the south to the Gulf of Finland in the north. The northern sector was codenamed 'Panther', the southern sector 'Wotan'. On 15 September Hitler gave permission for German forces to withdraw behind this line and to meet the onrushing Soviet enemy. The strategy was a failure from the start. On 22 September Soviet forces breached the Dnepr and established a bridgehead behind the Wotan line. The bridgehead was counter-attacked by German forces but in early November the Red Army successfully moved a large striking force into the marshy areas to the north of Kiev, the Ukrainian capital, and was able to outflank the German defenders. Hoth's Fourth Panzer Army was unable to hold them and Kiev fell on 6 November 1943. Despite desperate German counter-attacks in December, the area west of Kiev was cleared and the springboard prepared for the drive into German-occupied Europe in 1944.

The final weeks of 1943 found Germany in a very different position from a year before. Italy was no longer an ally, but was now an ally of the enemy. German forces had been driven out of North Africa, Sicily and southern Italy with heavy losses. The submarine war had failed and over 80 per cent of German submariners died in the course of the conflict. Heavy bombing placed growing strains on the home front and a heavy toll on German civilian lives. In the east the whole area of southern Russia and Ukraine, whose resources had been deemed essential for the German war effort, were lost in a few months of campaigning.

Hitler reacted to the crisis by trying to find alternative ways of stemming the tide of defeats. On 26 November 1943 Hitler, in the presence of Hermann Göring, visited the Insterburg airfield where he inspected a series of entirely new weapons, which promised to take Germany in one bound beyond the technical achievement of its enemies. The Fieseler Fi 103 'flying bomb' (which came to be known as the V1) and the Messerschmitt Me262 jet fighter were the kind of weapons that Hitler wanted. He ordered the Me262 to be converted to a bombing role; the flying bomb became one of the new 'vengeance weapons' which German propaganda had been announcing with declining conviction during the second half of 1943. The prospect of developing a German atomic bomb had been suspended earlier in 1943 but great expectations were aroused about the new generation of vanguard weapons among both the German leadership and the public at large. Hitler also laid great emphasis on creating a spirit of endurance and sacrifice among the German armed forces for the struggles of the following year. On 22 December 1943 he issued an order for the creation of a National Socialist leadership staff, whose job was to organize ideological indoctrination and fanatical commitment in the armed forces. A year later there were 50,000 officers to carry the message to the troops. National Socialism came to dominate all areas of public life in the last stages of Hitler's war to the death.

Above: A German Tiger 1 tank in action during Operation Citadel in July 1943. The attempt to cut off the large salient around Kursk ultimately failed, but German tank losses were much more modest than Soviet. The German side lost an estimated 278 tanks and self-propelled guns, the Red Army some 1,600.

Below: A leaflet dropped over German lines by Soviet aircraft in 1943 promised German officers and soldiers who voluntarily surrendered better food and conditions, preference in choosing what labour they did and a quick repatriation after the end of the war. The reality for all German prisoners was a long post-war period of forced labour in the Soviet Union.

CHAPTER 7

THE RUINED REICH

1944–1945

In the last two years of the war the Third Reich lurched from defeat to defeat until it finally collapsed in an orgy of violence in the spring of 1945. The inevitable defeat of Germany and her Axis allies became clear once the Western Allies had invaded northern France in June 1944. The same month Rome fell to advancing American armies in Italy and the Soviet high command launched a devastating operation against the Germany Army Group Centre in Belorussia. From then until final defeat in May 1945 German forces were continually in retreat. As defeat stared the German people in the face a group of high-ranking conservative opponents planned to assassinate Hitler. The attempt failed and in July 1944 the apparatus of terror was turned on the plotters, and on anyone else who hinted at defeatism or defied the regime. In the last year of the war thousands of Germans died at the hand of their own regime as well as under the hail of Allied bombs, most of which were dropped in the last twelve months of the conflict. Prisoners in the vast network of concentration and labour camps were forced to work on the most dangerous projects. When Allied armies approached they were subjected to long 'death marches' to the German interior. The 7 million forced labourers and prisoners-of-war working in Germany kept the German war economy going under ever more difficult conditions. When the final battles were lost in the winter and spring of 1945, Hitler retreated to his bunker in Berlin, where he shot himself on 30 April rather than face capture and humiliation. He left a country of ruins behind him and over 6 million Germans dead.

1944 The Lull before the Storm

Hitler expected 1944 to be the decisive year for the future of the Third Reich. In his New Year's Day address he told the German people that in the next twelve months 'this momentous war will approach its climax'. He was exhilarated by the scale and significance of the impending struggle. In his annual broadcast for the anniversary of the Reich, 30 January 1944, he warned his listeners that German defeat would mean the end of the old Europe and the triumph of Soviet barbarism. German propaganda began to play on the theme that Germany was the bulwark of civilization against the dark forces of crude Western materialism and Soviet primitivism, both of them the offspring of the worldwide Jewish conspiracy.

The sense of a system dangerously poised between triumph or destruction was the message at the core of Hitler's directive which he sent to Field Marshal Kesselring when the American and British armies mounted a major amphibious invasion of the area around Anzio on the western coast of southern Italy on 22 January 1944. 'The battle,' he wrote, 'must be waged in a spirit of holy hatred for an enemy conducting a pitiless war of extermination ...' Within days of the Allied landings, which had been almost unopposed, Kesselring had managed to put together a six-division army under the command of Col. General Eberhard von Mackensen. In five months of bitter trench warfare he succeeded in containing the Allied bridgehead. The plan for Anzio had been to land north of the main German line and drive a wedge behind it, encircling much of the German army. Instead the Allied force was almost expelled from Anzio by a vigorous German counter-offensive on 16 February. Strongly supported by sea and air, Allied armies managed to hold on to the narrow perimeter they had established, while Mackensen was never strong enough to complete the rout in the face of overwhelming Allied air power. Further south, the approaching British Commonwealth and American armies (supported now by Free French and Polish units) were also held up for months along the heavily defended Gustav Line, which ran through Cassino. The campaign in Italy reached a stalemate which was only broken six months later.

The more dangerous situation was on the Eastern front where the Red Army continued to exploit the offensive that had developed across the Ukraine during the autumn and winter. In the first weeks of January one Soviet army group pushed further west of Kiev, under heavy German attack. In the south Soviet forces made bolder progress, crossing the Dnepr in force and trapping a large German force at Korsun, near the city of Cherkassy, in late January. Although large numbers of the encircled German force managed to battle their way out, von Manstein's depleted Army Group South could not force through a rescue corridor. 18,000 German soldiers were captured in the pocket, with thousands killed in a gruesome encounter

Pages 318–9: A queue in Berlin waits for emergency food rations outside the Vaterland Haus on Potsdamer Platz in 1945. The destruction of Berlin by bombing and the final Soviet assault left the population short of all essential supplies.

MONTE CASSINO

One of the bloodiest battles of the war in the West was fought for the small town of Cassino and the ancient Benedictine monastery, Monte Cassino, which stood on a hilltop above the town. Cassino lay in the path of Allied armies as they tried to force a way through to Rome in early 1944 against entrenched German forces in the mountain passes of the southern Apennines manning the so-called Gustav Line. The weight of the Allied attack was taken by the 14th Panzer Division commanded by one of Germany's leading tank generals, Fridolin von Senger und Etterlin. The campaign lasted a gruelling five months and involved four major Allied operations, the first one launched on 17 January 1944. The German side promised to respect the monastery and left it unoccupied, but the Allies thought it housed a German garrison and, despite arguments over the morality of destroying a major architectural and religious centre, on 15 February 229 bombers utterly destroyed the site. Only after it had been reduced to rubble did the Germans occupy it, using the ruins as a useful defensive position. Two further Allied operations in February and March resulted in heavy casualties for the attacking Allied force and not until May, when Free French units to the west had begun to break through the Gustav Line, did the Polish Second Corps commanded by General Wladyslav Anders finally storm the hill and seize the monastery on 17 May. By then von Senger und Etterlin had moved most of his forces as the German army began a phased withdrawal to the Gothic Line north of Florence. Though an ultimate defeat, Cassino was a tactical victory for the German side, holding up the Allied advance for almost five months while new defensive positions were created to the north, and exacting a heavy toll of the enemy. A British inquiry in 1949 confirmed that there was no evidence that the German army occupied the monastery at the time the campaign began.

where German soldiers were cut down by Cossack sabres or run over by Soviet tanks. The German armies in the south retreated rapidly westward while Soviet forces under Marshal Ivan Konev reached the border with Moldavia on 19 March 1944, and on 7 April crossed the Romanian border. Further south the German forces were expelled from the rest of the Ukrainian steppe; Odessa was liberated on 10 April and the Romanian border reached a few days later. The southernmost German armies were placed under the command of General Ferdinand Schörner, a fanatical though effective commander, who enjoyed Hitler's confidence. At almost the same time, on 25 March 1944, Hitler finally sacked von Manstein for what he regarded as persistent insubordination.

The front finally stabilized by April 1944, with Soviet armies exhausted and overstretched by months of continuous mobile warfare. The long Axis retreat created a crisis among Germany's wartime allies who now stared at huge Soviet armed forces poised for entry into Central Europe. During January and February Hitler received high-ranking delegations from

Romania, Hungary and Croatia. In late February at Klessheim Castle, near the Austrian city of Salzburg, Marshal Antonescu assured Hitler of Romania's continued allegiance to the Axis pact. On 16 and 17 March Hitler met with the Bulgarian ruling council at Klessheim to discuss Bulgaria's policy in the face of the Soviet advance. The most dramatic encounter involved Admiral Horthy, Regent of Hungary. For some time in early 1944 the Hungarian government had been considering the options available as a result of Axis defeats, and had put out peace feelers to the Western powers. On 18 March at Klessheim Horthy was subjected to an angry tirade of insulting threats from Hitler and was told to accept a German occupation of his country the following day. Operation 'Margarethe' had been prepared some time in advance and was quickly carried out. A pro-German government was installed in Budapest along with a German plenipotentiary. Hungary pledged to send new military formations to help the Germans in the east and Gestapo officials were able to begin the mass deportation of Hungarian Jews, which until then Horthy had resisted. Within four months over 400,000 were deported to their deaths in Auschwitz-Birkenau, more than half Hungary's Jewish population.

On the home front the priority was to sustain domestic morale in the wake of a year of defeats and to extract as much as possible from the war economy for the final decisive battles. In 1944 the economic reforms begun two years before were bearing fruit in very much larger output of almost all major weapons. During the early months of 1944 Albert Speer undertook a further centralization of the wartime organization of the economy by demanding that all the armed forces accept a radical simplification of production so that industry could concentrate on a narrow range of easily produced, but high-quality, weapons. On 25 January 1944 the army published its recommendations: anti-tank weapons were reduced from 12 to just one; anti-aircraft guns from 10 different types to two; artillery from 26 models to 8; tanks and vehicles from 18 to 7. Throughout German industry rationalization experts and time-and-motion officials toured each plant to look for ways of saving time and materials. By 1944 production time on the Panzer III tank was cut in half; the time it took to make an Me109 fighter and the number of man-hours needed to build it both fell by 50 per cent. The one area over which Speer could still not exert sufficient control was aircraft production. In the spring of 1944 he manoeuvred to take over direct control of the mass production of fighters, which were essential to Germany's efforts to keep the bombers from destroying production altogether. On 1 March 1944 Speer, together with Erhard Milch, set up a 'Fighter Staff' to accelerate the production of fighter planes. The move achieved impressive results despite the bombing. In 1944 Germany produced 39,000 aircraft against 24,800 in 1943, the great bulk of them fighters.

The most pressing shortage remained labour. It was estimated that Germany needed at least 4 million more workers in 1944 to achieve the greatly expanded production plans. Increased conscription of male labour for the armed forces could be met only by forcing more women to work, or by finding more workers from outside Germany. By 1944 over 3 million more women (many with children) were working six-hour part-time shifts in addition to the almost 15 million women working in industry, agriculture and services. The bombing made it difficult to recruit more since many women, particularly those with children, had been evacuated from the threatened industrial areas and could not easily be brought back. The efforts to recruit foreign workers were accordingly stepped up during 1944. At the peak that year there were 5.3 million forced labourers and 1.8 million prisoners-of war working in German industry and on German farms, almost 20 per cent of the total workforce. Most of them were Poles, Russians and Ukrainians. They lived for the most part in crude work camps where they could be properly disciplined. There were an estimated 20,000 labour camps throughout Greater Germany and an army of half-a-million Germans was needed to guard, supervise and train the foreign workforce.

By 1944, with a shrinking area of occupation, there were limits to how much labour could be deported back to Germany. Instead German industry turned to the exploitation of concentration camp labour. Prisoners had been contracted out to local businesses or for road-building and construction work from early in the war, but only in 1944 did the camp population (swollen by a large influx of foreign prisoners) reach a scale where it could make a difference to the labour force. By August 1944 there were 524,000 prisoners; by January 1945 over 714,000, many of them young Jewish workers transferred from the ghettoes as they were liquidated. The SS, who ran the camps, had their own industrial and building projects where prisoners were often worked to death. These included the notorious Mittelbau-Dora site at Nordhausen where the V2 rockets were constructed, where 10,000 prisoners died digging out the underground installations. Himmler was also willing to loan out prisoners to the armaments industry, for which the SS charged a scale of fees. The slave workers often enjoyed better conditions away from the main camps because employers needed to keep them alive, but they were still treated more harshly than the foreign workers. By early 1944 there were an estimated 1,600 sub-camps of the main concentration camps, set up near the building site or the factory, and around 230,000 camp prisoners worked for private German industry. The SS used their position as labour-suppliers to increase SS involvement in the war economy; Xavier Dorsch was appointed head of the Todt Organization in place of Speer, while Hans Kammler was given responsibility for the programme of dispersing German industry to safer underground sites in response to the bombing.

The bombing of German industry and cities, which had been temporarily eased as a result of heavy bomber losses, began again in the early spring of 1944. The situation was changed with the introduction of the P51 Mustang long-range fighter; fitted with drop tanks for extra fuel, the Mustang could fly far into German airspace, not only to protect the bombers but to destroy the German fighter force. The British and American bomber forces agreed in January 1944 to mount a concerted assault on the German aircraft industry under the codename

---

An elderly Berliner sits on her chair outside the burnt-out ruins of her apartment block. The Battle of Berlin was launched by RAF Bomber Command in autumn 1943 and continued until the early spring of 1944, by which time one-quarter of all Berlin's homes had been destroyed or badly damaged.

Operation 'Argument', though better known as 'Big Week'. The operation began on 20 February 1944 and lasted for six days, during which almost 20,000 tons of bombs were dropped on fighter production targets and the urban areas that housed them. The bombing succeeded in damaging two months of German fighter supply, but the attacks that followed also undermined the German fighter force, which by May was losing 25 per cent of its pilots per month and around half its fighter strength. The attacks forced more than 80 per cent of German fighters to remain in Germany to defend industry, starving the German fighting fronts of air support.

The one factor that dominated German thinking, both leaders and led, was the expectation of invasion in the West. The Allied occupation of Sicily and southern Italy in 1943 had ruled out a serious operation in France that year, but it was evident that at some point the Western Allies would choose the shortest and most geographically favourable route, across the English Channel and the northern French plain. Hitler saw the invasion as yet another possible turning-point. The defeat of an invasion attempt would 'decide the war', freeing up substantial forces for a renewed offensive in the East. On 3 November 1943 he released the last of his formal war directives, No. 51, to prepare a major defensive zone ready to absorb and destroy the Allied landing. All forces that could be freed would be concentrated on the single strategic goal of throwing the enemy 'into the sea'. Preparations to meet invasion had begun in 1942 with orders to construct the Atlantic Wall along the western and northern coast of occupied France. Hitler himself helped to design the fortifications, which included 15,000 strong-points defended by machine-guns and artillery. The programme was too ambitious for German resources, and the most heavily defended sector ran between the mouth of the River Seine and the River Schelde in north-east France and Belgium, which was regarded by most senior German commanders (and Hitler too) as the most likely route for an invasion force. The army and air force were also weak along much of the coastline. The Commander-in-Chief West, Field Marshal von Rundstedt, commanded 46 divisions in late 1943, spread out thinly throughout France and Belgium, with the greatest concentration around the Calais sector.

On 15 January 1944, Hitler appointed Rommel as commander of Army Group B along the threatened coastline. He had at his disposal Seventh Army around Normandy and Brittany and 15th Army from Le Havre to the Dutch border. Rommel immediately ordered the strengthening of the Atlantic Wall defences. He demanded the building of concrete bunkers as resistance centres, 50 million mines along the beaches and large new minefields in the Channel, and a whole range of obstacles along the shoreline to hold up the initial landings. Much was done in the vulnerable area around Calais but further west the programme could not be completed. Instead of 50 million mines he was given only one-tenth the number asked for. Rommel shared Hitler's view that the Allies would probably land in force around Calais, but mount a major diversionary attack in Normandy. He favoured the idea of building a firm static defence sufficient to destroy any landing on the beaches themselves, leaving most of the German force at or just behind the coast. The commanders in Paris, von Rundstedt and the armoured forces commander-in-chief, General Geyr von Schweppenburg, preferred the creation of a powerful mobile reserve held well back from the coast, which could be sent at

once to the area of Allied assault to help drive the beachhead back into the sea. The argument was finally addressed by Hitler in May 1944 when he divided the available armoured divisions between both strategies: four divisions formed a reserve under von Schweppenburg while the remainder were stationed at the coast or in southern France. In Normandy there was only the 21st Panzer Division to meet the expected diversionary attack.

The distribution of German forces reflected the extreme uncertainty surrounding Allied intentions. An elaborate intelligence hoax, Operation 'Fortitude', had been mounted by the Allies to persuade the German side that a large army group was stationed in south-east England, waiting to cross the Channel at its shortest point between Dover and Calais. The hoax worked and German intelligence insisted right up to the invasion in June, and well beyond, that the bulk of Allied forces would be released against the Calais sector. Timing was also a problem for the German side. Hitler expected a possible invasion from January onwards, but the realistic date seemed some time in May. From April standing patrols were

A scene on a beach in northern France in June 1944. Obstacles like these were placed along the whole French coast in the months leading to the Normandy invasion, in the hope that they would impede the movement of vehicles and equipment onto the beaches. In the event the Allies were well-prepared for what they would meet and the network of obstacles achieved little.

mounted all along the coast. When nothing happened in May, it was speculated that invasion would come from mid-June, but perhaps as late as August. The German public was made aware of the coming contest by a constant diet of propaganda on the formidable strength of the Atlantic Wall. In May the bombing eased over Germany as the heavy bombers were diverted to the destruction of communications and bases in northern France, and throughout the month there was a growing sense of the lull before the storm. Viktor Klemperer, observing his fellow citizens in Dresden, found mixed opinions among them about the coming invasion: 'They probably won't land, they've got time, they don't need to make this sacrifice. Or if they do come, then probably not at the Atlantic Wall...'

The Allies had long planned to land in Normandy on five designated beaches. The date was determined by the moon, the tides and the fickle weather of the Channel. The date finally chosen was 5 June 1944, but the weather was stormy and overcast for some days. The forecast persuaded the German side that invasion could not be imminent. On 4 June the naval command in Paris cancelled naval patrols the following day because of the weather. Rommel took the opportunity to drive back to Germany for his wife's birthday. The junior officers of the German Seventh Army were sent away on an exercise. Hitler was at the Berghof on 5 June hosting a discussion with Goebbels and Bormann on whether to permit the popular lynching of Allied airmen who came down on German soil. News had come in the day before that the American army had entered Rome, but there was little anxiety about what was happening in France. At 10 o'clock in the evening news came in that radio intercepts suggested invasion the following day but Hitler, according to Goebbels, was 'unperturbed'. Firm news from Normandy arrived during the night but Hitler was only roused at 10 o'clock the following morning to be told about the landings. 'Right in the place where we expected them,' he announced.

Invasion in the West

There was in reality a great deal of confusion about what the invasion in Normandy signified. For a long time commanders in France, and Hitler's headquarters, assumed that the operation in north-western France was a feint and that the real assault would then be mounted further east around Calais. As a result reinforcements were slow to be sent to the Normandy front and the Allies established a firm bridgehead within a few days. Rommel's strategy of fierce shoreline resistance was destroyed almost at once, but he commanded 34 divisions against the Allies' initial lodgement of five divisions. Allied success, however, depended not on the army units but on overwhelming air power and the support of a large armada of heavy warships, whose fire proved devastating against the defending forces. On 6 June the German Third Air Fleet in northern France could muster only 170 serviceable aircraft against 12,000 Allied planes, including a complement of 5,600 fighters. Even with these advantages the Allied advance slowed after the first few days as German forces were brought up to strength and a firmer line established inland. When British and Canadian armies tried to capture Caen in mid-June they failed; American forces were able to penetrate the Cotentin peninsula and isolate Cherbourg, but they too could make no further progress south. A heavy storm on

19/20 June destroyed one of the artificial harbours used to supply Allied forces and produced a temporary crisis of supply. If the divisions of 15th Army, still waiting for the expected main invasion towards Calais, had been diverted to help Rommel in Normandy, the outcome of the campaign might have been very different.

While the Western Allies were held in the Normandy bridgehead, Rommel and von Rundstedt met Hitler at his French headquarters, Wolf's Lair II at Soissons, near Paris, where they tried to persuade him to allow a withdrawal to a more defensible line. Hitler insisted that the line should be held at all costs and when they asked again on 29 June, Hitler sacked von Rundstedt and replaced him with Field Marshal von Kluge, who was instructed on no account to withdraw. By then the strategic situation had changed again. On 22 June 1944 the Red Army launched a major offensive, Operation 'Bagration', against German Army Group Centre in Belorussia. The German army in the east had expected the attack to come further south, where Soviet forces had made great progress by the spring, or north towards the Baltic States. Tanks and artillery were removed from Field Marshal Ernst Busch's Army Group Centre to reinforce the flanks. The Soviet side mounted a major deception campaign like the Western Allies, placing dummy tanks and air bases in the southern sector while the real vehicles and aircraft were moved into position with the greatest secrecy. On 10 June a diversionary attack was mounted in the north, but on 22 June the full weight of the Soviet offensive was unleashed. The German army group could muster only 1.2 million men, 900 tanks and 1,350 aircraft against 2.4 million Soviet soldiers, 5,200 tanks and 5,300 aircraft.

The German front rapidly collapsed and withdrew back to Minsk, the Belorussian capital. On 28 June Hitler replaced Busch with Field Marshal Walter Model, whom he regarded as a reliable man for any emergency. The front stabilized, but not enough to prevent the loss of Minsk on 4 July. Soviet forces then unleashed further offensives north and south, driving the whole German front back towards Poland and into the Baltic States. Over two months of fighting Army Group Centre had been destroyed; for the loss of 179,000 men the Red Army had imposed losses of 589,000 on the German enemy, the largest single defeat suffered by the German army during the war.

The collapse of the German army in the east was in sharp contrast to the situation in France where, despite pouring one and a half million men and 330,000 vehicles into the bridgehead, the Allies could make slight progress. Although possessing overwhelming air superiority (and by mid-July around 4,500 tanks to the German 850), they faced a German army with years of combat experience. On 7 July the British and Canadian forces began the battle for Caen, where the great bulk of German armour was concentrated, with a devastating raid by heavy bombers. Rommel's main defensive line, however, was further to the south of Caen and it was here that the German army made its last stand. On 18 July Operation 'Goodwood' was launched against the ridge of hills occupied by Rommel's forces, but two days later, on 20 July, torrential rain turned the battlefield into a quagmire and the operation was abandoned. Further to the west the American forces, under General Omar Bradley, were preparing to break out against a much more weakly held front around St Lô. Operation 'Cobra' was designed to pierce the German line and open the way for a large encircling

LT. COLONEL CLAUS SCHENK VON STAUFFENBERG (1907–1944)

The man who attempted to assassinate Adolf Hitler on 20 July 1944 was descended from an ancient aristocratic family and had during the early years of the regime shown some sympathy for the National Socialist revolution. He turned against Hitler and contemplated his death only when he realized that the future of the idealized Germany he favoured would be destroyed by Hitler's reckless military ambitions. His early career was a conventional one for a young man of his class. In 1926 he joined an elite cavalry regiment and rose rapidly to become a General Staff officer by 1938. He served on the staff of the 16th Panzer Division in the campaigns in Poland and France and was then posted to the Army High Command. His devout Catholicism and his attraction for the romantic nationalism of the mystical poet Stefan George provoked revulsion against the violence he witnessed on the Eastern Front and he joined the military resistance circle based in Army Group Centre. He began to see a future Germany in terms of social justice and favoured what he termed a genuine 'national' socialism rather than the traditional conservative nationalism of many of the other conspirators. He was severely injured in Tunisia in 1943 and posted to home duties where he served as chief-of-staff first to the deputy of the Home Army, General Friedrich Olbricht, a fellow conspirator, and then to General Friedrich Fromm, commander of the Home Army. It was in this role that he plotted Hitler's death, and it was Fromm who ordered Stauffenberg's execution when the plot failed. A memorial marks the spot where Stauffenberg was killed in the former courtyard of the German War Ministry building.

movement behind the German forces opposing Montgomery at Caen. The bad weather also made it impossible to launch 'Cobra' and it had to be postponed from 20 July, first for a day and eventually for over a week.

The July Plot: Assassination and Terror

While Allied forces stalled in Normandy, on 20 July a major political drama was unfolding inside Germany. At Hitler's headquarters in Rastenburg a senior staff officer, Colonel Claus Schenk von Stauffenberg, attempted to assassinate Hitler and launch a *coup d'état*. Hitler survived the attempt and as a consequence the apparatus of terror inaugurated a wave of increasingly unrestricted victimization that lasted until the defeat of the Reich ten months later.

There had been a number of assassination attempts earlier in the year. In February 1944 Ewald von Kleist planned to arm himself with a bomb beneath a new uniform which he would be modelling for Hitler, but although the event was scheduled three times, Hitler failed to turn up. On 9 March 1944 a further attempt was made by Eberhard von Breitenbruch at the Berghof, but he was denied access to the meeting room. In the early part of the year some of the conservative resisters were rounded up by the Gestapo. On 19 January 1944 Count

Helmuth von Moltke was arrested. A German lawyer who worked in Hitler's headquarters, he organized what became known as the 'Kreisau Circle', named after his country estate where the conspirators occasionally met. He was sent to a camp, then tried before the People's Court in Berlin and executed on 23 January 1945. Others in contact with the Circle were arrested in July; Julius Leber, a socialist who was to be the interior minister in a post-Hitler government, was seized on 5 July; the same day Adolf Reichwein, a history professor who was to be minister of culture, was also taken into custody. Leber was executed in 5 January 1945, Reichwein on 20 October 1944, the same day that sentence was passed on him in the People's Court. The one group that the Gestapo had not yet touched was the circle around Beck and Goerderler, which by July 1944 involved a range of senior German soldiers and officials committed to the idea that only the murder of Adolf Hitler would create the conditions for a successful takeover of power.

The failure of numerous assassination attempts created a sense of disillusionment among the conspirators. Lacking support from the contacts they had made abroad in the West, and uncertain about whether the German population would approve a conservative coup, they focused their energy on creating a network of sympathizers who could play a part in creating a post-Hitler political system. The choice for a suitable assassin finally fell on von Stauffenberg who, despite suffering severe injuries in Tunisia which left him with only one eye, destroyed his right hand and left him with only three fingers on his left, was one of the few conspirators with the will and determination to see the act through. On 1 July he was appointed chief-of-staff to the commander of the home army, which gave him access to the conferences with Hitler. The plan to kill Hitler was put into place immediately; after his death it was planned to activate 'Operation Valkyrie', a contingency plan originally drawn up by the Hitler regime in case it proved necessary to impose civil order in an emergency. The plan would allow the conspirators to issue orders and control any possible opposition, but it hinged on enough of the armed forces and police accepting the new authorities, for which there was no certainty.

Stauffenberg tried to carry out the assassination three times in the first half of the month, on 6, 11 and 15 July. The attempts were abandoned because he wanted to be able to kill Himmler and other senior Party men at the same time. Finally, on 20 July, it was decided that he would carry out the deed regardless. He arrived at the Wolf's Lair headquarters with a time bomb in his briefcase. He succeeded in taking it into the meeting with Hitler, which had been transferred from a concrete bunker, where the effects of the blast would have been deadly, to a small wooden building on the surface. Stauffenberg primed the bomb with his three remaining fingers, pushed his briefcase under the oak map table and left the meeting to

Overleaf: A photograph taken shortly after the failed bomb attempt on Hitler's life, 20 July 1944. Hitler was shaken and his arm injured but he survived the attack. He changed his shredded clothes at once and is seen here walking with General Keitel (left), Hermann Göring and Martin Bormann (right).

answer a fictitious telephone call. Another of those present, irritated at stubbing his foot on the case, pushed it further under the table, behind a thick oak support. The explosion killed four people, destroyed the building, leaving Hitler dazed, deaf, with a limp left arm and his clothes in shreds, but alive. Stauffenberg had seen the building blown into the air and assumed the assassination had worked. He bluffed his way out of the compound and made for Berlin by plane. He arrived at the War Ministry where he and co-conspirators tried to take over the building. As news began to filter through that Hitler was not dead, the situation was suddenly reversed. Stauffenberg was shot but not killed, and he and his co-conspirators in the Ministry building were arrested, taken to the courtyard and executed by firing squad. Stauffenberg cried out 'Long live eternal Germany' as he was killed. Ludwig Beck, who was also present in the War Ministry, tried to shoot himself twice and was then helped the third time by an army sergeant. Carl Goerdeler was arrested some weeks later, condemned to death on 8 September and finally executed in prison on 2 February 1945.

The announcement that Hitler was still alive was made a little after six o'clock in the evening on the radio. Hitler promised to address the nation and finally did so after midnight, in the early hours of 21 July. He blamed a clique of 'ambitious, conscienceless and criminal and stupid officers' and promised merciless extermination. 'This time,' he continued, 'an accounting will be given such as we National Socialists are wont to give ...' That day the security services began a ruthless roundup of everyone implicated in the plot. Some of the conspirators were based in Paris and Prague, where it had taken longer for the news of Hitler's survival to arrive. The German military governor of France, General Karl von Stülpnagel, was part of the conspiracy to kill Hitler and then try to negotiate a deal with the West. A large number of Gestapo and SS had been arrested in Paris but the coup petered out when the truth was learned. Stülpnagel tried to commit suicide, but only succeeded in blinding himself. He was taken to Berlin and executed among around 200 other conspirators. On 1 August an order was made that family members of the conspirators should also be arrested, part of an estimated 5,000 caught up in the angry terror of the regime. The first executions occurred on 8 August and were filmed by a propaganda ministry film crew. Goebbels intended to distribute the film, titled 'Traitors before the People's Court', but found he could not watch the scene of the hanging using steel bands suspended from meat-hooks, through which the condemned were slowly and painfully strangled. The film was only shown to a select few Party leaders.

The July Plot opened up new opportunities for the SS, the security apparatus and the armed forces to act in increasingly lawless ways. Himmler was appointed commander-in-chief of the Home Army, which he added to the post of Minister of the Interior, acquired in October 1943. The radicalization of the justice system in the second half of 1944 made it possible to place anyone in a concentration camp on the recommendation of a Gestapo officer, while many crimes were punished on the spot by execution. Looters, defeatists, foreign workers guilty of sleeping with German women, could be shot or hanged without trial. On 30 July Hitler signed a decree that removed any need for a military court to investigate acts of 'terror or sabotage' committed in occupied Europe and permitted immediate execution by the army or the security police. Lawless terror now not only applied across what remained of the

NEWS OF HITLER'S DEATH, 20 JULY 1944

Thursday 20 July [Berlin] This afternoon Loremarie Schönburg and I sat chatting on the office stairs when Gottfried Bismarck burst in, bright red spots on his cheeks. I had never seen him in such a state of feverish excitement. He first drew Loremarie aside, then asked me what my plans were. I told him they were uncertain but that I would really like to get out of the A.A. [Foreign Office] as soon as possible. He told me I should not worry, that in a few days everything would be settled and we would all know what was going to happen to us. Then, after asking me to come out to Potsdam with Loremarie as soon as possible, he jumped into his car and was gone.

I went back into my office and dialled Percy Frey at the Swiss Legation to cancel my dinner date with him, as I preferred to go out to Potsdam. While I waited, I turned to Loremarie, who was standing at the window, and asked her why Gottfried was in such a state. Could it be the *Konspiration*? (all that with the receiver in my hand!) She whispered 'Yes! That's it! It's done. This morning!' Just then Percy replied. Still holding the receiver, I asked: 'Dead?' She answered: 'Yes, dead!' I hung up, seized her by the shoulders and we went waltzing round the room. Then grabbing hold of some papers, I thrust them into the first drawer and shouting to the porter that we were off on official business, we tore off to the Zoo station. On the way out to Potsdam she whispered to me the details and though the compartment was full, we did not even try to hide our excitement and joy.

Count Claus Schenck von Stauffenberg, a colonel on the General Staff, had put a bomb at Hitler's feet during a conference at Supreme H.Q. at Rastenburg in East Prussia. It had gone off and Adolf was dead. Stauffenberg had waited outside until the explosion and then, seeing Hitler being carried out on a stretcher all covered with blood, he had run to his car, which had stood hidden somewhere, and with his A.D.C., Werner von Haeften, had driven to the local airfield and flown back to Berlin. In the general commotion nobody had noticed his escape.

On reaching Berlin he had gone straight to the O.K.H. [Army High Command] in the Bendlerstrasse, which had meanwhile been taken over by the plotters and where Gottfried Bismarck, Helldorf and many others were now gathered. (The O.K.H. lies on the other side of the canal from our Woyrschstrasse.) This evening at six an announcement would be made over the radio that Adolf was dead and that a new government had been formed...

By the time we had reached the Regierung in Potsdam, it was past six o'clock. I went to wash up. Loremarie hurried upstairs. Only minutes had passed when I heard dragging footsteps outside and she came in: 'There has just been an announcement on the radio: A Count Stauffenberg has attempted to murder the Führer, but Providence saved him...'

Source: Marie Vassiltchikov *The Berlin Diaries 1940–1945 of Marie 'Missie' Vassiltchikov* (Chatto & Windus, London,1986), pp. 189–90, entry for 20 July 1944

'V' FOR VENGEANCE

In the search for weapons that would stop the remorseless bombing of Germany in 1943 and 1944, Hitler favoured novel inventions or 'wonder weapons'. Since they were to exact revenge for the bombing of Germany, they were given the general title of weapons of vengeance (*Vergeltung*) and given designated numbers as 'V' weapons. The most important were the V1 flying bomb developed by the Fieseler aircraft company and the V2 rocket, developed at the Peenemünde research station by a team led by Major-General Walter Dornberger, who subsequently worked for the American military after the war. The V1 was developed first and launched for the first time on 13 June against London. It was completely inaccurate, as was the V2, and only a few of the flying bombs and rockets hit London, 2,419 out of approximately 10,000 V1s fired and 517 out of 6,000 rockets produced. The campaign, which had been designed to raise domestic morale in Germany and persuade the Allies to suspend area bombing of German cities, backfired. The Allies dropped thousands of tons of bombs in an effort to disrupt the programme, while the strategic effect of the campaign was slight. Other V-weapons such as the V4 Wasserfall anti-aircraft missile might have had a much greater effect on the bombing offensive but it was given a lower priority beside the V1 and V2. The V3 was a heavy long-barrelled gun designed to fire high-velocity shells a great distance. Two sites were set up near Calais in late 1943 to bombard London with ten shells a minute but the promised range of almost 100 miles was never achieved and both sites were too heavily bombed to allow the programme to be completed.

new German empire but was also introduced into the German homeland itself, where unnumbered ordinary Germans were killed over the final months of war as part of the Party's struggle against the kind of defeatism they had always blamed for German collapse in 1918.

The radicalization of the home front was also manifested in the decision taken by Hitler to appoint Goebbels on 25 July to the post of Plenipotentiary for Total War, the position he had wanted in the spring of 1943. Goebbels sought to use a mixture of Party power and propaganda persuasion to extract the ultimate efforts from the bombed and dispirited German population. The popular reaction to the assassination attempt gave some ground for thinking that the German people would nevertheless continue to fight as long as they could. Secret police reports made it clear that apart from the orchestrated demonstrations of Party loyalty, many

Above: A notice displayed in front of bombed-out ruins declares 'Looters will be shot'. The civil and military police imposed severe penalties on anyone caught taking advantage of the bomb destruction. Crime increased with the bombing but the risks were very high. By the end of the war looters could be shot on the spot, without trial.

Opposite: A group of concentration camp labourers from the Mittelbau-Dora camp working on the V2 rocket in an underground installation in the Harz mountains. The V-weapons programme relied on slave labour for constructing the underground factories and for building the finished rockets, but many of the finished products were found to be the object of sabotage.

AUSCHWITZ-BIRKENAU IN 1944: A MEMOIR

Mengele is out of work, there's no more 'left line, right line.' Almost all the transports [of Hungarian Jews] wind up in the gas chamber: men, women, children. The labor camps are stuffed to bursting; they wouldn't know what to do with more workers. In summer, death takes longer to skim off its share....

The crematoria are going full-bore around the clock. We hear from Birkenau that they've burned 3,000, then 3,500, and last week up to 4,000 bodies a day. The new *Sonderkommando* [special duty unit] has been doubled to keep everything running smoothly between the gas chamber and the ovens, day and night. From the chimneys, flames shoot thirty feet into the air, visible for leagues around at night, and the oppressive stench of burnt flesh can be smelled as far away as Buna [the factory at Auschwitz-Monowitz].

By an amazing paradox, while this last massacre is going on and the system is approaching, industrially speaking, absolute perfection, the camp regimen has become less harsh. They have eliminated the morning roll call and shortened the evening one. There hasn't been a public hanging for the last three months.

The SS no longer come inside the camp as much, and even Rakasch only kills a man occasionally now.

Our diet hasn't improved, though, but most of us have some sort of fiddle going on and can wangle an extra liter of soup. Plus the work is less exhausting, since we're sheltered from bad weather.

We have become acclimatized. Those of us who couldn't bow low enough have long ago gone up in smoke. Time itself no longer has much meaning; it's subdivided into independent fractions that don't add up and must be negotiated one by one.

Horror has become an everyday thing for us. We don't talk about those convoys of Hungarians, or the dead, or our lives elsewhere, or the future, which logic demands that we ignore. We speak only of the here and now.

Source: Paul Steinberg *Speak You Also: A Survivor's Reckoning* (Allen Lane, London, 2001), pp. 98–9

ordinary people expressed 'profound indignation and rage' at the news, even among those known to be unsympathetic to National Socialism. Goebbels was able at last to redeem the pledge he had made the year before about 'wonder weapons' when the first VI flying bombs were launched at London on 13 June. The first rockets followed on 8 September 1944. Although the immediate effects were unimpressive, the idea that the war could perhaps be rescued for Germany kept at least a portion of the population willing to fight. Goebbels was also keen to ensure that the final struggle should be much more the responsibility of committed National Socialists. The regional Party leaders were also Reich Defence Commissars (a title they had been given in 1939), and in this capacity Goebbels tried to get them to bypass military and bureaucracy and mobilize local resources and willpower on behalf of the movement.

The remorseless wheels of genocide continued to turn all through the military reverses and assassination crisis. At Auschwitz-Birkenau the killing peaked during 1944 as the Gestapo apparatus reached out to northern Italy and Hungary, and the remotest areas of German occupation in the Greek islands. Between 15 May and 9 July around 438,000 Hungarian Jews arrived at the rate of about 10,000 a day. Some 15 per cent were selected for labour, the rest killed. The former commandant, Rudolf Höss, who had been sent off for other duties in 1943, was reinstated to supervise the major task of murdering the Hungarians. At the end he was awarded the War Merit Cross first class and posted back to Berlin on 29 July 1944, his job complete. In September and October Jews from the Lodz ghetto, the last to be dismantled, arrived in Birkenau and around 20,000 remaining Jews from Slovakia. The last trainload of Jews arrived on 30 October 1944. A few weeks before, on 7 October, a group of Jewish camp workers, whose task it was to help in the destruction and disposal of the bodies, staged a sudden revolt, blowing up one crematorium and killing three SS guards. The rising was put down with savage brutality, but it was one of the last gestures of the oppressed Jewish camp population. In November Himmler ordered an end to the gassing and Auschwitz-Birkenau began to be dismantled. The prisoners were sent on forced marches to other camp destinations in Germany, including the young Dutch girl Anne Frank, who ended up in Bergen-Belsen, where she died. By this stage an estimated 5.7 million European Jews had been killed.

To the Frontiers of the Reich

A week after the July Plot it was possible to launch Operation 'Cobra'. The fragile nature of the German defence was finally exposed when American forces prised open the line and then raced south and east to liberate large parts of western France in a matter of days. Facing the powerful American army group were 10 weak divisions of German Seventh Army and 110

Overleaf: A group of American soldiers pose for a photograph with a captured German flag in the French town of Chambois, the last area defended by German forces in the 'Falaise Gap' through which tens of thousands of Germans fled from the advancing Allies in August 1944.

THE WARSAW RISING, AUGUST–OCTOBER 1944

In August 1944 Polish resisters launched a major operation against the German occupation of Warsaw. Polish resistance was first organized in 1940 as the Union of Armed Struggle, then in 1942 was renamed the Polish Home Army (*Armia Krajowa*). In January 1944 the Home Army launched a nationwide campaign, Operation 'Tempest', against German communications and supplies. The decision to mount a rising in Warsaw was a response to the rapid approach of the Red Army from the east and fear that the Soviet Union would impose a communist government unless the Poles helped to liberate themselves. On 1 August the commander-in-chief of the Home Army, General Tadeusz Bór-Komorowski, ordered the rising to begin. Around 37,000 Poles took part, both men and women. The Germans responded immediately with savage reprisals. A force of 21,300 troops and security officers supported by tanks and artillery, led by Lt. General Erich von dem Bach-Zalewski, the SS commander of the anti-partisan campaign in Russia, began to murder the civilian population systematically. Within days 40,000 had been killed but Himmler reined back the violence and insisted on the defeat of the rebels. On 25 August a major offensive was launched against the areas still in Home Army hands and street by street the Home Army was driven back to a small area of central Warsaw. On 1 October 1944, Komorowski negotiated surrender and a day later the rising ended. Around 225,000 Poles were killed, including 15,000 of the Home Army. The remaining population was deported from the city, which was then destroyed, block by block.

SS General Erich von dem Bach-Zalewski (1899–1972) was put in command of the German forces deployed to put down the Warsaw uprising in August 1944. He had previously distinguished himself as commander of the anti-partisan campaign in the Soviet Union. He was responsible for the mass murder of hundreds of thousands of Soviet civilians and Poles. He avoided indictment in the Nuremberg trials by posing as an expert witness, and was finally imprisoned by the West German authorities for his part in the Night of the Long Knives in 1934. He died in a Munich prison in 1972.

tanks. When the blow fell on 28 July, prefaced by a massive air bombardment from 1,500 heavy bombers, the German defences crumbled. By 30 July the enemy had reached Avranches on the Atlantic coast, moving on to occupy the whole of Brittany in the first week of August. The heavily defended ports of Lorient and St Nazaire were isolated, their German garrisons bottled up until the end of the war. A new American army, the US Third Army, was activated under the flamboyant General George Patton and sent east behind the German front line towards Le Mans, Chartres and Paris. The whole German force in northern France suddenly faced the prospect of encirclement.

Hitler's reaction to the crisis was characteristic. Field Marshal von Kluge was denied the chance to pull back the German front and ordered to mount a counter-offensive against the American flank at Avranches, using all the tanks he could find. The battered armoured divisions were gathered at the town of Mortain, thirty miles from the Atlantic coast, and on 7 August in early morning mist the counter-attack began. The Allies had been alerted by intercepted Enigma messages and had prepared an anti-tank trap. The Mortain offensive collapsed and von Kluge was replaced by Walter Model, who had a few weeks before stabilized the disastrous retreat in Belorussia. Model saw at once that the situation could not be rescued; the Mortain offensive had taken tanks from Caen and allowed Montgomery's army group to break through at last from the north. On 15 August a strong Allied force landed in southern France and this news finally persuaded Hitler that the position in France was hopeless. As the jaws of the Allied armies closed around 200,000 German soldiers, Hitler ordered a retreat. Model organized a remarkable escape through the narrow gap around the town of Falaise between the two approaching Allied armies. Around 45,000 German soldiers were captured and 10,000 killed, but the rest escaped and made their way as best they could towards the Seine and eastern France. The Falaise pocket was sealed on 19 August; by this date Patton's army had already reached the Seine north and south of Paris, which was liberated with little conflict on 25 August. Somehow Model got 240,000 men across the Seine, though with almost none of their equipment; the battered divisions retreated across France until they reached a defensive position running from the Belgian coast, along the German frontier, down to Switzerland. Here the German army turned to defend the Reich.

In the East the Soviet front now made greater progress in the north and the south. In the Baltic states the commander of German Army Group North was replaced on 23 July by General Schörner, whose fanatical commitment to the National Socialist cause also led him to be promoted to head the National Socialist Leadership Staff set up to make the army more ideologically committed. It was his task to try to hold the German position in the Baltic States and close off the Red Army's path into East Prussia. On 13 September 1944 the Soviet assault on Estonia began and by 23 September the German army abandoned the capital and the rest of Estonia apart from a small garrison that held out on the island of Saare until 24 November. During the course of the Estonian battle, the Finnish government sued for an armistice on 19 September and left the war. The battle for Latvia and Lithuania was more prolonged and bitter as German forces attempted to forestall a Soviet invasion of German territory. A Soviet attempt to seal off Army Group North by seizing Riga was spoiled in mid-August but a second heavy

Soviet offensive towards the Baltic coast at Memel (a city taken over by Germany in March 1939) succeeded in cutting off Schörner's Army Group North in the area of Courland in western Latvia. Here it held out until after the end of the war, only surrendering on 10 May 1945.

In the south the military and political situation continued to deteriorate for the Axis. After the collapse of Army Group Centre it was the turn of Army Group South (now renamed Army Group North Ukraine) to face a massive Soviet offensive. On 13 July the Red Army launched its fourth major offensive of the summer towards the Polish city of Lvov. Major cities of Germany's 'New Order' fell one after the other: Lublin on 23 July, Brest-Litovsk on 26 July and Lvov itself a day later. Soviet forces liberated the camp at Maidanek in the process, where they found the first hard evidence of the Jewish genocide. In ten days the whole German position in southern Poland had been destroyed. The German army under Model, who had not yet been posted to France, retreated to the river Vistula where German troops had arrived victorious five years before in the war with Poland. By late July the Red Army, exhausted after six weeks of heavy combat, reached the far bank of the Vistula opposite the Polish capital of Warsaw. The Polish Home Army, hoping to liberate the city before the Soviet forces arrived, staged an uprising on 1 August which led to two months of bitter fighting. A vengeful force of German soldiers and mercenaries were responsible for killing 225,000 of the city's population, the largest single atrocity of the war.

The last major Soviet offensive of the summer came in the direction of the Balkans and destroyed what remained of the German system of alliances. The campaign against German Army Group South Ukraine began on 20 August 1944 and within days won striking successes, isolating and encircling a large Axis force and occupying most of Romania by early September, including Germany's main source of natural oil in the Ploesti oilfield. On 23 August the Romanian government of Marshal Antonescu was overthrown by a military coup led by the young Romanian King Michael, and the following day Romania formally joined the Allied side and abandoned the Axis. Romanian soldiers now fought against the Germans remaining in Romania, killing around 5,000 and taking 53,000 prisoners. On 12 September a formal armistice was signed with the Soviet Union. By that stage the vanguard of the Red Army was already at the edge of Hungary. The rapid collapse of Romania opened the way to invasion of Bulgaria. German bases were stationed here but Bulgaria was not a belligerent against the Soviet Union. On 8 September the Red Army entered, reaching the capital Sofia on 15 September. The Bulgarian army then joined the Soviet side and undertook operations against German units in Yugoslavia and Hungary. The German high command now realized that the large German forces still stationed in Greece and the Mediterranean islands were threatened with being cut off and they were evacuated from 10 October onwards, shortly before a combined Soviet and Yugoslav partisan force captured Belgrade on 20 October.

By the late autumn the remaining Axis state, Hungary, was all that was left of the German alliance system. Here too the political situation was confused. Admiral Horthy signed a preliminary armistice with the Soviet side on 11 October and on 15 October announced publicly that Hungary was seeking an end to the war. Hitler needed to keep control of Hungary and sent Otto Skorzeny, who had rescued Mussolini in 1943, to seize Horthy and force Hungary to stay in the war. Skorzeny's unit tricked their way into Horthy's palace in Budapest, took his son hostage, and forced him to reverse the armistice decision. A fascist Arrow Cross government was installed and most of the Hungarian army kept fighting alongside the Germans until the spring of 1945. On 28 October, in response to the changed Hungarian position, a major Red Army offensive was launched against Budapest, which was strongly defended by four German and two Hungarian divisions under the command of a senior SS police official, General Karl von Pfeffer-Wildenbruch. The city was surrounded but not taken and Hitler ordered the garrison to stand and fight to the last. The city only fell in February 1945 with the loss of 160,000 men.

The crisis on all fronts in 1944 left Germany almost entirely isolated and facing the prospect of heavier bombing and invasion of the homeland. The Western Allies began to think that the war would be won in a matter of weeks, but the German armed forces and population continued to fight and work under the most difficult and dangerous conditions. The liberation of most of France in August 1945 brought American, British Commonwealth and Free French forces to the point where they could mount the next wave of offensives towards the German homeland. In the north Montgomery launched a major offensive from bridgeheads over the Seine, and by 4 September had liberated Brussels and the port of Antwerp. American forces further south pushed towards Luxembourg, which was liberated from German rule on 15 September. The next target was the city of Aachen in German territory. It was subjected to heavy bombing which destroyed much of the city, but a fierce German defence held up the American advance for five weeks. Aachen was finally captured on 21 October. After that American and French forces fought across Lorraine until by mid-December they were along the Rhine and the line of German defences, the Westwall, poised for the final battle for Germany.

The Allied confidence that Germany might be invaded or forced to surrender in 1944 prompted Montgomery to launch an airborne operation around the Dutch city of Arnhem in the hope that he could force crossings over the Rhine and open the way for a major thrust into Germany. Allied armies, unlike German forces, were now at the end of very long supply lines, which stretched all the way back to Normandy. There were limits to how much further they could advance without securing a major port. Le Havre was bombed heavily and occupied on 12 September 1944, and Calais two weeks later, but neither could function quickly as a major supply base. Antwerp was in Allied hands but still subject to German fire from the opposite side of the Scheldt estuary. On 17 September the British army launched Operation 'Market Garden', but poor intelligence had failed to find two SS Panzer divisions resting in the area. The German defence proved too strong and the operation was abandoned on 26 September. Montgomery instead concentrated on clearing the Scheldt estuary to make it possible to use Antwerp, which was now under attack by V2 rockets as well, and on 8 November finally cleared German forces from the estuary region. The Allied advance came to a halt as German armies dug in for the final defence of the Reich.

For Hitler the situation in the West was not regarded as beyond rescue. He placed exaggerated confidence in the effect of the V1 and V2 in persuading the Allies to abandon bombing of German cities. He believed it possible to divide the Allies from each other, hoping to the last that the strange alliance of capitalism and communism ranged against Germany would fall apart at the critical moment. He wanted the final mobilization of all German manpower, young and old, and on 25 September drafted a decree, eventually published on 18 October, for the creation of the *Volkssturm*, a people's militia that would take its part in the coming showdown with Germany's enemies. Above all, Hitler persuaded himself that it was possible to mount a decisive military counter-stroke in the West that mirrored the German victory there in 1940. From September the armed forces prepared an operation initially codenamed 'Watch on the Rhine'(*Wacht am Rhein*) but finally given the title Operation 'Autumn Mist' (*Herbstnebel*). German commanders were reluctant to take risks at a time when they saw the priority as defensive, but Hitler insisted. A force of 500,000 men, 1,000 aircraft and 1,000 tanks, spearheaded by the Sixth and Fifth Panzer Armies, was assembled in secrecy in the area facing the same Ardennes forest that German forces had penetrated so successfully for the defeat of France. The object was to drive a wedge between the American and British Commonwealth army groups and to drive for, and capture, the port of Antwerp. The point chosen was the weakest link in the Allied line, held by four inexperienced American divisions numbering only 83,000 men. Planning was completed in October and November and a date set for December when the weather was poor enough to prevent the Allies from using their overwhelming superiority in the air.

The attack was finally launched on 16 December in cold winter conditions. The Allied line was soon pierced, but did not collapse entirely. A large bulge (hence the Allied name for the battle) was carved out, 40 miles wide and 60 miles long. Allied forces were quickly deployed on the southern and northern flank and when the skies cleared, German troops were faced with pulverizing air strikes. The neck of the bulge began to close as Allied forces moved forward. Hitler at first refused to permit retreat but relented on 8 January to prevent a defensive disaster. When the battle ended in early February the German army was back where it had started, with the loss of 100,000 men, 850 tanks and almost all of the 1,000 aircraft. Operation 'Autumn Mist' destroyed the defence capability in the West and opened the way for final invasion. On New Year's Day 1945 Hitler called on the German people to join him in 'the merciless struggle for our very existence'.

Opposite above: A photograph of Hitler with other leaders taken in front of a newly-built bunker at his headquarters at Rastenburg, in East Prussia, on 18 September 1944. Hitler, back to camera, is talking to Grand Admiral Karl Dönitz (far left), General Keitel (centre) and foreign minister Joachim von Ribbentrop (right). Threatened on all fronts, Hitler refused to consider any suggestions for a compromise peace.

Opposite below: German troops pass a burning Allied tank during the operation 'Autumn Mist', known on the Allied side as the Battle of the Bulge. The campaign, launched in December 1944, was the last attempt by Hitler's armies to reconquer lost territory and it ended in dismal failure a few weeks later.

THE VOLKSSTURM DECREE, 25 SEPTEMBER 1944

Decree of the Führer on the Formation of the German Volkssturm

After five years of the heaviest struggle the enemy, thanks to the betrayal of all our European allies, stands on some fronts near to or on the German frontier. He exerts all his strength in order to destroy our Reich. His final aim is the extermination of the Germans.

As in autumn 1939 we stand against the front of our enemy quite alone. Then in a few years, thanks to the first major application of our national strength we succeeded in solving the most important military problems, the position of the Reich and of Europe too safeguarded for years thereafter. While the enemy now believes he is able to strike the final blow, we are determined to complete the second great mobilization of our people. Building as in the years 1939 to 1941 exclusively on our own strength, we must and will succeed in breaking not only the will to destruction of the enemy, but to throw him back and to hold him far away from the Reich until a secure peace is guaranteed for the future of Germany, her allies and Europe itself.

We set against the total will to destruction of our Jewish-international enemy, of which we are well aware, the total mobilization of all German men.

In order to reinforce the active strength of our armed forces, and in particular in order to conduct an unremitting struggle everywhere where the enemy wants to tread on German soil, I summon all German men capable of bearing arms to join the fight.

I order:

1. In every Gau in the Greater German Reich is to be formed a German Volkssturm from all those men aged from 16 to 60 capable of bearing arms. It will defend the homeland with every weapon and means, insofar as they appear suitable for it.

Source: *Reichsgesetztblatt*, Teil I, 20 October 1944, p. 253

1945 In the Jaws of Defeat

The overriding question facing all Germans by the beginning of 1945 was how to cope with the reality of a coming defeat. The popular mood had been sustained to some extent by propaganda about wonder weapons and unexpected offensives during 1944, but only the most fanatical or ill-informed could shield themselves from the prospect of defeat. Even Goebbels, who orchestrated the propaganda, was plagued by doubts and failing health. For most ordinary Germans there was little room for manoeuvre, caught between powerful and looming enemies who insisted on unconditional surrender and a regime utterly committed to fighting to the bitter end, for whom surrender was not negotiable.

The final four months of the Third Reich were among the most deadly for the German people. Around 1.1 million German servicemen lost their lives between January and April, most

A young Waffen-SS officer surrenders in December 1944 to a unit of the US army during Operation 'Autumn Mist'. Some SS units were sent behind the front dressed in American uniforms, but those who were caught were shot as spies.

SURVIVING THE DRESDEN FIRESTORM, 13/14 FEBRUARY 1945

It rained, the storm blew, I climbed up a little further to the partly broken-down parapet of the Terrace, I climbed down again out of the wind, it kept on raining, the ground was slippery. Groups of people stood or sat, the Belvedere was burning, the Art Academy was burning, in the distance there were fires everywhere – I was quite dulled. I had no thoughts at all, no more than occasional scraps rose up in my mind. Eva – why I am not worried about her all the time – why can I not observe any details, but see only the theatrical fire to my right and to my left, the burning beams and scraps and rafters in and above the stone walls? Then the calm figure of the statue on the Terrace made a strange impression on me again – who was he? But most of the time I stood as if half asleep and waited for dawn…It grew lighter and I saw a stream of people on the road by the Elbe. But I did not yet have the courage to go down. Finally, probably at about seven, the Terrace – the Terrace forbidden to Jews – was by now somewhat empty, I walked past the shell of the still burning Belvedere and came to the Terrace wall. A number of people were sitting there. After a minute someone called out to me: Eva was sitting unharmed on the suitcase wearing her fur coat. We greeted one another very warmly, and we were completely indifferent to the loss of our belongings, and remain so even now. At the critical moment, someone had literally pulled Eva out of the entrance hall of no. 3 Zeughausstrasse and into the Aryan cellar, and she had got out to the street through the cellar window, had seen both numbers 1 and 3 completely alight, had been in the cellar of the Albertinum for a while, then reached the Elbe through the smoke, had spent the rest of the night partly looking for me…Once, as she was searching, she has wanted to light a cigarette and had had no matches; something was glowing on the ground, she wanted to use it – it was a burning corpse. On the whole Eva kept her head much better than I, observed much more calmly and gone her own way, even though pieces of wood from a window had struck her head as she was climbing out. The difference: She acted and observed, I followed my instincts, other people, and saw nothing at all. So now it was Wednesday morning, the 14th of February, and our lives were saved and we were together.

Source: Victor Klemperer *To The Bitter End: The Diaries of Victor Klemperer, 1942–1945* (Weidenfeld, London, 1999), p. 392. Entry for 13/14 February 1945, written 22–24 February.

of them on German soil. Thousands of civilians died fleeing from the advancing Red Army, while thousands more died at the hands of German military and civil police, security men and the SS, accused of malingering or defeatism, even though defeat was staring the German people in the face. German military resistance, often now to the death, had about it a suicidal quality; German civil policing, on the other hand, was homicidal. On 6 February, Heydrich's successor as head of the RSHA, Ernst Kaltenbrunner, issued a decree that allowed policemen to decide when someone deserved to be shot, without having recourse to any judicial process. On 15 February the Minister of Justice published a further decree which virtually abolished the regular judicial system, replacing it with a system of kangaroo courts staffed by a judge, a Party official and a soldier who could also decide on execution without any due process of law. The victims were likely to be foreign workers, many of whom were singled out for savage treatment for the failure of the war effort they had been forcibly recruited to serve. On 31 March 87 Italian workers were shot in Kassel on suspicion of looting a food-train. Prisoners in the regular

Above left: A German officer hanged in Vienna on the orders of a 'flying court martial' for daring to plan the surrender of the city to the approaching Red Army. Thousands of soldiers were killed by their own side in the last months of war for desertion or defeatism. The placard in this case reads 'I connived with the Bolsheviks'.

Above right: The burning of bodies in the main marketplace in the Saxon city of Dresden following the firestorm generated by air attacks on the night of 13/14 February 1945. After the attack German propaganda suggested that 250,000 had been killed but the latest estimates suggest that the figure was around 25,000. Bodies were still being found in the ruins of the city two or three years after the raid.

prisons were also murdered in large numbers in the last weeks of the war as a further act of retribution against the powerless. In Kiel around 200 prisoners were killed, in Frankfurt an der Oder some 750; an estimated total of 10,000 were murdered before the end of the war. The number of ordinary Germans killed for defeatist comments or alleged sabotage or desertion has not been calculated. In every city and town in Germany the regime left a grim epitaph of decomposing bodies swinging from improvised gallows.

The deadliest fate was reserved for the ever-growing camp population. As the enemy approached, the camp prisoners were forced into long marches to camps in the interior, or were loaded into goods wagons open to the elements. The so-called 'death marches' exacted a high toll from the more than 700,000 prisoners. No exact figure can be found but estimates suggest that between 200,000 and 350,000 perished from hunger, cold and deliberate killing between January and May 1945. The guards in the camps saw the collapse of the Reich as a time for revenge. Some of the camps were evacuated at the last moment; prisoners who could not move were shot or burned alive, while those who could still move were forced at gunpoint to march often hundreds of miles with almost no food or water. Those who dropped on the way were finished off with a shot. Many died of cold and hunger before they arrived at their destination. At the Mittelbau-Dora works the number of prisoners increased by 50 per cent in the first months of 1945 but on the open trains that arrived packed with prisoners denied food for days, the dying and the dead – frozen and brittle – outnumbered the survivors. In Auschwitz the largest death-march, of 58,000 prisoners, began on 17 January, just ten days before the arrival of the Red Army. They marched or were put in goods vans to camps in the Reich, but 15,000 died on the way. The terrible scenes of starving, ill-kept prisoners in the camps liberated by the Western Allies in April and May were the product of the final orgy of violence and neglect indulged in by an SS apparatus that cared nothing whether the prisoners survived or died.

For those who avoided the violence from their own side, there remained the ever-present threat from the air. From the autumn of 1944 the Allied bomber forces had been able to roam almost unopposed over the Reich, supported by large fleets of fighters and fighter-bombers designed not only to destroy the German air force but to bomb fleeting targets on the ground – a train, lorries, stations – and to strafe civilians. In October 1944 the air forces embarked on two operations, Hurricane I and Hurricane II. The first was a heavy assault on the Ruhr and

Opposite above: A view common over Germany during the five-year bombing campaign conducted against German cities by the RAF. Tracer fire from German anti-aircraft guns light up the sky over the German naval base at Kiel on the north German coast. By 1944 there were 14,500 heavy guns and 42,000 light guns defending German targets.

Opposite below: As the Red Army neared the German capital in spring 1945, the population made desperate efforts to defend the city. Here German women dig an anti-tank trench on 9 April 1945. The defences crumbled in a matter of days when the Soviet assault began.

HITLER REFLECTS ON WAR, FEBRUARY 1945

6th February 1945

After fifty-four months of titanic struggle, waged on both sides with unexampled fury, the German people now finds itself alone, facing a coalition sworn to destroy it.

War is raging everywhere along our frontiers. It is coming closer and closer. Our enemies are gathering all their forces for the final assault. Their object is not merely to defeat us in battle but to crush and annihilate us. Their object is to destroy our Reich, to sweep our *Weltanschauung* [world view] from the face of the earth, to enslave the German people – as a punishment for their loyalty to National Socialism. We have reached the final quarter of an hour.

The situation is serious, very serious. It seems even to be desperate. We might very easily give way to fatigue, to exhaustion, we might even allow ourselves to become discouraged to an extent that blinds us to the weaknesses of our enemies. But these weaknesses are there, for all that. We have facing us an incongruous coalition, drawn together by hatred and jealousy and cemented by the panic with which the National Socialist doctrine fills this Jew-ridden motley. Face to face with this amorphous monster, our one chance is to depend on ourselves and ourselves alone; to oppose this heterogeneous rabble with a national, homogeneous entity, animated by a courage which no adversity will be able to shake. A people which resists as the German people is now resisting can never be consumed in a witches' cauldron of this kind. On the contrary; it will emerge from the crucible with its soul more steadfast, more intrepid than ever. Whatever reverses we may suffer in the days that lie ahead of us, the German people will draw fresh strength from them; and whatever may happen today, it will live to know a glorious tomorrow.

Source: François Genoud *The Testament of Adolf Hitler: The Hitler–Bormann Documents* (Cassel, London, 1961), pp. 38–9

Rhineland, already virtually destroyed by earlier bombing, and the second a sustained campaign against oil and transport targets. On 27 January 1945 the priority shifted to attacking cities with the full force available, in Operation 'Thunderclap'. A quarter of all Allied bombs were dropped in the last few months of the war, 477,000 tons out of the 1.9 million that fell on Europe altogether, and almost the whole of this weight was dropped on German cities. Among the most devastating was the raid on the Saxon city of Dresden on the night of 13/14 February 1945 when a force of 796 Lancaster bombers attacked in two waves carrying a large load of incendiaries. Meeting little resistance, the force concentrated its bomb load on the centre of the city, creating the conditions for a firestorm like the one that devastated Hamburg in 1943. The death toll of 25,000 people was the worst since Hamburg and the assistance to the advancing Soviet armies, which had been the justification for the raid, was minimal. Dresden was only one of the German cities subjected to unrestrained raids in the last weeks of the war. The tens of thousands of victims were magnified by the breakdown of civil defence services, and the large number of refugees and evacuees trying to escape the war at the front. The very last raid by Bomber Command was mounted on 2 May against the port of Kiel, but on 25 April a large force of Lancasters had also attacked and destroyed much of the area of Berchtesgaden and Hitler's Berghof, from fear that he might use his southern headquarters as a rallying point for a fanatical last stand. By the end of the war almost half a million people had been killed by Allied bombs.

Hitler was almost certainly deluded enough by early 1945 to think of a final redoubt, but he made the decision to stay in Berlin. On 16 January he returned to the ruins of the Reich Chancellery and the large underground bunker and stayed there for the remainder of the war, surrounded by valets, secretaries and his faithful entourage. His health was evidently failing; his left arm and hand shook, his body was pale and drained and his face sallow and swollen. He nevertheless exuded, according to Goebbels who also stayed in Berlin, 'incredible certainty and strength of belief'. He remained wedded to delusions of victory drawn from the lessons of history, which showed that time and again victory had been snatched from the jaws of defeat by a chance intervention. His favourite example was Frederick the Great and the Seven Years' War, in which the Prussian king was saved at the last moment by the sudden death of the Russian empress and the collapse of the alliance against him. The sense of unreality was tempered by the decision, taken on 1 February, to declare Berlin a fortress city. Inhabitants were made to dig trenches and set up barricades. *Volkssturm* recruits guarded the stations and main buildings as the capital braced itself for Hitler's last stand.

Invading the German Homeland

By January 1945 there was no prospect of German victory, nor of a negotiated settlement, and the last stand when it came lasted only a matter of weeks. German forces were still engaged in a bitter struggle in Italy, which now bore little relation to the principal battlefield further north. By December 1944 the Allied armies had painfully fought their way to a line just below Bologna, in northern Italy. While they waited for spring weather to complete the destruction of German forces, around 80,000 Italian partisans were isolated in the northern provinces. Since the Allies were not intending to move forward, six of Kesselring's 26 divisions could be used to conduct anti-partisan sweeps which matched in ruthlessness the behaviour of German forces in Russia. Around 40,000 partisans died, while villages suspected of partisan sympathies were burned down and their inhabitants slaughtered. The Allied offensive opened again in April 1945 and within three weeks the German position was demolished. Bologna was captured on 25 April, Verona on the 26th and Venice was liberated on 29th. For some time SS Lt. General Karl Wolff had been trying to negotiate an armistice with the Western allies, but it was not agreed until 29 April and came into effect on 2 May.

The final battles on the eastern and western fronts of Germany were fought with greater determination but the outcome was never in doubt. In the east, after months of careful preparation, the Red Army launched its largest campaign of the war, the Vistula–Oder operation. Around 2.2 million soldiers, 7,000 tanks and 5,000 aircraft were deployed to drive a wedge towards Berlin. In the Red Army's path lay German Army Group A, commanded by the trouble-shooting General Schörner, with 400,000 men, 1,136 tanks and a paltry 270 aircraft. There was no way to compensate for the disparity and when the campaign opened on 12 January, the Red Army advanced at great speed. In East Prussia the German troops defended with a new ferocity now the Russians were on German soil, but were soon restricted to the city of Königsberg. Hitler declared it a fortress city and the population had to endure six weeks of relentless bombardment which reduced the place to rubble, until the German commander, General Otto Lasch, finally surrendered on 9 April. He was condemned to death *in absentia* for not fighting to the finish. The same fate befell the Silesian city of Breslau, which was declared a fortress on 22 January and surrounded by the Red Army on 15 February. In this case the city was not surrendered, despite requests to Hitler from the beleaguered commander. It held out until 6 May, but only at the cost of 10,000 German civilians, 6,000 German soldiers and the destruction of much of the historic town.

In the centre of the Soviet drive the forces of Marshal Zhukov reached the Oder River at Küstrin by 31 January, only 40 miles from Berlin. On 2 February a small bridgehead was made across the river. Wherever the Red Army advanced it was preceded by a stream of desperate German refugees, some of them colonists who had been shipped east to farm the New Order, others local inhabitants terrified of the vengeance of Soviet soldiers. The first Soviet units to enter German territory in East Prussia perpetrated their own atrocities against the local population after witnessing for months the ruins of the Soviet land they had liberated. Thousands of German women were mass-raped by Soviet soldiers all over the conquered areas. A mass exodus was attempted by sea from the East Prussian coast and 450,000 refugees were rescued, many to be left further down the vulnerable coastline. In the end over one million refugees and wounded soldiers were successfully evacuated westwards. In other areas of Western Prussia and Pomerania a second wave of refugees sought the safety of the sea, and in total 2.1 million were moved to western Germany between January and May. Less fortunate were the 10,000 passengers crammed on to the Strength Through Joy ship *Wilhelm Gustloff*, which was sunk on 30 January with the loss of all but 1,239 of those aboard. In Silesia, including the area seized from Poland in 1939, some 3.2 million Germans fled the arrival of the Soviet regime. Some went to Bohemia or to the Sudetenland, from which they were subsequently brutally

expelled after the war. Those who stayed and those who fled were the victims of unrestrained looting and random violence by Soviet soldiers. After years of dominating and exploiting the East, it was the turn of German populations to taste victimization.

The final campaign in the West began later, in March 1945, though bombing and strafing by British and American aircraft spread out across Germany in the months of preparation for the final offensive. Between the two Allied forces lay Berlin. By agreement, the German capital lay in the Soviet zone of occupation, and although Western armies could almost certainly have reached Berlin by the end of April, the Western supreme commander, General Dwight Eisenhower, respected the agreement. The German defence in the West rested on three main army groups but they could muster only 26 divisions, while in the East there were still an estimated 214, though they were much weakened by losses of manpower and material. The German forces in the West could mount only a token resistance, though many units fought with a desperate

Above left: An anxious youth and an older man, both members of the newly formed *Volkssturm*, await the Red Army in a street in Berlin, armed with the portable 'Panzerfaust' anti-tank bazooka. The *Volkssturm* was formed in October 1944 as a popular militia made up of German men and boys who had not been conscripted for the front, but their military value was negligible.

Above right: Russian road signs on a city street in German Pomerania in April 1945. The signs to the left point to Moscow (1,875 km) and other Soviet cities, the ones to the right point to Berlin (142 km) and the port of Stettin (32 km).

MARTIN BORMANN (1900–1945)

Among Hitler's immediate circle his secretary Martin Bormann was the person he came to rely on most by the end of the war. Bormann was the son of a Prussian sergeant-major who left school to work on a farm. After brief service at the end of the First World War, he joined the notorious Rossbach Freikorps and was imprisoned briefly as accessory to a political murder in 1924. He joined the National Socialist Party in 1925 and rose rapidly to become a senior SA officer and, in October 1933, a party Reich Leader. From July 1933 he was assistant to Rudolf Hess, Hitler's deputy. He was liked by Hitler and soon gained wide influence in party affairs. Like Stalin, Bormann learned how to manipulate the Party machinery and to increase his own responsibility while more ambitious party leaders underestimated the vulgar, obedient and brutal young secretary. In 1941, after Hess had flown to Scotland in May to try to broker a peace deal, Bormann succeeded him as head of the Party Chancellery and became Hitler's personal secretary. In this role he gradually came to play a central political part, playing off one powerful Party boss against another, influencing key appointments and controlling access to Hitler. He was a fanatical National Socialist, utterly committed to the racial and political ambitions of the regime and a fierce anti-Semite and anti-Christian. He was more committed to the 'socialism' of the Party than Hitler and favoured extensive nationalization of business during the war. Bormann was responsible for taking down Hitler's final dictated testament in 1945 and was with him in the bunker in 1945. Hitler ordered him to try to escape but he was killed in the attempt. For a long time there was uncertainty about his fate, but DNA tests on bones found during excavations in Berlin confirmed that he had died in Berlin.

Hitler's secretary and head of the Party Chancellery, Martin Bormann. He was an early member of the party, blindly loyal to Hitler and an ambitious and unscrupulous politician. By 1944 he had become one of the most influential men in Germany, controlling who had access to the *Führer*.

ferocity. The Allied armies reached the length of the Rhine by 7 March and forced a river crossing. By 1 April the forces of Army Group B under Walter Model were encircled in the Ruhr pocket and compelled to surrender on 21 April. Model, unable to cope with the scale of German defeat, walked into a nearby forest and shot himself. The Western Allies then spread out into the rest of northern and southern Germany. Many Germans had had enough of the conflict and hung out white sheets and cloths to signify their willingness to surrender. In some cases they were shot by local policemen or SS men minutes before the enemy arrived.

On 12 April the US Army reached Magdeburg on the River Elbe and on 26 April they met advance units of the Red Army, which had bypassed Berlin and reached the Elbe at a village near the town of Torgau. They were units from the final Soviet assault on eastern Germany and Berlin, which began on 16 April 1945. The German army in the east was large but increasingly short of fuel and weapons as the bombing finally destroyed the integrated transport and distribution system of the Reich. The final defence of Berlin was improvised; an Army Group Centre under Schörner and an Army Group Vistula under Col. General Gotthard Heinrici tried to direct units that increasingly lacked cohesion and fighting power. Hitler, in his bunker in Berlin, waited for reports and moved phantom armies around on the map table. The reality was the rapid destruction of what was left of German resistance. South of Berlin the Red Army quickly dispensed with Army Group Centre and reached the Elbe; to the north an offensive launched on the 18 April reached the Elbe and the North Sea coast, where it met up with Montgomery's 21st Army Group which had captured Hamburg on 3 May. Berlin itself was the target for Marshal Zhukov. The capital was surrounded by 25 April, but the first units of the Red Army reached the suburbs of Berlin on 20 April. German defeat was now only a matter of days away.

The End of the Reich

While the battles for Germany raged through March and April, Hitler became increasingly divorced from reality. He spent long hours with Bormann dictating his version of recent history. The war was, he told Bormann, 'typically Jewish'. He spent most of his time in the extensive underground bunker beneath the Chancellery. Above ground, Berlin was reduced street by street to rubble under constant air bombardment. On 3 March Hitler made his last trip to the front when he visited commanders along the Oder, awaiting the onslaught on Berlin. On 19 March he issued the 'Scorched Earth' decree in which he demanded that everything should be destroyed rather than fall into the hands of the enemy, but in many areas of Germany even Party fanatics hesitated to further alienate the population and the order was ignored or modified. The following day Hitler made his last public appearance when he reviewed Hitler Youth volunteers in the Chancellery gardens. Thereafter he withdrew into the isolation of the bunker, linked to the outside world by telegram, telephone and the few officers and civilians still able to fly into Berlin.

On 12 April news arrived of the death of President Roosevelt. Hitler hailed the news as a historic turning-point, comparable to the death of the Russian empress that had saved Frederick the Great, but baulked at Goebbels's suggestion that Albert Speer should be sent as a personal emissary to the new President, Harold Truman, to broker peace. While Hitler issued

proclamations calling for suicidal resistance many of those around him were seeking a political solution. Himmler had tried to begin negotiations with the West through the head of the Swedish Red Cross, Folke Bernadotte; Ribbentrop had also put out feelers to the West; in Italy the SS had tried to negotiate an armistice for several months. None of the negotiations were accepted in the West, which clung to the commitment to unconditional surrender, evidently only weeks away. On 20 April, as Soviet guns could be heard battering the capital, Hitler celebrated his birthday with his intimate circle in the bunker. He speculated on leaving Berlin to lead a final rally from his base in Bavaria, but no decision was made. He gave permission to Himmler, Speer and Göring to leave Berlin while they still could. Goebbels decided to stay with his Führer and moved with his family into the bunker on 22 April. That same day Hitler had finally realized that there was no army ready to do battle for Berlin and made the decision to stay in the capital and die there. His mood worsened with the realization that no final apocalyptic conflict would take place above ground. When Göring telegrammed from Berchtesgaden on 23 April to ask if he should assume Hitler's role now he was trapped in Berlin, Hitler flew into a rage and ordered his arrest. A few days later news arrived that Himmler was trying to offer surrender to the British, and Hitler ordered his arrest as well. As long as he was still alive, his word remained law.

The photograph alleged to be the last picture of Hitler before he committed suicide on 30 April 1945. Hitler stands looking at the ruins of the new Reich Chancellery building together with his adjutant Julius Schaub. The Chancellery, built at great expense in the late 1930s, lasted just six years.

Outside the conflict for Berlin reached a climax. On 25 April Zhukov's forces had reached the River Spree, nearing the centre of the city. By 29 April they were storming the Tiergarten, close to the government zone, and the following day began the fight to capture the Reichstag building. In the bunker the atmosphere was morbid, as Hitler arranged his affairs in anticipation of his death. On 28 April he asked for a priest to be brought so that he could marry Eva Braun, his female companion, who had flown from Bavaria to be with him in the bunker. At 1 a.m. in the morning of 29 April they were married. The following day Hitler took leave of all his staff and in the afternoon withdrew into his study with Eva. He shot himself in the head, she died of cyanide poison. As the bodies were brought out wrapped in carpet, those present raised their hands in a final 'Heil Hitler' salute. The two corpses were taken to the Chancellery garden, where they were placed in a shallow pit and doused with petrol before being set alight. In his testament Hitler had appointed Goebbels his successor as chancellor and Grand Admiral Karl Dönitz, who had fled north to the port city of Flensburg, as president.

The following day, 1 May, Goebbels tried to arrange a ceasefire and negotiation with the local Soviet commanders, but Stalin refused anything but unconditional surrender. When the news arrived, Goebbels finally let it be known outside Berlin that Hitler had died. That same day he arranged with his wife, Magda, the death of their six children, who were poisoned with cyanide

HITLER'S REMAINS

There has long been dispute about what happened to the remains of Adolf Hitler and Eva Braun after their bodies were dumped in the Chancellery garden and set on fire. Soviet soldiers found the remains of jawbones and dental work which were positively identified by one of the technicians who worked for Hitler's dentist. These remains were then taken to Moscow, along with other remains found at the Chancellery site, where they were kept sealed from the public throughout the period of the post-war Soviet state. Although Stalin knew about the dental remains, he insisted to his Allies in the summer of 1945 that Hitler had probably escaped from Berlin, and even implied that the Western states had colluded together to shield Hitler from justice. There were numerous reports and rumours about post-war sightings of the Führer. British intelligence organized a detailed investigation in 1945 led by the intelligence officer and future historian, Major Hugh Trevor-Roper. The British research confirmed the story of Hitler's suicide and the destruction of his body. He also insisted that Hitler had shot himself, while the Soviet side made the case that he took cyanide, an argument that they sustained long after 1945 because it made Hitler seem more of a coward. Later, in 1970, Soviet KGB operatives dug up what they believed to be the bones of Hitler and Eva Braun, buried in boxes on a Soviet base near Magdeburg, East Germany, burnt them again, reduced the remains to powdered ash and scattered them in a nearby river. These remains were almost certainly not those of Hitler and Eva Braun. The dental work remains the single reliable evidence of their death in April 1945.

SAYING GOODBYE TO HITLER, APRIL 30 1945

30 April begins like the days that went before it. The hours drag slowly by. No one knows just how to address Eva Braun now. The adjutants and orderlies stammer in embarrassment when they have to speak to the 'gnädiges Fräulein'. 'You may safely call me Frau Hitler,' she says, smiling.

…Then we eat lunch with Hitler. The same conversation as yesterday, the day before yesterday, for many days past: a banquet of death under the mask of cheerful calm and composure. We rise from the table, Eva Braun goes to her room, and Frau Christian and I look for somewhere to smoke a cigarette in peace. I find a vacant armchair in the servants' room, next to the open door to Hitler's corridor. Hitler is probably in his room. I don't know who is with him. Then Günsche [Hitler's SS adjutant] comes up to me. 'Come on, the Führer wants to say goodbye.' I rise and go out into the corridor. Linge fetches the others. Fräulein Manziarly, Frau Christian, I vaguely realize there are other people there too. But all I really see is the figure of the Führer. He comes very slowly out of his room, stooping more than ever, stands in the open doorway and shakes hands with everyone. I feel his right hand warm in mine, he looks at me and isn't seeing me. He seems to be far away. He says something to me, but I don't hear it. I didn't take in his last words. The moment we've been waiting for has come now, and I am frozen and scarcely notice what's going on around me. Only when Eva Braun comes over to me is the spell broken a little. She smiles and embraces me. 'Please do try to get out. You may yet make your way through. And give Bavaria my love,' she says, smiling but with a sob in her voice. She is wearing the Führer's favourite dress, the black one with the roses at the neckline, and her hair is washed and beautifully done. Like that, she follows the Führer into his room – and to her death. The heavy iron door closes.

Source: Traudl Junge *Until the Final Hour: Hitler's Last Secretary* (ed. Melissa Müller, Weidenfeld, London, 2003), pp. 186–7

Col. General Alfred Jodl signs the document of unconditional surrender in a schoolhouse in the French city of Rheims where General Eisenhower, Allied Supreme Commander, had his temporary headquarters. The Soviet government objected and a second surrender ceremony was arranged for the following day in Berlin. Below: Jodl's signature on the surrender document, which was signed at 2.40 in the morning of May 7.

THE END OF THE WAR IN BERCHTESGADEN

A rare clear voice on the radio confirmed Hitler's death. Profoundly shocked, Mutti absorbed the news, not so much because she mourned Hitler but because she felt deeply betrayed. Our only hope now was that the Führer's suicide would speed up the end and stop the bloodshed.

The changing tune of the daily chatter made my head spin. My mind was filled with Nazi propaganda assuring certain death to all of us if the enemy won the war. I was eager to be persuaded otherwise and could have hugged Tante [aunt] Susi for saying that perhaps we would all survive somehow…Our fear mounted when we heard that the Russians were approaching from Vienna at about the same rate as the U.S. troops from the northwest….Young women in Berchtesgaden planned to hide in the mountains in case of a Soviet occupation. Mutti gave me a tiny, light-yellow paper envelope that contained a teaspoon of ground pepper and told me to carry it in my apron pocket at all times. If any enemy soldier threatened to harm me, I should throw the pepper into his eyes. I said I would try but that I would surely escape anyway because I was a fast runner….

On May 3, 1945, a messenger from the mayor's office walked from house to house. Hang a white sheet over your balconies or out of the windows, he instructed us, stay inside and open the door without resistance to any foreign soldier who wants to enter. He also told Mutti that as far as he knew the American troops were poised to take Berchtesgaden. Tante Susi promptly fetched several large white bedsheets and draped them from the balcony of Haus Linden, while I stood below to make sure they were hanging straight.

Inside, Mutti slowly took Hitler's portrait – the smallish, dark red wax relief created by Schego – from the wall where it had hung since 1933. That night we melted the portrait down. Hitler's face dissolved like a mirage at the bottom of the hot aluminium pan. Later the wax provided us with some desperately needed candles.

Source: Irmgard Hunt *On Hitler's Mountain: My Nazi Childhood* (Atlantic Books, London, 2005), pp. 225–7, 236

during the late evening. Then Goebbels and his wife took cyanide themselves and had their bodies burned. His last reported message for Dönitz was to inform him that National Socialists 'understood not only how to live and fight but also how to die'. The following day the commander of the Berlin garrison, Lt. General Helmuth Weidling, surrendered Berlin to avoid further bloodshed.

The fall of Berlin was swiftly followed by the surrender of other German armies. The final process was uncoordinated and confused. Hostilities ceased in Italy on 2 May with the capture of 490,000 German troops; in northern Germany on 4 May Admiral Hans-Georg von Friedeburg signed the surrender of German forces in the Netherlands and northern Europe; the following day German forces surrendered in Bavaria. On 5 May Dönitz ordered Hitler's chief of operations, General Alfred Jodl, to travel to meet General Eisenhower and surrender all German forces unconditionally. In a schoolhouse in the French city of Rheims, at 2.40 in the early morning of 7 May, the document was signed. Stalin was furious that the surrender was made to the Western powers and insisted on a second ceremony in Berlin. The Soviet surrender document had to be made to match the one produced by the Western Allies, and was not ready until late on 8 May. A little after midnight, on 9 May, Field Marshal Keitel signed the document of surrender. Even then German forces continued fighting. Field Marshal Schörner's Army Group Centre surrendered in central Czechoslovakia over the course of 11–12 May. German garrisons isolated in the British Channel Islands, Brest, Lorient and Dunkirk were told of the surrender and finally abandoned resistance.

This did not yet constitute the end the Third Reich. At Flensburg, close to the Danish border, Dönitz continued to operate as if he really did lead the vestiges of the regime. He set up a cabinet and was allowed to keep his own armed force. When visitors arrived in Flensburg they were given a guard of honour and escorted by German and SS soldiers still permitted to bear arms. The foreign minister in the new German government was Hitler's finance minister, Count Schwerin von Krosigk; Speer became economics minister; Franz Seldte resumed his post as labour minister, and Julius Dorpmüller retained his post as transport minister. The group played out a charade of governing. The new president held meetings, issued declarations and on 11 May drew up a draft memorandum recommending to the Allied occupiers of Germany that his government should be recruited to help run the new Germany to avoid the danger of 'hunger, chaos and the radicalization of the masses'. The Allies were at first uncertain what to do with the new German regime, but on 23 May it was decided to terminate it. A detachment of British soldiers arrived, disarmed the German garrison and arrested the ministers, some of whom were on the list of wanted major war criminals. With the end of the brief Dönitz government the Third Reich finally came to an inglorious conclusion.

Overleaf: A crowd of Danish men and women watch as German soldiers and vehicles of the occupation army withdraw into Germany following the surrender of all Germany's northern armies to Field Marshal Montgomery at Lüneburg Heath on 4 May 1945. The streets are patrolled by armed members of the Danish resistance movement.

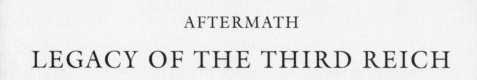

AFTERMATH

LEGACY OF THE THIRD REICH

The destruction of the Third Reich still left the 'German Question' unresolved in Europe. The Allies were uncertain about how to educate the German population out of National Socialism, while the German population expected the worst to happen. In the end German sovereignty was restored quickly with the creation, in 1949, of the German Federal Republic in the western zones of occupation and the German Democratic Republic in the Soviet zone. In the 1950s both German states experienced an economic miracle, while each was integrated into the defence and alliance system on either side of the Cold War divide. The crimes of the regime were highlighted through the decision to establish an International Military Tribunal at Nuremberg, to try both major and lesser war criminals. Millions of other Germans were subjected to denazification proceedings and sacked from their jobs. But by the 1950s many former National Socialists had won back their jobs and in some cases played an important part in the development of the two new German states. The shadow of the Third Reich hung over Germany as the population struggled to come to terms with the scale of the crimes committed by the regime. The problem of 'overcoming the past' has remained a central feature of German culture since 1945, despite the long period of economic success and the establishment, in 1990, of a reunited democratic Germany as a full partner in the development of the European Union. A few Germans were attracted to the memory of the Hitler years, but neo-Nazism has remained to this day a tiny fringe movement. Popular fascination with Hitler and the history of the Third Reich is, by contrast, an international phenomenon that shows no sign of ebbing away.

The End of the Third Reich

The Third Reich disappeared almost overnight in May 1945. The institutions set up by the regime ceased to function. The SA and SS melted away, hoping to avoid retribution. The Party itself, made up of around 8 million members, seemingly vanished as Germans destroyed their membership documents and hid their Party badges and medals. The hour of defeat was named *Stunde Null*, Hour Zero.

The place of the Third Reich was taken by four zones of occupation, agreed well in advance by the Allied powers. Britain's zone comprised the most heavily populated and industrial rich areas of the north and north-west; the United States governed the area south of Cologne down to the Austrian border with Bavaria; France had a smaller sector comprising the Saarland and Baden; the Soviet zone extended across the whole of eastern Germany from Dresden to the Baltic Sea (though much of Prussia was absorbed into the new territory of Poland or directly ruled from Moscow). Berlin, although it lay in the Soviet sphere, was divided into four national zones, with an area of shared administration in the city centre. Austria and Vienna were also divided into separate zones of occupation. Each zone established its own administration but also relied on existing German institutions and personnel to help run services and local businesses. There was nevertheless no doubt left in the minds of the defeated population that they had to accept Allied authority and Allied justice. German sovereignty was suspended in 1945 with no plan in place to restore it.

Most ordinary Germans, surviving in ruined cities, struggled with the simple problems of daily life, in many cases too apathetic or stunned to constitute any threat to the occupiers. However, many of those who had directed the criminal activities of the regime made good their escape. Some went into hiding in disguise but were subsequently uncovered. Julius Streicher, the editor of the savagely anti-Semitic journal *Der Stürmer* and former Party leader in Nuremberg, was exposed by chance when an American officer in a routine interview joked that he looked like the notorious *Gauleiter*. Streicher immediately confessed and was taken into custody as a major war criminal. Rudolf Höss, former commandant of Auschwitz, lay low on a farm but his hiding-place was given away and British soldiers arrested him on 11 March 1946. Hans Frank, the Party governor of Poland, his identity unknown, was rounded up and put in a prisoner-of-war camp. Here he slashed his wrists and neck, but survived this suicide attempt. His identity was then established and he was taken to the main collecting centre for major criminals set up by the Western Allies in Luxembourg. Others managed to escape detection entirely, fleeing to destinations overseas in North and South America. Adolf Eichmann, assisted by an escape network organized by Catholic clergy in Italy, arrived in

Previous pages: German leaders sit in the dock at the Nuremberg Trial of the major war criminals held between November 1945 and October 1946. In the front row, far left is Hermann Göring, to his left Rudolf Hess, Hitler's deputy.

BLASTS OF FATE:
A PARTY MEMBER LOOKS BACK ON THE REICH, 1947

We haven't deserved these blasts of fate…But it is too late. The best people are gone, above all those who should be the leaders of our young people. Mutual trust is lacking. How those who wanted the best were betrayed and deceived. Now, Alfried, we must show that the spirit of those days is not dead. Trouble and want bind us closer together. We must go on living, for our life's work for the young people has not yet succeeded and must be carefully sifted. My boys are enthusiastic about the camp life of those days and think wistfully of those times. There are thousands of different opinions re A.H. here. I myself spoke to a U-boat sailor, who says that 2 boats of his flotilla were set aside which took him to SP [Spain?]. One of the two, either 88 [code for Hitler] or M.B. [Martin Bormann], is said to have lost a leg. Even English people are of the opinion that both are alive. I can well believe that 88 was mentally or physically broken. Is it surprising?…But fanaticism will come again. I too was despairing…but today in spite of poverty, restrictions and work I am very satisfied, when I feel my head will burst I go to the old, faithful fighters and we give each other courage. My boys are with an old PG [party comrade] getting their bellies filled again. I myself go once a week to a very good comrade to eat. It is the old true comradely spirit of the SA. How I think back to that unity.

Source: The National Archives, WO 208/3791, Censorship Civil Communications, letter from J.J. to A.K., 25 October 1947, pp. 1–2

Opposite above: After the liberation of the concentration camp at Bergen-Belsen by the British army, female SS guards are made to help transport and bury the corpses that littered the camp. Thousands died there in the last months of war as food supplies for the camps dried up. Hundreds more died of malnutrition after liberation.

Opposite below: At a German Air Force base at Bad Abling, between Munich and Salzburg, the American army has constructed a temporary prisoner-of-war camp for 80,000 German troops who surrendered in the Austrian Alps in May 1945. Poor provision had been made to accommodate and feed the millions of German military prisoners and many were left for weeks in primitive camps with little shelter.

A LOST WAR

Heim: Could the war have been won at all, even if no military mistakes had been made? My opinion is: no. From 1941 onwards *at the latest* it was just as much lost as the Great War because the political aims bore no relation whatsoever to GERMANY's military and economic possibilities. The only thing HITLER's particular method of waging war cost the German people, was millions too many people killed. That's the only thing – the war could not be won. The remarkable thing is this, a thing which I am always thinking: how is it that a country like GERMANY, which is situated in the middle of the continent, has not developed politics to an art, in order to maintain peace, a sensible peace, in this much more difficult situation, than, for instance, the English situation; that on both occasions we were so *fatuously* stupid as to think that we could challenge the world – which is of course what it eventually amounts to when the war has been lost – without seeing that that is absolutely impossible in the situation in which we find ourselves in GERMANY. What are the reasons for it? Is it lack of political understanding, is it lack of political experience – I am no politician, no historian, I don't know, I only see the question. We never could have won the war.

Source: Transcript of talk by Generalleutnant Heim to fellow German POWs, 23 May 1945 in S. Neitzel (ed.) *Tapping Hitler's Generals: Transcripts of Secret Conversations, 1942–45* (Frontline Books, Barnsley, 2007), pp. 159–60

Argentina in July 1950, while the Gestapo chief, Heinrich Müller, disappeared completely. His whereabouts have never been discovered. Joseph Mengele, the young doctor who experimented on live subjects at Auschwitz, also ended up in Latin America, where he survived undisturbed until his death.

The other form of escape taken by thousands of Germans at the very end of the war was suicide. The wave of self-inflicted deaths began earlier in 1945 when it became clear that the Reich was doomed. Many of the major figures of the regime chose suicide as the way out, from Hitler and Goebbels in the Berlin bunker to the suicide of Heinrich Himmler, who tried to evade capture with a group of SS companions. He was caught by a British patrol and, in the course of being searched, killed himself with a concealed cyanide capsule. Other prisoners in Allied hands also chose suicide. Robert Ley, head of the vast Labour Front organization, hanged himself in his cell in Nuremberg on 24 October 1945, using the hem of his towel attached to a toilet cistern. Even Hermann Göring, who remained a defiant leader of the cohort of war criminals tried at Nuremberg, killed himself on the night before he was

German prisoners-of-war in northern Italy in May 1945. These were the first armies to surrender unconditionally to the Allies, on 2 May 1945.

due to be hanged, 15 October 1946. The last suicide of a leading Party figure was of Rudolf Hess, serving a life sentence in Spandau jail in Berlin. He hanged himself on 17 August 1987, at the age of 93.

Alongside the suicides of key actors in the Third Reich, there were thousands of suicides by more junior officials, Party organizers and servicemen. Some 78 generals and admirals committed suicide, over 10 per cent of the senior officer corps. The German commissar in Norway, Josef Terboven, spectacularly blew himself up with 50 kilograms of dynamite at the end of the war. Odilo Globocnik, the organizer of the Operation Reinhard mass killings of the Jews, took cyanide before he could be captured. In some cases suicide simply reflected a personal belief that defeat would only bring a disastrous end to Germany and German culture, and life under those conditions was not worth living. In other cases a guilty conscience clearly played a part. For thousands of women who committed suicide in eastern Germany and Berlin, it was a reaction to the mass rapes perpetrated by Soviet soldiers against any women they found, young or old. In Berlin in 1945 there were over 7,000 reported suicides, a rate of suicide five times higher than normal. Of these, half were women.

The wave of suicide ebbed quickly once defeat was an accomplished fact. For former members of the many Party organizations, and officials of the regime, there then followed a period of mass arrests and internment. The Western Allies' supreme headquarters in Paris issued an 'Arrest Categories Handbook' which listed all the organizations, from the SS down to the League of German Girls, which involved automatic arrest and imprisonment. The American Counter Intelligence Corps arrested 117,500 by the end of 1945; the British interned around 100,000, the French 21,500. In the Soviet-occupied areas 122,000 were arrested and sent to camps, in some cases the same camps that had been used to hold prisoners of the Reich. A combination of poor food and hygiene, harsh labour and cold – the features of the German camp system – led to the death of 42,800 prisoners in Soviet hands. All of those subject to arrest had to undergo a process of interrogation to establish what role they had played, and to mete out a measure of Allied justice.

By far the largest category of prisoners were military personnel, most of them captured in the last months of the conflict. The British and Americans had not expected to take such a large number of prisoners, but by the time the war ended there were 8.7 million prisoners-of-war in Western hands. Many of them were put in large, overcrowded and improvised camps, in open fields without adequate shelter. The death rate among the prisoners was higher than among those in permanent camps in the United States, Canada and Britain, largely because there was too little food and medical care. The difficulties of processing such a large number accelerated the decision to release the prisoners as soon as possible. By the end of 1945 there were still 5.5 million, by the end of 1946 2.6 million. Those that remained in captivity were used as labour in Britain or France, in violation of the Geneva Convention, and were not finally repatriated until 1947. The Soviet Union captured fewer soldiers, but again had poor facilities to accommodate those that surrendered at the end of the war. Altogether there were 2.88 million Germans (as well as many Axis troops) in Soviet hands of which 356,000 died of malnutrition, cold, neglect and disease. These prisoners, too, were

REFUGEES FROM THE EAST

'The soldiers didn't lose the war,' he said bitterly. 'It was the leadership and particularly the SS. They ruined our morale. I was in the Wehrmacht since '38. It was not long before I started trying to quit – promotion, everything was just one big racket. But you couldn't get out. In 1941 I was badly wounded, near St Petersburg [*sic*], and had to have my right leg amputated. (He pulled up his trousers and showed me a hideous bright pink shiny limb.) I spent six months in various field hospitals in Russia. When I was invalided home I tried once again to get a discharge. Instead, they sent me back to the Russian front with my wooden leg, at the age of forty-eight. On the way I passed through Elbing, my home town, and there were the healthy unwounded SS wandering around the streets. In Russia, whenever we in the Wehrmacht captured prisoners, the SS took them over from us and shot them. The SS had everything – all the food they wanted and the best, the warmest clothes. They got mad drunk and raped the Russian women and ruined our morale. While we watched this kind of thing going on, we heard from home that German women with one child and a husband at the front (that was me!) were being ordered to sleep with other men and so increase the German population. That was the Führer's *Schweinerei* and it ruined our morale. So did the speeches in which Hitler, Goring, Himmler and Gauleiters Koch and Giesler swore that every German village would be defended to the last man. We had seen what that meant. Ha! But what did they do? Here in Kempten [Bavaria], Bürgermeister Brändler – that drunk who used to go round boasting of the thousands of Bavarian women he'd had – at the last minute he ordered the SS to blow up all the bridges, not to stop the Americans getting in, but the population from getting out! Then brave Herr Brändler pulled off his uniform and tried to escape in priest's clothes. But they got him – the people of Kempten got him and bound him and stuck him on a wagon, drove him round the town and pelted him with stones! Then the Americans came in, the SS disappeared, the Nazi bigshots and the *Hilfspolizei* [auxiliary police], they tore off their insignia, burned the records and put white flags out of their windows – the brave boys. And where are they now? Most of them are sitting right here, in the best apartments, helping the Americans to occupy and keep order. Brändler's adjutant is among them. I saw him the other day, wandering about. He lives in his own apartment, while we refugees – my wife, myself and our child – live in an unheated attic…'

Source: James Stern *The Hidden Damage* (Chelsea Press, London, 1990), pp. 240–1. Stern was employed by the US Army to interview Germans about their wartime experiences in 1945.

made to labour on building projects in the shattered cities of the Soviet Union. Around 1.8 million were repatriated to Germany by 1948 but the last were not released until 1956, following years of forced labour.

For millions of other Germans, spread out over eastern and central Europe, the end of the war marked the start of an often violent programme of forced resettlement. All over the areas of occupied and Axis Eastern Europe the new regimes took their revenge on the German 'master race'. German settlers and businessmen were deprived of their land and goods; many were herded into makeshift camps or forced on long, strenuous marches westwards, towards what was left of Germany. Many were murdered by the angry victims of occupation, or their possessions looted or destroyed. The forced expulsion of over 11 million Germans was one of the most enduring and traumatic consequences of German defeat. They arrived in the Western and Soviet zones of occupation with almost nothing, forced to rebuild their lives from scratch.

A German woman and her family cooking on an improvised hearth in the open in Berlin in July 1945. More than half the urban area of Germany's major cities had been destroyed by the end of the war, forcing the population to eke out a desperate and impoverished existence in the first years of peace.

Almost 8 million came to the Western zones, 4 million to the east, and 470,000 to Austria. Until the early 1960s they were represented by their own political party, the Bloc of Expellees, founded in 1950, which campaigned on a traditional nationalist agenda. They were not warmly welcomed by the German population, which was itself suffering from high unemployment, chronic inflation and a serious deficiency of food. The average calories per day consumed in Germany declined from almost 2,000 in 1944 to 1,412 in 1945–6. The daily lives of all Germans, residents and expellees, were harsh in the years that immediately followed the end of the war. Only economic revival allowed the refugees to be integrated into West German society, but the legacy of expulsion and dispossession was a trauma hard to overcome for the generation that experienced it.

The Nuremberg Trials

The Allies had decided earlier in the war that they would punish the leaders of the Third Reich, as well as their military and industrial collaborators. In addition they were committed to a programme of what came to be called 'denazification' – the identification and penalizing of all those Germans who had actively participated in the regime and its crimes. For the rest of the population there were plans for positive programmes of re-education to make the Germans better democratic citizens. In the Soviet zones this meant creating a new cohort of enthusiastic communists and heavy penalties for anyone associated with fascism.

The most spectacular trial was planned for those deemed responsible for plunging Europe into war. In early May 1945, at the founding conference of the United Nations Organization in San Francisco, the wartime Allies agreed to set up an International Military Tribunal to carry out the prosecution of a list of prominent war criminals. The first trial was intended to be a showpiece of international justice and came to be known as the Trial of the Major War Criminals. Other trials were to follow on from the first, directed at key organizations or individuals who had played a part in sustaining the regime of crime. The document authorizing the tribunal was finally agreed and signed at the Potsdam Conference on 8 August 1945, and a detailed indictment was prepared for the cohort of senior prisoners in Allied hands. The indictment was finally presented to twenty-two prisoners on 19 October and the trial began on 20 November, without the figure of Robert Ley, who had committed suicide four weeks previously, or Martin Bormann, who was tried in absence. The trial was based on categories of international crime which had not existed before 1945. Crimes against humanity and crimes against peace were not defined as such when they were committed by the leaders of the Reich. The defence lawyers for the major war criminals contested the legality of the trial throughout its entire eleven months, but international opinion (and much of German popular opinion too) was united in the desire to have a symbolic reckoning with National Socialism and its allies. Of the twenty-two indicted, twelve were sentenced to death (including the absent Bormann); three were acquitted, including Hjlamar Schacht and Franz von Papen, and the rest subject to long prison terms.

The major trial was only the start of a period of more than a decade in which trials were mounted against camp guards, leading industrialists, military commanders and a host of lesser

BRUEGGEMANN, Dr.M · TER MEER, Fritz · OSTER, Heinrich · GATTINEAU, H.

GAJEWSKI, Fritz · SCHMITZ, H. · SCHNEIDER, Dr.C. · von SCHNITZLER, G.

AMBROS O. · LAUTENSCHLAEGER · MANN, Wilh. R. · BUETEFISCH, Heinrich

DUERRFELD, W.H. · HOERLEIN, H. · Dr. KRAUCH, K.

JUSTICE JACKSON AT THE NUREMBERG TRIAL

The privilege of opening the first trial in history for crimes against the peace of the world imposes a grave responsibility. The wrongs which we seek to condemn and punish have been so calculated, so malignant, and so devastating, that civilization cannot tolerate their being ignored, because it cannot survive their being repeated. That four great nations, flushed with victory and stung with injury stay the hand of vengeance and voluntarily submit their captive enemies to the judgment of the law is one of the most significant tributes that Power has ever paid to Reason....

In the prisoners' dock sit twenty-odd broken men. Reproached by the humiliation of those they have led almost as bitterly as by the desolation of those they have attacked, their personal capacity for evil is forever past. It is hard now to perceive in these men as captives the power by which as Nazi leaders they once dominated much of the world and terrified most of it. Merely as individuals their fate is of little consequence to the world.

What makes this inquest significant is that these prisoners represent sinister influences that will lurk in the world long after their bodies have returned to dust. We will show them to be living symbols of racial hatreds, of terrorism and violence, and of the arrogance and cruelty of power. They are symbols of fierce nationalisms and of militarism, of intrigue and war-making which have embroiled Europe generation after generation, crushing its manhood, destroying its homes, and impoverishing its life. They have so identified with the philosophies they conceived and with the forces they directed that any tenderness to them is a victory and an encouragement to all the evils which are attached to their names. Civilization can afford no compromise with the social forces which would gain renewed strength if we deal ambiguously or indecisively with the men in whom those forces now precariously survive.

Source: *Trial of the Major War Criminals before the International Military Tribunal*, (Nuremberg, 1947), vol ii, pp. 98–9, opening statement by Justice Robert H. Jackson, Chief US Prosecutor, 21 November 1945.

Opposite: A picture gallery of the senior directors of the German chemical giant I. G. Farben who were tried by the Allies between May 1947 and July 1948 for aiding and abetting German imperialism and endorsing crimes against humanity. There were 24 defendants in total, of whom 13 were found guilty and sentenced to prison terms ranging from 18 months to eight years.

cases concerned more directly with war crimes in the original sense of crimes committed in the course of battle. At Nuremberg there were twelve trials in all, indicting 184 senior military, bureaucratic, industrial and medical personnel. Most were given prison sentences, but the last executions under Allied law were carried out in Landsberg prison (where Hitler had written *Mein Kampf*) on 6 June 1951, to wide German protests. Altogether the United States authorities conducted 489 trials against 1,600 people. Most of those arrested were not subjected to a full trial but forced to take part in the denazification process. This was conducted not only by the Allies, but also with the involvement of German judicial and administrative authorities working alongside. In the British zone between 1945 and 1949 there were 24,000 hearings in front of German *Spruchgerichte* (Investigation Courts), which found two-thirds of those indicted guilty of active association with National Socialism and its goals. Most of the 3.66 million Germans subject to denazification proceedings were not prosecuted, and a large proportion were given the special status of *Mitläufer*, someone who went along with the Party, but did not actually do anything active. For those who were closely associated

Mathilde Ludendorff, widow of General Erich Ludendorff, argues her case before a German denazification tribunal in Munich on 23 November 1949. Millions of Germans were examined for their links with the Hitler regime and its crimes but only 35,000 were classified in the most serious category of collaborator.

MISSION AND OBJECTIVES OF THE US OCCUPATION

1. DENAZIFICATION: Removal of Nazis from all positions of power. Largely accomplished but continuing in SPRUCHKAMMER courts

2. DEMILITARIZATION: Removal and destruction of all German military power. Continuing

3. DEINDUSTRIALIZATION: Removal and destruction of German industrial capacity to a level agreed upon at Potsdam. Continuing

NEGATIVE

A FREE, PEACEFUL AND DEMOCRATIC GERMANY

POSITIVE

1. RE-EDUCATION: By example the soldier is showing the German what it means to be a citizen of a democratic country

2. SELF-GOVERNMENT: The US has given the responsibility for the governing of the US Zone to the German people

3. FREE ELECTIONS: In 1946 many Germans voted for the first time. In the US Zone, constitutions for each state were voted upon late in the year

4. ACCENT ON GERMAN YOUTH: German youth are the ones we may educate to a free and democratic way of life – this is being accomplished through the German Youth Program

5. BALANCED ECONOMY: Germany is to be treated as an economic unit – steps are being taken to make the US Zone as self-sustaining as possible

The American occupation authorities took seriously the task of re-educating the conquered German population to be good democrats. This poster from January 1947 highlights American aims at denazifying and demilitarizing Germany while encouraging the development of democratic institutions.

with the regime, investigation usually brought demotion or sacking and the loss of the right to vote. The process of re-educating Germans into a democratic way of life, which was pursued with most enthusiasm by the American administration, seldom involved more than lectures, leaflets and propaganda. By the end of 1945 the Western Allies began to abandon plans for a major programme of education, focusing on reviving the shattered German economy and creating institutions which democratic Germans could run for themselves.

The New Germanies

The first years after 1945 were marked for most Germans, but particularly those who lived in the cities, by problems of sheer survival. Millions lived in temporary housing, or the cellars of ruined houses, often for years. They ate poorly and depended on the Allied administrations for any additional welfare. The Allies stripped Germany of much of its technical equipment (and many of its top scientists and engineers), and in March 1946 set up a Level of Industry Schedule which prevented Germany from producing many heavy industrial and chemical products and limited its steel output to around one-fifth of what it had been during the war. The shortages of all products led to a lively black market and rampant inflation. In 1948 the western zones suspended the inflated currency and established a new one, which became the present-day Deutschmark. In 1947 the western zones were recipients of Marshall Aid to speed up the recovery programme. By 1950 the western area had reached the level of output achieved before 1939; by 1955 industrial output was double the level of 1936.

MARSHALL AID

In June 1947 the American Secretary of State, General George Marshall, launched a European Recovery Program to provide assistance for the war-torn states of Europe, including defeated Germany. The states of the new Soviet bloc refused to participate and the funds were largely made available to the major states of Western Europe, Britain, Germany, Italy, France and the Netherlands. An estimated total of $12.7 billion was provided between 1948, when the plan was activated, and 1951, when it came to an end two years earlier than intended. A further $12 billion of aid had already been given by the United States between 1945 and 1948. The assistance was targeted at major industrial and infrastructure investment, with the aim of kick-starting the European economy. The aid was not intended as a gift, but was to be paid back when the European economy was in a healthier state. In practice very little of the money was ever repaid except by Germany. Under the terms of an agreement negotiated in London in 1953, Germany was obliged to repay only $1 billion of the aid it had received and completed the repayment by June 1971. By this stage all Western European economies had experienced the longest and most significant boom in European history and German repayment did not have the same effects that reparations had had after World War I. Marshall aid played a part in providing funds needed for investment, but there were also other explanations for economic expansion, particularly increased state management of the economy and the introduction of freer trade between capitalist countries.

The need to rebuild the bombed cities and improve living standards dominated German public life, and quickly blunted memories of the Third Reich. There was little to be gained by dwelling on a past that could not be recovered and, unlike the 1920s, most Germans did not look back to a more golden age, but forward to a promised 'economic miracle'. Germans also benefited (at least in the western zones) from the onset of the Cold War. The United States, Britain and France agreed that Germany needed to be restored as a sovereign state, but there was no prospect of doing that in collaboration with Stalin's Soviet Union. No peace treaty could be agreed between the former wartime allies, and so two separate German states were constructed: out of the western zones the Federal Republic of Germany (West Germany), with a founding constitution, or Basic Law, which tried to avoid the mistakes of the 1920s by

Opposite: In postwar Germany there was a desperate shortage of all kinds of goods as well as food. This elderly couple are searching through garbage bins in Berlin in 1945 in the hunt for anything usable. By the autumn the German diet in most of the occupied area had fallen to around 1,000 calories a day, just over one-third of the wartime level.

granting the right to ban parties committed to subverting the constitution; out of the Soviet zone there arose the German Democratic Republic (East Germany), ruled by a socialist coalition, but in effect by the dominant East German communist party, supported directly by the Soviet Union. Berlin remained divided, and in 1960 the East German government of Walter Ulbricht built a high wall across the city to separate the capitalist zones from the communist capital. The old Germany of Bismarck and Hitler was divided and remained so down to the collapse of Soviet Communism in 1989/90.

The effort to construct a new and progressive western Germany encouraged many Germans to put the past behind them in an act of collective amnesia. On 20 December 1949 the new West German parliament agreed an Amnesty Law for those penalized by denazification, or about to be processed. The Western Allies concurred and it became law on

Above left: The first chancellor of the German Federal Republic, Konrad Adenauer, a Catholic politician from the Rhineland. He led the newly-founded Christian Democrat Party (CDU) and played a critical part in stabilizing post-war Germany and reintegrating Germany into the wider European community.

Above right: The first leader of the German Democratic Republic (DDR) set up in 1949 was the German communist leader Walter Ulbricht. As chairman of the Socialist Unity Party (which included both communists and social democrats) he imposed many of the conditions of the Soviet model on the new German state. He dominated East German politics until his death in 1973.

31 December 1949. By 1951 around 792,000 Germans had benefited from the amnesty and could be allowed back into office. During 1951–2 a great many had voting rights restored, and it was also agreed to give back pension rights to over 400,000 who had lost them as a result of the post-war hearings. The first chancellor of West Germany, Konrad Adenauer, who had been mayor of Cologne before 1933 and an opponent of Hitler, pressed the Allies to accept further concessions and on 17 July 1954 a general amnesty law was passed which helped a further 400,000 people. In 1954 only 183 further investigations were carried out. At the end of 1954 the western Allies set up three 'Pardon Commissions' to release the remaining war criminals in Allied hands. By 1955 there were only 94 left, and by 1958 all had been freed. By the mid-1950s tens of thousands of former Party members were active in all areas of public life – politics, industry, universities and the law.

The economic revival made the Federal Republic into the power-house of the booming European economy. The 'economic miracle' owed something to the coming of the Korean War in 1950, which required Germany to expand its industry well beyond anything envisaged by the Allies in 1945. The war also encouraged the West to abandon the idea of German disarmament and to get the Germans to play a part in confronting the threat from the Soviet Union. In 1955 new defence forces were set up, despite wide pacifist protest among a public

GERMAN REARMAMENT

After the Second World War the victorious Allies were determined that any post-war German state would have to remain disarmed to avoid a repetition of the 1930s. Many Germans also welcomed this decision. The situation changed with the emerging Cold War and the threat posed to Western Europe by the Soviet bloc. The Russian-controlled East German state began concealed rearmament in the early 1950s, while in West Germany plans were secretly begun in 1950, at the instigation of a number of senior officers from the war period, to prepare for the re-establishment of a German army. In 1955 Britain, France and the United States decided that it was important for the confrontation with the Soviet Union to allow West Germany to rearm. Despite popular protests in Germany against militarism, the new German army (*Bundeswehr*) was founded on 12 November 1955. The same year West Germany became a member of the North Atlantic Treaty Organization (NATO), set up in 1949. In 1956 conscription was reintroduced. The West German state was also allowed to rebuild an air force and a small navy. The armed forces numbered around 500,000 at the height of the Cold War. Although German forces took part in combined NATO exercises, the German constitution prevented the service of German military personnel abroad, or active engagement in combat operations. Only since 1990 and the age of German reunification have German forces begun to participate in peace-keeping missions outside German territory.

ERP

Inter-europäische Zusammenarb
für bessere Lebensbedingung

which no longer wanted to be reminded of war, and West Germany was integrated into NATO. In 1957 West Germany also became a founder member of the European Economic Community, forerunner of the European Union. As a major player in Europe, both the German public and wider international opinion worried about the revival of political extremism. In 1956 the West German Communist Party was banned under the terms of the new constitution; in 1952 the neo-Nazi Socialist Reich Party had been banned under the same provision. During the 1970s and 1980s other extreme-right fringe groups were subjected to the same ban, while in the 1970s the emergence of radical Marxist terrorism (the most well-known of which was the Baader-Meinhof group) was contested vigorously by the

Left: The symbol of Germany's economic recovery after 1945 was the famous Volkswagen 'Beetle', here on the assembly line at the main plant in Wolfsburg, northern Germany. The British allowed the Germans to start production in 1946 because they assumed it would never be a commercial success. By 1960 one million Beetles had rolled off the production line.

Right: German politicians were keen to reintegrate with the rest of Western Europe. Financial assistance from the United States and initiatives to found pan-European organizations, such as the Council of Europe, helped Germans to find a new European role. This poster from 1947 celebrating the European Recovery Program carries the caption 'Inter-European Collaboration for Better Living Conditions'.

social-democratic government of Helmut Schmidt. Although there has remained a small and vociferous neo-Nazi presence in Germany, political extremism has posed no threat to the survival of an increasingly secure and prosperous democratic society.

The Long Shadow of the Third Reich

The Third Reich was nevertheless not so easily set aside. In 1949 the first president of the new West German parliament, Paul Löbe, warned that 'we will have to bear its consequences for an unforeseeable period'. During the 1960s the West German government returned to the issue of crimes committed under the Third Reich, but did so on its own behalf rather than at the behest of the Allies. Hundreds more cases were prosecuted against camp guards, the members of police battalions active on the Eastern Front murdering Jews, senior SS personnel and others clearly implicated in the perpetration of particular crimes. Part of the explanation for the renewed pursuit of justice against those implicated in terror and genocide can be found in the interest generated by the kidnapping of Adolf Eichmann by Israeli security agents in the Argentine capital of Buenos Aires on 11 May 1960. Eichmann was taken to Israel, where he was put on trial in front of the world's media on 11 April 1961. The fourteen weeks of the trial at last gave an opportunity to explore in detail the entire nature of the genocide of the Jews, which until then had not been widely discussed either inside or outside Germany. Eichmann insisted that he was only obeying orders. He was eventually found guilty of assisting genocide and executed on 31 May 1962.

The same year as his trial the first comprehensive history of the genocide was published by the Austrian-born scholar Raoul Hilberg, who had left Austria for America in 1938 after the *Anschluss*. His three volumes on *The Destruction of the European Jews* broke new ground in explaining the genocide as a fully integrated and organized process, but Hilberg had difficulty finding an American publisher and his work was translated and published in German only in 1982, an indication of just how sensitive the many issues raised by the history of the genocide were in Germany in the 1960s and 1970s. Only later was the term Holocaust widely used to describe what Hitler's Reich had done to the Jewish population, as Hilberg's concept of a unitary mass murder came to be widely accepted both in Germany and abroad. The screening of the four-part fictional American television series *Holocaust* in Germany in January 1979 was another important step in showing the German public the nature of the crimes of the Third Reich. The German parliament reacted to the series by removing the restrictions on how long after the event murder could still be punished.

Two years after the Eichmann judgement, the West German authorities mounted a series of trials of camp guards and personnel who had served at Auschwitz-Birkenau. The Auschwitz Trials, based at Frankfurt am Main, lasted from 20 December 1963 to 10 August 1965. They involved 22 of the approximately 6,000 SS who worked at some time or other in the camp, resulting in the imprisonment of 17 of the defendants. The trial (like the Eichmann trial) provided the opportunity to present in public the full history of the horrors at Auschwitz-Birkenau, which until then had been known mainly from the unreliable testimony and autobiography of the camp commandant, Rudolf Höss. The moving account of the camp

EICHMANN INTERROGATED, 6 JUNE 1960

EICHMANN: One thing is certain Herr Hauptmann [Captain Avner Less]: IV B 4 [Eichmann's department for Jewish affairs] never decided anything on the strength of its own judgment and authority. It never would have entered my head to mess myself up with a decision of my own. And neither, as I've said before, did any of my staff ever make a decision of his own. All decisions were based on (a) the relevant Reich laws and accompanying implementation orders; (b) the police regulations, the decrees, orders, and instructions of Himmler and the head of the Security Police – those were our legislative bases – if you don't mind the term – in quotes, of course. The loyalty oath in itself called for unquestioning obedience. So naturally we had to comply with the laws and regulations.

LESS: Did the law of the Reich provide for the final solution of the Jewish question?

EICHMANN: The final solution itself – I mean, the special mission given to Heydrich [on 31 July 1941] – to put it bluntly, the extermination of the Jews, was not provided for by Reich law. It was a Führer's Order, a so-called Führer's Order. And Himmler and Heydrich and Pohl, the head of Administration and Supply – each had his own part in the implementation of this Führer's Order. According to the then prevailing interpretation, which no one questioned, the Führer's orders had the force of law. Not only in this case. In every case. That is common knowledge. The Führer's orders have the force of law.

Source: Jochen von Lang (ed.) *Eichmann Interrogated: Transcripts from the Archives of the Israeli Police* (Da Capo Press, New York, 1999), p. 124

written in 1945–6 by the Italian chemist and former prisoner Primo Levi, under the title *If This Is a Man*, was not published in German until 1961. Over the years that followed other perpetrators were brought to trial, though few were given extensive sentences. The search for criminals slowed from the 1970s but was sustained by a growing consciousness outside Germany that escaped criminals and non-German perpetrators, taking advantage of the mass migrations at the end of the war, had found sanctuary in the West and ought to be identified and, if possible, brought to justice. The trials have been intermittent but the last ones have taken place in the twenty-first century, with men now in their late eighties or nineties.

The problem confronting many Germans during the 1970s and 1980s was coming to terms with the reality that a German regime had launched world war and perpetrated genocide. The problem of 'overcoming the past' became a public debate when in the 1980s a dispute between historians (*Historikerstreit*) erupted in the German media. Some older German scholars wanted the Third Reich to be put into context, both as something that had to be understood as a product of German history, not merely an aberration, but also as part of a wider European world of racism, dictatorship and terror, of which Hitler's Germany was one example. The historical revisionism provoked bitter disputes as younger Germans wrestled with the idea of coming to terms with the Third Reich as a 'normal' historical story, with its counterparts elsewhere, particularly in Stalin's Soviet Union. These issues were opened up again by the collapse of Soviet Communism and the end of the German Democratic Republic in 1990. In the Soviet bloc the story of the Third Reich had been told differently, as a product of capitalist imperialism. Class terror was seen as more important than the racism of the system, so that many East Germans had only a vague understanding of what Hitler's Germany had been responsible for. The two Germanies were formally merged on 3 October 1990, amidst some international anxiety that a large united Germany might pose a renewed threat to European security. The term used to describe the union, 'German Unity', was itself the product of much debate in an attempt to avoid any comparison with the Pan-Germanism of Hitler's Reich.

The creation of a single German state opened up further debates about the nature of German identity after Hitler. It also gave the opportunity for a new surge of ultra-right protest and propaganda in the wake of the collapse of communism. In 1991 there were an estimated 37,000 members of right-wing extremist parties and associations (including 2,100 overtly neo-Nazi); in 1994 there were 54,000, including 3,740 neo-Nazis. Unification also prompted a reassessment among the public about continued preoccupation with the National Socialist past. An opinion poll in 1994 showed that 56 per cent of respondents living in former West Germany thought that too much attention was given to the Holocaust and that it would be better to 'draw a line through the past'. But in the former eastern areas, where knowledge of the Holocaust was still being absorbed, the percentage was only 36 per cent, while 54 per cent thought that it was wrong to try to forget what had happened. The difficult question of how much prominence to give to memory of Hitler and the Third Reich fifty years after their destruction was opened up by two major events in the mid-1990s.

The first was the launching of an exhibition titled 'Crimes of the Armed Forces', which opened in Hamburg on 5 March 1995. The display included a large number of original photographs of German soldiers taking part in atrocities, largely on the Eastern Front, but also in the Balkans and Italy. The exhibition aroused strong sentiments for and against, because for the first time the public was forced to confront the established view that only Himmler's SS had carried out crimes, while the armed forces had fought a clean war. The organizers took the exhibition to 23 German cities and it was viewed by 700,000 people. There were strong protests against what was seen as a slur against ordinary soldiers, but there was also strong support among the younger generation of Germans who felt that for too long they had not been told the entire truth about what their grandparents' generation had done. The second event was the publication in 1996 of a book by a young Jewish American scholar, Daniel Goldhagen, under the title *Hitler's Willing Executioners* (in Germany it had the less

CONFRONTING THE GERMAN PAST

Bundestag Debates, 163 Session, 13 March 1997: stenographic report
[Debate over Exhibition: 'War of Destruction: Crimes of the Armed Forces 1941 to 1945']

Gerald Häfner (Greens) My honourable ladies and gentlemen! Dear colleagues! The debate today is about our attitude towards the worst and decisive phase of our own German history, and it concerns how we today can contribute to ensure that the planned destruction of people, of whole races simply on the ground of their race or their convictions, is never repeated. There has been for a long time in this House and in this republic a consensus between the democratic parties, that we do not allow the extreme right, the ultra-right, the neo-Nazis to put a foot more on the soil of this republic, or press through the door of this republic. This consensus has in recent weeks been abandoned, and by a party that sits in this House and takes part in this government: the CSU [Christian Social Union]. I think a clear statement is required about this from responsible members of the Christian Social Union and from this government.

How has it come to this? The cause is an exhibition which has already been shown in 15 German cities – it can be seen at the moment in Munich – an exhibition about the crimes of the armed force from 1941 to 1944. This exhibition is no sweeping condemnation of all members of the armed forces. They know that, considering the whole period of the Second World War, 18 million Germans served in the armed forces. Among them are many who did this out of conviction, but certainly also many who fulfilled their military service against their will and could not go through with the deeds or refused them, when they could not approve them or find them justified.

It is not therefore about a general condemnation. It is much more to do with stopping the lie that only the SS was responsible for all the bad deeds and that the armed forces in the East conducted a clean, noble, and brave campaign, that had nothing to do with the brutal, racist ideas of Hitler and nothing to do with the cruelties of this war. The truth is that the armed forces in the East engaged precisely in a war of conquest and destruction and in this war, under the responsibility of the armed forces, millions of civilians, women and children were murdered for no reason. Whoever denies this truth, whoever wants to suppress it, whoever falsifies our history, thereby contributes to spreading a deliberately biased account of history in this country, thereby contributes to bringing back real myth building again with a vengeance. Exactly this is what is happening in Munich.

(applause from the Greens and the SPD)

Source: Hans-Günther Thiele (ed.) *Die Wehrmachtsausstellung: Dokumentation einer Kontroverse* (Edition Temmen, Bremen, 1997), pp. 170–1

provocative title of 'Hitler's Willing Helpers'). The book exposed, often in excessively graphic detail, the sheer horrors of the genocide and the apparent pleasure that many German soldiers and security men had taken in the task of mass killing. The central thesis was simply that millions of ordinary Germans had been possessed by an embedded hatred of the Jews and that this explains how something like genocide was possible. Goldhagen toured Germany in staged debates with German historians, who were in the main hostile to the idea of German collective guilt, but the audiences were generally enthusiastic for Goldhagen and critical of the efforts of Germany's historical elite to mask the physical reality of the Holocaust.

In the years since 1996 there has been an increasing effort to expose all those areas of the history of the Third Reich that had either lain dormant or had been glossed over in the existing history. The result has been a painful effort to finally come to terms with the National Socialist past. In the early 1990s lobby groups campaigned to get a memorial constructed to the Jewish victims of the Third Reich and it was finally approved by the German parliament. The construction began on 1 April 2003 but the difficult nature of the German past made it a contested project. The area chosen was once the site of an SS barracks, which provoked the first protests. It was then discovered in October 2003 that one of the firms involved in supplying the memorial, Degussa, had been the parent company of the firm that produced

A photograph of the young American political scientist Daniel Jonah Goldhagen, whose book *Hitler's Willing Executioners* became a runaway bestseller in Germany in 1996. He provoked controversy with his claim that all Germans had an embedded dislike of the Jews, inherited from the past, which predisposed them to endorse the Holocaust.

393

NEO-NAZISM

Although the National Socialist Party disappeared completely in 1945, political groups sympathetic to the values of the Third Reich re-emerged after the creation of the new West German state. A few small fringe right-wing parties succeeded in gaining seats in local assemblies, but the first real neo-Nazi party was the Socialist Reich Party, founded in 1949. It was banned in 1952 as unconstitutional and laws in West Germany made it an offence to display the Swastika or to publicly endorse any of the ideology of the Hitler regime. A new nationalist movement, the National Democratic Party of Germany (NPD), was founded in November 1964 and at its peak won just under the 5 per cent of votes in a general election necessary to give it seats in the national parliament. During the 1970s and 1980s a host of small right-wing splinter groups kept the ultra-right alive, though their total membership was never more than around 20,000. The rise of violent neo-Nazism was most evident in the years after German re-unification in 1990, particularly in the recently emancipated regions of former East Germany. There was a sharp increase in race-related murders and assaults in the early 1990s. Most ultra-right groups have been banned under German constitutional law or their leaders prosecuted for violating laws limiting ultra-right activity. The recent revival of the National Democratic Party under its leader Udo Voigt has been matched by the growth of other neo-fascist or racist parties in other parts of Europe, most notably in Britain, Italy, the Netherlands, Austria and Hungary.

Zyklon B for the gas chambers at Birkenau. Work was suspended while a public debate took place. In the end work was renewed, but opinions over the monument remained divided. The Berlin memorial was formally opened on 10 May 2005, but it bears no words to indicate what it is commemorating. The German Interior Ministry now holds a public conference each year on approaches to the genocide to coincide with Holocaust Memorial Day, 27 January – the date when the Red Army liberated the camp. The willingness to open up German public space to memorializing the genocide has had its counterpart elsewhere, including Austria, where a monument put up in the Vienna Judenplatz in 2000 provoked similar arguments.

One of the reasons why Germans have been unable to avoid coming face-to-face with the legacy of the Third Reich has been the wide popular appetite in the Western world for the whole history of the Hitler period. The intense curiosity was expressed in the international acclaim for the German film *Downfall*, screened in 2004, which chronicled the last days in Hitler's bunker and grossed earnings of more than $92 million. The film immediately provoked hostile criticism for making Hitler, however briefly, into an object of sympathy, but its popularity reflected how international the memory culture of the Third Reich has become. The wide media attention given to the libel case brought by David Irving against Deborah Lipstadt and Penguin Books in 2000 demonstrated how much the history of Hitler has been appropriated by the rest of the Western world. The decision of the court in London to confirm the judgement that Irving was responsible for distorting the history of the Holocaust was the first time that the English judicial system had been required to make a historical rather than a legal judgement.

The sustained interest in the history of Hitler's Reich is not only a German problem, but it has more complex echoes for German society. The Third Reich symbolizes a great deal about human capacity for grotesque violence towards other humans on a scale still difficult to fathom or explain, even after the intervening seventy years of further wars and genocides. It is the unique character of Hitler's Reich, set in the heart of progressive Europe, which explains at least part of its grim fascination even today for an international audience. For Germany, brought to the brink of destruction by Hitler's hubristic ambition, the weight of just twelve years of its history remains an unavoidable burden on the present.

Opposite: A neo-Nazi rally in the American city of Orlando, Florida on 25 February 2006. Neo-Nazi movements have flourished in numerous countries outside Germany, recruiting white supremacists and anti-Semites who try to keep alive the memory of the Hitler years. Many states now have legislation against Holocaust denial or incitement to racial hatred which has severely limited neo-Nazi activity.

Overleaf: A view of the Holocaust Memorial site in Berlin, opened in May 2005 at a cost of 25 million euros. The monument took a little over two years to build but was the object of regular controversy over the site chosen, the contractors used on the project and its design.

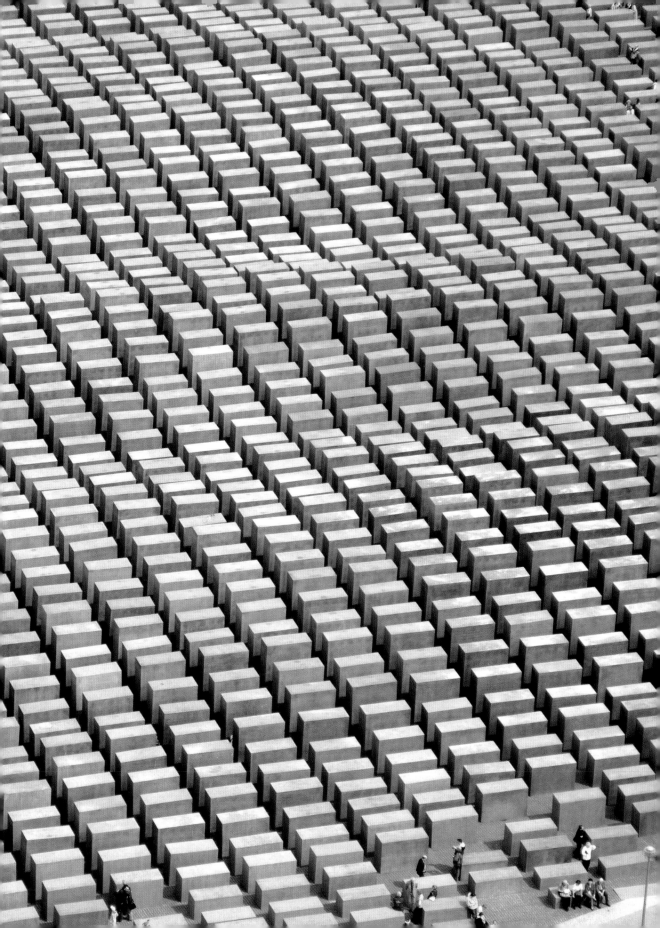

Bibliography

The following list is intended as a short guide to further reading and to acknowledge the English-language books that proved helpful in constructing this narrative. A great many books in German have also been consulted and the author would like to give a general acknowledgement to the valuable work that is being done on the Third Reich by German scholars.

Adam, P. *Arts of the Third Reich* (London, 1992)

Allen, M. T. *The Business of Genocide: The SS, Slave Labor, and the Concentration Camps* (Chapel Hill, NC, 2002)

Aly, G. *'Final Solution': Nazi Population Policy and the Murder of the European Jews* (London, 1999)

Aly, G. *Hitler's Beneficiaries: How the Nazis Bought the German People* (London, 2007)

Barnes, J., Barnes, P. Hitler's *Mein Kampf: Britain and America: A Publishing History 1933–1939* (Cambridge, 1980)

Barnett, V. *For the Soul of the People: Protestant Protest Against Hitler* (Oxford, 1992)

Barnouw, D. *Germany 1945: Views of War and Violence* (Bloomington, 1996)

Bartov, O. *Hitler's Army: Soldiers, Nazis and War in the Third Reich* (Oxford, 1991)

Bessel, R. *Germany 1945* (London, 2009)

Bessel, R. *Nazism and War* (London, 2004)

Bloch, M. *Ribbentrop* (London, 1992)

Boog, H. et al *Germany and the Second World War: Vol IV: The Attack on the Soviet Union* (Oxford, 1998)

Broszat, M. *Hitler and the Collapse of Weimar Germany* (Leamington Spa, 1987)

Broszat, M. *The Hitler State: The foundation and development of the internal structure of the Third Reich* (London, 1981)

Browning, C. *Ordinary Men: Reserve Police Battalion 101 and the Final Solution* (Cambridge, 1992)

Brustein, W. *The Logic of Evil: The Social Origins of the Nazi Party, 1925–1933* (New Haven, 1996)

Burden, H. T. *The Nuremberg Party Rallies: 1923–39* (London, 1967)

Burleigh, M. *The Third Reich: A New History* (London, 2000)

Burleigh, M., Wippermann, W. *The Racial State: Germany 1933–1945* (Cambridge, 1991)

Caplan, J., Wachsmann, N. (eds) *Concentration Camps in Nazi Germany* (London, 2010)

Caplan, J. (ed.) *Nazi Germany* (Oxford, 2008)

Corni, G. *Hitler's Ghettos: Voices from a Beleaguered Society* (London, 2002)

Dean, M. *Collaboration in the Holocaust: Crimes of the Local Police in Belorussia and Ukraine, 1941–1944* (London, 2000)

Dederichs, M.R. *Heydrich: The Face of Evil* (London, 2006)

Deist, W. et al *Germany and the Second World War: Vol I: The Build-Up of German Aggression* (Oxford, 1990)

Deist, W. *The Wehrmacht and German Rearmament* (London, 1981)

Eberle, H., Uhl, M. (eds) *The Hitler Book: The Secret Dossier Prepared for Stalin* (London, 2005)

Engelmann, B. *In Hitler's Germany: Everyday Life in the Third Reich* (London, 1988)

Evans, R. J. *The Coming of the Third Reich* (London, 2003)

Evans, R. J. *The Third Reich in Power* (London, 2005)

Evans, R. J. *The Third Reich at War* (London, 2008)

Fischer, C. *The Rise of the Nazis* (Manchester, 2002)

Fischer, C. *Stormtroopers: A Social, Economic and Ideological Analysis, 1929–1935* (London, 1983)

Fleming, G. *Hitler and the Final Solution* (London, 1985)

Frei, N. *Adenauer's Germany and the Nazi Past. The Politics of Amnesty and Integration* (New York, 2002)

Frei, N. *National Socialist Rule in Germany* (Oxford, 1993)

Friedländer, S. *Nazi Germany and the Jews: The Years of Persecution 1933–1939* (London, 1997)

Friedländer, S. *The Years of Extermination: Nazi Germany and the Jews, 1939–1945* (London, 2007)

Fritz, S. G. *Endkampf: Soldiers, Civilians and the Death of the Third Reich* (Lexington, Kentucky, 2004)

Gellately, R. *Backing Hitler: Consent and Coercion in Nazi Germany* (Oxford, 2001)

Gellately, R. *The Gestapo and German Society: Enforcing Racial Policy* (Oxford, 1990)

Goeschel, C. *Suicide in Nazi Germany* (Oxford, 2009)

Goltz, A. von der *Hindenburg: Power, Myth and the Rise of the Nazis* (Oxford, 2009)

Hamerow, T. *On the Road to the Wolf's Lair: German Resistance to Hitler* (Cambridge, Mass., 1997)

Hancock, E. *Ernst Röhm: Hitler's SA Chief of Staff* (London, 2008)

Hauner, M. *Hitler: A Chronology of His Life and Times* (London, 2008)

Heer, H., Naumann, K. *War of Extermination: The German Military in World War II, 1941–1944* (Oxford, 2000)

Herf, J. *The Jewish Enemy: Nazi Propaganda during World War II and the Holocaust* (Cambridge, Mass., 2006)

James, H. *The German Slump: Politics and Economics, 1924–1936* (Oxford, 1986)

Jarausch, K. *After Hitler: Recivilizing Germans, 1945–1995* (Oxford, 2006)

Johnson, E. A. *Nazi Terror: The Gestapo, Jews and Ordinary Germans* (New York, 1999)

Kater, M. *The Nazi Party: A Social Profile of Members and Leaders, 1919–1945* (Oxford, 1983)

Kershaw, I. *Hitler: 1889–36: Hubris* (London, 1998)

Kershaw, I. *Hitler: 1936–45: Nemesis* (London, 2000)

Kershaw, I. *The 'Hitler Myth': Image and Reality in the Third Reich* (Oxford, 1987)

Kirk, T. *Nazi Germany* (London, 1995)

Koch, H. W. *In the Name of the Volk: Political Justice in Hitler's Germany* (London, 1989)

Koonz, C. *The Nazi Conscience* (Cambridge, Mass., 2003)

Kurthen, H., Bergmann, W., Erb, R. (eds) *Antisemitism and Xenophobia in Germany after Unification* (New York, 1997)

Large, D. C. *Nazi Games: The Olympics of 1936* (New York, 2007)

Large, D. C. *Where Ghosts Walked: Munich's Road to the Third Reich* (New York, 1997)

Lauryssens, S. *The Man who Invented the Third Reich* (Stroud, 1999)

Lewy, G. *The Nazi Persecution of the Gypsies* (Oxford, 2000)

Longerich, P. *Holocaust: The Nazi Persecution and Murder of the Jews* (Oxford, 2010)

Longerich, P. *The Unwritten Order: Hitler's Role in the Final Solution* (Stroud, 2001)

Matheson, P., *The Third Reich and the Christian Churches* (Edinburgh, 1981)

Maier, K. et al *Germany and the Second World War: Vol II: Germany's Initial Conquests in Europe* (Oxford, 1991)

Mawdsley, E. *Thunder in the East: The Nazi–Soviet War, 1941–1945* (London, 2005)

Mazower, M. *Hitler's Empire: Nazi Rule in Occupied Europe* (London, 2008)

McDonough, F. *The Holocaust* (London, 2008)

Merkl, P. H. *Political Violence under the Swastika: 581 Early Nazis* (Princeton, 1975)

Müller, I. *Hitler's Justice: The Courts of the Third Reich* (London, 1991)

O'Neill, R. J. *The German Army and the Nazi Party, 1933–1939* (London, 1966)

Overy, R. J. *Dictators: Hitler's Germany and Stalin's Russia* (London, 2004)

Overy, R. J. *Interrogations: The Nazi Elite in Allied Hands* (London, 2001)

Overy, R. J. *The Nazi Economic Recovery, 1932–1938* (Cambridge, 1996)

Overy, R. J. *War and Economy in the Third Reich* (Oxford, 1994)

Padfield, P. *Himmler: Reichsführer SS* (London, 1990)

Pelt, R. J. van, Dwork, D. *Auschwitz: 1270 to the Present* (New Haven and London, 1996)

Pine, L. *Nazi Family Policy 1933–1945* (Oxford, 1997)

Quinn, M. *The Swastika: Constructing the Symbol* (London, 1994)

Reuth, R. *Goebbels* (London, 1993)

Roseman, M. *The Villa, the Lake, the Meeting: Wannsee and the Final Solution* (London, 2002)

Rossino, A. B. *Hitler Strikes Poland: Blitzkrieg, Ideology and Atrocity* (Lawrence, Kansas, 2003)

Rürup, R. (ed.) *Topography of Terror: Gestapo, SS and Reichssicherheitshauptamt on the 'Prinz-Albrecht-Terrain'* (Berlin, 2003)

Salkeld, A. *A Portrait of Leni Riefenstahl* (London, 1997)

Schoenbaum, D. *Hitler's Social Revolution: Class and Status in Nazi Germany, 1933–1939* (New York, 1966)

Scholder, K. *A Requiem for Hitler and Other New Perspectives on the German Church Struggle* (Philadelphia, 1989)

Schulte, T. *The German Army and Nazi Policies in Occupied Russia* (Oxford, 1989)

Snowman, D. *The Hitler Emigrés: The Cultural Impact on Britain of Refugees from Nazism* (London, 2002)

Sofsky, W. *The Order of Terror: The Concentration Camp* (Princeton, 1997)

Spotts, F. *Hitler and the Power of Aesthetics* (London, 2002)

Stachura, P. *Gregor Strasser and the Rise of Nazism* (London, 1983)

Steinbacher, S. *Auschwitz* (London, 2005)

Stephenson, J. *The Nazi Organisation of Women* (London, 1981)

Stern, J. P. *Hitler, the Führer and the People* (London, 1976)

Szejnmann, C-C. *Nazism in Central Germany: The Brownshirts in Red Saxony* (Oxford, 1999)

Tooze, A. *The Wages of Destruction: The Making and Breaking of the Nazi Economy* (London, 2006)

Turner, H. A. *Hitler's Thirty Days to Power: January 1933* (London, 1996)

Wachsmann, N. *Hitler's Prisons: Legal Terror in Nazi Germany* (New Haven, 2004)

Wegner, B. (ed.) *From Peace to War: Germany, Soviet Russia and the World, 1939–1941* (Oxford, 1997)

Weitz, E. D. *Weimar Germany: Promise and Tragedy* (Princeton, 2007)

Welch, D. *Propaganda and the German Cinema* (London, 2001)

Westermann, E. B. *Hitler's Police Battalions: Enforcing Racial War in the East* (Lawrence, Kansas, 2005)

Wistrich, R. *Who's Who in Nazi Germany* (London, 2002)

Zitelmann, R. *Hitler: The Politics of Seduction* (London, 1999)

Picture acknowledgements

akg-images: 19, 26, 31(ullstein bild), 36-7 (ullstein bild), 49 (Westfälisches Schulmuseum, Dortmund), 73, 74, 77 below (ullstein bild), 84 (ullstein bild), 88 right, 96 (ullstein bild), 98, 107 (Album), 118, 119, 122, 127 (ullstein bild), 160, 183 below, 209, 218, 235 above, 246-7 (ullstein bild © DACS 2010), 251 above, 252, 255, 269 left, 271 below, 276, 288 below right, 293, 299, 314 (ullstein bild), 317, 318-9, 351 right, 353 below, 357 left (ullstein bild), 358, 375, 386, 388 left, 396-7. Alinari Archives, Florence (© DACS 2010): 30. Bridgeman Art Library: 315 (Private Collection/Peter Newark Military Pictures). Bundesarchiv: 15 right (183-R01217), 17 below (102-00204), 59 (003-022-005), 91 below (183-R31497), 145 (003-009-040), 240 right (183-J08516), 281 below (003-009-223), 288 above (183-B22478), 288 below left (169-0367), 342 (183-S73507), 383 (004-004-008-T1/2). Corbis: 211 above, 257, 304-5, 327, 332-3, 340-1, 347 below, 349, 363, 366-7, 373 below, 388 right. Heritage Images: 47, 139, 204-5, 263, 285. Mary Evans Picture Library/Weimar Archive: 27, 41, 43 above, 53, 70, 111, 112-3, 116, 201, 226-7, 237. Paphotos: 393 (John Zich/AP), 394 (John Raoux/AP). Rex Features/Roger-Viollet: 28. Topfoto/Granger Collection: 50, 174 left. ullstein bild: 15 left, 22, 43 below (Imagno), 56 (Hoffmann), 57, 61, 64-5 (V.Pawlowski), 69 (Hoffmann), 77 above (Archiv Gerstenberg), 88 left (SV-Bilderdienst), 91 above right (Archiv Gerstenberg), 93, 105 (Imagno), 109, 130 left, 130 right (Imagno), 132, 135, 136, 137, 144, 148-9, 152 (Heinz Fremke), 156 above (Max Ehlert), 156 below (SV-Bilderdienst), 159 (Hoffmann), 161, 168-9 (Wolff & Tritschler), 171, 174 (Hoffmann), 177 (Imagebroker.net), 180 right (SV-Bilderdienst), 183 above (SZ Photo), 185, 195, 199 (SV-Bilderdienst), 211 below, 222, 229, 232 (Hoffmann), 235 below, 240 left, 251 below (Archiv Gerstenberg), 261 (SV-Bilderdienst), 266-7, 269 right (W. Frentz), 271 above (SV-Bilderdienst), 281 above left (W. Frentz), 281 above right (SV-Bilderdienst), 283 (SV-Bilderdienst), 295, 298, 303, 307 (SV-Bilderdienst), 312-3 (W. Frentz), 317 above, 336 (W.Frentz), 337 (SV-Bilderdienst), 347 above (W.Frentz), 351 left, 353 above (SZ Photo), 357 right (Voller Ernst), 360, 368-0 (LEONE), 373 above (Archiv Gerstenberg), 378 (AKG Pressebild), 380 (dpa), 382, 384(dpa). Wiener Library: 6, 9, 10-11, 17 above, 25, 34, 81, 91 above left, 103, 147 (Hoffmann), 153, 200, 223, 325.

Text acknowledgements

The publishers are grateful for the permission to reproduce material from the following:

Fred Breinersdorfer (ed) *Sophie Scholl: Die letzten Tage* Fischer (Taschenbuch Verlag)

Margarete Buber-Neumann *Under Two Dictatorships: Prisoner of Stalin and Hitler* Trs. Edward Fitzgerald originally published by Pimlico and reprinted by kind permission of The Wylie Agency

Henrik Eberle, Matthias Uhl (eds) *The Hitler Book: The Secret Dossier Prepared for Stalin from the Interrogations of Hitler's closest personal aides* (John Murray Publishers)

Konrad Elmshäuser, Jan Loker (eds) *'Man muss hier nur hart sein…': Kriegsbriefe und Bilder einer Familie (1934-1945)* (Edition Temmen, Bremen 2002)

Rudolph Höss *Commandant of Auschwitz: The Autobiography of Rudolph Höss* (Weidenfeld & Nicolson, an imprint of The Orion Publishing Group, London)

Irmgard Hunt *On Hitler's Mountain: My Nazi Childhood* (Atlantic Books)

Traudl Junge and Melissa Muller *Until the Final Hour: Hitler's Last Secretary* (Weidenfeld & Nicolson, an imprint of The Orion Publishing Group, London)

Victor Klemperer *To The Bitter End: The Diaries of Victor Klemperer, 1942-1945* (Weidenfeld & Nicolson, an imprint of The Orion Publishing Group, London)

George Klukowski (ed) *Diary from the Years of Occupation 1939-44: Zygmunt Klukowski* (University of Illinois Press, Chicago.)

Richard Overy *Interrogations: Inside the Minds of the Nazi Elite* (Penguin UK)

Theo Schulte *The German Army and Nazi Policies in Occupied Russia* (Berg Publishers, an imprint of A&C Black Publishers Ltd)

Albert Speer *Inside the Third Reich* (Weidenfeld & Nicolson, an imprint of The Orion Publishing Group, London)

Paul Steinberg *Speak You Also: A Survivor's Reckoning* (Allen Lane, an imprint of Penguin UK)

H. Trevor-Roper (ed) *Hitler's War Directives 1939* © Hugh Trevor-Roper 1964 originally published by Sidgwick and Jackson and reprinted by kind permission of PFD and the estate of Hugh Trevor-Roper

H. Trevor-Roper (ed) *Hitler's Table Talk 1941-44* (Weidenfeld & Nicolson, an imprint of The Orion Publishing Group, London)

Marie Vassiltchikov *The Berlin Diaries 1940-1945 of Marie 'Missie' Vassiltchikov* reprinted by Chatto & Windus, a division of the Random House Group Ltd and reproduced by kind permission of PFD.

Fuehrer Conferences on Naval Affairs, 1940 (Greenhill books, an imprint of Pen & Sword Ltd)

The publishers have been unable to trace the copyright holder for the following titles and would be delighted to make restitution at the earliest opportunity:

Walter Warlimont *Inside Hitler's Headquarters 1939-145* originally published by Weidenfeld & Nicolson, an imprint of The Orion Publishing Group, London

François Genoud *The Testament of Adolf Hitler: The Hitler-Bormann Documents* originally published by Cassell Plc., a division of the Orion Publishing Group (London)

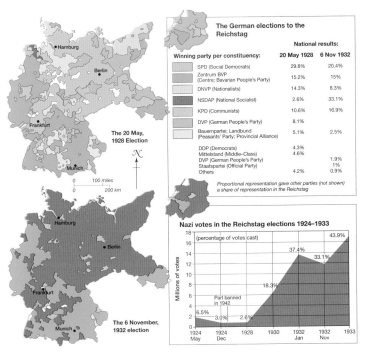

The German elections to the Reichstag

		National results:	
Winning party per constituency:		**20 May 1928**	**6 Nov 1932**
	SPD (Social Democrats)	29.8%	20.4%
	Zentrum BVP (Centre; Bavarian People's Party)	15.2%	15%
	DNVP (Nationalists)	14.3%	8.3%
	NSDAP (National Socialist)	2.6%	33.1%
	KPD (Communists)	10.6%	16.9%
	DVP (German People's Party)	8.1%	
	Bauernpartei; Landbund (Peasants' Party; Provincial Alliance)	5.1%	2.5%
	DDP (Democrats)	4.3%	
	Mittelstand (Middle–Class)	4.6%	
	DVP (German People's Party)		1.9%
	Staatspartei (Official Party)		1%
	Others	4.2%	0.9%

Proportional representation gave other parties (not shown) a share of representation in the Reichstag

The 20 May, 1928 Election

0 ____ 100 miles
0 ____ 200 km

The 6 November, 1932 election

Nazi votes in the Reichstag elections 1924–1933

(percentage of votes cast)

Millions of votes

43.9%
37.4%
33.1%
18.3%
Part banned in 1942
6.5%
3.0%
2.6%

| 1924 May | 1924 Dec | 1928 | 1930 | 1932 Jan | 1932 Nov | 1933 |

German Expansion 1936–1939

MEMEL March 1939
RHINELAND March 1936
SUDETENLAND September 1939
March 1939
AUSTRIA March 1938

0 ____ 300 miles
0 ____ 450 km

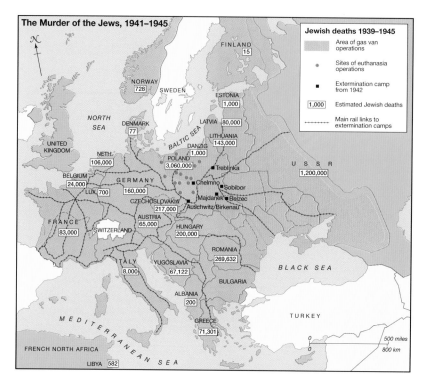

The Murder of the Jews, 1941–1945

N

Jewish deaths 1939–1945

Area of gas van operations

Sites of euthanasia operations

Extermination camp from 1942

1,000 Estimated Jewish deaths

Main rail links to extermination camps

FINLAND
15

NORWAY
728

SWEDEN

NORTH SEA

ESTONIA
1,000

DENMARK
77

LATVIA
80,000

BALTIC SEA

LITHUANIA
143,000

UNITED KINGDOM

DANZIG
1,000

NETH.
106,000

POLAND
3,060,000

U S S R
1,200,000

Treblinka

BELGIUM
24,000

GERMANY
160,000

Chelmno

Sobibor

LUX. 700

Majdanek   Belzec

CZECHOSLOVAKIA
217,000

Auschwitz/Birkenau

FRANCE
83,000

AUSTRIA
65,000

SWITZERLAND

HUNGARY
200,000

ITALY
8,000

YUGOSLAVIA
67,122

ROMANIA
269,632

BLACK SEA

BULGARIA

ALBANIA
200

TURKEY

MEDITERRANEAN SEA

GREECE
71,301

FRENCH NORTH AFRICA

0   500 miles
0   800 km

LIBYA 582

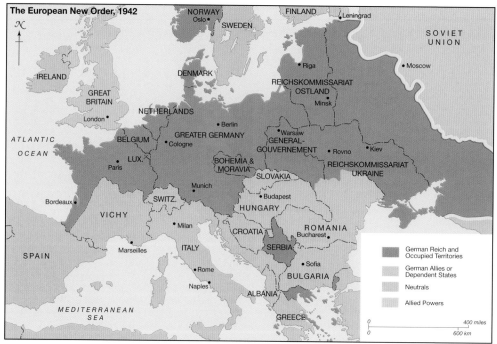

The European New Order, 1942

N

NORWAY
Oslo

FINLAND

Leningrad

SWEDEN

SOVIET UNION

IRELAND

DENMARK

Riga

Moscow

REICHSKOMMISSARIAT OSTLAND

GREAT BRITAIN

NETHERLANDS

Minsk

London

Berlin

BELGIUM

GREATER GERMANY

Warsaw

GENERAL-GOUVERNEMENT

ATLANTIC OCEAN

Cologne

LUX.

Rovno

Kiev

Paris

BOHEMIA & MORAVIA

REICHSKOMMISSARIAT UKRAINE

Munich

SLOVAKIA

Bordeaux

SWITZ.

Budapest

VICHY

HUNGARY

Milan

ROMANIA

SPAIN

CROATIA

Bucharest

Marseilles

ITALY

SERBIA

Rome

Sofia

BULGARIA

Naples

ALBANIA

MEDITERRANEAN SEA

GREECE

German Reich and Occupied Territories

German Allies or Dependent States

Neutrals

Allied Powers

0   400 miles
0   600 km

The Defeat of the Reich, 1944–1945

Axis or occupied territory liberated to March 1945

under German/Axis control, March 1945

site of battle

Dec 1941 date of battle

Allied attack

FINLAND
surrendered to USSR
Sept 1944

Lake
Onega

lake
Ladoga

Helsinki

Leningrad

Narva

Novgorod

U S S R

Dec 1941

Riga

Tula

NORTH
SEA

BALTIC
SEA

NORWAY

SWEDEN

DENMARK

Feb–April 1945
Königsberg

Minsk

June–Aug 1944

Orel

Voronezh

Lübeck

Stettin

May 1945

Vistula

Bialystok

Kursk

Stalingrad

D-Day
6 June
1944

GREAT
BRITAIN

London

Rotterdam

Arnhem
Sept 1944

Berlin

Warsaw
Jan 1945

Nov 1943

Kharkov

Don

Calais

NETH.
Antwerp

BELGIUM

Brussels

Dec 1944

May 1945
Prague

Kiev

Krivoy Rog

Stalino

Rostov

Caen
July 1944

Dieppe

Paris

G E R M A N Y

Danube

Vienna

SLOVAKIA

Carpathians

Dniester
Odessa

Metz

1944–45

April 1945

Budapest

ROMANIA

Ketch

Sebastopol

St. Nazaire

SWITZ.

Alps

Trieste

1944–45

Bucharest

B L A C K   S E A

Caucasus

FRANCE

Lyon

Milan

Genoa

Žagreb

Belgrade

CROATIA

SERBIA

Danube

Rimini

Cannes

Marseilles

Toulon

Florence

Livorno

ITALY

*Allies land
Jan. 1944*

Istanbul

T U R K E Y

SPAIN

Allies land Aug. 1944

Corsica

Rome

Anzio

Cassino

Sofia

BULGARIA

Index